LEADERSHIP IN GOVERNMENT: STUDY OF THE AUSTRALIAN PUBLIC SERVICE

*For our parents,
Elfrieda and George Kakabadse,
and Mila Lisa and Dmitar Korac,
with deep love and respect.*

Leadership in Government: Study of the Australian Public Service

ANDREW KORAC-KAKABADSE
and
NADA KORAC-KAKABADSE
International Management Development Centre
Cranfield University
Cranfield School of Management

LONDON AND NEW YORK

First published 1998 by Ashgate Publishing

Reissued 2018 by Routledge
2 Park Square, Milton Park, Abingdon, Oxon, OX14 4RN
711 Third Avenue, New York, NY I 0017, USA

Routledge is an imprint of the Taylor & Francis Group, an informa business

Copyright © A. Korac-Kakabadse and N. Korac-Kakabadse 1998

All rights reserved. No part of this book may be reprinted or reproduced or utilised in any form or by any electronic, mechanical, or other means, now known or hereafter invented, including photocopying and recording, or in any information storage or retrieval system, without permission in writing from the publishers.

Notice:
Product or corporate names may be trademarks or registered trademarks, and are used only for identification and explanation without intent to infringe.

Publisher's Note
The publisher has gone to great lengths to ensure the quality of this reprint but points out that some imperfections in the original copies may be apparent.

Disclaimer
The publisher has made every effort to trace copyright holders and welcomes correspondence from those they have been unable to contact.

A Library of Congress record exists under LC control number: 97077552

ISBN 13: 978-1-138-33497-7 (hbk)
ISBN 13: 978-1-138-33501-1 (pbk)
ISBN 13: 978-0-429-44407-4 (ebk)

Contents

Figures and tables	viii
Preface	xii

1	Introduction	1
	Overview	1
	Structure of the book	3

Part 1: Overview of leadership — 9

2	Leadership: an overview	11
	Introduction	11
	Character of individuals	19
	Context	24
	Developmental perspective	38
	Culture: bridging goals, circumstances and developmental pathways	56
	Power and politics: bridging traits, context and meaning	65
	Information technology development: the leader's changing role	72
	Discretionary leader	75
	Transformational leadership revisited	79
3	From public administration to public management to?	86
	Global diffusion of public administration	87
	Information technology and public administration	97
	Managerialist reforms of the APS	106

Part 2: Australian public sector leadership survey   117

4   The survey   119
       Demographics   120

5   Culture of the Australian Public Service (APS)   133
       Overview   133
       Attitudinal factors   134
       Values factors   135
       Organizational performance factors   136
       Information technology (IT) factors   137
       Impact of culture   137
       Differences by level of organization   140
       Summary   141

6   Impact of the Centre   143
       Styles of management   143
       Summary   150

7   Leadership   151
       Introduction   151
       Valuing leadership in the APS   152
       Emerging leadership philosophies   162
       Leadership in action   171
       Benchmarking leaderships: private sector comparison   183
       Summary   189

8   Recommendations for management development   193
       Overview   193
       Areas needing attention   196
       Developing leaders   209
       Summary   245

References   247

Appendix 1   Culture of organization factor analysis: APS   299
    Attitude factors   300
    Values factors   301
    Organizational impact factors   303
    Information technology factors   304

Appendix 2 Leadership factors: APS	306
APS top team's demography measures	307
Length of time in organization (organizational tenure)	307
Number of senior appointments (senior management tenure)	308
Length of time in current position (top team tenure)	308
Organizational size	310
Team players	311
Radicals	313
Bureaucrats	315
Appendix 3 Leadership factors: private sector	317
Drivers	318
Politicians	319
Strategists	320
Appendix 4 Impact of culture of organization on organizational performance: APS	322
Appendix 5 Impact of the Centre	328
Appendix 6 Top team impact	334
Appendix 7 Impact of leadership philosophies on the APS	338
Team players	339
Radicals	342
Bureaucrats	345
Appendix 8 Impact of private sector leadership philosophies	349
Appendix 9 Leadership impact on organization: regression analysis	353
Service delivery	354
Performance of people	355
Strategic direction	356
IT training	357
IT application	358
IT skills	358
IT impact	359
Private sector: strategic direction	360
Private sector: management of structures	361
Private sector: people management	362
Private sector	362
Index	363

Figures and tables

Figure 2.1	Pathway through leadership	18
Figure 5.1	Impact of culture on performance of organization	138
Figure 6.1	Leadership wheel: impact of Centre on regions - organizational performance	146
Figure 6.2	Leadership wheel: impact of Centre on regions - attitudes, values and effectiveness of delivery	149
Figure 7.1	Top team impact: APS	161
Figure 7.2	Leadership wheel: team players' impact on organization	172
Figure 7.3	Leadership wheel: top team impact on team players	174
Figure 7.4	Leadership wheel: radicals' impact on organization	176
Figure 7.5	Leadership wheel: top team impact on radicals	178
Figure 7.6	Leadership wheel: bureaucrats' impact on organization	180
Figure 7.7	Leadership wheel: top team impact on bureaucrats	181
Figure 7.8	Leadership wheel: leadership impact on the Centre	182
Figure 7.9	Leadership wheel: private sector	188
Figure 8.1	Leadership wheel: impact of top teams on the APS	194
Figure 8.2	Leadership for effectiveness (APS)	214
Figure 8.3	Leadership for IT adaptation (APS)	215
Figure 8.4	Private sector: leadership for effectiveness	217
Figure 8.5	1990s leadership: a paradox	222
Figure 8.6	Aftermath of downsizing	224
Figure 8.7	Discretionary leader behaviour	244

Table 2.1	Comparing manager versus leader attributes	55
Table 3.1	Contrasting domains: private versus public sector	95
Table 3.2	Reinventing organizations: the costs	102
Table 4.1	Level in organization	125
Table 4.2	Years in job	126
Table 4.3	Years in the organization	127
Table 4.4	Years in the APS	127
Table 4.5	Number of senior management appointments	128
Table 4.6	Appointments outside the APS	129
Table 4.7	Structure of organization	129
Table 4.8	Age of respondents	130
Table 4.9	Background	131
Table 4.10	Gender of respondents	131
Table 4.11	Qualifications	132
Table 5.1	Differences of perception by level	140
Table 6.1	Leadership demographics	144
Table 7.1	Benchmarking leadership in the APS (1 low - 5 high)	153
Table 7.2	Fundamentally different views concerning the direction of the organization (%)	154
Table 7.3	Sensitivity of dialogue (%)	155
Table 7.4	Managerial behaviours: comparative response by seniority (%)	156
Table 7.5	Reasons for poor dialogue and lack of cohesion over vision (%)	162
Table 7.6	Profile of leadership: private sector	184
Table 7.7	Leadership: sample distribution (valid cases)	184
Table 8.1	Need for change in leader behaviour: views of SESs and SOs - % of responses	196
Table 8.2	Comments highlighting improvements (SESs)	198
Table 8.3	Comments highlighting improvements (SOs)	199
Table 8.4	Impact of restriction of dialogue (APS)	200
Table 8.5	Sensitivities related to IT issues (APS)	201

Table 8.6	Impact of top team (private sector) on people and organization - Poor quality of dialogue and visioning	202
Table 8.7	Impact of top team (NHS Trusts) on people and organization - Poor quality of dialogue and visioning	203
Table 8.8	Enhancement of quality of dialogue (APS)	204
Table 8.9	Key job related values and attributes	207
Table 8.10	Slotting team players, radicals and bureaucrats: transformational	210
Table 8.11	Slotting team players, radicals and bureaucrats: transactional	211
Table 8.12	Subordinate managers' views of the top team	219
Table A4.1	Impact of culture of organization	323
Table A4.2	Impact of values on performance of organization	326
Table A5.1	Impact of corporate Centre's management style on demographics of organization	329
Table A5.2	Impact of Centre management's style on organizational culture and performance	331
Table A6.1	Top team impact (organizational) on the APS	335
Table A6.2	Top team impact (people) on the APS	336
Table A7.1	Team players' impact on organization performance	339
Table A7.2	Team players' impact on IT effectiveness	340
Table A7.3	Top team impact on team players	341
Table A7.4	Radicals' impact on organizational performance	342
Table A7.5	Radicals' impact on IT effectiveness	343
Table A7.6	Top team impact on radicals	344
Table A7.7	Bureaucrats' impact on organizational performance	345
Table A7.8	Bureaucrats' impact on IT effectiveness	346
Table A7.9	Top team impact on bureaucrats	347
Table A7.10	Leadership utilization of the four key styles of management	347
Table A8.1	Impact of drivers	350
Table A8.2	Impact of politicians	351

Table A8.3	Impact of strategists	352
Table A9.1	Regression analysis: leadership factor influence on organizational impact measures	354
Table A9.2	Regression analysis: leadership factor influence on organizational impact measures	355
Table A9.3	Regression analysis: leadership factor influence on organizational performance measures	356
Table A9.4	Regression analysis: leadership factor influence on IT training	357
Table A9.5	Regression analysis: leadership factor influence on IT application	358
Table A9.6	Regression analysis: leadership factor influence on IT skills	358
Table A9.7	Regression analysis: leadership factor influence on IT impact	359
Table A9.8	Regression analysis: leadership factor influence on clarity of strategic direction	360
Table A9.9	Regression analysis: leadership factor influence on effective management of structures	361
Table A9.10	Regression analysis: leadership factor influence on effectiveness of people management	362
Table A9.11	People management (Alpha .81)	362

Preface

The study reported in this book formed the basis of a report submitted to the Australian Commonwealth Government.

The study was not commissioned by the Australian Government and hence was a totally independent piece of work. However, the study received full support and cooperation from the civil servants in Canberra. The completed report was submitted to Dr Peter Shergold, Public Service Commissioner, Public Service Commission and Merit Protection Board, Canberra, Australia, May 1996.

We would like to acknowledge all those in Canberra who helped make this Study possible, especially, Dennis Ives, former Public Service Commissioner, Dr Peter Shergold, Jenni Colwill, Edward Attridge, Brian Joyce, Jenny Cahill and Derek Volker, former Secretary of the Department of Employment, Education and Training, and all those civil servants who gave their time to take part in this survey or who assisted in the process of administration, data collection and distribution of feedback once the survey was complete. Nada and I are deeply indebted to you.

At the Cranfield end, we also wish to thank Andrew Myers and Leo Murray for their support, help and guidance throughout the project. Thanks also to Dorothy Rogers, Jenny Ford and Alex Britnell for their patience and perseverence in typing draft after draft.

We thank you for all the care and assistance you gave to make this project possible.

Andrew Korac-Kakabadse
Nada Korac-Kakabadse

1 Introduction

Overview

Leadership is one of those few topics of management and organization behaviour that has a history far greater than the subject matter heading within which it is housed. The writings of Confucius, Aristotle and Plato emphasize the transformational interpretation of leadership, highlighting the visionary or superhero nature of the great man or woman. From the ancient philosophers, to more modern great philosophers as Hobbes and Nietzsche, to current scholars, transformational leadership has dominated thinking. Further through postulation and/or enquiry, the search has been on to identify those elements that lead to super human drive and extraordinary impact, in the hope that others can replicate or be trained in such attributes. Historically, it is assumed that transformational leaders make the big strides and break out of existing moulds and on to new worlds.

With the onset of large, structured work organizations needing to be responsive to market and/or community/political influence, leadership has equally been viewed from the perspective of action and making major strides forward, and from being strongly influenced by context. Different circumstances in different organizational settings provide parameters around which the leadership contribution is actioned. Effectiveness of leadership would be determined by being able to recognize appropriateness of action and influence relevant to the dynamics of that context. Hence, in any analysis of leadership, when taking into account context, attention needs to be paid to understanding followership and culture of organization. Unless the requirements of colleagues and subordinates are appreciated, any leadership effort could be ineffective or even counterproductive, as the followers would not have given their tacit 'permission' for their leaders to act. Add the modern day phenomena of speed of information, the rise of multi national and multi cultural organizations, the fact that revenue streams and key client accounts can be enhanced or damaged by subordinates irrespective of the behaviour of the boss, then contextual considerations can be of paramount importance.

With these thoughts in mind, this book reports the results of surveys conducted within the Australian Public Service (APS), in private sector organizations spanning 12 industries, and in the National Health Service Trusts (UK).

The theoretical framework adopted in these studies attempts to capture the reality of demands made on managers and their response and contribution to improvements and changes of their circumstances. In effect, context and person are taken into account. Further, from a developmental perspective, exploration is undertaken as to whether managers can be grown to be effective leaders, sensitively balancing their wishes with the dynamics of the demands they face in their situation. Taken into account are the individual manager's attitudes, values and behaviour, organizational circumstances and the feelings and views of others within the organization. Such analysis provides insights as to current leadership practice and its impact on present day dynamics. In turn, such enquiry highlights pathways for improvement that would be contextually relevant and useful.

As it is assumed for this text that leadership in today's work organizations requires examination of attributes of individuals, namely behaviour, attitudes or deeper personality dimensions and job/role related dynamics or pressures which would take account of context, the concept of discretion provides for the conceptual bridge between individual behaviours and role demands. The discretionary element of role refers to the choices the role incumbent needs to make in order to provide shape and identity to his/her role and that part of the organization for which the person is accountable. The contrast to the discretionary element of role is the prescriptive side, namely the structured part, which is predetermined and which focuses and restricts the individual's behaviour. In effect, the prescriptive part of a manager's job is that part over which the manager has little choice, other than to undertake the duties that are required of him/her.

Hence, the underlying philosophy of the Cranfield surveys is to refer to the senior manager's job as unevenly split between the leadership elements (discretionary) and the managerial elements (prescriptive), with the discretionary component predominating. Such distinction is particularly pertinent, as providing leadership in circumstances of substantially conflicting priorities is likely to make considerable demands on senior managers. The individual senior manager will need to make choices between unclear alternatives and is equally likely to need to devote considerable attention to nurturing key interfaces which influence internal and external stakeholders, in order to ascertain their commitment to a meaningful way forward.

What choices are made and how commitment is negotiated, highlight the impact the stakeholders have on the organization, as well as the capabilities of senior managers to effectively respond to such challenges. There is no reason to assume that even if the capacity of top management in the organization is considerable, each of the members of the Senior Executive would form similar conclusions as to the shape, size, direction, desired qualities of the total organization and thereby the shape and cost of each of the key functions/divisions/units within the organization. Hence, senior managers' beliefs concerning what to lead, how to lead and when to lead, highlight one key question: To what extent do senior managers share their views and concerns with each other?

On this basis, fundamental to effectively leading an organization is to ensure a high quality dialogue amongst the members of the 'Senior Executive'.[1] The preliminary results of interviews and case study analyses, examining the behaviours and capacities of senior managers, indicate that where the quality of dialogue is high and the relationship amongst senior managers is positive, the issues and concerns facing the organization are likely to be more openly addressed. Where, however, relationships are tense and the quality of dialogue restricted, certain issues and problems tend not to be raised, because to do so would generate unacceptable levels of discomfort, amongst certain or all of the members of the Senior Executive. In effect, such discomfort would be experienced as unwelcome and too overwhelming to face up to the problems confronting the organization. Ironically, the case studies in both the private and public sector highlight that unless the top team is working reasonably effectively, issues which need to be addressed are not.[2] That is to say, the senior management of the organization knowingly allow the organization to deteriorate because they feel too uncomfortable to jointly discuss and attend to key issues and challenges facing the enterprise.

Structure of the book

This book consists of eight chapters and nine appendices.

Chapter 1 provides for a brief overview of leadership and the structure of the report.

Chapter 2 strongly emphasizes that leadership needs to be viewed in two alternate modes, transactional and transformational. A comprehensive review of the literature, although highlighting these two terms as crucial to understanding leadership, also shows a mix of meanings and understandings as to the finer points of distinction between the two. For this reason, the literature on leadership is configured in the additional categories of individual, contextual and developmental. An assumption is made, namely that transformational leadership only holds meaning in the individual and developmental categories, whereas transactional leadership thinking principally addresses contextual issues. The concept of 'individual' refers to those persons supposedly born with particular qualities of leadership, the identity of which has been the quest amongst philosophers and researchers in this and past centuries. It is postulated that the ultimate accolade of the 'born to be a leader' perspective is charisma, again a desired but as yet to be discerned determinant of leadership.

The 'contextual' category refers to the managerial accomplishments leaders need to have in order to manage operational matters (daily transactions). Within this category are placed decision theory, goal theory, contingency and situational theories, culture of organization and the challenging topics of power and politics. As the essence of contextual development is transactional, on the premise that transformational approaches alter the fundamentals of context, it is emphasized that topics such as culture of organization, situational leadership, decision processes and even power and politics, require incremental application of leadership (i.e. managership).

The 'developmental' category assumes that anyone can develop the characteristics, philosophy, behaviours and ways of leaders. Development in this sense highlights the human being as capable of ordinary as well as extraordinary steps and achievements, an assumption of such ancients as Socrates and Plato. It is postulated that crisis brings out certain latent elements which can transform individuals and circumstances in ways that could not have been foreseen. The developmental category, although placed as an essential element of transformational leadership thinking, allows for examination of pathways to continuous improvement. The developmental philosophy rejects the quest for those innate characteristics that lead to greatness. As all people, potentially, can develop themselves to greater and greater ends, the search for the elements of greatness amongst those few, is viewed as futile to pursue.

Chapter 3 explores developments in public administration over the last two/three decades. A point that is felt strongly is that the field of public administration has been, and is being, transformed globally to adopt concepts of public management. The rationale of economics has influenced governments worldwide, inducing a greater awareness of costs and more effective utilization and deployment of resources. Inevitably, the benchmark has been the private sector, whereby managerial experiences and skills, and strategic tools promoting change, such as the use of information technology (IT) and re-engineering, have been transported into the public sector domain. As emphasis is given to examining the changing landscape of public administration, equally attention has been given to those voices of caution that would consider the transfer of private sector practices unwelcome and further, for some, damaging. The question that still remains purposely so unaddressed in this chapter is that of direction. Where are all these changes and developments taking us? A question that the programme of research reported in this book can only, in part, address.

Chapter 4 outlines the structure underpinning the surveys and reports on the findings of 11 demographic characteristics of leaders in the APS. Certain differences exist between the members of the Senior Executive Service (SESs) and Senior Officers (SOs) concerning years spent in the APS, years on the job, number of senior management appointments held, age and qualifications. The majority of SESs and SOs have no working experience other than in the APS. Also the greater proportion of respondents in this survey are male.

Chapter 5 explores the impact of the culture of the APS, interpreted as the key attitudes and ways of working and the values held by SESs and SOs, against measures of organizational performance and the effectiveness of IT application in the organization. It is concluded that a performance oriented culture is supportive of the nurture of desired and shared values but both only marginally impact on the effectiveness of organization performance.

Chapter 6 examines the impact of the Centre on regional/outlying offices. Four key styles of management are identified: people sensitive styles, power oriented styles, styles promoting rules and regulations, and styles valuing performance and professionalism. Most positive impact occurs when managers at the Centre practise styles that value the performance and professionalism of others. Most negative impact on the regions is made when managers at the Centre practise styles that promote rules and regulations and pursue approaches that are interpreted as power oriented.

Chapter 7 comprehensively explores the subject of leadership and the manner in which it is practised in the APS. Current leadership practice within the APS is considered as a subject needy of attention, as senior management are viewed as seriously divided on issues of strategy and mission, suffering from poor quality dialogue and ineffectively communicating, when benchmarked against the private sector and NHS (UK) survey respondents. Three contrasting philosophies of leadership are identified in the APS, and their impact on the organization is examined and contrasted against similar findings in the private sector.

Chapter 8 provides recommendations for enhancing leadership performance within the APS. Particular areas needing attention are highlighted and examined in detail in terms of those issues the respondents feel merit examination. Comparison is also drawn between the APS respondents' views and the views of the private sector and NHS top managers. Attention is also drawn to particular issues cited by the respondents as inhibiting the providing of attention to overcome these challenges. However, these inhibitions are considered to be more myths than reality. Highlighted are the two paradoxes of leadership, which if poorly managed lead to the phenomena of the leadership gap made worse within circumstances of downsizing. These are considered as powerful reasons for improving leadership performance within the APS. On the job recommendations to improving leadership performance are offered, emphasizing key leader behaviours and the need for effectively promoting the mission of the organization. Considerable discussion is offered as to the off the job development experiences that should be considered for the training and development of current and future leaders.

Appendix 1 provides for a more detailed breakdown of the factor analysis results of the attitude factors, the values factors, the organizational performance factors and IT factors.

Appendix 2 provides for a more detailed breakdown of the factor analysis results of the three leadership philosophies identified in the APS.

Appendix 3 provides for a more detailed breakdown of the factor analysis results of the three leadership philosophies arising out of the private sector survey.

Appendix 4 provides for a detailed statistical breakdown of the impact of the culture of the APS on the measures of organizational performance and supports the conclusions reached in Chapter 5.

Appendix 5 provides for a more detailed statistical breakdown of the impact of the Centre on outlying regions/departments and supports the conclusions reached in Chapter 6.

Appendix 6 provides for a more detailed statistical breakdown of the impact of top management on the APS and supports certain of the conclusions reached in Chapter 7.

Appendix 7 provides for a more detailed statistical breakdown of the impact of the three APS leadership philosophies on the organization and supports certain of the conclusions reached in Chapter 7.

Appendix 8 provides for a more detailed statistical breakdown of the impact of the three leadership philosophies emerging from the private sector survey and supports certain of the conclusions reached in Chapter 7.

Appendix 9 provides for a detailed regression analysis of the impact of leadership on measures of organizational impact and the four IT measures, and supports certain of the conclusions reached in Chapter 8.

Notes

1 The term 'Senior Executive' embraces those senior managers who occupy discretionary leader roles. These managers may be members of one team, a number of teams (e.g. boards of a company and the committee of executive directors who may not sit on the board), a number of interlinking committees. It is assumed that the manner in which discretionary leader roles are configured varies from organization to organization.
2 'Top team' refers to the members of the Senior Executive and as such is used as shorthand term to refer to those senior managers who occupy discretionary leader roles.

Part 1
OVERVIEW OF LEADERSHIP

2 Leadership: an overview

Introduction

Leaders have been referred to as 'captains of the ship' to denote their stewardship role in operating the organization entrusted to their care. Their primary tasks are to balance competing requirements and align organizational goals with a diversity of human needs and behaviour, exhibited internally and externally to the organization. Historically, the source of wisdom and direction for leaders stemmed primarily from their position in the organization, whereby subordinates were simply required to comply (Manz and Sims, 1990).

Leaders of the 1990s still retain some elements of organizational stewardship. However, the focus has shifted increasingly to the role of the 'organizational architect'. The principal contributing skills of architects are an ability to design and develop organizations; skills that require considerable creative insights and technical knowledge about how to analyze, design and stimulate complex, increasingly globalizing social networks supported by rapidly advancing information technology (IT) (Boettinger, 1989; Forester, 1989; Korac-Boisvert and Kouzmin, 1994a, 1994b).

In order to effectively cope with a variety of dynamic demands such as aggressive competition, employee needs, market demands, IT advances and global economic shifts (Porat, 1977; Dizard, 1985; Forester, 1989; Keen, 1991; Marceau, 1992; Nohria and Eccles, 1992), the contemporary leader continuously contends with the tasks of redesigning, renovating or reinventing existing organizations. Even those who have the luxury of designing an organization from scratch need their design skills on a continuous basis, as organizational planning is an ongoing activity that requires the same attention as is given to other strategically significant processes in organizations, such as new product and service developments or quality improvement. Organizational designers need to lay the groundwork for designing or redesigning infrastructure, for vision setting, for facilitating the flow of information, and for ensuring the continuous review of the nature of jobs, employee development, career paths and rewards for all stakeholders critical to the functioning of the organization.

Leadership, one of the oldest crafts, is currently enjoying a revival. To date there is no record of the counterpart to the modern day manager among the social groups of a more ancient and simpler past. Tribal chiefs, priests, generals and kings did not manage others; instead they led their followers. They led because they persuaded their followers to believe that they received inspiration and wisdom from somewhere, usually from above (Fairholm, 1991). Possibly because of its personal nature and the increasing social and organizational complexity of this century, leadership lost its appeal in favour of management and managers who experience a classical, rhetorical education. The transition from revelation to logic and from charisma to control, presents the history of the rise of management to pre-eminence in social and organized settings (Weber, 1920; Kouzmin, 1980; Fairholm, 1991).

Over time, leadership has come to mean a variety of things, with the usual definition that considers leadership either as a personal property (courage, stamina, power, charisma) or a property of position. Considered as a vital commodity since the beginning of humanity, leadership remains a topic of central interest, vested with the trappings of myth, legend and imagery. A review of the leadership literature suggests that there are almost as many different definitions of leadership as there are scholars who have attempted to define the concept (Stogdill, 1974). Further, leadership is applied to a diversity of behaviours, ranging from that of supervisor to that of prophet. Perhaps the closest to consensus over a definition of leadership is that of a social influence process, although the same may be said for most experiences that involve more than one person (Pondy, 1978).

In this book, leadership is considered as a concept used to identify actions which yield social change and improvement. As such, leadership is conceptualized as a temporary property of the person, and as such it resides neither in the person nor in the situation. Thus, leadership is conceptualized as a transient phenomenon, one which can be practised equally well by different individuals, depending on the circumstances and their strength of ideas. It should be noted that not all agree with this viewpoint and for that reason alternative viewpoints are outlined in this chapter.

A century of scholarly literature has produced a myriad of leadership and management theories and models and at the same time has muted the leadership and management terminology to the synonymous definition of 'good management'. In order to differentiate the contrasting theories of leadership, an overview of the field is initially necessary before further indepth analysis is undertaken.

Overview and definition of leadership

Selznick (1957) examines leadership by distinguishing it from management. The leader, in his view, is concerned with 'critical' as opposed to 'routine' decisions in the organization. Critical decisions have to do with the definition of the purpose of the organization. However, the definition of purpose, for Selznick (1957), is not simply the linkage of means to ends, but more the balance between the two, 'the cult of efficiency in administrative theory and practice is a modern way of over stressing means and neglecting ends' (Selznick, 1957, p.135). Furthermore, purpose is not concerned with human relations' efforts designed to develop a 'harmonious team'. As such, leadership is not equivalent to position, rather, it is concerned with statesmanship. Therefore the 'institutional leader' is primarily an expert in the promotion and protection of values (Selznick, 1957, p.28). Selznick's (1957) generative ideas for the conceptualization of leadership are expressed by three premises:

- 'Leadership is a kind of work done to meet the needs of a social situation' (Selznick, 1957, p.22). That is, leadership may involve the interaction of leaders on behalf of the organization or institution. However, 'it does not follow that the nature of leadership varies with each social situation. If that were so, there would be nothing determinate about it, its study would be a scientific blind alley' (Selznick, 1957, p.23).

- 'Leadership is not equivalent to office holding or high prestige or authority or decision making' (Selznick, 1957, p.24). That implies that leadership may or may not be exerted by those in position of authority.

- 'Leadership is dispensable' (Selznick, 1957, p.24). The idea suggests that not everything that occurs in an institution can be called 'leadership'. The assumption is that there exist social processes which occur without any need for leadership.

Selznick's (1957) construct of leadership explains certain human actions in the organization, emphasizing in particular the maintenance or transmittal of values which steer the direction of the institution.

In contrast, Burns (1978, p.12) sees leadership 'as a special form of power', where power is the mode of utilizing resources to achieve certain goals. Power, however, is not interpreted in any mechanical sense and as such is not always coercive. The most powerful influences consist of deep human relationships, in which 'two or more persons engage with one another' (Burns, 1978, p.11). For Burns, power is a basic aspect of humanity, and occurs in practically all relationships where there are motivations and resources. However, power need not be 'power over' but it can reflect a host of motivations such as the motive to achieve as opposed to the motive to dominate. For Burns (1978) leadership is 'purposive and oriented towards a goal, a vision or a change'. It involves competition and accepts that followers have motives of their own. Burns (1978, p.8) defines leadership action as the action that a 'person with certain motives and purposes mobilises, in competition or conflict with others, institutional, political, psychological, and other resources, so as to arouse, engage, and satisfy the motives of followers'. For Burns (1978, p.19) leadership 'unlike naked power wielding, is thus inseparable from followers' needs.'

In his reformulation of leadership, Burns (1978) classifies leadership as 'transactional' and 'transformational'. He considers that transactional leadership involves the exchange of valued goods, such as the exchange of votes for particular programs on the part of politicians and the electorate. Transactional leaders may be found as leaders of small groups; opinion leaders in political parties; and in legislative and executive leadership.

Transformational leaders do not simply engage in an exchange of valued goods, as they engage followers and transform the followers' vision of the world. Thus transformational leaders are 'moral but not moralist' (Burns, 1978, p.455). In this sense 'leaders engage with followers, but from higher levels of morality; in the enmeshing of goals and values both leaders and followers are raised to more principled levels of judgement' (Burns, 1978, p.455), where much of leadership 'asks sacrifices from followers rather than merely promising them goods' (Burns, 1978, p.455). Transformational leadership can occur as intellectual leadership, using ideas to transform and reform leadership, reforming particular structures of governance; revolutionary leadership, heroic leadership and ideological leadership. Such leaders use 'charisma' and 'enticing ideas' to sway followers, where the task of leadership is conscious raising on a wider plan' (Burns 1978, p.43).

Burns' (1978) work served to re-acquaint scholars with a critical distinction first raised by Weber (1947), namely the difference between economic and neo economic sources of authority which served as one basis for Weber's (1947) discussion of charisma. Burns' (1978) amplified and focused this important definition, using leadership illustrations such as Ghandi and

Roosevelt, that made the distinction between leaders and managers too striking for such assertions to be ignored.

While Burns' (1978) leadership definition excludes political leadership, namely that which is coercive or dictatorial, Tucker (1981) sees politics as leadership where politics is considered as the active direction of a political community and can thus be equated with leadership. For Tucker (1981), politics is not simple power seeking, though it can involve power. Therefore dictators can exert political leadership which is power based and power seeking. Tucker (1981) defines the political leader's task as a threefold function:

- Diagnostic: defining situations authoritatively for the group;
- Prescriptive: prescribing courses of group action that will meet the defined situation;
- Mobilizing, or diagnostic: policy formulating and policy implementing (Tucker, 1981, p.18).

For Tucker (1981) leadership involves activities which are political in nature and are responses to addressing problem situations.

Bennis' (1984) study of corporate leaders reinforces some of Burns' (1978) and Tucker's (1981) works. Bennis (1984) finds that leaders need to share vision, which involves clarifying the present and proposing a view of the future; communicating and gaining support for the vision; being persistent, consistent and focused, in order to maintain the vision; empowering, creating a 'social architecture' which allows for the expression of energy and organizational learning and the ability to monitor performance and learn from errors. Bennis (1984) argues that a combination of these factors provides 'transformative power'; the ability to 'translate an intention into reality and sustain it' (Bennis, 1984, p.64). He argues that the transformational power of leadership is the 'ability of the leader to reach the souls of others in a fashion which raises human consciousness, builds meaning and inspires human intent' (Bennis, 1984, p.70). Bennis (1988) identifies five qualities that are essential for successful leadership, conclusions reached through his study of chief executive officers:

- Technical competence defined as the combination of knowledge, broad experience and the ability to do whatever one does, as well as possible. These are people who are usually pragmatists and who have risen through the ranks as smart, insatiable and tireless workers.

- People skills defined as the possession of self understanding of one's talents and flaws, plus the ability to eliminate the latter or to compensate for them; also the capacity to understand and work with others in terms of common needs.

- Conceptual skills consist of a viewpoint and vision that permits one to capitalize on existing opportunities and anticipate future ones.

- Judgement defined as the artful mix of cognitive capabilities and intuition that translates into understanding and steadiness. With such judgement, leaders see and understand what's happening, responding immediately, decisively and intelligently.

- Character, that is defined as the perfect balance of ambition, ability and conscience; capable of doing the right thing and taking full responsibility for one's actions and those of his/her organization.

While Burns bypasses the key question of what it is that leaders do, or how they function as leaders, apart from interacting motivationally with followers, Kakabadse (1991) redefines and operationalizes Burns' leadership classification into the categories of 'discretionary' and 'prescribed'. Where discretionary leadership activity involves attending to non prescribed tasks, comparable to Selznick's (1957) 'critical' decisions, Kakabadse's (1991) discretionary leaders concern themselves with tasks such as setting agendas and vision, and the establishment and maintenance of relationships. Prescribed leadership involves spending time on more structured tasks, such as activities within functions as sales and marketing, or implementation of strategies or tasks that Selznick (1957) calls 'routine' decisions in the organization. Effective leadership for Kakabadse (1991) is one where the leader adopts a philosophy that is discretionary and developmental in nature. Like Bennis (1984), Kakabadse (1991) focuses on the operationalizaton of leadership in private and public sector organizations, at both the individual and team level.

While Selznick (1957), Burns (1978), Tucker (1981) and Bennis (1984) studies made advances from the functionalist approaches to leadership, in so far as they account for political and social action in more than objectivistic terms, they still contain an implicit hierarchical definition of leadership, which abstracts leadership as property possessed by some individuals (Sayles, 1979). In so doing, they do not address the essence of leadership, the critical spirit, that aspect which is necessary for a leader to be able to understand contexts. Furthermore they treat leadership as a volunteristic trait, where one simply chooses to exert leadership. Kakabadse's (1991) model goes a step further and addresses the essence of leadership, raising human consciousness by creating meanings and evaluating motives and goals against existing and emerging structures and vision that is located in the near and far future.

The overview of definitions of leadership has provided for two distinctions in the subject that clearly need to be taken into account, namely transformational and transactional. In essence, transactional leadership refers to the interactions between individuals and groups and by so doing, the context within which the intervention occurs needs to be taken into consideration. Context is a powerful force, for it can influence both the quality of the interaction and the parameters that bind its beginning and end. By being so context bound, transactional leadership more neatly equates with management.

In contrast, transformational leadership is proactive but beyond particular contexts. Transformational leaders may not only extend the boundaries of particular contexts but may equally dismantle the very pillars of that contextual framework. By so doing, transformational leadership is individualistic by nature with, at times, little respect paid to the maintenance of existing contextual patterns of interaction, a hallmark of transactional leadership. With transformational leadership, boundaries are broken and rebuilt, with the uncomfortable occurrence of scant attention being paid to the ensuing human cost. Within the bounds of transactional leadership, incremental adjustment to boundaries highlights its conceptual underpinnings and fundamental philosophical precept of 'get the best out of the people you've got!' (Thomasma, 1993).

Hence, context is a fundamental differentiation between transactional and transformational leadership, attributing the former to the management camp. A second differentiation requires highlighting within the transformational category, and that is, the nature of individualism. Is the individual 'born with' a greatness that transcends boundaries, or is an individual of 'normal' propensities required through circumstance and crisis to redefine direction and contextual parameters, with a superiority that is not based on a formality of command? From the so called 'great man theory' (Bernard, 1926; Tead, 1935) to the more current flavour of 'developed from humble beginnings'; both of which underly the transformational leadership thesis (Tichy and Devanna, 1986; Avolio, Waldman and Yammarino, 1991), which includes 'new age' value leadership (Bennis and Nanus, 1985; Banner and Blessingame, 1988; Fairholm 1991; Senge 1992), the debate of 'was I born great', or 'was greatness thrust upon me', continues.

Figure 2.1 provides for a pathway through leadership and captures the key distinctions of leadership, namely transformational and transactional. sub divided further into individual, contextual and developmental. These sub

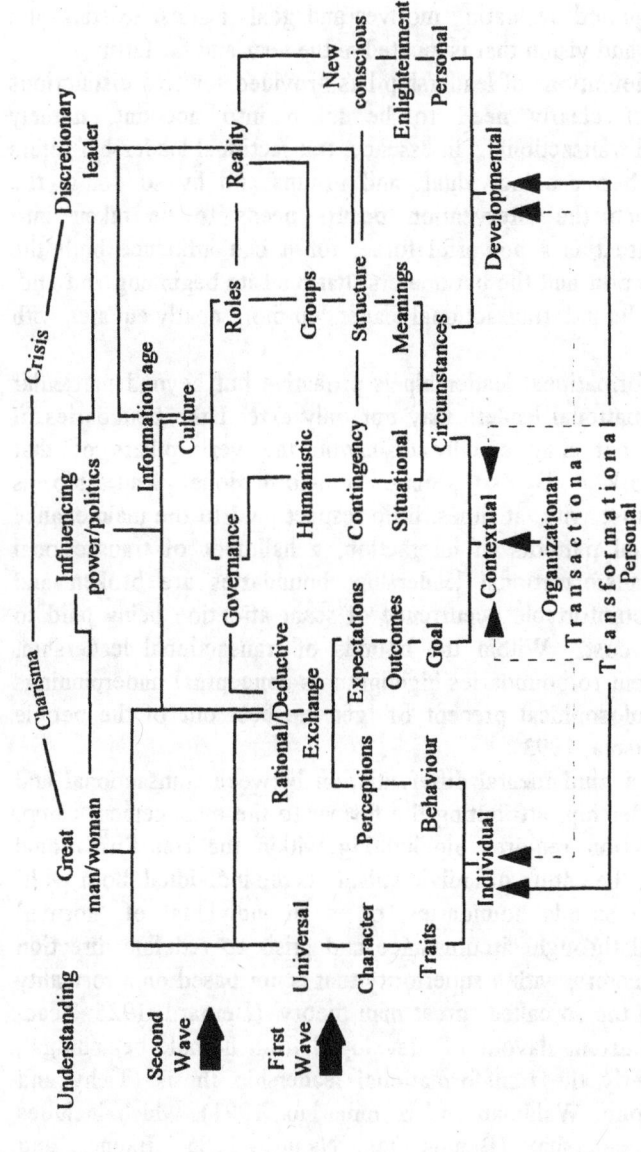

Figure 2.1 Pathway through leadership

18

divisions reflect the drifts in the literature, whereby transactional leadership draws somewhat upon both the inherent characteristics of individuals and the developmental routes to enlightenment schools of thought, but principally reflects contextualism. The emphasis throughout the transactional model is whatever organizationally works, use it. Transformational leadership enquiry draws on individual character and routeways to development, emphasizing the nature of big time leadership. However, transformational leadership also requires contextual appreciation, as it is assumed that leaders cannot continually lead, but do need to be exposed to the management of daily transactions. Hence, transactional and transformational leadership are linked, in terms of behaviour but substantially different in terms of philosophy and perspective.

The 'Pathway through leadership' model (Figure 2.1) also highlights the building block nature of leadership, whereby certain basics need to be understood (first wave understanding), in order to progress on to more interesting and sophisticated concepts (second wave understanding). Hence, the Pathway model (Figure 2.1.) not only attempts to sketch out the breadth of the leadership arena, but equally assumes a hierarchy of intellectual, psychological and moral complexities, which desire elucidation, but progress bottom up.

In order to better understand such contrasting perspectives and mix of terminologies of leadership, detailed attention is given, for the remainder of this chapter, to the contextual, individual and developmental subgroupings, thereby providing far greater meaning to the transactional and transformational distinction.

Character of individuals

The individual or personality view, exemplified by the great man theory, trait theory and a variety of psychological theories, deals with leadership in terms of personality characteristics seeking to discover 'who the leader really is'. This perspective focuses on the leader's traits or characteristic responses occurring independently of the stimulus context. The leader's personality characteristics or categories of characteristic response patterns are assumed to be stable structures within the person that dispose that individual to act in certain ways (Freud, 1922, 1953; Bernard, 1926; Bingham and Davis, 1927; Tead, 1935; Barnard, 1938; Jung, 1953; Davis and Warnath, 1957; Lazarus, 1963; Kets de Vries, 1977; Kotter, 1982).

Great man (person) theory

This approach centres on identifying and measuring the specific personal characteristics of elders, under the assumption that great leaders are born, not made. A number of studies have been conducted under the assumption that there are certain, specific, measurable personal traits and characteristics that clearly distinguish such leaders.

Trait theory

The view that a leader endowed with special qualities postulated by the great man theory, provided the basis for trait theory. The theory explained leadership in terms of traits of personality and character (Bernard, 1926; Bingham and Davis, 1927; Tead, 1935; Kilbourne, 1935). Examining 20 lists of so called leader traits, Bird (1940) found that none of the traits consistently appeared on all 20 lists. Davis and Warnath (1957), however, stated they identified four traits related to leadership: intelligence; social maturity and breadth; inner motivation and achievement drives; and human relations attitudes.

Analyzing the results of more than 25 years of research Stogdill (1948) reached two conclusions. First, that there are no specific traits or personal characteristics that stand out as strong determinants of leadership. Second, he identified five clusters of personal characteristics that were consistently associated with leadership across many research studies. Stogdill (1948) suggested that traits can be used to identify leaders from followers, effective from ineffective leaders and high level from lower level leaders.

Research on personal characteristics closed for a 25 year period, until House (1977) suggested that charisma might be based on specific, personal traits and characteristics. From these followed further enquiry. Four personal categories of traits: needs/motives, temperament, cognitive orientation and interpersonal orientation and two general categories: knowledge and relationships (Yukl, 1981; Kotter, 1982) have been influential in the literature. Although, searching for the inherent characteristics of leadership has swung in and out of popularity, currently, identifying the trait and personality dimensions to leadership has received a contemporary revival in the quest for a 'new age' leader (Banner and Blessingame, 1988; McAller, 1991; Senge 1992).

In contrast to trait thinking, psychological approaches have been equally popular in the development of leadership theory. Understanding leaders is undertaken through an analysis of their childhood experiences/deprivation, cultural experience, parental relations and their needs to fulfil among their followers (Freud, 1922; Frank, 1939; Fromm, 1941; Erikson, 1964; Levinson,

1968). Burke (1964) postulated that followers with a strong need to achieve are happier with asocially distant leaders. He contends that psychological distancing (psychic distance) between leaders and followers can enhance the leader's power and effectiveness by showing equal concern for task and people. De Vries (1977) suggested that leaders' interactions in situations intensify by crisis. He contends that the charismatic leader arises in times of crisis, due to the leader's own superego and the group's sense of helplessness and dependency. Barnard (1938) argues that followers attribute to leaders' exceptional abilities, even latent ones that are as yet undemonstrated, in order to have a reason for their dependency. However, the theme underlying character personal property quests is that, once found, these characteristics are effectively universally applicable, irrespective of context or ethnicity (Korman 1968; Yukl, 1981), a point that is strongly contended by behaviouralists.

Behavioural theories

The behavioural perspectives, epitomized by interaction expectancy role theories, exchange theory, perceptual and cognitive theories, address leadership issues in terms of acts, or 'what leaders do', and focus on overt behaviour and behaviour in relationships (Skinner, 1953; Homans, 1958, 1961; Tannenbaum and Schmidt, 1958, 1973; Likert, 1961; Fiedler, 1967; Jacobs, 1970; Vroom and Yetton, 1973; Pfeffer, 1977; Katz and Kahn, 1978; Peters and Waterman, 1982, Yukl and Van Fleet, 1982; Misumi and Peterson, 1985). The behaviouralist perspective draws attention to the intentions of people in a manner similar to Weber's (1949) category of 'Verstehen', assuming that individuals possess two capabilities: the ability to reason and the ability to know self interest. Through using reason to determine the nature of self interest, the behaviourist perspective examines people's actions, in terms of managerial or administrative style. Certain behaviour theorists, as Tannenbaum and Schmidt (1973), see leader behaviour as a continuum from manager centred to subordinate centred behaviour and have developed, arguably, the most commonly used approach to behaviour theory. Likert (1961) expands this basic model. Building on Theory X and Theory Y assumptions, Likert (1961) relates leaders' behaviour to a scale ranging from highly job centred to highly people centred. His emerging topography consists of four grid like categories: exploitative/authoritative, benevolent/authoritative; consultative/democratic and participative/democratic. Others such as Blake and Mouton (1964) extend the grid structure approach based on the discrete orientation of concerning of people to the tasks they need to accomplish and the relationships they need to form in the workplace. Their grid became a pillar in leadership development training. However, the theoretical foundations of the model's predictive integrity has been accused of being weak.

In contrast, Scott (1977) uses reinforcement as the basis for behavioural change. He suggests that defining leadership behaviour is more dependent on a logical analysis of circumstances than casting leaders in power terms. Davis and Luthan (1979), on the other hand, suggest that leaders merely set the occasion or provide a situation for the evocation of follower behaviour but do not cause follower behaviour. Thus, Davis and Luthan (1979) provide for one dimension of behaviour theory, follower expectations. The other is formative context, analyzed later in this chapter.

Interaction expectancy theories

The interaction-expectancy perspective emphasizes the expectancy factor in the leader-follower relationship. Homes (1956) developed a leader role theory based on three variables: action, interaction and sentiment. In his model, the leader's actions initiate structure-facilitating interaction, where leadership is the act of initiating such structure. In keeping with this line of thinking, Stogdill (1974) developed an expectancy-refinement theory of role attainment. In his model, the leader's role is to set mutually confirmed expectations concerning the follower's performance and intentions, so as to satisfy group aspirations. Along this track, Bass (1981) introduced reinforcement change theory. For Bass, leaders gain their position because of their perceived ability to rein in on the behaviour of the group members, by granting or denying them rewards and punishment. Equally, Evans (1970) contended that leaders can determine followers' perceptions by controlling the rewards available to them. In turn, Yukl (1981) postulated that the leader's capability to initiate decision decentralization increases subordinate motivation and skill, which in turn increases followers' effectiveness.

Perceptual and cognitive theories

Perceptual and cognitive theories focus on analysis and rational-deductive approaches to leadership. These theories are based on the work of Simon (1947), March and Simon (1958) and Cyert and March (1963) exploring parallels between human decision making and organizational decision making. The argument is that organizations can never be perfectly rational, because their members have limited information processing abilities. Thus organizations elect a 'bounded rationality' of 'good enough' decisions based on simple heuristics, rules of thumb, and limited search and information. Much of these theorists' work has focused on how organizations deal with the complexity and uncertainty presented by their environments.

Gilbraith (1974, 1977) and Thompson (1967) have given attention to the relationship between uncertainty, information processing and organizational design. Attributional analysis enters into this perspective. Attribution theory holds that to understand a leader, one must understand the leader's thoughts and intentions about a given situation (Pfeffer, 1977). Thus from the leader's behaviour, one can infer causes of exhibited behaviours to various traits or external constraints, where causes are a function of a rational process internalized by the leader's personal experience.

Pursuing this line of analysis, the open system perspective holds that the leader-follower relationship can be an open social system to the outside environment and sensitive to external influences and constraints (Katz and Kahn, 1978). Leadership is defined in terms of quality analysis, whereby the system imports energy, power and information, changes it and exports goods and services. The change process involves power, information and feedback to the system from the effects of the impacts made on the environment. The brokers of that change are the leader(s) of the organization (Katz and Kahn, 1966; Kast and Rosenzweig, 1973; Beer, 1980).

Exchange theory: bridging individual and context

Exchange theory sees leader-follower relationship in terms of economic transactions (Homans 1958). Group interaction continues because members find societal exchange mutually rewarding. Many kinds of social exchange take place. Such exchanges can be of material benefits, psychological benefits, approval, respect, esteem or affection. Pettigrew (1973) suggests that one way leaders can help their subordinates is to develop and maintain a network of contacts inside and outside the organization. That is, leaders assist followers to attain their expectations in exchange with others. Motivation becomes, at least, partially a function of fair exchange.

Bridging focus and action: the rational/deductive perspective applied to decision making

A contemporary contingency model developed by Vic Vroom and Phil Yetton (Vroom and Yetton, 1973) represents a rational deductive analysis of how decisions should be made by leaders. Using a decision tree, Vroom and Yetton developed five possible decision styles, ranging from an autocratic, leader decides style, to a participative, group decides style. The particular style chosen is a function of the needed quality of the decision, the need for group acceptance of the decision and the allotted time for making a decision. Thus, if a decision does not have a quality requirement and if subordinates are not involved in carrying out the decision, the style of the leader, in terms of participation, is more likely to be autocratic. The style(s) adopted by leaders depends on the answer to several questions dealing with the three factors of quality, acceptance and time. This model has received critical review, particularly with respect to the use of managers' self reports when testing it and its inability to distinguish between what managers say and do and what they are perceived as doing by subordinates (Fiedler, 1987).

Context

The contextual perspective, exemplified by situation theory, contingency theory, and humanistic models, determines leadership in terms of the situation or 'where leadership takes place' (Figure 2.1). The focus is on leader-member relations, task complexity, power, (Fiedler, 1967; Hickson et al, 1971), agency size, work maturity, structure of organizations (Child, 1973; Pugh and Payne, 1976) and goal attainment (House, 1971; Filley, House and Kerr, 1976). Certain theorists have even provided a historical perspective, for example Sashkin and Morris (1984) who have illustrated human work needs from a historic perspective of the nature of work over the past 100 years. Deeply rooted in the contextual perspective are the concepts of unity and harmony; the 'natural' order of things. Concepts as these are couched in Parson's (1959) structuralist-functionalist imperatives of adaptation to other systems and the physical environment; the attainment of system goals; task completion and order integration; and the maintenance of stability and consistency. The contextual perspective explains leadership in terms of situational traits or effective response in specific circumstances with subordinates.

Path/goal theory

Path-goal suggests that the function of the leader is to clarify for subordinates the paths available to achieving valued goals (House, 1971). Built on an expectancy theory framework, the path-goal model argues that a leader's style (task or person orientation) is effective when it clarifies linkages between subordinate effort and valued subordinate outcomes. The leader helps followers to achieve organizational goals by behaving in a manner contingent on the nature of the followers (need for direction, need for support, skill level) and the nature of the work setting (clarity of procedures, type of task, group relations). The hierarchical leader is concerned with structuring and consideration behaviour, adjusting his or her style in order to increase motivation and satisfy needs. While the empirical status of this model is equivocal, the application results have been mixed (Bass, 1981, p.446-7; Jago 1982, p.326).

Outcomes and leadership

The results of the early studies relating to leadership and performance are mixed. The early studies do not offer a constant theory about the impact of leadership on organization performance (Bass, 1981; Hunt, 1991). Some researchers cite poor empirical evidence as to the relationship between managerial behaviour and organizational performance (Pfeffer, 1981; Meidle and Ehrich, 1987). Lieberson and O'Connor (1972) investigate the influence of leadership on the sales, earnings and profit margin of 167 organizations from 1946-1965. They found that leadership explained from 6.5 per cent to 15 per cent of the variance of performance. Salancik and Pfeffer (1977) examine the influence of mayors on income and expenditure variables in 30 US cities. They concluded that managers' influence accounted for only about ten per cent of the variance.

Pfeffer (1978) proposes that organizational performance depends primarily on factors beyond the leader's control, such as the economic conditions, market conditions, governmental policies and technological change. Similarly, Kerr and Jermier (1978) identify forces detracting leadership influence, such as subordinates, task and organization. These detractors restrict the leader's ability to make any significant impact on organizational performance. Similarly House (1988, p.248) argues that leaders may have an impact on organizational performance. However, he cautions that the 'leader's effect' will be conditional on several factors such as the leader's ability, followers' ability, organizational or technological constraints and environmental demands. Others incorporate a number of contingency factors which may affect the leader succession-performance relationship. These factors include source of selection whether internally or externally appointed (Brown, 1982), size of organization (Scott, 1992), external environment (Haveman, 1993), age of organization and managerial characteristics (Carroll, 1984).

Although Drucker (1973) proclaims that the management is the 'life blood' of any enterprise, it took considerable research to provide more consistent findings that organizational effectiveness was the most influential domain of firm performance by executive leadership. Organizational effectiveness performance refers to general stakeholders' satisfaction and includes employees' satisfaction, personal development, public image and goodwill. This is in line with Pfeffer's (1981) view of leaders as ones needing to project symbolic qualities, as well as Meidle and Ehrich's (1987) proposition that leadership is a romantic concept; and even with the most extreme view presented by Weick and Daft (1983, p.90-1) that the 'job of management is to interpret, not to get the work of the organization done'; as well as Tsui's (1994), who postulated that leaders' decisions and behaviour are directed primarily towards the symbolic outcome of organizational existence.

Hambrick and Mason (1984) propose an 'upper echelons' perspective in which the upper echelon is a significant predictor of firm performance. Terry (1989) attributes the impact of change on an organization to the leader's actions, while Javidon (1991) claims that enterprises fail most often because of poor management. Weiner and Mahoney (1981) found that stewardship accounted for 44 per cent of variance in profitability of major firms. Similarly, Thomas (1988) used large retail firms and designed research to overcome the methodological problems of Lieberson and O'Conner's (1972) study and found that individual leaders do make a substantial difference. Day and Lord (1988) in their review claim that executive leadership can account for up to 45 per cent of the variance in terms of relevant organization outcomes. Lohman (1992) supports the idea that leaders have a positive impact on corporate performance and increase the capability of the organization, which may be translated into tangible results at a later time. Sonnenfeld (1988) suggests that symbolic acts of leadership have practical applications and that leaders stimulate others to achieve goals by inspiring actions, and exchanging information in informal ways. Bower (1983a, 1983b) finds that CEOs use their symbolic rules to persuade and, along with their actual power, can initiate actions in others.

The enduring question attempted to be answered by many, 'do leaders make a difference to organizational performance?', is most realistically and appropriately answered by Hambrick (1989, p.6) who states that 'some do, some don't, and a lot more could'. As the category of those 'who could make a difference but do not appear to' is the largest grouping, it is recognized that there is urgent need to enhance leader development and enable top people to unleash their potential in order to make the difference in terms of individual, team and organizational performance.

Succession research suggests that CEOs are able to exert a moderate effect on organizational performance over a period of several years (Thomas, 1988). Similarly, Romanelli and Tushman (1988) emphasize that executives have special timing effect on organizational activities. For example, leaders have an impact on the level of employees' commitment which influences their efforts and this, in turn, may influence the level of productivity of the organization. Consequently, it can be inferred that leaders have direct impact on organizational outcomes (Iaccoca and Novak, 1984).

The reason this debate on input, outcomes and effectiveness has raged is that strands of research have focused on more narrowly defined managerial behaviour and its linkage to leadership effectiveness, without necessarily exhibiting the impact of such behaviour on organizations. Hence, researchers have attempted to draw more direct links between leadership and organizational performance. For example, Yukl, Wall and Lepsinger (1990) show that clarifying goals is related to effectiveness. Hambrick (1982) states that the external boundary spanner role is another major aspect of the effective leader. Motivating behaviour is also related to leadership effectiveness, as this emphasizes the importance of employees being inspired and enthusiastic (Yukl, Wall and Lepsinger, 1990). Kotter (1988) provides an indepth study distinguishing between effective and ineffective leader behaviours. He found that effective leaders in complex organizations are engaged in creating an agenda for change and building strong implementation networks and relationships sufficient to elicit cooperation, compliance and team work. Integrating four decades of research, Yukl (1989) found a great deal of convergence among researchers. He separated leadership behaviour into four general categories: making decisions, influencing others, giving-seeking information, and building relationships. Although all these behaviours are relevant to leadership effectiveness, their relative importance varies across context and social time. A study by Quinn, Denison and Hooijberg (1989) validates the eight emerging executive leadership roles (producer, director, coordinator, monitor, facilitator, mentor, innovator and broker), developed by Quinn (1988) by extending the work of Yukl (1989) and Luthans and Lockwood (1984). Hence in drawing linkages between leadership outcomes and organizational impact, distinction needs to be drawn between opportunity costs and harnessing potential (leadership) and operational costs and day to day control (managerial), a boundary all too often blurred by the host of practitioners and academics, too linearly oriented in their search to justify ends and means (Kakabadse, 1991). The point being made is that insufficient attention is drawn to the distinction between leaders and managers in the research on organizational impact. It is more difficult to draw a direct relationship between the impact of a leader, as opposed to a manager, on the organization, as leaders are more concerned with broader strategic issues and less with operational matters, the latter being easier to measure in terms of outcomes.

Situational theory

Hersey and Blanchard (1988) developed a learning model for managers that provides an eclectic view of leadership by consolidating the major theories in the field into a behavioural based situational leadership model. The model is centred on the concept of leadership effectiveness according to the demands of the situation, with varying emphasis on task accomplishment and maintenance activities. Task activities may be formal (work assignments) or informal (unofficial leader) and include setting the direction for subordinates and influencing peers, while maintenance includes leader effect on group morale, performance and results. The model combines four basic styles of leadership with the four typologies of followers. By defining the follower situation, the most appropriate leadership style emerges: directing, coaching, supporting and delegating. The model emphasizes that the greatest impact on choice of style are followers' needs. That is, the amount of direction or support that a leader may provide to the follower(s) depends on the development level that the follower(s) exhibits on a specific task. By learning to enact the various leadership styles, and by learning to define the follower situations, appropriate leadership behaviour can be adapted. In effect, the model envisages a management development perspective of leadership skills in terms of understanding, diagnosing and influencing human behaviour at work. Hersey and Blanchard (1988) argue that effective leaders are those exhibiting the greatest range of style flexibility.

A number of the leadership research programmes have attempted to categorize a wide range of leadership behaviour in a few simple categories (structure, consideration); define the situation with a few simple categories focused on only the immediate situation (task, group) and the interpersonal relations between leader and led. The end result is that leadership outcomes are measured solely on the basis of group effectiveness. Some like Mintzberg (1973) extend the classification of leader behaviour beyond the two basic styles of structure and consideration. Mintzberg generates ten basic rules which he argues are typical of most managerial jobs, of which only one he calls 'leader'. The Mintzberg leader focuses exclusively on the leader-subordinate interaction, while the other nine encompass such activities as monitoring and disseminating information, acting as a figurehead, negotiating, handling disturbances, etc. In contrast, Pfeffer (1982) argues that leadership is not as important a factor as the impact of other factors such as budgets, economic conditions, changes in top executive positions, and role set expectations. Such influences, it is contended, frequently override the effects of leadership on organizational outcomes.

Well within the philosophy of situational theory, but extending the range of variables that can influence leader/member relations, Filley, House and Kerr (1976) postulate that the following factors have an impact on leadership effectiveness.

- History of the organization
- Age of the previous incumbent in the leader's position
- Age of the leader and his previous experience
- Community in which the agency operates
- Particular work requirements of the group

- Psychological climate of the group that is led
- Kind of job the leader holds
- Size of the group that is led
- Degree of cooperation between leader and group members
- Cultural expectations of subordinates
- Group member personalities
- Time required and allowed for decision making and implementation

Filley, House and Kerr (1976) argue that leader behaviour is effective in only certain kinds of situations, depending on which organizational and situational factors predominate at the time.

Overall, situational theory is more acceptable today. What is constructive is that the situational factors are finite in number, and although they vary according to the leader's personality, task requirements and follower expectations, needs and attitudes, as well as the environment in which they all operate, the concept is attractive because it is practically useable.

Contingency theory

Fiedler's (1967) contingency model of leadership has been reported as the most widely researched and most widely criticized framework for studying leadership (Bass, 1981, p.341). Fiedler (1967) postulates that the effectiveness of a group depends on the leader's motivational orientation (person versus task) and on the nature of the situation determined by: the structuredness of the task (high or low); the position power of the leader (high or low); and the quality of leader-member relations (good or poor). The model assumes that individuals have a leadership 'style' that is virtually unchanging. Furthermore, it assumes that the effectiveness of the leader in a particular situation will be contingent on the match between style (whether one's style is task oriented or relationship oriented), the existing relationship between the leader and the group being led, the nature of the task (whether the task is unambiguous and clearly structured or not), and the position power of the leader (whether the leader has strong versus weak authority over the group). The interaction between these elements yielded four combinations or 'octants' with the contention that it is possible to predict that where leader-group relations are good, the task is structured and the position power is strong, then the most effective leadership would come from a task oriented approach. The same would hold true if the conditions were reversed; the relations oriented person would only be effective when the favourableness of conditions were mixed. The model contains a continuum of situational favourableness (from highly favourable to highly unfavourable) that suggests that task motivated leaders are effective in a highly favourable and unfavourable situation, while person motivated leaders are effective in the moderately favourable situations. Fiedler's (1967) answer to leadership is the 'leader match concept', where the 'right' individual for the existing organizational conditions can be inserted or, barring that, can change the conditions themselves. Thus the model measures leadership in terms of task versus person orientation, as a measure of cognitive style, of attitude, and as a measure of the motivation in terms of leader match concept.

Overall, contingency theory and leadership match concepts have provided for considerable debate with a variety of empirical findings (Hoskings and Schriesheim, 1978).

Humanistic models

Humanistic theories attempt to ameliorate the basic tension between the individual in the group and the group, for the benefit of both the organization and its people. Such theories assume that people are by nature self motivated beings and that organizations are by nature structured and controlled. Humanistic theories combine both behaviour and situational elements to define an organizational surround that is essentially antagonistic to human desires. The central theoretical probe is to devise a theory of leadership that allows for needed control without unduly thwarting the individual motives of people. Two different research programmes concentrate on examining the behaviour of leaders within particular organizational circumstances, one at Harvard and the other at the Ohio State University, and both attempt to provide new paths to leadership thinking. Bales (1958), working with college undergraduates at Harvard, identifies two critical dimensions of behaviour: behaviour centred on task accomplishment; and behaviour that is directed toward interpersonal relationships, which he labels 'socio emotional relationship' behaviour. Individuals who consistently exhibit high levels of both of those types of behaviour in small group discussions are typically reported as leaders by their peers. Those individuals who engage only in high volumes of socio emotional relationship behaviour are designated as the leaders by their peers, but post discussion. Bales's (1958) work suggests that effective leadership consists of high levels of behaviour in both of these categories.

Adapting this line of thinking and in a seminal book on the human side of enterprise, McGregor (1960) describes two fundamentally different philosophies of leadership, Theory X and Theory Y. Theory X holds that the average person has an inherent dislike of work and avoids it and responsibility when possible, because most individuals have relatively little ambition. Thus, workers prefer to be directed, controlled, coerced or even threatened with punishment in order to make them perform effectively. McGregor (1960) argues that this type of management was replaced in the post industrial period with a management style based upon different assumptions about human nature, which he called Theory Y. Theory Y holds that the expenditure of energy in work is as natural as play or rest, and that high performance depends on self direction and self control. Thus commitment to organizational objectives is a function of rewards associated with their achievement. Leaders lead according to the assumptions they hold concerning work and people, and arrange the workplace to control or to liberate. Given the right organizational environment, the average worker learns to accept and seek responsibility. The leader's task is to create those conditions that unleash the human capacity for imagination, ingenuity and innovation.

The contrasting independent study conducted mostly in factories at Ohio State by Sashkin and Burke (1990) also identifies two types of behaviour on the part of foremen and supervisors. Their two categories 'initiating structure', giving task directions, and 'consideration' of employees and their feelings are, in essence, the same two dimensions identified by Bales (1958). Their study suggests that the most effective leaders exhibit high levels of both task and relationship centred behaviour, while leadership itself is characterized by a high degree of task oriented activity.

The ideas behind these two studies have been extensively applied in terms of management development, and a number of training programmes have been designed to help managers learn how to be 'high-high' or '9.9' leaders (Blake and Mouton, 1964), on the assumption that high levels of both types of behaviour, have performance relevance. Fleishman and Harris's (1962) study, for example, suggests that high-high supervisors have lower grievance and turnover rates from their subordinates. A further 20 years of research has failed to confirm that effective leaders actually engage in such high-high behaviour, leading one group of scholars to call it the 'high-high leadership myth' (Larson, Hunt and Osborn, 1976).

However, that does not mean to say that these contributions should be dismissed. Durkheim (1987) points to the dangers of anomie at work. Mayo (1933) emphasizes the positive significance of supportive interpersonal work relationships. McClelland (1955, 1958) supports these sentiments and illustrates the need for interpersonal contact in the context of work and meaningful achievement (McClelland, 1961; McClelland and Winter, 1969). The value of these studies is twofold: to highlight the importance of work relationships and also to provide guidance as to when directive or supportive leadership behaviour is desired according to the maturity of the followers (Blake and Mouton, 1964; Hersey and Blanchard, 1969; Argyris, 1957, 1962). They argue that as maturity increases, the leader should reduce control. The aim is to develop the follower to a level of maturity to do the required work mostly unaided.

Pursuing the theme of context and personal development, Argyris (1957, 1962, 1976) holds that organizations tend to structure merely to control performance in their own interests. He argues that an individual's nature is to be self directive, to seek fulfilment using initiative and responsibility. Thus leadership needs to create an environment within which the follower can make a creative contribution to the organization, as an outgrowth of their search for satisfaction, growth, self expression and maturity. Likert (1961), on the other hand, finds leadership to be a relative process, in that leaders must consider expectations, values and the interpersonal skills of followers. He argues that leaders must be supportive, involve followers in key actions and decisions, build group cohesiveness and provide freedom for responsible decision making.

The humanistic philosophy tends to have fallen in and out of favour, but recently experienced a revival with Peters and Austin (1985) who return to a humanistic view to explain much of current organizational behaviour, especially to explain the contempt that some customers and employees have for some of their leaders. Although for them the humanistic view smacks of a religious and ideological flavour, nevertheless they emphasize the caring context view within which one can rationalize individual action, and courses for corrective action.

Time: a managerial lever for leaders

Considerable empirical work on leadership has focused on the leader and the immediate work group, suggesting that the relationship between the leader and the led is an important aspect of the leadership process. Such work has been situated within the conceptual categorization of teams. Dubin's (1962) review indicates that foremen spend between 34 and 60 per cent of their interactions with subordinates. Mintzberg's (1973) study of top executives identifies that they spend 48 per cent of their contact time with subordinates and that the subordinate groups contained most of their required organizational relationships.

Equally these studies also highlight that managers can spend between 40 and 66 per cent of their time with non subordinates, such as superiors, peers, professional colleagues, members of other departments and units, and outsiders. Further, managers themselves spend only one fifth and usually closer to one tenth of their time with their superiors (Mintzberg, 1973).

Studies of foremen by Ponder (1957) suggest that foremen average between 200 and 270 activities per eight hour day. Similarly, a study of a Swedish top executive found that the individual was undisturbed for 23 minutes or so, only

12 times in 35 days (Carlson, 1951). Mintzberg (1973), observing five top executives, found that half of their activities lasted nine minutes or less, and only one tenth lasted more than one hour. He concludes that a manager's activities are 'characterized by brevity, variety and fragmentation' (Mintzberg, 1973, p.31).

Currently, literature suggests that there is an emerging need for more service, stockholder participation and special attention to disparate segments of a diverse populace requiring proficiency in 'inter spectral management', 'across border' or 'networking'. The profile and character of stockholder groups are changing, with highly educated and professional actors becoming the norm and resulting in a shift from organizing by division of labour to organizing by division of knowledge.

Professionals devalue management skills and management's mandate to curtail professional autonomy. Increasingly they demand to share decisions and directly influence the organizational agenda. Shared governance and not just the provision of inputs for decision making management control, the coordination of stockholders' interaction, and decision making occurring in teams rather than in the hierarchy, are expected features of such organizational contexts. The quality of performance rests on the quality of interactions, communication and coordination of stakeholders. Leaders will be challenged to share their leadership with stakeholders and will gradually evolve into joint or shared leadership where stakeholders will share authority and responsibility as needed at different stages and for different tasks contextually determined. Furthermore, adaptation to the globalization of organizations will further induce the proliferation of the networked organization of partnerships and joint ventures based on collaboration through situational authority.

This line of argument emphasizes the need for 'new age skills' such as creative insight, influence, sensitivity, visionary focus, caring, versatility, patience as well as commitment, empowerment and communication but all to be enacted within a circumstance of time constraint.

Governance: one bridge for spanning context

A currently topical aspect of leadership is corporate governance (Cadbury, 1992), a subject which has arisen due to the evolving views concerning the nature of the social, responsibility of companies whilst at the same time promoting the economic progress of the enterprise. Within the sphere of corporate governance, contrasting views exist as to the nature, morality and extent of leadership. One perspective is that economic performance is considered to be the basis for business, as without it a business cannot discharge any other responsibilities or be a good employer (Friedman, 1953).

Thus, the criterion for organizing commercial transactions is assumed to be strictly instrumental, one of cost, economizing on production expenses; and economizing of transaction costs (Williamson, 1981). Notwithstanding that the corporation is first and foremost an efficiency instrument, it does not preclude that firms also seek to monopolize markets (Williamson, 1981).

However, economic performance is not the sole responsibility of a business. Firms must allow for a balanced perspective (Drucker, 1974). The demands for the corporate social responsibility are increasing. The argument is that an organization needs to display full responsibility for its impact on the community and society, from the effluents it discharges into a local river, to the traffic jams its work schedules create on the city streets.

With this philosophy in mind, Drucker (1974) argues that management are 'trustees' accountable to no one single group and that in large publicly owned firms, 'management' should act in the 'best balanced interests' of a number of constituencies; shareholders, employees, suppliers, plant, communities, etc., all currently referred to as 'stakeholders'. Drucker (1974, 1993) continues that a lack of management accountability, exemplified by the current governing organs of corporations, has led to 'impotent ceremonial and legal fiction' at top management level, which in turn is largely responsible for the frantic financial manipulations for the mid 1970s and 1980s. Boards are too often seen as not being in control of their companies and as having failed to prevent either disasters or malpractice. Boards are often accused of not running their business as efficiently as they should and more generally of being answerable neither to their shareholders nor to society at large (Cadbury, 1992). The poor performance of some major corporations; hostile takeovers; the leveraged buyouts; the acquisitions; and the divertissement have created a 'bubble economy' that has collapsed in a series of financial scandals (Drucker, 1993). Changes through takeovers have resulted in an above normal level of turnover among executives (Martin and McConnell, 1991). The perception of irresponsible corporate behaviour is widespread and is not confined just to company boards, but to boards of non profit organizations as well (Cadbury, 1992). In addition to the main concerns of incompetence, boards have been criticized for ignoring the interests of shareholders, being self perpetuating bodies, and drawing their membership from too narrow a section of society (Cadbury, 1992). Cadbury (1992) argues that provided a company produces acceptable results, its board can in practice become self perpetuating, resulting in the legitimacy of the board as the appointee of the shareholders and therefore carrying out duties which are based on something of a fiction. Cadbury (1992, p.59) sees the lack of a keen and consistent sense of accountability to shareholders to be a basic reason for boards failing to achieve the results that they should have attained. He attributes lack of accountability to the inability or unwillingness of shareholders to exert effective pressure on boards to improve their performance.

While Drucker (1973) argues that board meetings rarely go beyond trivia, Lorsch and MacIver (1989) see that directors are at a disadvantage in trying to carry out their legally defined responsibilities. These disadvantages include the directors' psychological reasons for serving, the limits on their time, how well they understand their role and responsibilities as directors and the relationship they have amongst themselves and with companies' chairmen. Lorsch and MacIver (1989) argue that the directors' only power advantage, other than their legal mandate, is their capability to act as a group by reaching a consensus, but doing this requires group cohesion and time for discussion which are often scarce commodities in typical boardrooms. As such, CEOs tend to canvass agendas in advance of meetings, rather than encourage open discussion and run the risk of disagreement. For their part, directors tend not to openly criticize the CEO on any issues, nor articulate the key issues on their minds, nor assert leadership over other directors, and consider themselves responsible to shareholders rather than a broader constituency (Lorsch and MacIver, 1989).

Thus, the 1990s see the emergence of a rationale of now managing exclusively to 'maximize shareholder value' (Drucker, 1993, p.8). Value driven organizations create credos and lay down rules about how employees will interact in the business interests of the organization. This interpretation is grounded in agency theory, which defines a corporation as a nexus of contracts, inherently imbued with conflicts of interest about risk orientations, time horizons, effort levels, and pay outs of cash (Jensen, 1986). Agency theorists identify boards of directors as a primary monitoring device protecting shareholder interests (Fama and Jensen, 1983) or 'the stockholders first line of defence against incompetent management' (Weisbach, 1988, p.431).

Notwithstanding that boards are not always an effective steward of organizational resources (Vence, 1983; Drucker, 1993), they can be vigilant and exert significant influence on the organization they oversee (Kosnik, 1987). Kosnik (1990) argues that boards are more vigilant when their outside members are more than token shareholders in the firms. Although, in recent times, the number of shareholders in the population has grown rapidly, the proportion of the shares of most public limited companies held by individuals has fallen dramatically. Individual investors have been taken over by institutional investors, such as pension funds and insurance companies (Cadbury, 1992). The effect of the rise of the institutional investor and the move to wider share ownership has been to increase the demand for information on companies and on their activities. It is Drucker (1993, p.81) who identifies the 'institutional investors paradox'. Institutional investors can neither manage a business, nor walk away from it, which in turn forces them to 'have to make sure that the business is being managed'. The paradox is created by the fact that institutional investors cannot act as 'owners/managers' whilst at the same time their holdings cannot simply be sold, except to other pension funds or insurance funds. In effect, they are not ordinary 'investors' who can just dispose of their holdings (Drucker, 1993). Cadbury's (1992) view is that institutions now own such a high proportion of the shares of public companies that it has given them both greater influence in company affairs and greater cause to use their influence. Collectively, they have a compelling incentive to improve the governance of the companies in which they have invested, rather than selling out, given that they broadly can sell only to each other (Cadbury, 1992, p.184).

An additional viewpoint is that boards of directors are charged with ensuring that chief executive officers (CEOs) carry out their duties in a way that serves the best interest of shareholders (Vence, 1983). From this standpoint, boards can be seen as monitoring devices that help align CEO and shareholders' interests (Fama and Jensen, 1983), and further to provide leadership and vision, ensure for the right balance of board membership; set the aims, strategy and policies of the company; monitor the achievement of the set aims; review resources and the hiring and development of people in the company, and ensure that appropriate information is provided. With such potentially wide ranging responsibilities, the structure of boards can be that of one tier or two tier. Both structures fulfil the same basic function, that of being accountable to the shareholders for the direction and management of the company. In the unitary board structure, all its directors (whether executive or non executive) share the same aims and the same responsibilities. In contrast, the two tier board structure rigorously separates the control function (a supervisory board which oversees the direction of the company) from the management function (management board which runs the business). The members of the one board cannot unilaterally be members of the other. Hence, to the extent that the CEO duality function 'signals the absence of separation of decision management and decision control' (Fama and Jensen, 1983, p.314), many boards are unlikely to favour the dual structure, because a CEO who is also the chairperson of a firm's board of directors, can dominate both the agenda and content of both board meetings.

However, market needs as well as legal requirements are pointing out the need for a two tier board system, which is inherently more robust from the shareholders' point of view (Cadbury, 1992). Furthermore, two tier board structures enable the interests of the employees to be represented on the supervisory board without directly being involved in the management control of the company. Cadbury (1992) argues that the effectiveness of the governance system depends primarily on the clarity with which responsibilities are assigned and the quality of the people who undertake those responsibilities.

Perrow (1992) argues that large organizations have significantly influenced the centralization of power and authority in modern societies. His view is that the larger the organization, the more power and authority resides at the top to hire and fire, develop or enfeeble workers, relocate staff, influence politicians, influence elections, pollute, eliminate competitors, invest money, buy from suppliers elsewhere, discriminate ethnically and sexually and to corrupt (Perrow, 1992, p.461). The bigger the organization, the more power is generated, and the more concentrated it becomes. The argument is that society is being absorbed by large organizations, public and private, and as such this development leads to an erosion of civil society. Large organizations, consciously or unconsciously in their role of employers, increasingly perform more societal functions, such as socialization, providing occasions for social interactions, handling personal crises, recreation, cultural productions, skill acquisition, and other social activities. Peters and Waterman (1982) postulate that good managers provide meaning for people, as well as money. Hence through societal structural development and considerations, the leadership of an organization faces a paradox, captured on the one hand by Williamson (1985, p.317) who argues that 'the principal function of the board remains that of providing a governance structure protection for the stockholders' and that 'management participation should not become so extensive as to upset the basic board purpose'; whereas Drucker (1993. p.80) warns that managing a business exclusively for the shareholders alienates the very people on whose motivation and dedication the modern business depends, the knowledge workers, as the knowledge worker will not be motivated to make shareholders speculatorly rich.

Cadbury (1992) argues that the Anglo-American and Continental European concepts of the nature of a company stem from two different assumptions, where the former is based on the assumption that the enterprise is based on the capital invested in it by the shareholders, and the latter as coalitions of interests serving a wider purpose than providing a return to shareholders. Therefore the Anglo-American view holds that the key relationship in a capitalistic enterprise is between owners and managers, thereby emphasizing the rights and responsibilities of shareholders. In contrast, the Continental European view is that such emphasis needs to be placed on relationships with employees and on the place of the company in the community. Furthermore, Anglo-Americans prefer self regulation than statutory control, while the concept of self regulation is alien to the Continental Europe tradition (Cadbury, 1992, p.198). However, the increasing pressure on enterprises to act on matters of governance that stem from two main constituencies: shareholders whose influence is increasingly growing; and the broader constituency which includes politicians, regulatory agencies, the professions and society at large, will intensify the debate on issues such as the balance between self and statutory regulation and how far governance structure and standards should be harmonized internationally (Cadbury, 1992; Drucker, 1993).

Depending on the perspective adopted, the implications for leadership are immense, ranging from seeing leadership as that of leading a business or that of being social leaders, that of representing economic interests or of representing the interests of broader based communities, and for leadership research, that of identifying the characteristics of leadership or continuous enquiry into the ever changing nature of social consciousness.

Developmental perspective

The developmental perspective exemplified by developmental theory (Bennis and Nanus, 1985; Kakabadse, 1991) and discretionary leadership (Kakabadse, 1991) focuses also on situational behaviour. However, developmental theory emphasizes a process of constantly learning a repertoire of capabilities and responses to varied circumstances and people (Hrebiniak and Joyce, 1985; Hunt, 1991). Concepts of development offer a more dynamic approach to leadership. The model holds that each person has leadership potential and that the capabilities of leadership can be and are learnt (Bennis and Nanus, 1985; Kakabadse, 1991). Within this framework those who do not develop their capabilities to the full either have no desire to or believe that they are lesser beings, having not been favoured with 'born with' strengths and skills. Those who hold the latter beliefs are accused of failing to recognize that history is in fact written by 'winners', in whose advantage it is to extol the myth of the favoured few.

Leadership is defined as a person's capability and commitment to perform leadership tasks, where capability is conceptualized as a function of knowledge and/or skills which can be gained through education, training and/or experience and commitment, the latter being a combination of confidence and motivation (a measure of a person's feeling of being able to do a task well without supervision, with interest and enthusiasm). The model indicates that the ability of the leader to influence the intervening variables may be assisted by personal skills and either helped or hindered by situational variables. The model recognizes that the leader's own behaviour and level of emotional maturity is important in setting values and examples and in establishing and maintaining high standards of performance. Considering that leadership is increasingly concerned with the influence of others, who may exercise political constraints, control allocation of resources within organizations and/or externally from it, it is postulated that the leader's (in)effectiveness, has a direct bearing on the strategic direction and success of the organization.

However, in applying a capability model, there is necessity to distinguish between behavioural skills, knowledge and personal characteristics or traits. While skills and knowledge are, for the most part, learnable, characteristics may or may not be modifiable and traits are typically thought of as relatively fixed aspects of an individual's personality structure (Phillips and Hunt, 1995). The capability concept distinguishes 'personal capabilities' from personal characteristics, decrying characteristics and emphasizing learning and adopting a philosophy of learning in order to become a leader.

The convergence of empirical studies (Kouzes and Posner, 1987; Kakabadse, 1991) and theory based examination of developmental leadership activities (Bennis and Nanus, 1985; Sashkin and Burke, 1990) highlights a relatively small set of behavioural categories emphasizing leadership capabilities, namely, cognitive complexity, and two motivational competencies, self efficacy and pro social power need.

Cognitive complexity (Jaques, 1979; Jacobs and Jaques, 1987, 1990; Phillips and Hunt, 1992) is a mental means for constructing social systems that can attain certain organizational aims or vision. As such, it is prerequisite for leadership success, but in itself not sufficient (Rosen and Brown, 1996).

Self efficacy (Bandura, 1977, 1982, 1986, 1988) refers to one's beliefs about oneself as an effective 'agent'. This construct provides the basis for agency theory and is similar to the construct of internal control (Rotter, 1966), and is interlined with the philosophy of the self fulfilling prophecy (Merton, 1968; Rosenthal and Kouzmin, 1993; Eden, 1990). Self efficacious individuals believe that they can control or have an impact on their world by what they do, by means of their own actions. Although self efficiency includes concepts of self confidence, which is based on hope and narcissism, it is equally based on life experiences that teach one that one can take actions that will effectively have an impact on one's environment. Without a strong sense of efficacy, it is unlikely that a person will willingly take on a leadership role or even wish to be a leader (Phillips and Hunt, 1992).

The pro social power need refers to the need for power for its own sake and not for the sake of achievement of quality of results. Pro social power need oriented people are characterized by exhibiting a need for coercion and control, irrespective of context or organizational requirement. The concept of pro social power is further explored in the power/politics section of this chapter.

The developmental perspective draws on the ancient philosophy and modern theory to build the platform for wisdom for developing leaders.

From Plato's philosophical King to Machiavelli's Prince, from Hobbe's Sovereign to Neitzsche's Superman, philosophy has set the search for the nature of the ideal leader. The very concept of the 'new age leadership' perspective, centred on the renewed philosophical leadership paradigm, pursues its quest down the road of wisdom whilst rejecting the route of 'I was born into greatness.'

Enlightenment

The troublesome and impossible to escape fundamental question of Socrates 'What ought one do?' (Plato's recording) projects the same force of ethical dilemma to contemporary leaders, as it may have done to philosophers in ancient times. For Socrates, the force of his original question lies in the fact that it demands some sort of account from individuals, as to why they choose one action over another. In fact, at its deeper level, Socrates' question requires people to articulate some sort of founding vision about what they consider to be a 'good'. However, there is not in any one truth enunciated by Socrates that where one can look for a sense of the essence of leadership. Instead, Socrates goes to great lengths to recall to his fellow Athenians the fact that he has no holding on this or any other truth. In the Apology, his defence against the charge of impiety and corruption of the youth of Athens at his trial in 399 BC, Socrates details the origins of his humility. In response to others' puzzlement at the declaration of the Delphi oracle that none is wiser than he, Socrates replies that he visited a wise man and that after conversing with him he went away thinking 'I am wiser than this man: neither of us knows anything that is really worth knowing, but he thinks that he has knowledge when he has not, while I have no knowledge, and do not think that I have' (Plato, 1956, p.36).

The Socratic 'ignorance' paradox serves as the basis for an understanding of philosophy concerned with the search for wisdom. The philosophy is not itself a body of wisdom but rather the aspiration towards the end. In this construct, philosophy is a way of living one's life, an 'active activity', a verb rather than a passive noun. Thus 'apriori' to the attempt to defining leadership, 'apriori' to all forms of human inquiry, must come the acknowledgement of an ultimate infinite interval separating the seeker from the wisdom sought. As Socrates claims 'an unexamined life is not worth living' (Plato, 1956, p.45), then it is incumbent on the philosopher to subject him or herself to the practice of an endless humility; the practice of opening oneself to the limitedness of one's perspective and thus, in effect, to the finitude of one's being. Socrates' affirmation of the centrality of the 'examined life' makes him the prototype of the philosopher as a leader.

As Socrates himself wrote nothing and the majority of his work was recorded by his student, Plato, there is a need to distinguish between the image of Socrates as philosopher in action and that of Socrates as mere spokesperson for the beliefs peculiar to Plato and to the Platonism of the Academy founded in the fourth century BC, Athens. This is not to deny the importance of the Platonic vision of leadership, nor the wisdom of the philosopher-king articulated in Book V of the Republic (Plato, 1956). However, Socratic teaching at its root could not be limited to and by the expression of one idea among many. As a living absolute, the Socratic message is continual movement of a freeing of oneself from a presumption to know. Thus leadership as the exercise of Socratic humility leaves nothing untouched. No one given set of characteristics attributed to a leader or set of circumstances out of which a leader-follower relationship is deemed to be born can, in themselves, give rise to the phenomenon of leadership without the presence of the willingness to aspire to wisdom, that openness to truth as a process. The Socratic message found in the Platonic dialogue *Theaetetus*, suggests that a leadership role is an awakening, which is precisely the birth of all learning. 'I am so far like the midwife that I cannot myself give birth to wisdom; and the common reproach is true, that though I question the other, I can myself bring nothing to light because there is no wisdom in me. The reason is this: heaven constrains me to serve as a midwife, but has debarred me from giving birth' (Plato, 1957, p.26). It is this image of the Socratic leadership which may well serve as a guide to contemporary leaders. Leadership, in the Socratic sense, is not to be equated with a hindering or postponement of action. The leader-follower relationship is one which empowers the followers and where both members of the relationship are led to the creative activity in which the horizons of meaning surrounding the issues at hand are perpetually stretched.

In keeping with Socratic teaching, but providing contrast in one area, Plato's philosopher-king rules the state not with authority but by virtue which is an authority derived from the knowledge of the one truth. For Plato, the possession of the 'wisdom' of an 'intellectual vision' informing the principles of government as it informs the principles of human conduct in general, distinguishes the leader from follower. In The Republic, Plato claims that, 'until political greatness and wisdom meet in one' and 'those commoner natures who pursue either to the exclusion of the other are compelled to stand aside, a leader will never have rest from their evils - no, nor the human race, as I believe' (Plato, 1956, p.431).

Although the presence of the philosopher-king does not in itself guarantee the realization of the state as the embodiment of absolute justice, it is nonetheless true that without the guidance of the one who knows the essence of justice, the state is condemned to be ruled in an arbitrary and capricious fashion. Thus in interpretative, ideological interactions, what distinguishes contemporary leaders from followers is the possession by the former of a degree of critical perspective which is developmental for the latter. The developer-leader, for example, can develop (lead forward) only insofar as he or she possesses a higher level of capability than the developing-follower in the infinite nature of the task of imparting capability (knowledge, or Socratic truth). Followers are thus followers only insofar as their inability to perceive an ever widening series of perspectives and hence are not locked into their followership. The very essence of development consists in the mutual offering of perspectives which allows and promotes the movement of followers into leaders.

Socrates, Plato, Aristotle and Kant promote a virtue approach which emphasizes the will, intentions and character of the individual. The virtuous person acts according to inner conviction and strength, irrespective of the consequences of the action and its impact on relationships, whether it be based on kinship, professional or friendship ties. This focus on the individual as the pillar of ethics has advantage in that the onus is clearly allocated. It also has the disadvantage of presuming that all that is needed to achieve an ethical society is for its members to act according to subjective notions of virtue.

The philosopher leader

There is an increasing recognition of the place of philosophy in management and leadership theory. The contemporary penchant for visioning as a prelude to missioning, is one manifestation of this recognition.

Upon examining leadership, Kouzes and Posner (1987, p.93-4) conclude:

> Envisioning and intuiting are not logical activities. They do not lend themselves to easy study and observation. They are extremely difficult to explain and quantify. So we have either ignored them or not taken them seriously. Even so, in recent studies, executives have reported that their intuition has been a guide in most of their important decisions. And yet, while the use of intuition is commonplace among executives, they are very reluctant to talk about it. Hard bitten senior managers see it as too soft and mystical to openly acknowledge. They appear to be afraid that their executive colleagues, all who use intuition, will think that they are weird. Intuition is like that big elephant in the middle of the room - everybody can see it, but since it isn't supposed to be there, no one will talk about it.

Senge (1990) identified the need for 'metanoia' (transcendence of mind), a shift of mind, if organizations are to make the transformation into learning organizations. Senge (1990a, p.13) ascertains: 'When you ask people about what it is like being part of a great team, what is most striking is the meaningfulness of the experience. People talk about being a part of something larger than themselves, of being connected, of being generative. It becomes quite clear that, for many, their experience of that part of their lives is a stimulus to looking for ways to recapture that spirit'.

Covey (1990b) also exhorts managers to some form of metanoia by advocating the resurrection of principles as the basis for leadership. Covey (1990b, p.42) in Socratic spirit, posits that an individual's character is the principle determinant of their personal/interpersonal effectiveness: 'it is a principle centred, character based, inside out approach to personal and interpersonal effectiveness'. Of Covey's (1990a) seven habits of highly effective people, driven from a set of principles that include integrity, humility and fidelity, the seventh habit, 'sharpening the saw', includes spiritual renewal, which he defines with the continual clarification of values and commitment to others.

In his book, *Maverick*, Semler (1993) describes how he went through the process of letting go in order to transform his company, Semco, into what has been described as the world's most unusual organization. Similar sentiments have been expressed by Arnold and Plas (1993) in their book, *The Human Touch*. In Socratic style they declare: 'Those of us who run businesses today need to raise our clenched fists, slowly extend our fingers, and let go of our organizations' (Arnold and Plas, 1993, p.18).

Modern western leadership literature suggests a philosophical turn to Socratic contemplation, that is to approach situations with an attitude of acceptance rather than control; letting go rather than holding on; listening rather than doing; humility rather than proficiency. As Peck (1983, p.91) puts it:

> The unconscious is always one step ahead of the conscious mind in the right direction or the wrong direction. It is therefore impossible ever to know that what you are doing is right, since knowing is a function of consciousness. However, if your will is steadfastly to the good, and if you are willing to suffer fully when the good seems ambiguous, ... then your unconsciousness will always be one step ahead of your conscious mind in the right direction. ... Only you won't have the luxury of knowing it at the time you are doing it. Indeed, you will do the right thing precisely because you have been willing to forego that luxury.

For example Senge's (1990b) concept of the learning organization embraces several basic principles: system thinking; personal mastery (developing openness and trust); mental models (reframing or finding new ways of thinking); shared vision (read as culture); and team learning (Senge, 1992; Dumaine, 1994) are in many ways based on the Socratic philosophy. Senge's (1994) representations of leadership in *The Fifth Discipline* also differs from the pragmatic leadership role. Instead of focusing on the heroic transformation (male) leader, the leadership is a form of stewardship and facilitation or what is now popularly termed 'post heroic leadership' (Huey, 1994). This stands in marked contrast to the images of leadership that dominated the 1980s particularly in the *Excellence* literature (Peters and Waterman, 1982).

Jaques' (1986, 1989) fifth or theoretical dimension of management is further developed by Senge who introduces 'new age' concepts that are later developed into specific tools of the learning organization, such 'scientifically' packaged devices as the Ladder of Inference, the Causal Loop, Left-hand/Right-hand Columns, and the Container (Senge et al, 1994).

The unconscious and organizational anxiety

Leaders are typically held responsible for many things that go wrong, even if they are not directly responsible for certain outcomes. By common unconscious consent, the leader is deemed the centre of all trouble, allowing others to find relief from their own persecutors. The process also allows the leader to be more easily idealized as a good protective figure.

However, being held responsible and providing protection holds disadvantages for effective communication and relationship building. The problem is that of distancing, a conscious need to keep apart.

In some situations, leaders are unable to develop close relations with their colleagues and subordinates because of unconscious fears, or because some form an unconscious anger or envy which leads them to resent any trace of rivalry. Often the unconscious fears prevent the leader from behaving ably to accept genuine help and advice (Tait, 1995). Often the relations between a leader and his or her subordinates are also the focus of unconscious projections of an Oedipal nature, with subordinates projecting their fantasy of replacing their parent into the leader, a factor which may reinforce the leader's anxiety (Morgan, 1986). Transference, the process in which followers transfer or place upon the leader the qualities (positive and negative) of another significant person in their life and behave towards the leader as if he/she were that person (Freud, 1922), may place the unwitting leader in the role of another important person in the subordinate's life. The leader comes to realize that the subordinate expects them to behave as if they hold a series of values which are alien to the leader. When such dysfunctional relationships dominate, the leader frequently becomes isolated, providing an ideal situation for subordinates to club together in a way that may actually lead to his or her demise. Adults, like children, can become overly committed to the comfort and security provided by their new teddy bears (the doll or blanket), can reject development, project a rigid commitment to a particular way of working, thus making it difficult for the person to move on and deal with the changing nature of his/her surroundings (Winnicott, 1958).

Meanings

A wealth of evidence exits in the psychological literature, which has relevance for leadership, that individual behaviour is driven by cognitive schema (Bartlett, 1932; Neisser, 1977), namely the manner in which individuals receive, organize, plan, regulate and transmit information to other humans is learnt through interaction with others and experience. That is to say, people are capable of choice and regulation. Initially, Kelly (1955) and later Slater (1976) developed the repertory grid technique as a mechanism for discerning the meanings held by individuals. Piaget (1978) and Bruner (1972) offer similar arguments in the field of developmental psychology.

Bandura (1977) and Mischel (1977) suggest that people use symbolic processes to represent events and to communicate with others (Morgan, 1986; Forester, 1989). Goffman (1974) suggests that 'frames' of individual reference are created through subjective interpretations of social interaction, whilst Mangham (1978) comes to similar conclusions, but uses the analogy of the theatre as the metaphor.

Tolman (1924) suggests that we structure our experiences through purposive ways, which drive behaviour. In addition, Salancik and Pfeffer (1977a, 1977b) offer a 'social' information processing model to describe how salient purposive ways can be developed and in turn drive behaviour. The principle is that behaviour can be explained in terms of reciprocal interaction between personal and environmental determinants. People are influenced by environmental forces, but they also make choices as to how they should behave. People are responsive to situations and also influence situations. Through personal values, thoughts and symbols, people anticipate future experiences and attempt to use experiences from the past in order to prepare for the present and for the future.

Symbolism and meanings have been incorporated in the leadership literature under the heading the praxis of leadership (Carnevale and Stone, 1994). Praxis stands for the ability of actors to engage in acts of leadership which assist in the maintenance of a way of life which incorporates critical values and irreversible commitments (Selznick, 1957). Leadership, in this respect, resides in actions, not in positions, and requires continuous (re)examination and learning within contexts. Effective leadership in organization begins with some perspective on organization in terms of enactment, power and structure.

Formal organizations are 'essentially processes of organizing enacted persons' (Brown, 1978, p.371); that is, an organization is a negotiated environment, though negotiated from positions of unequal status, power and authority. Weick (1969) uses the term enactment to highlight the way in which organizational members construct and negotiate the 'reality' of the organization, using such concepts as role definition and acceptance and the affirmation of the symbolic universe within which people operate. Enactment requires the organizational member to make sense of organization (Weick, 1979), that is, to join in the conventional cultural and normative processes and to carve out a meaningful place. It is in this sense that the rationality of the organization is a 'post hoc' interpretation of events where rationality 'turns out to be an achievement, a symbolic product that is constructed through actions that in themselves are non rational' (Brown, 1978, p.370). The organization itself becomes a paradigm which incorporates rules of actions, including a rule regarding the application of rationality to events (Brown, 1978). As such, enactment occurs in the context of historically constructed social processes. It is a dialectic between the material and the ideal. All social conduct involves the interplay of the basic conditions which frame the action, the rationalization by actors of what they do, and the consequence (perhaps not intended) of their actions. It should be stated that Weick (1979) now postulates that sense making need not be a post hoc experience and can, in fact be a useful lever for aiding understanding and stimulating appropriate action in circumstances of diversity. The manner in which people sensibly corner the nature of their diversities, he terms shared sense making, thus making leadership the conceptual and emotional capacity to provide for understanding (sense making), thereby enabling others to function.

The dialectical interplay between these conditions yields structure; yet structure 'is both the medium and the outcome of the reproduction of practices' (Giddens, 1979, p.5). Thus structure in organization can be seen both as a feature of individuals interacting and as an outcome of such an interaction - structure in action. Enactment, therefore, occurs within the paradigmatic confines of the dynamic of power, class and ideological consciousness. That is, organizations restrict alternatives, they impose a system of control on members' outlooks which originates in the political and economic relations of the contemporary state of affairs. Thus organizational structures are composed of individuals who can be located within differential power structures and who represent historically notable dissections of control. Therefore, the structure of organization becomes a dialectical process, wherein basic relations of power are confirmed through rules which are absorbed through what might be considered ideological rituals in the workplace. Despite the conceptual anxieties underpinning structure, the topic became a subject in its own right, emphasizing its forward, goal attaining nature.

Structure of organizations

With the merit of attaining maximum productivity and efficiency, numerous theorists have planned an enquiry of the underlying forces which drive behaviour (Silverman, 1971; Sofer, 1972; Mouzelis, 1967) towards the attainment of organizational goals. In the broader organizational setting, this line of exploration has been identified as structural theory, driven by Weberian thinking (Weber, 1947) but nevertheless parallel to demographic analysis in ascertaining the predetermined nature of circumstances. Agreement as to which variables to pursue, namely task allocation, specialization, standardization, formalization, centralization and configuration, has been paramount, with the emerging view that emphasis should be on how to measure structural attributes, rather than which attributes want examination (Pennings, 1973).

Particularly influential has been the Aston School (Pugh et al, 1963; Pugh, 1969; Hickson, Pugh and Phesey, 1969) which originally examined 52 organizations in the English Midlands, with the study being replicated by Inkson, Hickson and Pugh (1970) and Hickson, Hinings, et al (1971). The overall conclusion is that four dimensions of structure, namely the structuring of activities, concentration of authority, control of workflow and size of supportive component, are particularly influential in determining the nature of the formative context of organizations. Other structuralist researchers (Child, 1972; Reiman, 1973; Donaldson, 1976; Blau, 1970; Hage and Aitken, 1966) dispute certain of the detailed findings of the Aston School but support the general overview that structural components are primary in the influence of formative context.

Leadership as definitions of reality

Leadership acts are therefore involved with the redefinition of reality and the creation of alternatives, although this occurs in the context of a social world that displays patterns of domination. Thus, any consideration given to leadership as a construct must incorporate an analysis of context, which in this case is equivalent to an analysis of the economic, political and cultural relations of modern societies. That is 'praxis' can become a unifying concept for leadership studies. Praxis is the recognition that theory must eventually be located in 'sensuous human activity' (Locke, 1971; Sternberg, 1985). The test of theory is its eventual relevance to improving human conditions: 'through practice and labour, the human species synthesizes and alters the material world and thereby transforms nature qua non as well as itself' (Held, 1980). Thus praxis stands for the ability of all people to engage in acts of leadership which help in the transformation to a way of life which incorporates participative principles. Leadership, in this sense, is both a critical and a shared leadership. It is aired because no one individual has the right way. Rather leadership is a communal endeavour wherein the direction of the society is discussed and debated. The need for leadership in the contemporary organization consisting of the knowledge workers, still persists. Knowledge work 'itself knows no hierarchy for there are no "higher" and "lower" knowledges'. Knowledge is either relevant to a live task or irrelevant to it' (Drucker, 1978, p.289). Thus the task at hand decides, 'who is in charge, when, for what and for how long' (Drucker, 1978, p.290). Therefore the knowledge needs to be organized as a team in which the task decides the leadership (Drucker, 1978).

As stated, leadership in this respect resides in actions and acts, not in persons or positions, but each act must also have critical audience. The critical spirit is the basis for leadership acts (Grob, 1984). Leadership needs to be conceived as critical reflection, critical action within the dialectic of enactment (Grob 1984). This proposition is based on the idea of action leadership, one that deals with organizational enactment, and which involves the demystification of structure (Berger and Luckmann, 1971); through being critically educative (Gramsci, 1971) and whose success and definition are conditioned by language (Pondy, 1978; Evered, 1983).

Because leadership influences 'enactment' (Weick, 1969) and sense making (Weick, 1979), namely ways in which organizational members construct and negotiate the 'reality' of organization, there is an urgency in leadership for 'boardroom' learning (Dror, 1980, 1984, 1987; Kakabadse, 1993). Enacted realities, including role definition and the acceptance and the affirmation of the symbolic universe within which organizational actors operate, are significantly different and more prone to distortion in crisis situations. Although organizations adjust to operate in the 'new' environment in crisis situations they do not necessarily learn, as they revert to old patterns of operation when threat is removed (Argyris and Schon, 1974, 1978; Argyris, 1982). Enactment requires, and also helps, actors to make sense of the organization by enabling actors to join in the conventional cultural and normative processes and to design a meaningful place (Ashby, 1952, 1960). In this sense, the 'rationality' of the organization is a post hoc interpretation of events or a 'symbolic product that is constructed through actions that, in themselves, are non rational' (Brown, 1978, p.370). Thus, leadership and organizational learning are both contextually defined and require different strategies in different circumstances (Pask, 1961; Belgard, Fisher and Rauner, 1988). For example, learning in the 'lean', but growing, organization will require different learning strategies from that in the 'lean', but mature, organization (Kakabadse, 1993). Furthermore, learning in organizations with dependencies on short term revenues requires different strategies to organizations with dependencies on long term revenue and competency requirements (Kakabadse, 1993).

Group dynamics

At the social level, organizations as networks cannot be understood without understanding the individuals who make up the organization (Granovetter, 1992). However, knowledge about the individuals often reveals little about the context of the network. The relationship between individuals and networks appears to be ambiguous, or at least paradoxical, as networks cannot exist without people (Ahrne, 1990). Networks are constantly being socially constructed, reproduced and altered as the results of the actions of people (White, 1992). Therefore, networks are as much a 'process' as they are structure; being continually shaped and reshaped by the actions of individuals who, in turn, are constrained by the structural position in which they find themselves within social time and space. There is a sense of emergence in understanding the essence of networks as properties emerging from the interactions of non linearly connected people in the social landscape (Ahrne, 1990).

Empirical evidence (Kanter, 1977; Fischer, 1982; Marsden, 1987; Burt, 1990) suggests that individuals develop relations with other individuals similar to themselves; thus forming a network group of kindred spirits with common social attributes embedded within 'formative contexts' (Unger, 1987) such as institutional arrangements, cultural values, ethnic tastes, training, background and cognitive frames that shape the daily routines of people's ideology and objectives (Lazarsfeld, Berelson and Gaudet, 1944; Faber and Seers, 1972; Erickson, 1988; Rice, Grant, Schmitz and Torobin, 1990; Rice and Aydin, 1991; Schmitz and Fulk, 1991). However, this relational proximity, or the extent to which individuals interact directly and indirectly, may lead to less discrepant social information processing, since people are more coherently linked, share a common perception (Van Maanen, 1978) and develop strong ties (Granovetter, 1973), which possibly leads to 'groupthink' (Janis, 1972; Janis and Mann, 1977; Janis, 1982; t'Hart, 1990).

Network structure does not predict attitudes or behaviour directly; it predicts similarities between attitudes and behaviours (Burt, 1992). People bring to the network a history of their previous interactions and carry away from a new interaction history and repertoire. However, they do not reconstruct social norms of interaction each time they meet, rather, they develop mutually agreeable means for the repetitive conduct of business

(Collins, 1987). With time, these patterns of exchange develop as a product of interaction and adaptation and become routinized, taken for granted or ideologized; creating a sense of security in conditions of uncertainty (Garfinkel, 1967; Giddens, 1984; Collins, 1987).

As such, people set the tone of network norms and become the receptacles of the network's shared idealism and may become less readily expendable (Selznick, 1957), and more inclined towards groupthink (Janis, 1982; t'Hart, 1990). Generally, networks provide the mechanisms by which actors are proximate to, or are exposed to, others' information, influence and behaviour (Hackman, 1983; Rice and Blair, 1984; Rice and Aydin, 1991). Actors who have had a part in the formation of the network norms or who become knowledgeable about them, develop a stake in their maintenance. Established norms make continuous interaction predictable and simpler than the constant negotiation of the terms of action (Collins, 1987). However, despite the seemingly routine character of networks, every interaction is fraught with uncertainty. Network order has potentially to be negotiated in each interaction concerning meaning and action, feelings and emotions (Cherry, 1978).

From the network individual's perspective, the most efficient form of interaction is action where the person is knowledgeable in the ways of the insiders of the network (Meyer and Rowan, 1983). Thus, actors interact effectively with each other by adopting a similar 'vocabulary of motives' (Mills, 1940). Through this vocabulary of motives, actors exchange information and develop similar perceptions and opinions (Rogers and Kincaid, 1981; Tichy, 1981; Hackman, 1983; Wellman, 1983; 1988) which often may lead to the network's 'darkside' or groupthink (Janis, 1972; Janis and Mann, 1977; Janis, 1982; t'Hart, 1990).

This is exemplified by Kennedy's advisory group during the Cuban crisis - an abortive invasion of Cuba at the Bay of Pigs by 1,200 US sponsored anti Castro Cuban refugee forces on 17 April 1961 (Bell, 1971; Morgan, 1986, Rosenthal, t'Hart and Kouzmin, 1991). The Bay of Pigs plan was developed so secretly and swiftly that only the selected few policy makers knew of what decisions had been made until it was too late to reverse them (Bell, 1971). President Kennedy and his advisers had unwittingly developed shared illusions and operating norms that interfered with their ability to think critically and to engage in the required reality testing. Strong rationalizing tendencies mobilized support for favoured opinions (Bell, 1971; Morgan, 1986). Had the information been subjected to dissident opinions, outside the advisory network group, the intended invasion may have been prevented (Bell, 1971). The influence of articulated dissident opinion is valuable in the decision making process, although it may often vary enormously from situation to situation (Bell, 1971). Similarly, the policy failure in the case of

Pearl Harbour, the escalation of US involvement in the Korean and Vietnam Wars, the Iran rescue mission and the Iran Contra Affairs can be attributed to group thinking (Janis, 1982; t'Hart, 1990; Rosenthal, t'Hart and Kouzmin, 1991).

Thus a paradox of leadership is to engender 'positivist' network norms and yet allow for challenge; to provide for stimulating but also secure environments thereby nurturing a healthy interplay of dissident opinion. It is that capability for the continuous reappraisal and yet maintenance of contra forces, that distinguishes leaders from managers, and as such distinguishes those exhibiting broader capabilities from those displaying more focused areas of competence.

Capabilities versus competencies: the differentiating leaders from managers debate

With significant advances in the understanding of the human psyche (Freud, 1922; Jung, 1953; Kets de Vries, 1977; Argyris, 1982); human behaviour (Asch, 1956; Zimbardo, 1970; Milgram, 1974); learning (Krebs and Miller, 1985); action (Argyris, 1957; Argyris and Schon, 1974, 1978; Argyris, 1982); and the unsuccessful attempt of the psychological perspective, through the 'age of psychological testing' (circa 1930-1940), to define universal traits of good leadership (Korman, 1968); the behavioural perspective, in the 'age of grid training' (circa 1950), to train managers to become good leaders and the contextual perspective, in the 'age of causality' (circa 1960-1970), to define an appropriate management style for the diversity of praxis situations exemplified by crisis (Wolfenstein, 1967; Staw and Ross, 1989; Rosenthal and Kouzmin, 1993) emerged the need for transforming managers into the leaders in the 'age of re-invention' (circa 1990).

The quest for new leadership has resulted in the theoretical distinction between leaders and the leadership role and managers and the management role (Levinson, 1981). The transformational leadership thesis flags this separation and opens the flood gates for a leadership revival through the reincarnation of the 'charismatic' leader (irrespective of whether charisma is a born with or developed characteristic). The 'age of value' (circa 1990) aids their distinct differentiation. The emerging argument holds that 'most leaders are good managers, but managers are not necessarily good leaders' (Warburton, 1993, p.29) and that the world beyond the 1990s will not belong to managers but to passionate driven leaders who are innovative path finders, able to empower others to lead themselves (Leavett, 1987; Manz and Sims, 1990; Fairholm, 1991; Warburton, 1993).

Managers are transactional technologists, maintaining balance in operations, are process - or means - oriented (Burns, 1978), are 'caretakers of the status quo' (Warburton, 1993, p.28) who think in terms of replicability with a focus on control and accountability (Bennis, 1984) and who relate to each other in role terms and favour loyalty, conformity, coordination and team spirit (Bradford and Cohen, 1984; Nibly, 1984; Manz and Sims, 1990; Fairholm, 1991). Managers prefer security and are effective in situations where they can direct the desired behaviour, control deviation from set norms and punish recalcitrance (Zemke, 1987). Managers favour proven technologies and hierarchical structures as they are predictable and are, in themselves, a form of control (McDermott, 1969, p.35). Managers from the more negative perspective avoid complexity and attempt to ensure tangible, detailed control to limit the danger and insecurity of uncertainty (McAdam, 1993, p.8), producing mediocrity and suffocating innovation and creativity (Fairholm, 1991), but from a positive viewpoint, build a culture satisfactory to those involved through daily, efficient transactions (Kakabadse, 1982; Kakabadse, Brovetto and Holzer, 1988).

Notwithstanding that 'rationality' and 'irrationality', human forces that seldom can be ordered and controlled, appear to be central to the human condition and the fact that rationality is often irrationality in disguise (Freud, 1922), managers tend to fear the irrational and use reason to bring its manifestation under control. The danger is that those adopting the mental set of manager often miss the hidden meaning and significance of actions that shape organizations (Morgan 1986).

For example, the rationality expressed by Taylor (1911) may have disguised an extreme form of compulsiveness, just as the contemporary manager's excessive concern for clear cut targets and goals may disguise a basic insecurity in life, anxiety, inferiority or insignificance (Kanter, 1977; Morgan, 1986; Manz and Sims, 1990). Psychologically powerless managers turn to the domination and control of others, invoking 'power tools' (status, rules and procedures) as a response to the restrictiveness of their own situation (Kanter, 1977). Thus, it is argued, considerable evidence supports the view that managers are autocratic leaders or 'strong men' (Manz and Sims, 1990) who, through their commands, exercise positional power in order to secure fear based compliance from others. In terms of leadership style, they are limbic leaders (instinctive, tangible and results oriented) dominated by left brain functions (analytical, elemental and rational) and exhibit behaviour that values analytical precision, close control and supervision, punitive and evaluative measures (Burgelman, 1990; McAdam, 1993). They are evaluative thinkers that are convergent in character, who, through the control of the flow of information and ideas, build emotional and physical blocks that prevent innovation (Henry, 1991). Managers are in action by 'operating the ship' or 'rowing the boat'.

Furthermore, it is argued that managers exhibit a Kantian (1901) attitude towards the world, characterized by hostility and distrust of everything that is new; they dread chaos. They, in a Kantian (1901) fashion, consider that both contextual parameters (Kant's external world) and human behaviour (Kant's internal nature) have to be formed, organized and dominated by rationality (Kantian understanding and reason) and by a rationality guided volition in order to make them safe (Kant, 1909). Thus, they share the Kantian (1901) fear of 'transcendental contingency'. They fear that the objects (actors, artefacts) could behave amongst themselves in a way quite different from the laws of their experience and thinking, unless they bind actors from the outset by these laws.

In contrast (perhaps influenced by the writings of Confucius, Aristotle, Plato and the Bible), leaders are considered to be transformational philosophers who are creative and outcome or ends oriented (Zaleznick, 1977; Burns, 1978; Peters and Waterman, 1982; Bennis, 1984; Bennis and Nanus, 1985). Their attitude towards the world can be characterized as loving, trusting, surrendering to it in affectionate vision of philosophical genius. They are designers who think globally the long term horizons in terms of renewal and operate outside the constraints of structure, often breaking the mould in order to create and achieve a set vision (Selznick, 1957; Bradford and Cohen, 1984; Nibly, 1984; Henry, 1991; McAller, 1991). They actively search for new frontiers and place a high emphasis on values, creativity, intelligence, integrity, cooperation and sobriety.

Leaders are self confident, mature individuals who understand themselves and how they differ from the group (Bennis, 1984, 1989; Bass, Avolio and Goodheim, 1987; Frey, 1993; Warburton, 1993). The behavioural responses of self assured leaders (Maslow, 1971; Ng, 1980; Bass, 1981; Metzger, 1987) generate an empowering, freedom enhancing environment (Kanter, 1977).

Leaders build socio psychological contacts with their followers that allow them to lead voluntarily towards common action, whether or not they are present to oversee the behaviour of followers and, as such, inspire innovation (Hodgson, 1988; Fairholm, 1991; Warburton, 1993). In terms of leadership style, they are cerebral leaders (conceptual, intellectual and design oriented), dominated by right brain functions (holistic, integrative and artistic/emotional) and exhibit behaviour that values a sense of identity, emotional integrity, flexibility and empowerment (Manz and Sims, 1991; McAdam, 1993). They are imaginative thinkers who are expansive in nature and who actively work on the removal of barriers to creative actions by fostering a creative formative context encouraging innovation (Henry, 1991). They are in the centre of action by 'steering the ship'.

It is argued that the contemporary leadership literature supports the view that leaders are 'ideological' (visionary or philosophical) super heroes, who can inspire and empower others to lead themselves. These super heroes have ascended from the first order of knowledge; knowledge for the sake of domination, also known as knowledge of positive science, to the second order of knowledge; the knowledge of essence or the knowledge of personal culture. 'New age' scholars express a need for an intellectual leap forward of transcendence from the pragmatic dimension of leadership to the philosophical dimension of leadership. The same values and traits that define leaders (creativity, vision, intelligence, integrity, energy) are screened out in the organizational selection process, in favour of conformity, loyalty, mediocrity, masculinity and team spirit (Fairholm, 1991; Korac-Boisvert, 1994a).

After a century of management control, measurements, systems, performance and productivity, managers predominate in contemporary organizations to the virtual exclusion of leaders (Fairholm, 1991; Korac-Boisvert, 1994b). The CEO of General Electric, Jack Welch (quoted in Manz and Sims, 1991, p.27), poignantly summarizes this situation by stating that 'we have to undo a 100 year old concept and convince our managers that their role is not to control people and stay "on top" of things but rather to guide, energize and excite'. Perhaps this scarcity of leadership resources is the 'raison d'être' for the quest for sensuous, knowledgeable, practical and active business athletes or 'new age' leaders (Banner and Blessingame, 1988; Senge, 1992) who can transcend mediocrity and provide synergies which excite and empower others, generate instability in institutional arrangements and yet still provide direction through the economical, political, ideological and social landscape (Ahrne, 1990).

The conventional wisdom of managerial control is seriously challenged as being appropriate to all social and organized settings, where contextual dynamics are intense, rapid or 'turbulent' (Emery and Trist, 1965) and, perhaps, even chronic (Korac-Boisvert and Kouzmin, 1994a).

Summarized below, in Table 2.1, are examples from the body of literature that emphasizes different characteristics of leadership as distinct from management (Selznick, 1957; Burns, 1978; Zaleznick, 1977; Bennis, 1984; Bennis and Nanus, 1985; Zemke, 1987; Fairholm, 1991; Kakabadse, 1991).

In the evolving organizational landscape where information is shared (Boettinger, 1989; Powell, 1990), the key aspect of leadership will be the leader's ability to influence the organization by winning the confidence of the stakeholders.

Table 2.1
Comparing manager versus leader attributes

Attributes	Leaders	Managers
Approach	Innovative, creates opportunity to imagine new areas to explore	Balance of operations
Interaction	Personal in their orientation to group members	Role bounded
Focus	Focus on vision, expectations and context	Focus on control, production and results
Influence	Within and outside the construct of structure and their immediate jurisdiction	Within the designated group
Motivates through	Volitional activity, emotion, offering suggestions	Formal authority mechanisms
Use	Influence (power)	Control
Values	Cooperation, unity, equality, justice and fairness in addition to efficiency and effectiveness	Coordination, efficiency, and effectiveness
Communicate	Indirectly and directly, give over lapping and ambiguous assignments	Directly giving clear direction solitary assignment
Represents	Direction in history	Process
Orientated towards	Ends	Means
Is	Philosopher	Technologist
Has	Transforming impact	Transactional impact
Role primarily	Discretionary	Prescribed
Main tasks	Defines and communicates goals, motivates	Implements goals, referees, coaches
Thinking time frame	Futuristic, tomorrow and the day after	Current, yesterday's output and today's problems
Thinking context	Global	Local
Main direction	Renewal	Maintenance
Source of authority	Non economic	Economic or quasi economic

The leader's capabilities for social networking depends on a variety of aspects of the cognitive phenotype. These include communicative ability, personality, background knowledge, generated trust, motivation, as well as the perceived status of the organization in the landscape (Thacker, 1990). In highly open information organizations, such as 'network organizations' characterized by lateral and horizontal patterns of exchange, interdependent flows of resources and reciprocal lines of communications (Nolan, Pollock and Ware, 1988, 1989; Powell, 1990), policy implementation will depend on the ability of the leader to communicate policies and visions to peers, followers and other stakeholders.

It can be argued that leadership action/inaction depends on a hierarchical interplay of causal elements. Increasingly, leaders require an ability to set the vision and energize the commitment of others through the creation of shared values and a shared understanding within the parameters of a 'global' context (Maier, 1967; Morgan, 1986; Keen, 1991). Leadership is becoming synonymous with 'networking' (Nohria and Eccles, 1992), 'framing' and 'bridging' processes (Morgan, 1986) that can energize and focus the efforts of people in ways that resonate with challenges and demands posed by their local and 'global' contexts. Contemporary leaders are required to be all round generalists who are able to achieve short and long term integration between technical, human, operational, socio cultural and creative areas of management and plan today's learning for future global activities (Morgan, 1986).

Culture: bridging goals, circumstances and developmental pathways

In 1980, many managers and scholars believed that organizations could become more effective if they built or developed the 'right' kind of culture (Schein, 1986). Some argue that 'strong' cultures are linked with effectiveness that can be deliberately created (Ouchi, 1981; Deal and Kennedy, 1982; Peters and Waterman, 1982). Others argue that strength of culture depends on the stage of evolution of the organization and its current capability for adaptiveness. Thus that strength is in understanding and using the existing culture (Schein, 1985, 1986; Kilmann, Saxton and Serpa, 1986a).

However, the strong culture organization has also a negative side, as it forms organizations with common social attributes which may lead to conformity (Janis, 1972; Janis and Mann, 1977; Janis, 1982; t'Hart, 1990) where others interact effectively with each other by adopting a similar 'vocabulary of motives' (Mills, 1940). Through this vocabulary of motives, actors exchange information and develop similar perceptions and opinions (Rogers and Kincaid, 1981; Tichy, 1981; Hackman, 1983; Wellman, 1983, 1988), which may lead then to the cultural 'dark side' (Korac-Boisvert and Kouzmin, 1994; Janis, 1972; Janis and Mann, 1977; Janis, 1982; t'Hart,

1990). Hence strength of culture encompasses both ends of the positive/negative continuum.

Negative culture is associated with a culture which promotes the growth of mistrust and contentiousness with uncertainty and confusion, where confidence in both the organization and its leadership diminishes (Davis, 1984). A strong belief may exist that favouritism rules, that success is not rewarded and that risk taking is penalized, which has a demotivating effect on the employees who lose enthusiasm and disregard pursuing a performance orientation. Those organizations deemed to have a more negative culture are frequently governed more by vested interests or political expediencies than by concerns for efficiency or effectiveness. Furthermore, actions and behaviour that get rewarded in negative cultures are often dysfunctional ones, such as 'playing politics', manipulating rules and policies and 'managing' impressions, (Kilmann, Saxton and Serpa, 1986).

A positive culture is one that integrates, shows high concern for people which is matched with strong performance expectations. The sense of fulfilment from meaningful and challenging work is one of the more important rewards of a deemed positive culture. Because performance is considered to be a core value, significant rewards are usually contingent on performance, especially on group performance rather than just on the individual (Kilmann, Saxton and Serpa, 1986b). Even if non performance criteria are taken into consideration pertinent to issues such as internal and external equity and the individual's potential, people are expected to make reasonable efforts in their day to day work. For example in the public sector, where everybody of a certain grade can expect similar increases, people are still expected to make reasonable efforts towards continuous improvement. Hence, irrespective of tangible rewards, actions and behaviour that are valued in a positive culture include self management, cooperation, teamwork, risk taking, innovation, experimentation and skill building, as well as conformity and receptivity to guidance from superiors (Kilmann, Saxton and Serpa, 1986).

Even organizations with 'right' or effective cultures that reinforce the mission, purpose and strategies of the organization, may find it necessary to change culture to foster greater cooperation across business units, as some parts of the business may have reached maturity. In attempting to develop further business, new artefacts are introduced that are positioned to persist in behaviours that may have worked well in the past but that clearly are dysfunctional today. The organization lives in a cultural age or 'cultural gap' (Kilmann, 1986). Therefore, although strong culture norms can make an organization efficient where everyone knows what is important and how things are done, those cultures are more difficult to change (Gordon, 1986; Kilmann, 1986). To be effective, the culture must not only be efficient but also appropriate to the needs of the business, organization and the employees.

Furthermore, if left alone, a culture eventually becomes dysfunctional as fear, insecurities, over sensitivity, dependencies and paranoia seem to take over, unless a concerted effort to establish an adaptive culture is undertaken (Kilmann, 1986).

However, changing culture in organizations is a slow, difficult and ongoing process. Some advocate leadership succession as the essential ingredient to culture change. Pettigrew (1979), for example, contends that since leaders are the 'creators' of culture, culture change is accompanied by a change in leadership. O'Tool (1979) argues that since culture is imbedded in organizational structure, such as a company's reward system, hierarchy or authority, then change of culture can be achieved by a change of structure, the new structure, supporting a regenerated culture. Others (Ouchi, 1981; Peters and Waterman, 1982; Sathe, 1983) argue that culture can be changed by developing a new set of values, or leadership philosophy which is then inculcated into employees. Where change processes involve the development of new organizational goals and ideals and the socialization of both old and new employees to the new set of beliefs, managing symbols and their accompanying meanings, is the agent of cultural change.

Thus the view of leadership as central in setting and changing culture cannot be over emphasized. Alongside visioning, communication and the creation of the mission, is the creation of the culture within the ethical dimensions and standards the leaders have set (Alderson and Kakabadse, 1994). A leadership which is badly out of touch with organizational values, negatively influences managers and employees but is still in charge of the organization. On the other hand, the good leadership, one which is 'in touch' with dominant values, creates momentum to make things happen (Gordon, 1986).

Thus, culture and its change appear to lie within the bounds of organizational leadership, as the organization's founders and leaders bring with them a set of assumptions, values, perspectives, philosophies and artefacts and impose them on their employees through interaction with one another in order to solve the fundamental problems of internal integration of group members and of environmental adaptation (Pettigrew, 1979; Schein, 1983; Dyer, 1984). The values organizations nurture and people exhibit are only manifestations of the culture, not the driving force of the culture. The driving force of culture are the deeply held assumptions that may be seen as the 'ideology', 'philosophy', 'charter', or basic 'credo' of the organization, nurtured by the adopted leadership philosophy. Where values are debated and discussed, basic assumptions, in most cases, are not. Values come from early conditioning, experience and significant events such as individual training and experience (Fairholm, 1991). As such values connote desirability, they are conclusive beliefs individuals evolve about what is true or beautiful or good about the world. As organization members accept a particular set of values and act upon them, these values become the truth for them.

Shared values, therefore, are strong determinants for group actions. Because assumptions have provided solutions for contextual problems that have worked consistently for a group in the past, assumptions are evolved on a 'taken for granted basis', dropping out of awareness and forming a group culture. The emerging culture is then positioned to new members as the correct way to perceive, think about, and feel in relation to the organization. The power of culture is derived from the fact that it operates as a set of assumptions that are unconscious and taken for granted. As such, culture does not only limit strategic choice, but strategies cannot be implemented if they run against powerful cultural assumptions (Schein, 1986; Kilmann, Saxton and Serpa, 1986b). To change culture requires leaders who have the determination and perseverance to effect change and find it necessary to remould the organization at any point in its history.

Cultural differences and leadership

In industrial and developing societies, both public and private organizations are joining forces with counter partners in recipient economies, in transitional joint ventures and in generating new joint ownership conglomerates, requiring dependency, collaboration and compromise of domestic technological skills and capabilities (Kevin, 1980). Contemporary executives operate within a global socio economic political network, where the internal organizational context (internal cultural values and work standards) are only a part of the diversified global context.

The reality of 'networked organizations' becomes synonymous with 'electronic networks', where remote, asynchronous and, often dysfunctional, communication may replace face to face communication, further redefining and distorting relationships, actions and formal roles. For example, the Society for Worldwide International Funds Transfer (SWIFT), shared by the growing international consortium of banks and other financial institutions, changes many of the basic dynamics of its members' core business, redesigning the meaning of organization within a context of tightly coupled and shared electronic business operations, worldwide. SWIFT necessitates competitors to cooperate by establishing close, structure independent, linkages between banks providing a range of business services, and to compete on the range of services they provide.

The globalization of work environments adds a new dimension to the cultural diversity of constituencies and stakeholders and adds additional complexity to the management of these interactions and intimate dependency relationships within global mindsets exemplified by multinationals and transnational organizations. 'New age' executives need to satisfy the needs of all groups and individuals who have a stake in the success of networked organizations. They must deal effectively with contradictions, ambiguities, different values and measurement standards, conflicting goals and a plurality of methods for the attainment of goals. They need to synthesize and reduce ethnocentrism and arbitrarily manipulate cultural relativism, because in their extreme forms, both sources of diversity pose equal dangers to transitional effectiveness. The former becomes insensitive to cross cultural differences, the latter becomes blind to cross cultural similarities.

For example, executives, operating even within those few multicultural organizations within multicultural Australia, need to consider the European respect for structure and chain of authority as well as the Asian concern for broad based involvement of all organizational participants. They also need to accommodate people socialized in cultures that accept intuition and fate as a key element of organizational life, along with others from diverse, sometimes antagonistic, cultures and learn to communicate effectively with individuals not overly familiar with the idiomatic Australian language.

Increased global mobility transforms predominantly ethnocentric organizations into multicultural ones. The past executive tendency to make independent decisions often poses difficulties in cross cultural relationships. Traditional management assumptions such as the fact that strategy and structure closely correlate, are increasingly invalidated by barrier breaking IT technology. The emergence of 'meta business' or network organizations, a quasi firm created through IT linkages and dependencies between organizations, leads to a situation where individuals are tightly coupled, making it impossible to define where the boundary of one organization ends and the boundary of another begins.

This is exemplified by General Motors' supply system and the interlocking relationships among economic institutions within Asian economies. These organizations provide a distinct form of coordinating economic activity, structure independent and flexible to the participating organization's structural redundancy, a situation in which the structural dynamic of one organization does not force structural changes in another. Rhetorical management actions (giving orders, setting procedures, supervision) are extrinsic and cannot be assumed to work in such networked structural futures. Executives will have to accommodate less arbitrary, more culturally ambiguous and, in the least, globally transacted, even collegial like decisions arrived through protracted cultural negotiation, formal discussion, compromise and high levels of residual and personal uncertainty.

Furthermore, leaders of multinational or multicultural organizations need to be sensitive to cross cultural issues in designing reward policies. For example, 'self actualization needs' appear to generate high preferences for reward items such as participation (power distance dimension) and work challenge (individualism dimension). However, participation may not work as well as a reward for those from a high power distance society. Similarly, work challenge may be ineffective as a reward in a collectivistic culture. Therefore, contemporary leaders must find psychological rewards and inspiration for people whose psychological development patterns are unfamiliar. Contemporary leaders must find new ways to tap the intrinsic motives of individuals to achieve optimum outputs.

Societies with Anglo-American work ethics have created value systems which emphasize that individuals can succeed if they have talent and commitment. There are also ethnic value differences within these work ethics that are often neglected in increasingly multicultural organizations. These differences are visible even in the cross cultural setting between 'psychologically close' cultures (Sappinen, 1992), as exemplified by Australian CEOs working in British subsidiaries, where cross cultural conflict appears to have been the unintended consequence emerging 'not in the start up period but when cooperation had become routine' (Meyer, 1993, p.101; Ouchi, 1980).

Notwithstanding the Australian heritage, as well as historically close cultural ties with Britain, manifested by a common language, and common political, legal and educational systems (Kanter, 1991), close similarity in terms of the four work related values (power distance, uncertainty avoidance, masculinity/femininity and individualism/collectivism (Hofstede, 1982, 1993); attitude dimensions (Ronen, 1986), and similar economic reform strategies, British and Australian management do not seem to have shared the same formative context experience. The similarities posed by close cultural ties (defined in the cultural, social and economic sense) led Australian foreign direct investment to flow predominantly towards Britain rather than to geographically proximate trading partners (Stevens, 1988). However, these same ties often lead Australian and British managers to 'inter cultural over confidence' (Meyer, 1993, p.93) and cognitive arrogance that overlooks the differences which may stem from the different fields of experience of each society (Kelley, Whatley and Worthley, 1987; Huo and McKinley, 1992).

Differences in national formative contexts may often impact on the interrelationship between business strategy; environment and control system attributes; and strategic management (Ouchi, 1981; Schneider, 1987, 1994; Douglas and Rhee, 1989; Porter, 1990; Huo and McKinley, 1992). Similarly, an organization's formative context (whether it has experienced organic and/or acquisition based growth), history and circumstance determine organizational success (Kakabadse, 1991, p.164). Naulleau and Harper (1993) posit that French managers require considerable attention in terms of social skills training, while an indepth study of senior managers in the UK, France, Germany, Sweden, Ireland, Austria, Spain and Finland suggest that the French, in particular, resent interference in their work or in the management of their functions (Kakabadse, 1993). They also find criticism difficult to take and display a high need for control in terms of implementing their views and intentions. A French view of interference is seen by managers of other European organizations as comments made by one colleague to another which might require some consideration (Kakabadse, 1993). Kakabadse and Myers' (1996b) study strongly supports this position. Ethnic culture affects the process of strategy formulation, particularly in scanning, selecting, interpreting and validating information as well as establishing priorities (Schneider, 1989). Differences in ethnic culture are likely to result in different interpretations and responses to the same strategic issue (Schneider and Meyer, 1991).

In the Australian case, geographic isolation (Blainey, 1966) may be instrumental in forming the Australian manager's proclivity for higher independence, egalitarianism (Western, 1983), dominance and assertiveness, than is the case with British managers (Barry and Dowling, 1984). Ignored differences in, or perhaps peripheral, cultural values between Australian and British managers are found to be of particular concern in the management of day to day activities, business etiquette and interpersonal interaction (Fenwick and Edwards, 1994). A comparison between Australian and American managers also reveals subtle differences in values, attitudes and beliefs about a range of management related topics (Dowling and Nagel, 1986; Posner and Low, 1990).

Similarly, Australian managers tend to make independent decisions, often posing difficulties in an increasingly cross cultural relationship where rhetorical management strategies (giving orders, setting procedures, supervision) are extrinsic and cannot always be assumed to work in the future. Australian managers need to learn to accommodate more collegial decisions, arrived through negotiation, discussion and compromise and to be sensitive to cross cultural issues when designing reward policies. For example, 'self actualization' needs (Maslow, 1962) appear to generate high preferences for reward items, such as participation (power distance dimension) and work challenge (individualism dimension) in Britain and its ex colonies (Hofstede, 1980). However, participation may not work as a reward for actors from a high power distance society (Hofstede, 1980, 1993). Similarly, work challenge may be ineffective as a reward in a collectivist culture.

In addition to technological development and the emergent gobalization of work environments, increased global mobility has transformed many ethnocentric organizations into multicultural and multinational organizations.

Although migration flows largely from non OECD countries to the OECD, there is considerable movement of member country nationals within the area (Garson and Puymoyen, 1995). Also, the consolidation or emergence of regional economic blocks (the European Economic Areas; Association of South East Asian Nations; American Free Trade Agreement and APEC), along with particular political developments (such as disintegration in the former Yugoslavia, Algeria and Haiti), have intensified and strengthened the regional aspect of migration (Garson and Puymoyen, 1995). Consequently, labour laws will receive more significance and be determined by global trading agreements (GATT) and individual trading block issues. Managing these interactions within intimate relationships and the global mindset perspective requires new skills from all stakeholders (Roobeek, 1990). Leaders in contemporary globalized organizations will need to synthesize ethnocentrism and cultural relativism, as, in their extreme forms, both pose equal dangers. The former becomes insensitive to cross cultural differences, the latter becomes blind to cross cultural similarities.

A willingness to learn to communicate effectively with people not familiar with the language system (jargon, context and cultural idioms) of the host society is also becoming increasingly a requirement (Keen, 1991; Foucault, 1965, 1979). Thus, motivation by personal success in the form of wealth, recognition and self actualization may produce increased productivity in organizations with predominantly British, Australian (and other former colonies) and American cultural backgrounds (Hofstede, 1980). These are cultures that value individualism (Hofstede, 1980), as exemplified by the number of Australian law firms and media organizations.

However, the same strategy may have no, or an adverse, effect within an organization which has a predominantly homogenized cultural background, such as a Japanese firm, which harbours consensus decision making and promotion of cohorts rather than individuals as an expression of Japanese 'groupness'. Similarly, motivation by individual job security may be successful amongst employees with a cultural proclivity for strong uncertainty avoidance, high power distance and a need for belonging, such as Greek, French, Spanish, Portuguese, Yugoslav and Asian peoples (Hofstede, 1980). Motivation by success and belonging, on the other hand, may produce higher productivity in organizations with a workforce which is predominantly of a North European culture (Hofstede, 1980; Keen, 1991).

It is considered that the impact of ethnic cultural factors may be felt most strongly in the belonging, affection and esteem needs of ethnically different actors. In organizations with a predominantly Greek culture, such as in labour intensive factories in Australia, these needs may interchange their positions and cause a reversal in the hierarchy because the Greek culture, characteristically, makes esteem contingent upon one's status in society

(Hofstede, 1980; Maslow, 1971, p.51-2). Self actualization needs determine intrinsic reward preferences, whereas needs below the level of self actualization appear to determine extrinsic reward preferences: the message is, different cultures value different reward preferences.

However, psychologically insecure people, irrespective of their ethnic and cultural background, hesitate to undertake challenging jobs. The acceptance of challenge is a key element in seeking a competitive edge. Often a reason for failure is the individual's inability to adjust to responsibility (Dowling and Schuler, 1990). Furthermore, psychological insecurity also generates resistance to learning new skills (Dowling and Schuler, 1990). In the process of rationalizing the irrational, to make people more secure and in control, psychologically insecure actors often miss the hidden meaning and significance of the actions that shape the organization (Morgan, 1986). The rationality expressed by Taylor (1911) may have disguised an extreme form of compulsiveness, just as a contemporary manager's excessive concern for clear cut targets and goals may disguise a basic insecurity in life, anxiety, inferiority or insignificance (Kanter, 1977; Morgan, 1986; Manz and Sims, 1990).

A comparative analysis of European manufacturers, with a total of 957 top managers (chairmen, CEOs, MDs, general managers) participating in the study, reveals ethnic differences in terms of job satisfaction, orientation to discipline, specialist versus general management orientation, team orientation, organizational orientation, other areas of business practices, as well as organizational and management performance which require improvement (Kakabadse and Myers, 1995). The study suggests that there are significant differences (positive and negative) in management perceptions of organizational orientation and change, as well as the quality of management (Kakabadse, 1993; Kakabadse and Myers, 1995a). Similarly, a comparative study of USA, Japanese and South Korean managers, and UK and Irish managers (Alderson and Kakabadse, 1994) reveals significant variations in attitudes towards work ethics. For example Hofstede's (1993) analysis of similar German, British and French organizations shows the Germans as having the highest rate of people in production roles and the lowest both in leadership and staff roles. He suggests that German workers do not necessarily need an American style manager to 'motivate' them, as they expect their boss to assess their tasks and to be the expert in resolving technical problems. Hofstede's (1993) view is that an uneasy relationship exists between national and organization cultures. National cultures differ primarily in the fundamental, invisible values held by a majority of people acquired in early childhood. Organizational cultures are a much more superficial phenomenon, driven mainly by the visible practices of the organization and supported by a process of socialization of the new members who join. Furthermore, while national cultures change only very slowly, the organizational culture may be consciously changed, even though it is not an easy task.

Social diversity, exemplified by differences amongst actors and the multiplicity of cultures within organizations needs consideration. Under estimating the impact of even subtle cultural differences on the establishment and maintenance of effective interpersonal relationships, may undermine the strategies for an effective information search and, thus, decisions, outcomes and organizational effectiveness. Considering that one of the criteria for the effectiveness of any social organization is its ability to utilize its resources (human and artefacts) to carry on a useful exchange with its environment and that socio cultural differences often cause the under utilization of the potential of an organization's human assets, overcoming cultural ignorance and increasing broader cultural understanding requires continuous attention. Since differences are subtle, impediments that are often left unaddressed lead to a creeping crisis. Until senior managers are willing to accept other values and behaviours that are dissimilar to their own, they will continue to carry a judgemental perspective that can, in spite of themselves, be prejudicial, discriminatory and oppressive (Carnevale and Stone, 1994, p.25).

Power and politics: bridging traits, context and meaning

It has long been contended that leaders use power (reward, referent (charisma), coercive, legitimate expert) to influence subordinates in order to gain their compliance, consented or coerced (French and Raven, 1959; Weber, 1968; Nyberg, 1981) by exercising archetypal power tactics such as force (French and Raven, 1959; Wrong, 1979; Yukl, 1981), authority (Barnard, 1938; Simon, Smithburg and Thompson, 1950; Krupp, 1961; Weber, 1968; Bell, 1975), manipulation (Dahl, 1961; Wrong, 1979), threats/promises (Neustadt, 1960; Bachrach and Baratz, 1970; Bell, 1975), persuasion (Goldhammer and Shils, 1972; Fairholm, 1993) and influence (Bachrach and Baratz, 1970; Fairholm, 1993) and through some 22 power behavioural intervention tactics (Fairholm, 1993). Furthermore, it has been argued that leadership, influence, charisma and control are substitutes for power, or at least are interchangeable terms. Papp (1984) contends that effective leadership abets power. Interwoven with power is the concept of politics, seen by some as an alternative term for power (Fairholm, 1993). Others view politics as a distinctly separate process of influence (Kakabadse, 1983), drawing heavily on contextual interpretations and social meaning (Mischel, 1977). Hence the power/politics conceptual span verges from prescriptive acts and the appreciation of elements of 'character' to ascertaining meaning, from an analysis of context and the needs and aspirations of the actors involved. That span is provided for in the ensuing discourse.

Leadership and the power dimension

Like leadership, power is the 'last of the little dirty secrets' (Bennis, 1974, p.62) in social science (the latest implicit component of social life to be exposed to systematic review and analysis), and provides a traceable theme in a rich and varied history of mankind from both the creationary and evolutionary perspectives (Pettigrew, 1975, 1987). For example, Cain's problem with Abel was that the latter had a power base (Laeyendecker, 1989), while Moses parried his power against the Pharaoh to let his people go, with the latter representing the epitome of leadership and organizational power as he sat in judgement over the people of Israel during part of their 40 year pilgrimage (Laeyendecker, 1989). Power underpins Darwin's (1964) thesis on evolution. Natural selection or 'survival of the fittest' is defined as a function of the ability (or power) of a species to defend itself from predators and to adapt to the environment. For Plato (1941, 1952), power is 'being', an experience that defines the real existence, or 'self', while for Russell (1938, p.12), power is the 'fundamental concept of social science'. Although leadership and management concepts (authority, influence, control, structures) all have power connotations, the power perspective evolved separately from the study of leadership (French and Raven, 1959; Mayes and Allen, 1977; Pfeffer, 1992). Because of power's antisocial connotations with manipulation, coercion, control and force, epitomized by the Machiavellian (1958) exploitive of the self serving use of power for achieving compliance, the power concept suffered from terminological taboos and negative undertones in organizational literature until the 1970s (Pfeffer, 1981).

Through group dynamic theories, the organizational power perspective received a contemporary awakening (Pfeffer and Salancik, 1978; Pfeffer, 1981a, 1992; Allan and Porter, 1983) when it was contended that power could be liberating, enhancing the individual and those they dealt with (Follett, 1942; Winter, 1973; McClelland; 1975; Kanter, 1977; Nyberg, 1981). Exchange theory and alignment theory have both acknowledged the use of power in the leadership context, assigning to power Russell's (1938) instrumental utility: the 'production of intended effects'. However, it may be argued that since terms such as 'influence' have been substituted for 'power' in the behaviourist literature, behaviourist scholars have in fact dealt extensively but implicitly with the power phenomenon. Notwithstanding, the positive dimensions of power have now received full attention in the transformational leadership literature (Schein, 1985; Beer and Walter, 1987; Dunphy and Stace, 1988, 1990; Fairholm, 1993).

Alignment and contingency theorists saw power as an instrument through which leaders could help followers achieve a compatible, congruent relationship between skills, personal values and the aims, methods, needs and the values of the host organization (Culbert and McDonough, 1980). Power itself is treated as having inherent scarcity value (Fiedler, 1967; Hickson et al, 1971; Szilagyl and Wallace, 1983) and is exercised only in situations where scare elements of the situation, real or perceived, are needed to achieve the desired results (Allan et al, 1979; Allan and Porter, 1983). Being a dynamic perspective, it holds that when criticality changes, those who control these evolving critical factors supplant former powerful organizational actors (Crozier, 1964; Kipnis, 1976).

Exchange theory defined power in terms of symmetry-asymmetry, as a system of control over information and affection, as a function of prestige and as a balance of values prominent amongst competing participants in an exchange relationship with the determinants of leadership (Bierstadt, 1950, 1974; Simon, 1957; Homans, 1958; Thibaut and Kelly, 1959; Gouldner, 1960; Cartright, 1965; Bacherach and Lawler, 1986). This perspective holds that organizations harbour subcultures where relationships can be both balanced and unbalanced (power concentrated in one party) and power being intercursive and integral respectively (Wrong, 1979). In unbalanced situations, the actor's lateral behaviour (exchange of favours, coalition organizing and networking with occupational peers outside the focal organization) is seen as strategies used to reduce power dependencies (Farrell and Petersen, 1982). In a relatively equal, balanced power situation, negotiation and bargaining strategies are used to reduce these interdependencies (Farrell and Petersen, 1982; Mitroff and Kilmann, 1984).

The transformational perspective sees leadership as the exercise of power in any of its manifestations in a group situation (Fairholm, 1991; Zey, 1992; Frey, 1993, Lewis, 1993). While the transformational perspective literature (Schein, 1985; Beer and Walter, 1987; Zey, 1992; Frey, 1993; Lewis, 1993; Warburton, 1993) recognizes that power coercion strategies in mature organizations possessing a well established culture may be necessary and that coercion may be the only alternative when speed is essential (Kotter, 1977; Kotter, Schelesinger and Sathe, 1979), relatively few works acknowledge and document the use of power coercive strategies as a legitimate primary strategy for change (Dunphy and Stace, 1988, 1990; Frey, 1993; Lewis, 1993). Dunphy and Stace (1988, p.321) contend that 'radical times may demand radical remedies' such as the use of power coercive strategies in short bursts of activity and 'discontinuous change' to achieve a desired transformation (Dunphy and Stace, 1988, p.322; Lewis, 1993). The transformation perspective confesses that power use or leadership may be perceived by group members and stakeholders differently depending on their particular construction of reality or unique philosophical persuasion (Zey, 1992). In this context, the power dimension, like the leadership thesis, is a subject of philosophical discourse today as it has been for generations and depends upon the way in which social action is viewed (Kouzmin, 1980, 1983).

Pursuing the perspective of social action, the concept of pro social power (Winter, 1973; McClelland, 1975; McClelland and Burnham, 1976; Winter, 1987) postulates that the need for power and not achievement characterizes successful managers in organizations; and that power has two faces. One that looks to some as the independent means by which organizational success is achieved and the other that looks to people as implements to be used for furthering one's own self centred desires (McClelland, 1975). Notwithstanding that the leaders' need for achievement is at least moderate, their greatest achievement is generally by means of power and influence. Considering that the leader recognizes that it is through power and influence that things are accomplished in an organization, rather than through social directive, the need for power reflects a sophisticated understanding of the nature of achievement in organizations. However, long lasting achievement through power requires a certain level of maturity and development by the holder (Kakabadse, 1991).

Hence, leadership analysis through the power perspective draws on salient ideas from distinct fields of power research; political power theory (Mills, 1957; Hunter, 1959, 1963; Dahl, 1961; Rose, 1967), psychological power theory (Weber, 1920, 1964, 1976; Hobbes, 1929; Barnard, 1938; Plato, 1941, 1952; Adler, 1956; Machiavelli, 1958; Nietzsche, 1976) and organizational power theory (Hobbes, 1929; Russell, 1938; Machiavelli, 1958; French and Raven, 1959; Maslow, 1971; Marx, 1973, 1976; McClelland, 1975; Daft, 1989), where freedom (at least relative) to act, independence, dependence, dominance and leadership are all inter related with power related concepts implicit in the structure of organized groups. As such, all social interactions are conceptualized in terms of power relationships between actors within the organizational context (Fligstein, 1992), where organizational structure represents a system of power that is organized to deliver goods to the ultimate consumers and provide benefits to all stakeholders (DiMaggio, 1986, 1988).

Although the distinction of each power related concept may be useful in specific discussion (Yukl, 1981), only the synthesis of these concepts, however, provides the 'semantic space' (Gardner, 1964) for the understanding of the leadership phenomenon. In this sense leadership, like power, has inherent instrumentality assumptions and is seen as an instrument to achieving some preconceived state, agenda, plan or desire (Nyberg, 1981). Like power, it arises out of a felt or perceived need. Like leadership, power implies a special kind of social relationship characterized by the concepts of:

- Intentionality: involving volitional (authority, control, persuasion, manipulation, force), not random action;
- Instrumentality: it is a means to desired ends;
- Action: it is apparent in use, not in mere possession;
- Dependency: it assumes that there is a freedom or dependency-interdependency factor inherent in any leadership action;
- Situation: specific leadership styles (like power tactics) are effective in specific relationships and not necessarily in others;
- Finite: results are measured and compared in a given situation or occurrence; and
- Difference (opposition): both assume difference or social opposition (leader/follower, power/powerless).

Leadership, like power, is both a relational and contextual concept (Papp, 1984) and has both emotional and ethical impacts (Fairholm, 1993). It is also pervasive and central to success in social functioning (Fairholm, 1993), where influence, direction, control, planning, coordination and correlation are all manifestations of power use in the organization (Handy, 1976; Mayes and Allen, 1977). Leadership utility, like the utility of power, lies in the action that can be exerted and in what others perceive can be exerted to do (Papp, 1984). Furthermore, power and leadership concepts are intermeshed; that is, rules facilitate power, and leadership structures rules (Greenleaf, 1977, 1983).

Given the relative nature of power and leadership, the contextual qualities of their application, their interpenetration and difficulties of assigning an objective value to even their most tangible elements, measuring the effectiveness of power (Papp, 1984) and leadership may be best assessed from an ethical perspective. Since Machiavelli (1958) draws attention to the ethical dimension of power use, ethics are still a central theme in organizational theory and praxis, although vague and incomplete (Fairholm, 1991). Social scientists have addressed various aspects of power ethics (domination, interdependence relationships, self discipline, justice, altruism, equality, personality), but with the view emerging that there are no truly sustained and comprehensive analyzes and syntheses of power ethics, either scientific, religious, fictional or pragmatic (Fairholm, 1993).

However, one perspective is clear and that is that a leader's action or use of the power strategy has ideological, methodological and procedural dimensions (Daft, 1989; Fairholm, 1993). The specific power strategy or mix that the leader adopts from the coercion consent continuum of archetypal power tactics, depends upon the individual leader, stockholders, situation (internal and global context) and the perceived availability of the scarce resources (Rogers, 1951; Fairholm, 1991). At one end of the continuum, the strategy relies heavily on coercion to secure compliance (Machiavelli, 1950). At the other end, power use relies on informed, cooperative consent as the basis for compliance (Fairholm, 1991). Whenever individuals are inter related in order to accomplish some planned activity, the power process is activated (Lukes, 1974). For example, agenda setting, the primary activity of leadership (Pfeffer, 1981b; Bass, Avolio and Goodheim, 1987; Frey, 1993), is a power process, as power is the resource lever most often used to accomplish the setting of goals (Kanter, 1977; Pfeffer, 1981a).

The power perspective provides support to the view that owners and managers of firms do not attempt to produce efficient organizations in an economic sense, as their intention is to attempt to greater control markets and to subdue or undermine the impact of competitors (Fligstein, 1992; Lamoreaux, 1985). The power perspective elucidates a salient social problem encapsulated in the mode of production, manifested as production for profit and as a response to putative demand. In this sense, it provides a useful framework for understanding the demise of managerialism and the emergence of large firms, conglomerates and a return to a neo leadership thesis.

A growing social conscience in the workforce, information sharing and the advent of global networks (multinational and transnational), further exacerbates issues of social stratification and focuses on common values, ideals and goals, indicating the need for a power use and leadership role redefinition. Thus, in time, the power perspective will, in turn, need to be critically re-evaluated.

Leadership and organizational politics

Mayes and Allen (1977) argue that power is the fundamental pillar of management's influence throughout organization, whilst personal influence (politics), again an integral part of leadership, is surely a form of power. Influence (politics) is a form of power, often subtle and indirect, by which organizational members impact on situations and on the behaviours of others (Fairholm, 1993). Since Hobbes (1929) points out that the power of the subject impacts on the sovereign, the debate has ranged from concern with the instrumental nature of power to its resource qualities and to its operating impact in group situations (politics).

However, different perspectives highlight that power and politics are separate conceptual entities and that organizational politics are not always negative and bad, but rather a process of getting what one wants, with the permission and approval of the others (Gross, 1996). If one's influence is perceived in a positive and favourable way then the receiving party is motivated (Kakabadse, 1983). However, if attempts at influence are not well received, then the receiving party may feel manipulated (Kakabadse and Parker, 1984). For the organizational leader, whose work is almost exclusively influencing others, to behave 'politically correct/appropriate', leadership in the political sphere is understood in the same manner as leadership within the context of participatory democracy. Although the external form in which such democracies manifest themselves may vary, the core of democratic process is embodied in the notion of leadership as an ideological activity. Thus moral leadership as an ideological activity is itself the realization of the essence of participatory democracy which requires political endeavour to weave through the differing needs and positions adopted by others.

Organizational reality is that stakeholders influence each other during each interaction. This is exemplified by the budget process, during which stockholders and stakeholders negotiate schedules, compromise goals, marshal support and compete for limited resources. Budgeting and associated activities can be seen as power tasks which organization participants accomplish via the use of power tactics, implicit in a political action process many call organizational politics (Fairholm, 1993).

Political activity became incorporated in organizational theorizing, in the 1960s when it was recognized as an inherent dimension of organizational activities. For example, Madison et al's (1980) research shows that 60 per cent of managers who have survived (continued) in the organization, concur that politics is 'frequently' or 'very frequently' a part of organizational life, while 95 per cent of all respondents agreed that office politics is necessary for achieving individual goals. The idea that organizational politics hinges on the relationship between interests, conflict and power has been addressed by many scholars (Burns, 1961; Burns and Stalker, 1961; March, 1962; Crozier, 1964; Jay, 1967; Pettigrew, 1973; Murray and Gandz, 1980; Pfeffer, 1978, 1981; Bower, 1983a) at least in an implicit way.

In fact scholars have examined organizational politics from a multi dimensional point of view, including elements as: actions taken by individuals through the organization (Mayes and Allen, 1977); influence of one actor towards another (Gandz and Murray, 1980); effort by one party to promote self interest over that of another and, therefore, threaten the second party's self interest (Rosen et al, 1961); action typically not sanctioned by the host organization or results sought that are not sanctioned (Plott and Levine, 1961); and some kind of exchange process with a zero sum outcome (Frost and Hayes, 1979). Some (Schein, 1977; Porter, Allen and Angle, 1981) treat power and politics as an additional variable in analyzing organizational behaviour, while others (Nord, 1974; Burke, 1976; Kakabadse and Parker, 1984; Fairholm, 1993) address power and politics explicitly as an integral part of organizational theory.

Such attention to the subject has been valuable, for certain theorists strongly argue that all organization members participate in politics (Kakabadse and Parker, 1984). Following this line of argument, Madison et al's (1980) research suggests that politics is used more by middle and upper levels of management than by lower level employees. Allan et al (1979) assess the personal skills and traits common to politically active people in organizations and conclude that all share some common characteristics. They are articulate, sensitive and socially adept, competent, popular, extrovert and self confident. They also exhibit aggressive tendencies, are ambitious and are highly intelligent and logical. They are willing to engage others in competition for available resources and for the dominance of their ideas and philosophy. Ironically, these attributes are also ascribed by transformational theorists to the new age leader.

Aristotle (1946) advocates politics as a means of reconciling the need for unity in the Greek 'polis' (city-state) with the fact that the 'polis' was an 'aggregate of many members'. For Aristotle, politics provide the means of creating order out of diversity while avoiding forms of totalitarian rule. In this original meaning, the idea of politics stems from the view that, where interests are divergent, society should provide a means of allowing individuals to reconcile their differences through consultation and negotiation (Kakabadse and Parker, 1984; Morgan, 1986). Considering that organizations are intrinsically political, in the sense that ways must be found to create order and direction among participants with potentially diverse and conflicting interests, 'politics and politicking' are essential aspects of organizational reality and are not necessarily optional and dysfunctional extras (Morgan, 1986). Thus, while power is the individual capacity to gain one's own aims in inter relationship with others, even in the face of their opposition, the process of continuous interaction people undertake in achieving their set aims, is viewed, by some, as politics (Kakabadse and Parker, 1984; Morgan, 1986).

Information technology development: the leader's changing role

The information revolution of the 1990s appears to be epic in its scale, moral in its significance and possibly frightening in its consequences. The dynamic aspect of IT may be conceived as a process of increasing complexity in the 'organizational landscape' (Ahrne, 1990), within which organizational actors must act. The kind of IT employed influences the patterns of interdependencies within the organization and hence the power relations between different actors and groups in the organizational landscape (Morgan, 1986; Ahrne, 1990). New IT creates possibilities of multiple points of access to common databases and the possibility of local, rather than centralized, information systems. The provision of a single fibre optic cable connection will accelerate this development (Boettinger, 1989). This, in principle, can increase the power of those at the periphery or local level by providing actors with more comprehensive, immediate and relevant data relating to their tasks, thereby, one assumption being the facilitation and enhancement of the self rather than centralized control (Korac-Boisvert and Kouzmin, 1996).

In practice however, IT is often used to increase power at the centre by decentralizing certain activities, whilst centralizing ongoing surveillance over performance (Morgan, 1986; Huber, 1990). In either instance, with increased centralization of managerial power, or alternatively, with greater decentralization of managerial power depending on the intent of the organization's strategy (Huber, 1990), IT has and will have an effect on the leadership role (Weill, 1992). Significant IT advancement has and will lead to the recognition of the need to implement new organizational design options (Boettinger, 1989; Forester, 1989; Limerick and Cunnington, 1993). For example, IT communication links, based on an email or bulletin board type infrastructure, facilitates communication between non linearly connected actors and increases the level of coupling between previously uncoupled entities in a 'network structure' (Boettinger, 1989; Korac-Boisvert and Kouzmin, 1996).

The combined effects of IT communication (increased flows of information), electronic brokerage (connection of many different buyers and suppliers instantaneously through a central database - electronic market) and IT integration (tighter coupling between interorganizational processes - electronic hierarchies) have resulted in emergent value adding partnerships - VAPs (Malone, Yates and Benjamin, 1987; Johnson and Lawrance, 1988; Boettinger, 1989), generating new patterns of interaction. These new patterns of interaction are as much processes as they are emerging structures; being continually shaped and reshaped by the actions of actors who are, in turn, constrained by the structural position in which they find themselves within a social space and time (Korac-Boisvert and Kouzmin, 1996).

In addition to design influence, IT knowledge is often used to weave patterns of dependency (Morgan, 1986). By possessing critical information at a critical time, having exclusive access to key data or by possessing the ability to synthesize in an effective manner, individuals can increase the power (influence) they wield within an organization (Korac-Boisvert and Kouzmin, 1996). For example, the fact that attempts to adopt new IT often create major conflict between stakeholders, is deeply rooted in IT's ability to produce a major impact on power relations. The application of IT often has both intended and unintended impacts on the performance and structure of organizations (Huber, 1990).

Adoption of new IT often requires roles to be fitted and adjusted in terms of rank and function. IT adoption affects organization and society itself, as it 'redefines the work content, changes managerial styles and culture, reshuffles power hierarchies and spawns a series of both man designed and spontaneous adaptations' (Zelany, 1982, p.58; Huber and McDaniel, 1986; Franke, 1989). In this sense, the problems of IT proliferation appear sharply as ideological conflicts over roles, often creating policy problems. IT policies become, to a large measure, the business of coping with role differentiation while integrating organizational structures and culture.

The proliferation of new IT that facilitates cross function and intra functional integration (Boettinger, 1989), or 'networks' (Powell, 1990), creates changes in the leadership role and in hierarchical differentiation. Leaders are faced with making the difficult call between what is local to their function and what is global to the business, to differentiate decisions that are operational for their tasks and strategic for the organization. The increase of stakeholders and thus interdependencies, creates a need for the increased sharing of tasks, information, roles and decision making accountability (Boettinger, 1989; Fairholm, 1991). These, in turn, produce changes in the planning and operational parameters, further promoting a need for leadership interaction with a wider range of stakeholders within the organizational landscape. Furthermore, IT provides real time information, generating a more rapid and frequent need to adjust to new situations. Thus it can be argued that with actors' growing awareness, IT development and distributed decision making accountability over a wide variety of organizational stakeholders, a mutation of traditional managerial prerogatives is likely to occur.

The IT potential to transform hierarchical organizations into 'information based organizations' (Drucker, 1988, 1990) or 'network organizations' (Powell, 1990) is at least fourfold. First, IT makes possible the reduction of management levels by providing a dramatically enhanced potential for control (Beniger, 1986). Second, network structures facilitate fluid, flexible and dense patterns of interconnections that cut across various intra and interorganizational boundaries (Drucker, 1988, 1990). Third, IT provides real time communication across social time and space (Sproull and Kiesler, 1991). IT also improves communication between systems, thus blurring the boundaries of organizations beyond market exchanges (Malone and Rockhardt, 1991). Fourth, IT contributes to flexibility through electronic storage and data manipulation (Walton, 1989). Emerging 'network organizations' (Powell, 1990) are characterized by relations that are based on neither authority nor market transactions (Powell, 1990), but on the network structure of ties (relationships) among actors in a social context. As such, they are radically different from the Weberian bureaucracy (Baker, 1992; Nohria and Eccles, 1992).

This mutation or continuous redefinition of the leadership role produces changes not only within management gratification patterns, but also within their attached values. The adoption of new IT has an impact on organizational design and relates to the core functions of an organization in its symbolic, sanctional, international and social aspects (Forester, 1989; Powell, 1990; Korac-Boisvert and Kouzmin, 1996). Furthermore, IT is linked to personal dimensions such as morality, purpose and meaning. How well the organizational roles are redefined will depend on organizational design choices which, in turn, depend on human, socio cultural and economic factors as well as perceived real benefits (Boettinger, 1989; Korac-Boisvert and Kouzmin, 1996). Thus the outermost significance of IT choice is not methodological in any narrow sense, but moral (Apter, 1965).

Discretionary leader

Emerging out of the Tavistock Institute, London, is the view that managerial work is strongly influenced by hierarchical position, in terms of the choices that need to be made in order to exercise the actual or potential discretion in an executive role (Jaques, 1951; Montenare, 1978).

The discretionary element of role refers to the choices that the role incumbent needs to make in order to provide shape and identity to their role and by implication to that part of the organization for which they are accountable. For example, one interpretation of the role of Director of Human Resources is that the incumbent needs to form a view as to the shape and size of the organization, the level of investment necessary for both production and R&D, the revenue potential of the distribution channels and/or channels to market, the measures of financial performance that are appropriate such as margins, profitability, revenue, and from that total business understanding, only then form a view as to how the human resources function should be developed in terms of its identity, shape and size in order to support the other line functions. In effect, the role incumbent may see their primary identity as business orientated, which in turn seriously influences the pursuit and practice of the functional components of their HR directing job.

The exercise of choice may be influenced by current issues of an operational or strategic nature or by future assumed concerns. Choice equally may be driven by more emotive experiences such as feelings of vulnerability, insecurity, anger or even 'difficult to justify' sentiments of not being able to cope. There is equally no reason to assume that those occupying discretionary roles of an operational and strategic responsibility will respond in a comparable manner to the more so called quantifiable 'objective' issues. Even if the emotive and mental capacity of the senior managers of the organization is considerable, why should similar conclusions be reached as to the shape, size, direction and key qualities of the total organization and, thereby, the configuration of each role incumbent's area of accountability?

Particularly evident is likely to be the potential disparity of choices during circumstances of more fundamental change. Argyris and Schon (1978) draw distinction between change that takes place within existing frameworks and more fundamental alterations disrupting established boundaries, in coining the phrases 'single' and 'double loop' learning. Johnson and Scholes (1993), Daniels, de Chernatony and Johnson (1993a, 1993b) and Daniels and de Chernatony (1993) highlight that no meaningful changes take place unless core behaviours, and valued ways of interacting, are displaced and substituted with alternative behaviours at the group or organizational level. Argyris (1991, 1993) continues the theme by highlighting that the approaches to learning adopted by individuals substantially influences subsequent behaviours.

The contrasting nature of discretionary leadership (Kotter, 1982; Boyatzis, 1982; Ghiselli, 1971; McClelland and Boyatzis, 1982) is highlighted in the observation of how dialogues emerge according to the predisposition of the actors involved. Dialogue is viewed more as quality processes or inhibitors of issues resolution. What happens to the senior executive grouping and the organization, if two or more top managers form substantially, deeply held, different views as to the current configuration and future organizational identity and shape? What if the experience of working within the senior management group is one of unworkable discomfort, whereby a restricted dialogue, debilitating tension at a personal level and minimal disclosure at the group level become the norm? How do such experiences and processes impact on leadership practice and the future development of the organization?

In attempting to address these questions, one aspect is clear, that fundamental to leadership and to learning within organizations is the concept of dialogue, involving a process of inner reflection brought about through the sharing of experiences, especially over contrasting or conflicting agendas. Only individuals who reflect on their experiences can develop a competence or ability to deal with new situations unsimilar to those they have already experienced. Through these rhythmic exchanges between participation and observation/distance, between action and reflection, knowledge grows (Korac-Kakabadse and Kouzmin, 1996). Thus, dialogue can be seen as the concept that expresses the dynamics of tacit knowledge. Therefore, fundamental to leadership and organizational learning are the quality, depth and breadth of dialogue. The quality of the dialogue encompasses the extent to which issues or relationships that are considered as sensitive within the group, inhibit the discussion of key organizational concerns and thereby affect the future of the organization, and in turn, how such experiences affect the extent to which the group members hold a shared view of the future direction of the organization (Myers, Kakabadse and Gordon, 1995). Depth refers to the level of sensitivity displayed concerning the difficult issues discussed, despite differences of view that may exist amongst individual members, possibly affecting their relationships and which may in turn negatively influence their openness of conversation concerning the organization (Myers, Kakabadse and Gordon, 1995). The breadth of dialogue refers to the variety of issues (internal and external to the focal organization), which are discussed.

Organizations need to ensure the existence of a high quality dialogue amongst and between both senior management and other organizational actors (Kakabadse, 1991). An international study of leadership capabilities indicates that when the quality of dialogue is high and the relationships amongst senior managers are positive, the issues and concerns facing the organization tend to be more effectively addressed (Kakabadse, 1991, 1993). In organizations where relationships are tense and the quality of dialogue restricted, certain issues and problems tend not to be raised, because to do so would generate unacceptable levels of discomfort amongst some or all of the members of the senior executive (Kakabadse, 1991). Such inhibition stimulates latent crisis or ever growing but creeping opportunity costs. In this context, dialogue encompasses understanding transfer through the content of the conversation concerning the present and the future of the organization, as well as external developments which may affect the organization and the views and responses of actors or groups within the organization (Kakabadse, 1991; Korac-Kakabadse and Kouzmin, 1995).

Therefore an audit of how issues are addressed or unaddressed by the senior management is crucial to leadership, organizational learning and vulnerability management. Senior managers are leaders, and within that framework also 'social wealth creators' (Kakabadse, 1991), who set the agenda and identify appropriate strategies, and at times, put operational methods forward. Thus they need to discuss issues thoroughly, explore alternatives and seek opinions through stimulating debate about the organization's present state and future prospects (Kakabadse and Myers, 1995a). Although research evidence suggests that high quality dialogue is not easy to attain, its importance cannot be overestimated (Westley and Mintzberg, 1989). Furthermore, the quality of the dialogue is contingent on the quality of the relationship amongst group members. Where strong and robust relationships promote a positive team spirit where even the most delicate of concerns are aired, with poor relationships undue attention is given to personalities and the issues that are deemed to be too sensitive to discuss tend to remain unaddressed, often with such dysfunctionality becoming a way of life (Kakabadse and Myers, 1995), and an avenue for creeping crises.

A complex organization consists of many social and cultural groupings, and so communication between and across these groups is likely to involve not only shared meanings but also contradictory and contested ones, thus requiring quality of dialogue as the means for improvement (Kakabadse, 1991, 1993). Furthermore, participants in communication may be equally active in (re)producing meanings, but they frequently do so from positions of unequal power (Korac-Kakabadse and Knyght, 1995). For example, in most contemporary western societies, a person's access to information and ideas can often depend on their class, gender, age and ethnicity, as can their access to means of communicating information to others (Korac-Kakabadse and Knyght, 1995). Similarly in organizational settings, actors' access to information and ideas can often depend on their position within the organization and their orientation as networking opportunists. Thus, quality dialogue is a resonance between the beliefs and cultural experiences of the participants, expressed through a shared familiarity with the codes in use. In these circumstances, communicated messages are effective at the explicit level and at the broader cultural level of connotation, as shared connotations arise from shared experiences (Korac-Kakabadse and Knyght, 1995).

Unlike the Great Man theories, resolution of conflicting agendas is not considered to fall within the remit of the most gifted to put right, but rather the best that leaders can do as a result of their development, perspectives on life and the organization, and their emotional and mental capability to shape and be flexible to the demands of their context. The analogy is that of USA President, John F Kennedy who, through the space programme, not only put a man on the moon, but created new technologies, expanded the country's economic horizon and equally met the challenge of adverse foreign interests, by doing things differently (Naisbitt, 1994). The development theorists would say that Kennedy was not born with greatness, but that endeavour and circumstances brought out the greatness in him (Smith, 1984). Today's organizational leaders face similar challenges, having to balance local and universal needs that overwhelmingly point towards political independence and self rule on the one hand and the formation of alliances on the other, a balance often attained with little guidance but still nevertheless achieved.

Transformational leadership revisited

Transformational leadership is considered as fundamental to identifying and pursuing vision (Kauppinen and Ogg, 1994); enhancing dialogue (Korac-Kakabadse and Korac-Kakabadse, 1996); promoting values (Conger, 1993); responding to crisis (Kouzmin and Jarman, 1994) and promoting the charisma to transform to a new and better world (Avolio, Waldman and Yammarino, 1991). What however remains unresolved is the prime dilemma of leadership, namely, are people born with the characteristics that lead to the successful transformation of circumstances, or, are people's experiences, coupled with their will to succeed, the principal forces for leader success? The question is of nature versus nurture. Following this question, one further issue remains unresolved, namely, do we have any way of differentiating between the two polar extremes of leadership, namely, the born with characteristics and free will and if not, do we know how these phenomena apply in our organizations? If not, do we herald any new development as positive simply because it is new, with the result that new leadership thinking is couched in similar language, with the paradox contrasts not being recognized by the authors involved?

The question of what is new in leadership, how it is defined and whether differences are highlighted so that managers are offered a language to distinguish unfamiliar experiences and phenomena in their world, is explored by examining two critically examined issues in the leadership literature, crisis (Trice and Beyer, 1993; Jarman and Kouzmin, 1994), and charisma (Ramos, 1981; Bass, 1985a, 1985b; Kozmetsky, 1985).

Leadership and the response to crisis

Historically, the driving motive of social organization in military and religious groups, the first large scale organizational models, was fear or perceived threat to loss of life (Fairholm, 1991). Epictus (1st Century AD) in his analysis of the power base is quoted as saying that, no one is afraid of Caesar himself, but is afraid of death, loss of property, prison, disenfranchisement (Krieger and Stern, 1968). The scientific management and neo classical models of organizational theory also raise the question of job security. The psychological factors generated by threat or crisis (real or perceived) exemplified by fear, anxiety, helplessness and dependency, evoke people's defence mechanisms such as repression, projection, displacement, rationalization, distraction, falsification and denial of reality (Freud, 1953; Kets de Vries, 1977; Trice and Beyer, 1993). While these mechanisms do not directly help each person to deal with external reality, they are adaptive since they maintain the internal tension at a manageable level leading to a commitment to change and shared vision (Kets de Vries, 1977; Trice and Beyer, 1993).

The acceptance of common objectives and motivation for change are most likely to occur when the alternative is perceived as acute dissatisfaction, loss or crisis (Apter, 1965; Wolfenstein, 1967; Manz and Sims, 1990, 1991; Reynolds, 1994). Often in situations where uncertainty and urgency are critically operational (Kouzmin and Jarman, 1989; Jarman and Kouzmin, 1990), leaders arise due to their own superego and group's sense of helplessness, dependency (Kets de Vries, 1977) and desire to reduce life's complexities (Freud, 1922, 1953).

In crisis, where perceived complexities frequently reach paramount dimensions, followers often attribute to leaders' latent abilities and special powers out of a need to defend their dependency (Barnard, 1938; Kets de Vries, 1977). The crisis situation implies threat and critical contingencies (Kouzmin and Jarman, 1989, 1994) and, in so doing, promotes the resort to power in interorganizational relationships (Salancik and Pfeffer, 1977). The more exceptional, unusual, uncertain, complex or non routine the situation is, as exemplified by a variety of crises (Rosenthal and Kouzmin, 1993, p.1-12), the more visible can power use be, as administrative authority is often forced to rely upon external control and formal power (Kanter, 1979; Kouzmin and Jarman, 1989; t'Hart, Rosenthal and Kouzmin, 1993).

The behavioural aspect of the transformational thesis, through the power lens, suggests that changes need to be modelled in people rather than in cultural or organizational forms (McPherson, 1990), and that 'people who change fastest and best are those who have no choice' (Frey, 1993, p.80). These views appear to echo May's (1953, 1972) existentialist perspective assertion that individuals in potential crisis become what human possibilities offer them to become.

Australian transformational leadership studies (Lewis, 1993; Parry, 1994) support this line of thought by arguing that under circumstances of urgency, even in the presence of a dissonant culture, it is necessary only to change patterned group behaviour through power coercive strategies to achieve short term organizational effectiveness. These studies support Bachrach and Baratz's (1970) position on power use in the decision making process, as a way of compelling obedience, even over resistance, which Lewis (1993) proposes induces the long term changes in culture.

In essence, the transformational leadership thesis provides a partial synthesis of the charismatic and trait leadership theory in crisis situations, but through a power perspective. The leadership is exercised through the power of a reward system, while the followers' consent is based on calculative compliance (Manz and Sims, 1990, 1991). The perspective is laden with the flavour of scientific management (Taylor, 1911; Münsterberg, 1913), paralleling the concepts of incentives to get work done, the need to change people's behaviour and job design; undervaluing cultural diversity in favour of a homogeneous perception of 'corporate culture' (Deal and Kennedy, 1982; Peters and Waterman, 1982) in an alignment perspective (Smirchich, 1983; Luis, 1992) and where the leader's role is to 'construct' the corporate culture. This concept of the unitary 'corporate culture', derived from anthropology and sociology, appears to have less applicability in contemporary contexts of fragmented, mobile and highly industrialized societies, where subcultures seem to enjoy a greater prominence (Van Maanan and Barley, 1985). However, with the rapid development of IT and the reality of a 'global village' (Toffler, 1980; Boettinger, 1989), the concept of a unitary culture and the concepts of charismatic leadership will require further re-examination.

Furthermore, the transformational perspective fails to provide an explanation for successful transformations by managers who happen not to possess the so called charismatic traits and yet have provided successful leadership. Also, other instances of organizational, non random adaptation to peripheral changes or 'realignment' (Hambrick and Finkelstein, 1987), implemented through changes in the structural context and reflecting deliberate and various degrees of leadership discretion in non crisis situations, go unexplained. Implicit and often mentioned in the transformational leadership literature is that eloquence, command of the facts, passionate commitment or sheer tenacity and endurance (Morgan, 1986; Cantoni, 1993) can, in the end, win the day. In this sense, the transformational perspective has a negative connotation as it echoes images of the 'strong man' view of leadership, emphasized by autocratic leadership, where strength is almost completely part of a patriarchal process (Pijnenburg and van Dain, 1991).

Leadership and charisma

Due to strong and explicit claims that only charismatic leaders transform an organization (Burns, 1978; Bass, 1985; Kozmetsky, 1985; Tichy and Devanna, 1986; Avolio, Waldman and Yammarino, 1991), one view of transformational leadership is that it is only perceived as a revived charismatic leadership theory. However, the transformational leadership thesis, has received not only charismatic leadership theory, it has also revived a trait leadership thesis and re-enacted behavioural leadership theory. The claim is that transformational leaders generate excitement in three primary ways: charisma, individualized attention, and face to face contact or managing by walking around (MBWA) (Bass, 1985a; Peters and Austin, 1985; Warburton, 1993).

Charisma, or a special magnetic charm, attractiveness or an ability to get compliance from others (Freud, 1922, 1953), is a concept that 'packs an emotional wallop' for followers above and beyond ordinary esteem, affection, admiration and trust' (Bass, 1985b). It underpins all transformational leader traits (Kotter, 1982) and observable behaviour (Kotter, 1982; Albrecht and Zemke, 1985). The charismatic leader's dominance, self confidence and strong conviction in the moral righteousness of his/her beliefs (House, 1977; Pauchant, 1991; House, Spangler and Woycke, 1991) are reflected in personal vision; communicating this vision in a manner that relates a compelling intoxicating image of ultimate goals and positive self regard (Bass, Avolio and Goodheim, 1987; Bennis, 1989; Frey, 1993; Warburton, 1993).

The leader's dominance or an 'assured sense of self power' (Maslow, 1971) encompasses concepts of self respect, pride, sureness, masterfulness, self esteem and an ability to get one's own way (Ng, 1980; Bass, 1981; Metzger, 1987). Leadership in this connection has a change of behaviour orientation. It is based on the leader's self concept and who the leader is in relation to context, determining a 'phenomenal field' (Rogers, 1951) or 'life space' (Lewin, 1966) for his/her behaviour; a kind of heroic and visionary figure who is somewhat able to create an almost larger than life vision for the workforce to follow. Furthermore, it is assumed that charismatic and intellectually stimulating leaders arouse in followers an awareness of problems and potential solutions (Bass, 1981; Albrecht and Zemke, 1985; Bass, Avolio and Goodheim, 1987; Fairholm, 1991). Thus, charisma, a transcendental idea of supernatural, superhuman, or at least, specifically exceptional qualities (Weber, 1968), also incorporates ideas of strong emotional bonding between charismatic leaders and followers.

The four trait categories that appear to characterize transformational leaders further reinforce the charismatic assumption. Transformational leaders are defined as having vision, a goal, agenda, results and expectations around which stakeholders can converge (Bennis, 1982; Bennis and Nanus, 1985; Gaernter and Gaernter, 1985; Bennis, 1989; Fairholm, 1991); an ability to communicate their vision through verbal, non verbal or symbolic means (Barbour and Sipel, 1986; Bennis, 1989; Fairholm, 1991); skills building trust, namely being constant, reliable, dependable and persistent (Brodie and Bennett, 1979; Drehmer and Grossman, 1984; Barbour and Sipel, 1986; Fairholm, 1991); and having a positive self regard through recognition of personal strengths, nurturing skills in others and developing talents (Bass, 1981; Kotter, 1982; Bradford and Cohen, 1984; Drehmer and Grossman, 1984; Gardner, 1987; Barbour and Sipel, 1986; Fairholm, 1991; Warburton, 1993).

The concept of charisma through personality traits is further reflected and reinforced by recent developments in behavioural analysis. Studies of worldwide transformational leaders (Kotter, 1982; Bass, Avolio and Goodheim, 1987) suggest that transformational leaders' behaviour reflects three activities: creating an agenda, interpersonal networks and implementation of an agenda.

An analysis of exceptional transformational leaders from the military (Bass, Avolio and Goodheim, 1987), and from industry, Henry Ford, who achieved his vision of mass produced automobiles; Lee Iacocca, who transformed Chrysler Corporation from bankruptcy to success; and Jan Carlson, who turned Scandinavian Airlines from an $8 million loss to a $71 million profit in a little over a year, reveals that all had acted in a situation of urgency when presented by threat to human or financial loss. It can be argued that successful organizational transformation in crisis situations is a serendipitous aspect of crisis (Jarman and Kouzmin, 1990; Rosenthal, t'Hart and Kouzmin, 1991; t'Hart, Rosenthal and Kouzmin, 1993). Interestingly, the 'I turned it around' tales are self written biographies (Harvey-Jones, 1988) whose reflections of their response to challenging events are that their history, background, development and convictions, unique to them, gave them the fortitude to turn losing circumstances into winning situations. Their accounts may lack the scrutiny of external analysis, but interestingly reflect a developmental philosophy of self determined stature in contrast to the born with predilection.

Paradox of progress

Constantly reported is that 'new age' executives need to satisfy the needs of all groups and actors who have a stake in the success of networked organizations (Conger, 1993; Block, 1993). It is construed that they must deal effectively with contradictions, ambiguities, different values and measurements standards, conflicting goals and a plurality of methods for the attainment of goals.

Increasingly they face demands to share decisions with other stakeholders who may be subordinates and who wish to directly influence the organizational agenda. Shared governance and not just the provision of inputs for decision making management control, surrendering to the coordination of stakeholders' intonation, and decision making occurring in teams rather than in the hierarchy, are expected features of such organizational contexts. The quality of performance rests on the quality of interactions, communication and coordination of stakeholders. The 'new age' leadership literature (Porter-O'Grady, 1984; Kozlowski and Doherty, 1989; Keen, 1991; Manz and Sims, 1991; Senge, 1992) in many surprising ways highlights the radical implications of the emergence of shared leadership and shared ownership (Higgins, 1988; Frey, 1993). Leaders will be challenged to share their leadership with stakeholders and will gradually evolve into joint or shared leadership, where stakeholders will share authority and responsibility as needed at different stages and for different tasks contextually determined. Furthermore, adaptation to the globalization of business will further induce the proliferation of the networked organization of partnerships and joint ventures based on collaboration through situational authority.

This line of argument emphasizes the need for 'new age skills' such as creative insight, influence, sensitivity, visionary focus, caring, versatility, patience as well as commitment, empowerment and communication. 'New age' leadership is defined by dimensions of caring (trustful and honest care of all stakeholders), service (facilitating co workers so that they can accomplish their tasks), innovation, productivity improvement, vision setting and self development. Thus the 'new age' leader is a 'visionary hero' who is able to capture the essence of the global context and express it in a purposeful vision that inspires followers to relate to and share the vision; a 'super leader' that possesses the strength and wisdom of many persons, helping to unleash the abilities of followers and empowering them to become self leaders (Stark, 1993).

Furthermore, the self development theme pivotal in all 'new age' leadership models is rooted in the notion of 'individualism' and an individual's self actualization need (Hofstede, 1980). Self developing leaders continuously transform their everyday experience into learning in order to improve performance and facilitate the self development of followers. They work on personal and organizational goals through the simultaneous processes of self analysis and problem solving. The agenda is to release one's potential to achieve excellence (Hofstede, 1980; Pedler, 1988). The contemporary literature fosters, again, a surprisingly transformational, or dialectical, model of advancement to a higher level of self development or human emancipation.

The 'new age' leader requires skills such as visionary focus, creative insight, commitment, sensitivity, caring, empowerment and communication (Hickman and Silva, 1984; Henry, 1991; Keen, 1991; McAller, 1991); demanding moral puritanism and superior knowledge. This moral standing reflects an ideological relationship between a higher development of human consciousness and more highly evolved forms of organization. The actor's commitment would be based on shared vision and ownership and the need for inner motivation or a passion to be involved in enterprise achievements for their own sake rather than being reward driven (Manz and Sims, 1990, 1991; Senge, 1992).

The emerging imperative for a leader's virtue in morals and values and the ability to have vision is a disguised but salient call for ideological leadership that enlarges the significance of organization for followers (Jeannot, 1989). 'New age' leaders are ideological leaders robed in the transparent cloak of visionaries. The language is that of the discretionary hero, pulling or cajoling both himself/herself and others through honest sharing of toil and challenge. However, the predilection to search for the unique set of personal characteristics is still as strong today (Howell, 1988; Warburton, 1993) as at the turn of the 20th Century, with the view that leadership, charisma and control are substitutes for power, if not sufficiently interwoven to allow for an interchangeability of terms (Papp, 1984).

The paradox is that substantially contrasting philosophies of leadership are attributed with the same symbols of progress, namely 'new age' and 'charisma' The paradox of progress is that conceptual and philosophical clarity are being overseen by an emerging temperament of political correctness, browbeating practitioners and theorists to not be seen to be revisionist in resisting what's new. To continue on this track, with loose language emphasizing 'newly emergent' but not 'substance', this generates the likelihood of a fundamental block in communication, namely, 'because you say it's new and right, it has to be, irrespective of my views and experience especially if I am not afforded a language to express my disquiet'. The danger is that 'new age' leaders may say they are good because they say so, fully convinced that they are enlightening and empowering, not recognizing that they are dumping, over loading and distracting already overburdened subordinates, who are not offered the means to voice their discontent. To not be able to express disquiet is bad enough, but when a lack of language and insight leads to confusion of philosophy and methodology (Skelton and Miller, 1993; Miller, 1995), inability to distinguish between the process of visioning and the implementation of a vision, then the concept of a creeping crisis in leadership and the social sciences more generally, seems particularly pertinent.

3 From public administration to public management to?

Already in the 1960s, a realization emerged that policy was not the only source of focus of public administration. The reformist work of the influential Brunel University Institute of Organizational and Social Studies (BIOSS), London, particularly in the Health Services (Newman and Rowbottom, 1968; Kogan et al, 1971; Kogan and Terry, 1971) and other works reaching different aspects of government, Bunyard (1978) highlight the breaking of new ground. Although the transactional nature of leadership epitomizes the structuralist and contextualist nature of BIOSS's philosophy (Brown and Jaques, 1964; Jaques, 1956, 1967; Kakabadse, 1977), the ground was set for fundamentally re-examining structuralist/functionalist assumptions and in turn exploring the role and contribution of individual action and choice, the prerequisites of transformational leadership. In effect, the basis for transformational leadership thinking in the public sector began to emerge in the 1960s, but is only just now being considered as a viable, if not painful and not clearly appreciated, alternative to structure and organizational form.

In this chapter, attention will be given to an analysis of the conceptual developments in public administration, culminating in an overview of how the current emphasis on management is crucially influencing a reconsideration of the developmental requirements of senior and middle ranking government officials. Attention is also given to exploring the impact of information technology (IT) as a tool of reengineering organizations, and its growing influence on the restructuring of government bodies. Throughout, certain attention will be given to changes and developments in the Australian context.

Global diffusion of public administration

Arguably, during the 1970s and 1980s, public administration and the public sector praxis in Australia experienced a period of 'normal science' (Kuhn, 1970), where the most common problems addressed consist of the 'policy process' (Rhodes, 1995). This phenomenon reflects rather dimly in many other economies during this period, exemplified by analysis of the Cuban missile crisis (Allison, 1971). It appears that research in the academic field of public administration was focused on 'the study of institutional arrangements for the provision of public services' (Hood, 1990, p.107), with only few reflections on the state of the discipline of provision. Much of the literature assumes a 'policy orientation', whilst concurrently adopting a traditionalist institutional approach in public administration (Hogwood, 1995). This is equally true of other developed economies such as the USA, UK, Canada and New Zealand, but with the UK breaking out of this mould earlier.

Since the end of the 1980s, however, the normal science of public administration has been increasingly replaced by crisis, announced by the emergence of the crisis management discipline. In economic terms, the notion that the public sector should provide 'value for money' became a concern for many economies in the 1980s. Liberal economies of the last decade have been experiencing fundamental structural change. In response to the emerging world economy 'characterized by the increasing crystallization of transnational markets and structures, the state itself is having to act increasingly like a market player, shaping its policies to promote, control and maximize returns from market forces in an international setting' (Cerney, 1990, p.230). The new transnational market setting, or the 'global' option (an advanced and complex form of internationalization that implies a degree of functional integration between internationally dispersed economic activities that have combined despite uneven effects across space and time) (Dicken, 1992, p.2), would have been inconceivable without the advancements of IT, particularly in telecommunications (Forester, 1985, 1987, 1989; Castelles, 1989; Henderson, 1991). Thus with increasing global competition, changing demographic and employment patterns, increasing demand for services, personal and community, the need to find innovative solutions at the local level to complex social problems (health, housing, community safety, unemployment), the pressure for reform and change in the public services, became inevitable.

These developments are producing profound effects on the management of public services. Indeed, these processes, while not uniform, are part of the liberation movement which has acted upon most parts of the world since the 1980s and has consequently seen a transformation, a redefinition and, in some respects, a blurring of the respective roles of public and private sectors

(Dunleavy and Hood, 1994). The role of the state and society in defining, protecting and promoting public interests is reshaped by a 'global campaign for value, emerging as privatization and public sector commercialization' (Korac-Boisvert and Kouzmin, 1994). At the very root of this global restructuring is a 'techno economic' process, with a range of new organizational possibilities facilitated by computer related technology, creating a world so different that it can only be understood as constituting a new techno economic paradigm (Freeman and Perez, 1988; Perez and Soete, 1988).

While these processes often have a different dynamic, they, nevertheless, are interlinked. Economic globalization combined with concepts of value added for communities has often forced politicians and 'bureau shapers' to restructure the state, and to hive off certain 'peripheral' functions thereby 'reinventing government' (Osborne and Gaebler, 1992). Thus, although the changes sweeping across the public services of developed and developing economies reflect particular aspects of the change agenda, and the rhetoric of 'flexibility', 'responsiveness', 'privatization', 'deregulation', 'reengineering' and 'quality service', all under the guiding principle of 'corporate managerialism', they equally represent much more than manifestations of policies of particular governments or ideologies. These changes require greater productivity; changing skill base boundaries; greater application of technology; greater inter agencies networking; and community agency networking. A closer examination suggests that, in the past few years, reinventing organizations has been brought about almost entirely through economic recession and low profitability. Research in the UK in the area of restructuring confirms that corporate reinvention is perceived by corporate leaders as synonymous with 'downsizing' and 'rationalization' (Currie, 1995, p.281), which suggests that reinventing organizations is almost entirely economically driven. Faced with 'growing red ink', Japanese industry also has adopted reengineering as a strategy for reinventing its organizations. Low growth, poor profits and the difficulties in raising capital from increasingly cautious banking institutions as well as having to compete with the emerging markets of the Pacific rim and China, have forced Japan to rethink its own business structures (Currie, 1995, p.267).

Politicians, policy advisors, senior civil servants and those who direct public services, approach policy and strategy formulation and its implementation in a variety of ways. From the late 1980s, they start looking for new ideas and solutions to complex problems from the private sector arena, and embark on the quest in earnest for better management in the early 1980s (Peters and Waterman, 1982). In the 1990s this search for new ideas becomes prominent (Osborne and Gaebler, 1992). Where the key motivation for change in the public sector is improved public sector performance, private sector management techniques become attractive even though based on the philosophy of economic rationalism (OECD, 1987, 1995).

Owing to their inherently purpose based division of labour, designed for achieving predetermined policies rather than responding to innovation, public sector organizations experience enormous difficulties in adapting to changes of contextual as well as core technological dynamics (Morgan, 1986, p.35). Thus, when new problems arise in public sector organizations, they are often ignored because there is no responsiveness to organizational technological uncertainties or complexities. Dynamic circumstances call for responses involving capacities for creative, flexible and timely action. Public sector organizations, especially, face the challenge of 'reinventing' themselves for the IT age (Osborne and Gaebler, 1992).

Experience of change in public administration

Like other ideologies, economic rationalism is a combination of discourse and practices. The discourse provides meaning which enables the practices to be developed and the practices provide a 'real world' which generates experiences that become topics of discourse, which in turn serve to validate the practices (Muetzelfeldt, 1992). This has led to somewhat superficially different strategies of change, but overall dominated by a neo Taylorist and post Fordist, 'control and command' frame of references, through the metaphor of an 'organizational machine', which critically embraces approaches to leadership, public learning and definition of meanings (Drath and Plaus, 1994). For example, Jenkins (1995) describes how the British Government has nationalized huge chunks of public services and voluntary activities, not by direct ownership but through their central control of power and finance and through their ability to appoint and control the huge increase in quangos. Not that this is unusual, as many governments' approaches to change are led from a top down, pragmatic and fragmented stance, where control can be exercised (so it is thought) through contract, 'agency', quasi markets, performance related pay and the pursuit of improvement and quality through an expansion of the audit inspection (Power, 1994) and arbitrary top down targets. In Britain, for example, a significant trend is the increasing centralization of power, particularly at the expense of local democracies and local pluralism (Marr, 1995), where many civil servants and their departments are left with the daunting task of implementing a never ending stream of reforms and fads.

Numerous authors draw attention to problems in the public administration discipline, although most of these view public administration as under threat of invasion from the 'hostile' paradigm of public choice and management (Rosenthal, t'Hart and Kouzmin, 1991). Thompson and Bates (1957),

Woodward (1965), Perrow (1967), Miletti et al (1978) and Ramos (1981) all specifically refer to the commodity bias in the large part of organizational experience and managerial prescription. Whereas these two perspectives arose separately and at different times in the USA, it is their confluence under the banner of public management and further the economic rationalists' influence which seem to have led to a fundamental questioning of assumptions in public administration in Australia and elsewhere in public sector management.

This political initiative for change has led to a number of characteristics which include a focus on public services as part of a government belief in 'social engineering' and 'reengineering' to correct market failure, and a concern to grow new structures as mechanisms for service delivery (Kass and Catron, 1990; Rhodes, 1991; Goodstell, 1994). For example, in Australia the deregulation of the labour market and the privatization of public sector activities are the central theme to the discourse. There is a move to replace centralized industrial relations mechanisms with labour contracts based on enterprise capacities, small groups or individual bargaining. The proponents of the New Right argue that workers should be as independent from the encumbrance of formal organizations as possible and that this independence should be achieved through subcontracting, franchizing and payment based on piece work and/or incentive payments (Muetzelfeldt, 1992). This is a fundamental shift from career service (Caiden, 1990), which until recently was arguably the single dominant source of continuation of employment in government.

Hood (1990), for example, argues that public administration has 'lost an empire' since 1970. He attributes this to a weakness of theory and methodology, as the theoretical elaboration in public administration was fairly limited. He argues that the method of analysis was centred on the 'historical case study, often based more on shrewd common sense than explicit theory' (Hood, 1990, p.109). The result was a vulnerability to rival paradigms, principally public choice and management. Hood (1990) asserts that the main impact of management is practical rather than academic. While senior public officials sought guidance in business practice, the intellectual challenge presented by management was weak. Hood (1990) questions whether the business management approach to public administration is really a 'professional' one at all, 'in so far as a profession involves arrangements for systematic and cumulative additions to the knowledge of the profession through published writing and research' (Hood, 1990, p.113). For Hood (1990) the managerial approach fails to provide a clear set of principles on which to organize public services. Therefore he argues that the management approach does not advance administrative theory beyond the collection of incompatible proverbs, 'to the extent it has no intellectual superiority over the old orthodoxy in public administration' (Hood, 1990, p.114).

By contrast, public choice theory acquires both practical relevance, and in Hood's view, academic respectability. The practical effects of public choice theory have come from its use (and abuse) by new right governments. Its academic status is such that 'it has undermined some of the traditional assumptions built into academic public administration, to the point of now constituting a major alternative approach to the subject' (Hood, 1990, p.116).

In contrast to Hood's (1990) measured evaluation of the ostensible decline of public administration, Kingdom (1990) provides a more strident and iconoclastic analysis. Kingdom's (1990) argument is that a number of contemporary forces conspire to place the study of public administration in a particular critical condition; 'the past 20 years have seen the development of certain intellectual fashions which necessarily threaten the discipline and its characteristic paradigm' (Kingdom, 1990, p.5). The 'contemporary forces' of government policies are such principles as privatization, commercialization and contracting out. The intellectual fashion consists of a new right ideology, in which Kingdom subsumes public choice management. Thus the source of the public administration decline is political rather than intellectual. Kingdom (1990) does not suggest that the old paradigm is a scientific failure, but rather that it is confronted by an inhospitable 'ideological' climate.

Rhodes (1995) on the other hand claims that the public administration discipline is poorly founded, 'relies on a restricted range of methods' and that it 'employs only descriptive and simple forms of inductive statistics; and eschews theory' (Rhodes, 1995, p.11). He claims that this disarray is partly caused by the presence of alien forces in the territory of public administration, 'the colonial or occupying powers include economists, accountants and business' (Rhodes, 1995, p.13).

Gray and Jenkins (1995) address the paradigmatic challenge of public management. They focus on the institutional structures and management processes but not on academic work because the 'changes to the study of public administration tend to follow those in the practice of the administration of government'. (Gray and Jenkins, 1995, p.75). They, like Rhodes (1995), argue that public administration has been 'open to colonization by marauding theoretical hordes and changing agendas, often driven by outside forces' (Gray and Jenkins, 1995, p.77). They argue that a more mature scientific paradigm would not be undermined by a change in the 'real world', its position would be stable provided that it had the theoretical power to explain, and the concepts and methods to evaluate, any changes that occur (Roszak, 1986). In the absence of such strength, public administration has suffered a theoretical onslaught led by 'economists and management scientists aided and abetted by those who argue more generally that the art of private sector management should be transported to the public sector' (Gray and Jenkins, 1995, p.80).

Gray and Jenkins (1995) launch an ideological attack on public management, assuming that because the conventional academic paradigm is associated with an ideological position that is sympathetic to state intervention, so a rival paradigm must be anti state. Gray and Jenkins (1995) claim that many of the advocates of public management 'are clearly true believers in the power and sanctity of markets or the ability of other nostrums to rescue what they perceive as the theoretically weak and misconceived field of public administration (Gray and Jenkins, 1995, p.82). They contend that instead of a paradigm shift, 'competing visions exist that in many ways remain separate and distinct' (1995, p.87). However they fail to reflect the purely scientific content of much of the public management paradigm or to support their assertion with academic reference (Pollitt, 1993). As some note, public choice theory has become detached from its politically rightward tendencies and fashioned into a powerful analytical tool (Lane, 1993; Pollitt, 1996; Boyne, 1996).

Although there is a widespread perception of a decline in public administration, the circumstances are not entirely consistent with Kuhn's (1970) argument that the principal reasons for an academic crisis are 'technical'; that is, are the accumulation of research evidence that undermines the ruling paradigm. Therefore, it is not the interpretation of the world that has changed, but the world itself (Rothstein, 1989). Instead of the traditional pattern of large line bureaucracies providing services directly, the public sector begins to consist of markets and contracts. Prior (1993), for example, contends that fundamental change in the public sector does not replace one broadly uniform set of arrangements with another uniform set, but with a plethora of different sets of arrangements with few common features. Prior (1993, p.459) questions whether the 'public sector is any longer useful as a generic analytical concept'. Perhaps more importantly for an applied discipline, public administration lacks the concepts and methods to evaluate the components of the new public management. By contrast, policies based on competition and performance are ready for evaluation by a paradigm drawn upon public choice and management. On this basis, it is held that public administration in Australia has been engulfed by concepts of public management.

This particular managerial shift in the public sector is not confined to Australia alone but applies to a number of economies, known as the 'management community', notably Britain, United States, Canada and New Zealand, with a wider group such as Japan, Germany and Spain engaged in privatization strategies, as opposed to the 'New Public Management' (NPM) techniques. Although it appears that the Westminster model of government is more readily absorbed by managerialist strategies, where power is centralized in a core executive and change can be implemented in a traditional top down fashion, the pressure for reform and change appears to continue irrespective of the political composition of government. For example, UK Conservative governments have pursued the managerialist agenda with substantial zeal. 'Swedish Social Democrats, Spanish and French socialists, untainted by the same ideological motivations, have been only slightly less zealous' (Wright, 1994, p.112). Similarly many managerialist elements have been adopted by Labour governments in New Zealand and Australia with equal zest (McAllister and Vowles, 1994).

France initially strongly resisted the application of management theory, and yet in some way France was ahead of Britain. According to Chevallier (1996, p.70) 'the movement of rationalizing budgetary choices, launched in 1967, constituted the first systematic and coherent attempt to experiment with management theory in the French civil service. This was closely related to the endeavour to formulate the principles of a new public management'. German bureaucracy is more resistant to the introduction of management thinking (Seibel, 1996), although the German administration shares with France and even Japan, considerable involvement in policy making. Even China has not been immune to managerialism. Selznick (1952) sees the Chinese bureaucracy as the 'organizational weapon' of the Communist party rather than the rational tool of administration of the country. Zhou (1995) argues that change has happened to the Chinese bureaucracy since economic reform began in 1978, where reforms were aimed at overcoming bureaucratic inertia and inducting the bureaucracy to be more of an organizational instrument than a 'weapon'. Some of the Chinese changes even mirror the managerialist agenda: the devolution of resources allocation from the central to local government; allowing the heads of 'work units' to allocate a large proportion of any surplus revenue; decentralization of personnel management, and in the work units, an encouragement towards the 'managerial responsibility system' which is aimed at eroding the authority and role of the 'politicrats' (Zhou, 1995, p.465). The influence of public management has extended to Eastern European economies, where foreign experts advise on privatization, and where new special purpose ministries have been established, separate from the 'regular bureaucracy' (Meaney, 1995). Thus there visibly exists a global pattern of reorganization, with more or less successful deliberate copying of the trajectory elsewhere.

Process of management

The public management terminology connotates a shorthand description of a variety of reinventing public sector initiatives, attempting to bring their management reporting and accountability approaches closer to that of business methods (Dunleavy and Hood, 1994). These attempts generally involve a shift in the design coordination of public sector organizations, making the public sector less distinctive as a unit from the private sector and reducing the extent to which discretionary power is limited by uniform and general rules and procedures (Dunleavy and Hood, 1994). Enhanced are the discretionary powers of public managers, empowering them with the new role of a manager instead of the old one of administrator. This is an outward manifestation of the design shift.

In contrast, some argue that managers in government organizations operate with less autonomy than their counterparts in the private sector (Pollitt and Harrison, 1992; McKevitt, 1993; Davis, 1994; David, 1995, p.73) as public enterprises generally cannot diversify into unrelated businesses or merge with another firm. Governmental strategy usually enjoys little freedom in altering the organization's mission or redirecting objectives, as legislators and politicians often have direct or indirect control over major decisions and resources. Furthermore, strategic issues get debated in the media and in the legislature, often becoming politicized, and resulting in fewer strategic choice alternatives. Pollitt and Harrison (1992) question how the artificially created internal markets of the public sector can be compatible with real markets and how balance can be achieved between the need to integrate service delivery with the espoused desirability to decentralization, in effect to try and make the organization more responsive to customers. McKevitt (1993) suggests that considering that the policy end is given by political direction, and the search options are restricted to the operational and implementation domain, public mangers are left in the role of only implementing political decisions.

Thus the arguments regarding the main differences between the private and public sectors are summarized in Table 3.1 below.

Table 3.1
Contrasting domains: private versus public sector

Organization	Private sector	Public sector
Purpose	• Profit driven • Market share • Clear objectives	• Socio political driven • Social values • Multiple objectives
Context	• Competitive market • Accountable to shareholders • Raise capital	• Artificially created internal market • Publicly accountable • Taxation
Management strategies	• Flexible/discretionary • Freedom to take risks • Goal setting	• Little scope for flexibility • Regulation/legislation • Pre defined goals

Notwithstanding those arguably valid concerns about the influence of politics in public sector management, public sector management can be impactful in dealing with generic situations found in both the private and public sectors.

In the provision of social services, for example, managing change in the external environment requires managing key stakeholders in order to reduce the potential conflicts of interest in a complex web of relationships and thereby making a significant contribution to the effective delivery of services (Tutt, Neale and Warburton, 1992). What is being postulated is that the management of relationships, both external and internal, is a crucial part of managing any organization. Management requires the 'creation and nurture of relationships of trust and respect between different levels of groups within an institution, and between the institution and other key actors in its environment' (Pollitt and Harrison, 1992, p.282) and as such, applies to the public and private sector. 'Relationship management' is, at very least, a spin off of 'stakeholder management', which is not only about managing relationships between the organization and its stakeholders, but also about the relationships between stakeholders, irrespective of whether there is a legitimate source of interest to the organization (Freeman, 1984). Management in the public sector thus can be viewed as the management of a community of stakeholders and interlocking political and resource interests. If the public organization may be characterized as including a large range of, sometimes, conflicting demands and priorities from stakeholder groups who have a variety of aims and objectives, then the rationing of resources is an inevitable key issue. Furthermore when those demands are increasing, but the resources are decreasing, then the issue forces the management to identify core activities and core competencies in order to establish a basis for achieving some sort of rationing of resources and prioritization (Choo, 1992). Although only a basis, it is an essential step in attempting to ensure equality and equity in the relationship between resources and services. Furthermore, a circumstance of increasing demands and reducing resources provides an opportunity for allowing public sector managers to acquire new skills and develop an understanding of 'strategic thinking' and its importance to the organization. For example, in many ways the management of a subsidiary or local authority operates as a multi business or diversified corporation. The 'centre' represents the political interests of the local authority, while the service is actually delivered from most of the service points. These services are often diverse with relatively little in common with each other and may be dominated by professional values which owe a greater loyalty outside the organization than within. Corporate management then, consists of an overview of the authority as a whole, determining the composition of its services, while the services pursue business strategies designed to satisfy their customers.

The 1990s, in particular, are seeing the flourishing of commercialization within the public sectors at all levels of government in many economies. The shift from the full privatization argument of the late 1980s to that which calls for varying degrees of commercialization (including corporatization of the public sector) does have significant organizational development and organizational change implications which, of course, have their effect on public management development needs. The actual implementation of commercialization is problematic if human factors in such reform processes are not taken into account.

Confronted with radical reforms, new roles and rapid change implied by the introduction of commercialization, public sector mangers are left to seek any strategy that will help them to cope with such change. The notion that people do not voluntarily, nor automatically, change behaviour in the most appropriate way merely because a reform has been formally set in place, has penetrated the public sector arena. New legislation and more regulation, again, do not automatically change behaviour. In the context of commercialization, the change in public sector development is to facilitate people to change behaviour in directions compatible with the directions of the reforms introduced. Such developments smack of the need for transactional leadership and not a mere mimicking of private sector assumptions and private sector performance indicators.

Information technology and public administration

The most fashionable strategic objective of contemporary Australian organizations, in both the private and public sector, is that of gaining competitive advantage (variously defined as establishing and maintaining market place advantage, improving performance, and gaining increased productivity) and is, in reality, driven by a need to reduce costs through the adoption of new IT (Wheatley, 1992). In keeping with such developments, many Australian Public Service senior executives have 'reengineered' their organizations and business in order to cut costs (Computerworld, 1992, p.58; Wheatley, 1992). The Australian economy, for example, embarked in mid 1980s on a decade of public service and industrial reforms that were technologically led (Dodgson, 1989; Australian Management Advisory Board, 1992). Technological change brought work restructuring to the public service and later to industry, although changes were also brought about in response to both domestic and international market pressures that reflected broad, community wide government policies and rapidly changing social and economic settings (Dodgson, 1989, 1991). The 1993 Australian government review of the public sector concludes that IT is a fundamental enabler for increasing government competitiveness (Commonwealth Government, 1993), while the 1995 Government Information Technology Review Group reviews 97 per cent of the public sector organizations to identify opportunities for taking advantage of IT developments (Commonwealth Government, 1995). IT is seen as the integral element in delivering the policies outlined in the 'Working Nation' initiative (Gibbons, quoted in Carroll, 1995, p.2).

In the competitive, and sometimes over enthusiastic, pursuit of cost reduction, managers often misunderstand the role of IT and select strategies for IT adoption that ignore the fact that technology transfer also produces cultural transfer (Soesastro, Pangestu and McKendrick, 1990; Geisler, 1993; Korac-Boisvert, 1993). Often IT investments are made in the belief that returns will eventuate. Many managers under this perceived pressure invest in IT based on a 'gut feeling' or 'media hype' assumption that value will be ensured, 'without having good measures to determine the performance effects' or a comprehension of IT's socio cultural effects on an organization or its associated human costs (Kauffman and Weill, 1990, p.337; Geisler, 1993; Korac-Boisvert and Kouzmin, 1994a; Garnett and Kouzmin, 1995).

A review of the recommendations of various government enquiries on IT's role in public management is in keeping with the assertions made that Anglo-American societies primarily focus on IT as an enabling tool for cost cutting and attaining competitive edge. The secondary focus is on information sharing. Other societies have a primary focus on initiatives for achieving a vision of an information society which would benefit the community and the economy. The Canadian Government's inquiry report, for example, concludes that IT is fundamental to the issue of public sector organizations' competitiveness and provides a blueprint for an integrated approach to improving government service delivery while significantly reducing costs (Treasury Board of Canada, 1994). Similarly, the US Government's National Performance Review suggests a need for reengineering the whole business of government through the use of IT (NPROVP, 1993). The report further suggests that the American Federal Government, with the exception of the Defence Department, is significantly behind the private sector in the identification and utilization of the best information systems and, as such, is virtually the only sector of American society that has yet to confront the need to reinvent itself for the information age (NPROVP, 1993; Reynolds, 1994).

At a state level, the report of the State of California's Task Force on Government Technology Policy and Procurement identifies an increase in the state's IT budget in the face of reductions in its statewide budget; a lack of enterprisewide planning and coordination in IT; a lack of performance information and a lengthy delivery time for solutions (State of California, 1994). These reports also reveal that the secondary focus of Australian, Canadian and USA governments is the creation of a national vision in which all citizens can exchange and receive information and by which government can more effectively use IT.

The European Community report advocates an action plan based on specific initiatives, highlighting a need to remove monopolistic, anti competitive environments; in effect the prime task of government being the safeguarding of competitive forces (The European Council, 1994). Similarly, the Swedish Government's Commission on Information Technology (1994) promotes the use of IT as a means of improving the quality of life and the nation's international competitiveness. It makes a series of recommendations on what is to be achieved and how, in areas such as education and research, the legal system and public administration (Swedish Prime Minister's Office, 1994). The Danish Government outlines a strategy and proposals for the year 2000. It covers issues such as health; data protection and privacy; education; libraries; mass media; telecommunications; and the impact of IT on the working life of Danish people (Danish Ministry of Research, 1994). Thus the role of IT has evolved from that of an administrative support tool to that of a major catalyst for change. Furthermore, IT adds a new element to the continuing debate of the Euro-American 'gradient' of public service management. It could be suggested that the Anglo-American public sector view of IT is more 'instrumental' (emphasizing IT as a tool for rationalizing tasks and cost cutting), whereas the North European view is more 'social' (emphasizing that IT is a tool that needs to be managed for the benefit of society).

IT, reengineering and public management

The metonym of the 1990s, 'reengineering' (Hammer and Champy, 1993, p.32) or 'strategic core reorganization' (Fairbrother, 1991), has become executive rhetoric in both private and public organizations. A survey in the USA reveals that most senior executives cite reengineering as their program of choice for achieving strategic goals (Gateway Information Service Inc, 1992). Ninety per cent of company executives in Canada and Britain, 98 per cent in Germany, 85 per cent in US and 69 per cent in Japan report that their organizations have undertaken some form of reengineering (restructuring, downsizing and/or cost reduction) since 1988 (Cascio, 1994, p.8).

Many executives perceive global competition; rapid IT development; sluggish economic growth; financial deregulation; privatization of public utilities; and cost cutting as the pressures driving them to reengineering (Osborne and Geabler, 1992; Wheatley, 1992; Forester Research Inc, 1993). In the Australian cultural setting, IT appears to be a pivotal dimension of the reengineering process in public sector organizations. The public 'wealth creators' (Kakabadse, 1991) view IT as a structural facilitator of market driven approaches to the conduct and delivery of public services. IT is used to build a 'social architecture' for change in order to reinvent, or at least revitalize, the public sector image (Hill, 1989).

A review of the literature (Hammer, 1990; Champy and Arnoudse, 1992; Stanton and Power, 1992; Hammer and Champy, 1993) suggests that the reengineering idea is built on an eclectic collection of pre existing concepts relating to competitive advantage, a process with degrees of implementation, rather than implying a fully fledged new organizational paradigm. The term 'reengineering' is used to refer to a strategy of 'downsizing'; 'delayering' (flattening of hierarchies); 'restructuring'; 'programming' (automating existing processes or the routinization of management tasks) and effecting 'lean production' (concentration of production on 'value added' activities and the elimination of 'no value added'/'waste' activities). It also refers to developing new business processes (decentralization, team production, reorganizing management information systems, adopting new IT); 'outsourcing' (reborn entrepreneurialism) (Gateway Information Service Inc, 1992; Babson, 1993; Cameron, Freeman and Mishra, 1993; Forrester Research Inc, 1993; Womack and Jones, 1994; Glasson and Rusli, 1994) or reorganizing in a top down fashion, through a coercive style of change management, possibly accompanying the further centralization of power in the hands of senior management and thereby engineering changes to a new set of ground rules (DuGay and Salaman, 1992) focused on structural change.

The impulse to restructure arises in response to a variety of tensions. Restructuring appears to be one of the most common approaches to organizational change, despite the fact that many restructures 'never produce the long run benefits' (Bolman and Deal, 1991, p.99). While organizational forms may diverge, both in terms of the overall division of functions and of the internal structure of work relationships, new IT (whether encapsulated in computer related technologies or in managerial strategies) is introduced with the 'rational' goal of increased productive efficacy and, as such, many 'old' choices continue to be made. Eccles (1992) argues against simple technological determinism and suggests that a cycle of change, such as delayering, is likely to be followed by relayering at some point and this, in turn, by further rounds of delayering. He suggests that the cycles of change may not merely be the reflection of business cycles, but that they are derived from organizational dynamics. However, these dynamics are influenced by the organizational structure that provides constraints on the interactions managers can make; structure defines combinations within which managers choose their interactions (Bourdieu and Passeron, 1990; Giddens, 1984).

While any one strategy on its own appears to be insufficient to gain an organizational competitive edge, reengineering often involves a complex variety and encompasses 'the fundamental rethinking and radical redesign of business processes to achieve dramatic improvements in critical, contemporary measures of performance such as cost, quality and speed' (Hammer and Champy, 1993, p.32).

Reengineering and human costs

Empirical data suggests two reasons for organizations choosing to reengineer; financial (to increase the organization's share value) and organizational (to reduce overhead and bureaucratic layers; increase speed of decision making processes; enhance internal communications; foster entrepreneurship; and increase productivity). Both are based on the economic criterion of productivity (Cascio, 1992, 1993). Thus, an economic criterion becomes of paramount importance when selecting new IT. However, whenever economic criteria act as selectors (focusing devices) for the adoption of new IT, development often follows old paths, in which an established technology has become the dominant paradigm instead of opening a bigger set of new possible paths and as such, the specific IT choice falls behind the newly emerging industry benchmarks (Dosi, 1984; Anderson and Tushman, 1990). At other times, the selection of new IT is based on the media hyped promotion of cost efficiency or personal choice. This occurs without understanding IT's broader implications, such as the less obvious human costs of organizational restructuring, exemplified by the emotional costs employees incur (stress related injuries); corporate 'memory loss' (contacts, tacit knowledge, experience); absenteeism and productivity loss as well as other organizational risks that can offset potential cost savings (Due, 1992; Australian Commonwealth Government, 1995).

Often the increase in expense in overtime, temporary and contract work can exceed the savings expected from job cuts (Greengard, 1993). Cost cuts in many cases are not achieved because the dominant feature of reengineering, downsizing, is often followed by the hiring of replacement staff or the use of former staff paid at consultant rates, with those who remain suffering the 'survivor's syndrome' (Brockner et al, 1993; Cascio, 1993, 1994). Low morale, lack of trust and a decline in commitment to the organization have multiple and ripple effects on virtually every human resource aspect of business activity, as survivors find themselves in 'new, and not necessarily friendly, environments' (Cascio, 1993, p.95). As a result, reengineering has 'fundamentally altered the terms of the psychological contract that binds workers to organizations' (Cascio, 1993, p.103). Fillipowski (1993) reports that the American Management Association's survey on reengineering in 1993 found that 80 per cent of surveyed companies that had reengineered reported decreased employee morale; 13 per cent reported no change in employee morale; and 2 per cent reported increased morale (Fillipowski, 1993). However even a two per cent increase in morale may not benefit an organization as indicted by the survivors' attitude studies (Brockner et al, 1993). Survivors are often worry laden managers and employees with low self esteem who direct their motivation to doing things to keep their jobs, but not to achieving organizational goals (Brockner et al, 1993). Survivors of retrenchments and layoffs become conservative and negative and abandon innovation as a risky strategy, often actively resisting further change in any form (Haydon, 1993). The negative attitudes are amongst the 'culprits' underlying productivity problems (Bowditch and Buono, 1982; Stuller, 1993). Reinvented organizations give rise to negative attitudes (Slem, Llevi and Young, 1986; Due, 1992) whereas employees with positive attitudes can increase their productivity from 50 per cent to 100 per cent (Stuller, 1993).

The effect of reinventing organizations has considerable human costs as well as costs to organizations. The most quoted factors (Slem, Llevi and Young, 1986; Marting and Shell, 1988; Slater, 1984; Schuler, Dowling and Smart, 1988; Stuart, 1993; Korac-Boisvert and Kouzmin, 1995) are summarized below (Table 3.2).

Table 3.2
Reinventing organizations: the costs

Employees	Organization
Stress	Stress related costs
Loss of self esteem	Low risk taking
Low morale	Low productivity
Loss of innovation and credibility	Low quality of work
Taking extra leave (including absenteeism)	Expenditure on extra leave (including absenteeism) Supplying leave relief Administrative work Supervisor's work
Counselling	Employee mental health (or employee assistance) programs
Retraining	Training
Transition employment	Transition staffing
Resignation	Resignation (including superannuation)
Loss of skills	Loss of corporate intelligence Loss of experience Loss of contracts/business
Redeployment	Redeployment policies
Retrenchment	Retrenchment (including voluntary redundancy) packages
Re-employment	Recruitment/re-employment
Sue employer	Employee litigation
Industrial disputes	Industrial disputes
Early retirement	Retirement packages
Survival syndrome	Survival syndrome

Staff cuts in organizations with a reengineering strategy range from ten per cent (Dilton, 1993) to 80 per cent (Coleman, 1993). A significant feature of reengineering involves the unprecedented number of white collar staff affected, with a relatively high proportion of them in middle management positions (Cascio, 1993). Although middle management comprises only five to eight per cent of the work force, they accounted for 17 per cent of the dismissals in the United States between 1989 and 1991 (Cascio, 1993, p.96). Thus, the profits of downsized organizations often do not increase as much as expected and very few report increases in the returns on funds invested (Brockner et al, 1993; Cascio, 1993). For example, surveys and case studies suggest that only 45 per cent of surveyed American organizations report increased profits, while 20 per cent actually report decreased profits (Fillipowski, 1993). Eighty per cent of American respondents to the Conference Board Survey and two-thirds of the largest organizations (employing more than 10,000) report lower morale after some forms of reengineering (Axel, 1993).

The Australian Government's review of public organizations with a reengineering strategy, reports that 82 per cent of downsized organizations experience no productivity increase, of which 22 per cent experience a decrease, with the productivity loss varying between 50 and 100 per cent (Commonwealth Government, 1995). The staff reduction ranged from 10 to 80 per cent and led to a loss of tacit knowledge, skills and experience. In one outsourcing case, an industrial dispute cost AUD$17,299 per affected staff member, while survivors were claimed to become conservative and negative (Commonwealth Government, 1995). The Australian Department of Employment, Education and Training (DEET), for example, in 1992-1993 (the year of reengineering) had a 61 per cent increase in workers' compensation premium (Comcare) from the previous year with a total claim of AUD$5.7 million (The Canberra Times, 1993). Although the stress related cases in DEET officially account for only 25 per cent of the compensation pay out, it is likely that other injuries were also due to stress (lack of concentration due to stress of imminent job loss) (Public Eye, 1993). One of the largest Australian reengineering exercises involving counter staff has been in the Australian Post, which transformed the traditional post office into retail postal outlets. In response to stimuli from external competition, Australia Post adopted IT as the cornerstone of new service delivery and a vital tool in attracting additional retail services, such as payment collection (using barcoding) for other agencies (Commonwealth Government, 1995). Although considerable staff training had been undertaken, there was a significant human cost in the process.

Notwithstanding that since 1990 the trend towards reengineering has resulted in job displacement at most of Australia's largest employers through compulsory retrenchments, early retirements and voluntary redundancies of managerial and specialist staff, Aungles and Parker (1992, p.72) find no evidence of de-bureaucratization of large organizations. Reengineering of Australian public sector organizations has resulted in decentralized coordination and operational dominance; de-specialization; and a shift away from the internal labour market (core periphery employment model). The outcomes of strategic core reorganization regarding policy development and program delivery in large Australian public sector organizations are still unclear.

Organizations reengineering, especially those with symbolic goods (knowledge intensive, social welfare and research and development based) need to closely link IT strategies to human resources strategies, as IT 'puts a heavy emphasis on organizational forms' (Dodgson, 1989, p.17) and culture (Gransey and Roberts, 1992). The inter dependency relationship between staff, management and the organization (people's needs, skills and values on one hand and the organizational objectives on the other) changes through fundamental changes to job profiles (individual job reclassifications to accommodate new and expanded roles and responsibilities), new skills to cope with new technology and new organizational orientations (Kriegler et al, 1988, p.23). The importance of staff involvement and participation for generating commitment to change, and for securing its implementation, should not be under estimated (Bolman and Deal, 1991). Muetzelfeldt (1988) argues that the acceptance of radical organizational change relies on broader cultural forces, including the technological ability to import into the workplace the ideology of consumerism and the sense of identity which goes with it.

The dark side of reengineering: the need for leadership development

The 'dark side' of adopting a reengineering management model is not its adoption per se, but its adoption without critical examination and adjustment to local context. The study of TQM as a reengineering strategy in the Canadian, British, American and Australian public sector organizations reveals 'contrapreneurship'; the deliberate resistance to implementation (MAB-MIAC, 1992; Morgan and Murgatroyd, 1994). Some reasons for the identified resistance are union fears about potential job losses; the breakdown of traditional union/management relationships; and rhetorical, but limited, active commitment from top management (Morgan and Murgatroyd, 1994). Other reasons are that the public sector is often culturally and structurally resilient to some of the quality management ideas.

For example, public servants generally, up to now, have not been paid or rewarded on performance even though some managerialist policies have attempted to introduce such a situation (MAB-MIAC, 1992, p.30-31; Morgan and Murgatroyd, 1994). In the Australian Public Service (APS), performance pay was equalized around merit pay for most, but is currently being replaced by agency bargaining mechanisms (formal equalization of performance pay). Similarly, the absence of a real market in the public sector usually means that so called customers are often involuntary clients of monopolistic or regulatory services or processes. Managing customers' expectations and attempting to set a service standard to satisfy them is far more difficult when public sector organizations do not have autonomy to vary service provisions (MAB-MIAC, 1992, p.30-31; Morgan and Murgatroyd, 1994).

While radical quality improvements are urgently needed in many public sector organizations, as well as the adoption of 'best practices', these need to be incorporated into organizational ideology that is sensitive to public sector culture which, amongst other things, is resistant to change; risk averse (because of potential political fallout and fear of innovation); lacks a clear objective, for example a profit motive; and has the problem of communicating leadership ideals from the top down and to other parts of the organization (Savoie, 1994).

Radical organizational change suggested in all encompassing and ill defined terms of reengineering requires change in the balance of power and the adoption and implementation of projects which decisively shifts power balances and re-orders entrenched organizational cultures (Higgins, 1988; Korac-Boisvert and Kouzmin, 1994). Change ideology, as a management tool, needs to challenge the basic premises on which organizations have been managed and requires organizations to make significant qualitative shifts away from traditional and outmoded modus operandi to new and innovative operations. The agenda for qualitative leaps or radical organizational changes is not essentially concerned with 'efficiency', however conceived, but with more fundamental transformations in the socio cultural quality of life (Higgins, 1988; Korac-Boisvert and Kouzmin, 1994).

Ideologies can play a significant role in the processes of organization creation because they have the potential to link attitude to action (Smelser, 1963). The link is made between broad, often moral, diagnoses of situations and actions at a specific level. Ideology mobilizes consciousness and action by connecting social burdens with general ethical principles. Improvements in quality and performance flow from a corporate ideology that systematically recognizes and rewards individuals, symbolically and materially, for identifying individual sense of purpose with the values that are designed into organization.

However, the potency of organizational ideology is not only contextually contingent, but is also contingent on how it is maintained and kept alive

(Pettigrew, 1987). As a tool of change, ideology is potentially superior to other mechanisms, such as economic rewards or formalized rules. This superiority drives from its combined subtlety and power to mobilize: it is a 'tacit' means of mining additional sources of 'mobilization and direction' towards organizational ends (Kilmann, 1985, p.ix). The strength of organizational ideology that shapes organizational culture provides the key for securing 'unusual effort on the part of apparently ordinary employees' (Peters and Waterman, 1982, p.xvii). Ideological management has greater acceptance and preference than old direct methods of control because it appears to be more inclusive, more pervasive and less identifiable (Selznick, 1957).

However, in today's multicultural organizations, ideology must celebrate diversity (Morgan, 1983; Van Maanen, 1994) and accommodate 'driven people whose ideas provoke and enrage the received ideas of a discipline and move the great lumbering cart of theory onwards. Ideology accommodates the idiosyncratic, exciting, innovative maverick thinker, the active deconstructionist and marginal people alike' (Weir, 1993, p.17); they are all 'social wealth creators' (Kakabadse, 1991).

Patterns of industrial and social conflict are likely to operate within the process of selection of new technologies, both as negative criteria (which possible developments to exclude) and as positive criteria (which technologies to select). Only through managerial choices are multi dimensional tradeoffs between the variables of technological trajectories made (Dosi, 1984, p.19). The policy design choice needs to be explicit, public and acceptable.

In addition to IT 'upskilling' of staff and management in order to gain a competitive edge in a 'sustainably developed' manner (development that meets the needs of the present without compromising the ability of future generations to meet their own needs (WCED, 1987), there is also a need for greater partnerships between government, educational institutions, industry, employees' unions and the community at large (Radford, 1994, p.2). The globalized world calls for greater cultural diversity of public management, the workforce and education (Radford, 1994, p.2). Public sector organizations need commitment to continuous learning and work ethics that respect differences in people and encourage them to perform.

Managerialist reforms of the APS

The extent to which such diversity of rationales has been introduced into the Australian public sector context is interesting.

Australia has undergone dramatic change in the way government policy is administered or, more controversially, managed. Within the Australian context, corporate managerialism connotes a radical reshaping of the culture and administrative structures of the public sector that has been pursued by both state and federal governments since the mid 1980s. With the increasing adoption of private corporate practices concerning the delivery of 'more with less', the rhetorical administrative reforms of restructuring and rationalization (variously defined) and management improvement measures (financial accountability, management of IT systems, human resource management) have been implemented with varying degrees of success.

While the focus of management improvement in Australia has been on structural, financial and planning techniques through the utilization of IT, the essence of this restructuring has been to reorient the business of Australia's largest 'firm', the Australian Public Service (APS), so that it no longer services a welfare state but, instead, services a state which defines its primary objective as one fostering a globally competitive economy. The central public policy objective has been to shift public policy from the 'social good' to the 'economic good'; from a 'welfare state' to 'the competitive state' (Cerney, 1990). This shift also redefined the public sector's role from the delivery of public services to the management of scarce resources. Furthermore, the decade of change has replaced the idea of a public service with one of management; the image of a public servant (above the clerical ranks of the public service) with that of being a 'public wealth creator'. Managerialism has spawned a de facto cultural formula of the control kind; derived from its 'rational, output oriented, plan based and management led view of organizational reform' (Sinclair, 1989, p.383).

The Australian Public Service (APS) has been engaged in a comprehensive reform process for more than 20 years (MAB-MIAC Task Force on Management Improvement, 1992). The seeds that would grow into a dynamic climate for change in the 1980s in Australia were sown in the early 1970s, when the reformist Labour Government (1972-1975) came to power and embarked on the largest inquiry into Australian public administration. The long undisturbed APS was confronted with the major review process (RCAGA, 1976) and with a set of administrative law reforms (Bayne, 1984). The Royal Commission on Australian Government Administration (RCAGA), consisted of a staff of 40, in addition to eight task forces. The Commission called on the service of some 50 consultant individuals and/or groups. For all the zeal of the reforms, little came of their work as the government that appointed them was out of office before they had reported and the post in house inquiry (the Bland Committee), appointed by the incoming Liberal Country Party Government (1975-1983), adopted the implementation of only a few of the Royal Commission recommendations.

Notwithstanding the untimely changes of political direction, the principles of access to equality and participation had begun to take root. The deliberations of the Administrative Review Committee in 1971 led to three pieces of legislation, the Administrative Appeal Tribunal Act 1975, the Ombudsman Act 1976, and the Administrative Decisions (Judicial Review) Act 1977 which led to the setting of the Administrative Review Council (RCAGA, 1976). Further debate was to proceed with the passage of the Freedom of Information Act in 1982.

This was followed in the 1980s by the introduction of a set of managerialist administrative reforms which have made the APS more decentralized and devolved in terms of authority and responsibility and which have demonstrably enhanced performance and accountability (MAB-MIAC Task Force on Management Improvement, 1992). Soon after gaining office, the Labour Government (1983-1991) introduced radical administrative reforms, under the influence of economic rationalists who were the dominant professional group in the APS management and who advocated 'managerialism', 'commercialization', 'deregulation', 'corporation' and 'privatization' as elements of their key reform vision (Coates, 1988; Pussey, 1991; Blandly, 1992). The bureaucracy becomes the focal point for change (Pussey, 1991) seeking to achieve cost effectiveness in all that it does; with the argument that traditional values such as job security are no longer affordable in a world dominated by chronic budget deficits and worrying public debate; and asserting, as an act of faith, that anything the public sector does the private sector can do cheaper and better (Pirie, 1985; Porter, 1986; Ansett, 1986). The reforms were of various types, from one that promoted accountability, through the ones related to workplace practices, organizational management efficiency and effectiveness to ones related to customer orientation. Australia followed, somewhat idiosyncratically, the path of public sector reforms first articulated in Britain and repeated, in various shades, in New Zealand, Canada and elsewhere (Caiden, 1991; Sherwood, 1992; Schwartz, 1994).

At the federal level, the logic of program budgeting becomes an integral part of the Financial Management Improvement Programme (FMIP) in the mid 1980s, aiming to improve the financial management performance of public service managers (Gleeson, 1986, Keating, 1988). The first budget cycle that adopted the broad principles of program budgeting was completed in 1992. A parliamentary review of the FMIP completed in 1990, concludes that the FMIP resulted in a streamlining of budgetary processes; established structures for programme management and budgeting; simplified public financial management and improved financial planning and accountability. As a result of the Efficiency Scrutiny Unit (established by the Australian Commonwealth Government in 1986) review recommendations to government, the APS underwent heavy departmental restructuring in 1987 (Hamilton, 1990, p.69). From the mid 1980s, reforms were introduced to establish consultative structures and processes designed to make public service managers more participative in their decision making style (Davis and Lansbury, 1990) and further to facilitate equal employment opportunities (Dickenson, 1986; Burton, 1990). The 1990s has seen the emergence of staff appraisals and individual development plans as mechanisms for improved workplace practices.

In addition to the accountability reforms, efficiency audits (Adams, 1986; Pugh, 1991) joint management reviews, performance bonuses and employer initiated retirement schemes, were introduced. Furthermore limited privatization measures were put in place to promote cost efficiency and cost effectiveness by exposing the public sector to market forces. In essence, the practice of contracting out government services to the private sector emerged in the late 1980s (Baker, 1988).

The deregulation of public agencies also began (Harman, 1989) as well as private sector competition on a limited basis with public agencies for government contracts (Dawkins, 1986; Porter, 1986). Under the pressure from policy imperatives to identify services for which charges could be either increased or imposed, there was a move towards greater cost recovery, which was attractive for public agencies with licencing and regulatory powers but not for those that existed to fill the gaps in a market that the private sector found unattractive to fill, legal aid service, public transport, welfare and housing (Kevin, 1987). Increasingly, APS agencies began sponsoring specific commercial ventures, to varying degrees of commercial expectation, involving the provision of 'common government services' (that is, goods and services traditionally provided to, and by, APS agencies without reimbursement) or the sale of goods and services related to, or derived from, budget funded core or incidental functions.

The growth in APS commercialization can be measured by the growth in commercial and quasi commercial revenue derived by APS agencies. Over the initial four year period of APS commercialization (1988-89 to 1992-93), such revenue increased from AUD$1.61 billion (14.7 per cent of total running costs) to AUD$3.17 billion (29.2 per cent of total running costs) (Australia Budget, 1990, 1991, 1992, 1993). Yet, by 1992-93, it still constituted only a relatively modest 7.6 per cent of total Portfolio Departmental Expenditure (Australia Budget, 1993). On a portfolio basis, expansions in the late 1980s were most significant in administrative services, followed by health, housing and community services. Most portfolios subsequently continued to expand their quasi commercial activities.

With the growing commercialization of the APS from the late 1980s, the relationship between civil servants, as APS commercial managers, and their minister began to change. The Auditor General set the context when he stated that the commercialization 'involves a Department of State remaining accountable to its Minister and subject to most public service administrative and financial controls and processes, but operating outwardly in a commercial manner' (ANAO, 1992, p.1). Indeed, the accountability implications of commercialization have only just began to emerge and must be viewed in the context of a redefining of accountability responsibilities of ministers and their civil servants (Dixon, Kouzmin and Korac-Kakabadse, 1996). Australia has seen an acceleration of the not too subtle turning away from the full accountability of ministers for the actions of their departments, towards managerial accountability. Faced with the accountability dilemmas generated by greater complexities of politico administrative realities, parliament has reconceptualized 'public accountability'. This has been most succinctly defined by the Senate Standing Committee on Finance and Public Administration as the 'obligations of persons/authorities entrusted with public resources to report on the management of such resources and be answerable for the fiscal, managerial and program responsibilities that are conferred' (Australia, Parliament, 1990, p.90).

The commercialization of the government sector in Australia has pursued two sequential, but inter related steps. The first step involves 'marketization' (Coward, 1990, p.67); the creation of monopoly, contestable or competitive markets for goods and services produced by APS agencies. This requires decoupling of an agency's policy advising and regulatory functions from its service delivery functions in order to allow it to identify those budget founded core and incidental service delivery activities for which markets can be identified (Dixon, Kouzmin and Korac-Kakabadse, 1996). By these means, agencies are faced with quasi commercial competitive pressures to enhance their productivity, to improve their service quality, to increase their extra budgeted revenue and/or to reduce their costs.

The second step involves an organizational reengineering that focuses on how agencies can best adapt to these marketization pressures. This is done either through establishing one or more integrated commercial (quasi commercial) units or creating a set of commercial procedures that permit and facilitate the conduct of commercial (quasi commercial) activities as an adjunct to budget funded functions. Both approaches require the adoption of commercial goals (profit, customer service), which necessitate the use of business oriented management practices. The form of commercialization pursued by each APS agency, however, depends on the extent to which market competition is permitted or expected; cost recovery is required or permitted; non commercial goals are simultaneously met; budget supplement is provided to APS clients; revenue retention is permitted, and the degree of mutual mix of the above elements (Dixon, Kouzmin and Korac-Kakabadse, 1996).

For changes of this kind, strategies and vision need to be kept open ended and dynamic and to be used as a focal point for inclusion both inside and outside the organization. There is strong empirically derived evidence (Kanter, 1984; Fullan, 1991; Pettigrew, Ferile and McKee, 1992; Hopkins, Ainscow and West, 1994; Heckscher, 1995) that successful visioning and implementation proceeds from very different frames of reference of organization than the 'bureaucratic machine' metaphor where policies and regulations 'make changes happen' (Hampden-Turner and Trompenaars, 1993). The frames of reference need to see organizations as multi layered, multi dimensional, pluralist, loosely coupled where causality is complex and non linear. Multi agency, cross boundary, ad hoc task teams need to be able to cut across formal levels and status, in order to work on the implementation of key business priorities, leading to new roles, relationships and responsibilities and in turn the development of new competencies, behaviour and attitudes. APS agencies endeavouring to reinvent their managers have come to recognize that in order to achieve the required management behaviour changes, they must create a context that encourages responsible administrative action, which is not just a matter of following written procedures and rules (Richards, 1991).

Responsible administrative action or public management in a situation where the routine application of rules is problematic, pre supposes an ability and willingness to perceive decision choices in a way that they may be informative by an appreciation for rules, but not determined by them - leadership through discretionary choice. Where action is perceived as determined by rules, prescriptive management, the sense of personal responsibility for that action diminishes greatly and thus the definition of problems to solve and challenges to address, are forced into preconceived and often arbitrary categories of meaning (Burk, 1989; Nagel, 1991).

The willingness of public managers to accept personal responsibility for their administrative decision and action depends on the psychological dimensions of their personal experience and its influence on their ability to take responsibility for the consequence of their decisions and actions (Kakabadse, 1991). The creation of an environment that supports the taking of responsibility for the consequences of decisions and actions has in effect been an important reform implementation priority. APS managers have increasingly been given more freedom to act. The question is, have APS managers been moved into a management environment in which they are required to operate within a paradox created as a bi-product of the managerialist reforms, anomalies, contradictions, confusions and uncertainties, which almost inevitably lead to inadequate or inequitable treatment of some stakeholders?

If this is the case, learning how to manage efficiently and effectively in a complex and perceived paradoxical context requires the inoculation of philosophies and paradigms that help public managers to cope with the ambiguities, complexity and indeterminacy of their role. This requires the nurture of wisdom, which allows for a more accurate apprehension of the true nature of the manager's organizational circumstances. Such a learning process, by nature, improves understanding of the relationship between knowledge, decision and action (Denhardt, 1987; Harmon, 1989).

Developing managers: the public sector experience

The managerialist driven Australian Labour Government fundamentally challenged the traditional doctrine of public administration by adopting the position that public administration is more about the management of services and responsive implementation of policy rather than about policy development and design (Howard, 1986). As stated, this provoked a debate and dispute over the role of political judgement. On the one hand, the managerialist orientation is intended to provide a far quicker and more community responsive service orientation at the local level. On the other, democracy is driven to a place of lesser consequence, whereby the managerialist oriented administration slowly determines the parameters to the policy agenda. However, whatever the merits of the arguments pursued, by the late 1980s it became axiomatic that there was a need within the APS for competent and confident managers with the management and leadership capabilities required to enhance their organizations' performance within the APS politico managerial environment.

As a result, public managers have been expected to adapt to ever changing external and internal conditions, which is especially challenging for those confronting the risks and uncertainties associated with commercialization and ultimate redundancies. The reforms that followed forced the APS managers to grapple with their own need to change behaviour. This meant exploring how to become more performance oriented and whether, to what extent and how to adapt business management practices (Attridge to the APS, 1991). One of the essential first steps was the need to become more entrepreneurial and thereby become more flexible and better able to cope with uncertainty. Public sector managers are not traditionally expected to model themselves on conspicuous examples of successful entrepreneurs, but they are increasingly being told to explore how private sector management behaviours could be adopted for application in the new public sector management environment.

In Australia, for example, the public sector may have considerable difficulties in recruiting new leaders from the private sector, considering that the Federal Government Task Force Inquiry on Leadership and Management Skills identified a lack of vision and strategic perspective; poor team work; inflexibility and rigidity; poor people skills and self management as major impediments to quality management in Australian organizations (Barraclough, 1993; Industry Task Force on Leadership and Management Skills, 1995). Additionally, the inquiry revealed that the levels of formal tertiary education of Australian managers, as compared with most OECD countries, is far behind that of other industrialized nations, especially at senior management levels (Industry Task Force on Leadership and Management Skills, 1995). The score for technical expertise (focused on educational attainment and specialist knowledge in key areas of business) of Australian management was behind the ranges for the Japanese and for US managers (Davis, 1994). Furthermore, Australian executives also ranked poorly in terms of people management skills; leadership; entrepreneurial drive in middle level management; and investment in new technology (Davis, 1994).

The concepts of flexibility, responsiveness, deregulation, commercialization and customer service are currently the focal element of public service structural adjustments in many societies (UK Department of Social Security, 1989; External Affairs and International Trade Canada, 1991; Australian Department of Employment, Education and Training (DEET), 1993, 1995a, 1995b; US National Performance Review, 1993). The public sector's leadership needs, like their counterparts elsewhere, require exploration and then tailored implementation. There exists a need to design organizations with structures that can withstand and effectively cope with a variety of dynamic demands such as increasing societal demands, employee needs, executive/political wishes, market demands as well as IT advances and global economic shifts (Porat, 1977; Dizard, 1985; Forester, 1989; Keen, 1991; Marceau, 1992; Nohria and Eccles, 1992). Furthermore, there exists an additional need to have the ability to eliminate, or at least minimize, inherent bureaucratic inefficiencies and maximize the organization's ability to serve internal and external stakeholders and control the resources needed to meet them. The transferability of client focused policies to praxis requires public sector staff and managers to carry out contextually defined tasks in a timely fashion and in an effective manner, instead of performing routine tasks merely well, or non routine tasks too late. This qualitative shift requires two generic corrections: averting the 'red tape' syndrome and the adoption of values for the effective practice of leadership to meet current and future challenges.

Averting the 'red tape' syndrome exhibited by unnecessary layers of regulation and control, requires the transition from a system that holds managers accountable for following rules, to a system of accountablility for results. However, the cultural shift from bureaucratic efficiency to decentralized authority, embraced in the labour management cooperation or the empowerment of leaders and followers alike, may require, as noted by President Clinton (quoted in Reynolds, 1994, p.21) a 'decade of change'.

New leadership values are based on cooperation, freedom, equity, justice and personal freedom, requiring actions that conflict with currently operating and deeply rooted bureaucratic values underpinning concepts of efficiency, professionalism and the need for secrecy. Furthermore, public sector leaders face the philosophical 'confidence gap' as they often lack the expertise, entrepreneurship and stewardship skills required for setting visions and transforming them into action (Mitchell and Scott, 1978). By reducing 'red tape', focusing on clients, empowering employees, re-examining fundamental work practices and embracing advanced IT, public sector leaders are likely to be better equipped to actively commence a revolutionary 'decade of change' towards a new era of organizational leadership (Reynolds, 1994, p.21). The new leadership skills must at least expand the traditional ones, where 'negotiating, bargaining, participating, assessing and convincing will, in future, be the central tools of public management' (Bohret, 1993, p.90).

Thus, management development for the public sector needs to adopt learning processes that facilitate the achievement of quantifiable management behaviour change. The key ingredients involve getting a critical mass of managers to develop a common picture of the future to which all can align and ground their actions. In order to effect change in the existing 'public service mindset' there will need to be a bottom up as well as top down movement, drawing from different approaches, with the very different assumptions about organizations, change processes, learning, leadership and motivation, and such diversity embraced through dialogue (Bohm, 1990). Learning must encourage both management and organizational values and perspectives to be formed, reframed or reconceptualized, in order to help make sense of the options available in relation to further courses of actions and the basis of their selection, which is often referred to as judgement incorporating 'instrumental' (management) (Beiner, 1983, p.163), moral (leadership) and political judgement (policy advice) (Anderson, 1988).

Judgement, a more than ever crucial element of leadership, bearing in mind the need to blend and reassess the requirements of professional, managerial and policy demands, requires a capacity to determine how best to synergize and blend management contradictory demands and pressures. Therefore management development must emphasize the enhancement of each individual's capacity to make judgements (Macadam and Bawden, 1986). In the art of judgement there is 'no science at all, either of organization or of anything else, which will help the executive much in performing his most essential and characteristic functions' (Banfield, 1960, p.27). That is, an effective management development process requires leadership as its primary focus, rather than the mastery of the knowledge of management techniques (Jenkins, Reizentein and Rodgers, 1984; Kakabadse, 1991). Considering that knowledge serves a variety of purposes and that there is no 'fundamental solution to the problems of knowledge, since uncertainty is a characteristic feature of the research process' (Morgan, 1983, p.389), it ultimately involves a choice, which in turn requires judgement. This in turn requires continued and concurrent enhancement of the person's ability to analyze relevant value frameworks (Bargo, 1980) and cognitive processes that transcend formal logic in order to explore 'dialectic operations' within a spirit of enquiry (Riegel, 1973) and discover important questions and problems as well as self understanding.

Organizational leaders occupy roles that are both personalized and institutionalized. The choices they make (moral/normative, social/structural, personal/behavioural) define their moral standing and influence principles of legitimacy and development, thereby effecting overall social stratification (Cavalli-Sforza and Feldman, 1981) and 'the moral character of society' (McPherson, 1984, p.76). The moral character of leadership and society at large represents a valuable economic resource, 'social wealth creator', where trust provides for important social cohesion (McPherson, 1984; Kakabadse, 1991). As such, leadership choices should be analyzed and conceptualized in respect of all three distinct dimensions: 'instrumental' (management), 'moral' (leadership) and 'political' (policy advice).

Within the newly emerging public service, the rhetorical management actions (giving orders, setting procedures, supervising) are extrinsic and cannot be assumed to work. Public sector managers will have to accommodate less arbitrary, more culturally ambiguous and collegiate oriented decisions through protracted cultural negotiation, formal discussion, compromise and high levels of residual and personal uncertainty. There is an emerging need for more service, stakeholder participation and special attention to disparate segments of a diverse populace requiring proficiency in 'inter sectoral management', 'across border' or 'networking'. The profile and character of stakeholder groups are changing, with highly educated and professional actors becoming the norm and resulting in a shift from organizing by division of labour to organizing by division of knowledge. As a result stakeholders will more share authority and responsibility with their leaders as needed. Furthermore, adaptation to looser organizational relationships will further induce the proliferation of partnerships and joint ventures based on collaboration.

Leadership skills are more likely to be defined by dimensions of caring (trustful and honest care of all stakeholders), service (facilitating co workers so that they can accomplish their tasks), innovation, productivity improvement, vision setting and self development. Thus the leader will need to be able to capture the essence of their current context, add value and express their perspective through a purposeful vision that inspires followers to relate to and share the vision. The ideal is of a leader that possesses the strength and wisdom of many persons, helping to unleash the abilities of followers and empowering them to become self leaders.

A broader consideration for public sector leaders will be the capability to address and promote values as fundamental parameters guiding thought and action.

Values are implicit in administrative action, structure and the application of technology (Fairholm, 1991, p.54), notwithstanding that values have always been a part of leadership and these are especially key in government. Indeed, at one level, government is a values displacement activity, as its key role is in ordering community values about how people will live together. Government sets social values, arbitrates disagreements, and validates changes in the process of guiding the value set the community adopts. Research carried out in the state of Virginia shows that a sample of 305 state and local government leaders in 1989 defines value leadership as quality of service and a focus on organizational vision, with a strong orientation towards innovation in improving performance (Fairholm, 1991).

Values leadership, therefore, holds strong, strategic connotations and is fundamental to prioritizing excellent performance (Brassier, 1985). The acceptance and enactment of values to suit new and challenging circumstances lies in the 'glue' promoted by leaders in terms of the intrinsic virtues they hold in common with their followers, values that guide the individual behaviour of both leaders and followers. As the leader articulates those common values, all group members can coalesce their work towards agreed upon results. Exploring the leadership paradox in management and performance, Denison, Hooijberg and Quinn (1991, p.5) introduce the concept of behaviour complexity which they define as the 'ability to exhibit contrary or opposing behaviours while still retaining some measure of integrity or credibility'. They contend that the leader continuously needs to negotiate and manage the management and performance paradox. Similarly, Quinn, Spreitzer and Hart (1991) define the concept of behaviour complexity as meeting the requirements of a diverse set of roles in a skilful and explicit manner. According to Hooijberg and Quinn (1992), leaders high in behaviour complexity are more able to perform many roles and play them to a greater extent, and are more able to demonstrate a balance amongst competing roles. The essence of management development for the public sector in the future would be to equip leaders to effectively address such a juxtaposition, and for followers to understand why contradictory behaviour from the top can, in fact, be strategically healthy (Kakabadse, Okazaki-Ward and Myers, 1996).

Part 2
AUSTRALIAN PUBLIC SECTOR LEADERSHIP SURVEY

Part 2

4 The survey

The survey conducted in the Australian Public Service (APS) is an adapted version of the results of considerable research carried out by the Cranfield Management Development Centre team over a number of years in the private and public sectors. In fact, over 5,000 general managers (GMs), directors, managing directors (MDs), chief executive officers (CEOs) and chairmen spanning 12 countries, and 515 chairmen, CEOs, directors (executive and non executive) of National Health Services (NHS) Trusts (UK) form the benchmark database of the:

- Demographics, namely size of organization, organization structure, gender, background of respondent, years spent on the job, years spent in organization, years spent in APS, experience outside the APS, qualifications and the number of senior management appointments held by each respondent.

- Culture of organization, identifying the shared views and attitudes SESs and SOs hold towards their organization, their role and work and the degree of support and constraint they experience in the discharge of their duties. Equally explored are values, namely the more deeply held feelings of the respondents concerning professionalism and conduct; the rights and duties of individuals in the workplace; workplace democracy; quality of relationships, internally in the APS and externally with clients, communities and other agencies; and the orientation of understanding towards provision of service to clients, communities and other agencies.

- The relationship between the Centre and regional and outlying offices and whether the styles of managers at the Centre are conducive and supportive to the effective functioning of regional offices.

- Leadership, namely the attributes of leadership displayed in the APS and whether such attributes are universal throughout the service or particular, according to whether specific factors influence leadership orientation and behaviour.

- Organizational performance indicators, such as the effectiveness of service delivery, the opportunity for the development of people, the effectiveness of the top team, the clarity of strategic direction, and the quality of internal interfacing and the effectiveness of utilization of IT in the organization.

Factor, cluster and regression analyses are used to identify discernible elements of culture, shared values and leadership orientation, and correlation analyses are utilized to explore the relationship between elements of these characteristics. Wherever relevant, comparison is drawn between the APS findings and the results emerging from the international private sector surveys and the NHS (UK) research programme.

Demographics

Organizational demography

Background Organizational demography is conceptualized as the distribution of organizational members along any demographic trait or any set of demographic traits (Pfeffer, 1983; Mittman, 1992). The foundations of organizational demography research is based on the structuralist sociological theories that emphasize the importance of numbers and proportions for understanding interaction processes in social aggregates (Simmel, 1955, p.125; Blau, 1977). These structuralist theories are built on the assumption that the positions among which social actors are distributed exert fundamental influence on social life, more so than cultural values and norms. Blau (1977) propositions that differentiation along significant dimensions of social position creates social structure, which reflects and affects social actors' role relations and social interactions and associations. The constructed social structure is conceptualized as a multi dimensional space composed of the various positions within which members of the population are distributed. These positions are most often defined by demographic attributes such as age, tenure, occupation, gender and ethnicity (Blau, 1977). Thus, the basic assumption underpinning demography theory is that demographic characteristics influence social dynamics, which in turn influence organizational outcomes (Pfeffer, 1983; Stinchcombe, McDill and Walker,

1986). Pfeffer (1983, p.348) argues that 'demography is an important, causal variable that affects a number of intervening variables and processes and, through them, a number of organization outcomes'.

Demography theory focuses on compositional characteristics that influence interpersonal and group dynamics, and is particularly relevant to understanding outcomes involving 'top teams' (Kakabadse, 1991; Kakabadse et al, 1996) and their impact and influence in organizations (Pfeffer, 1983). Group demography attributes such as age, tenure, occupation, gender and ethnicity, may be used as surrogate measures for the common experiences and background that shape human development and influence, amongst others, the language, quality and frequency of communication (March and Simon, 1958; Pelz and Andrews, 1966; Allen and Cohen, 1969; Rogers and Shoemaker, 1971). Group demography reflects similarity and dissimilarity among individuals, making it a meaningful perspective for understanding the processes affected by group dynamics, such as the level and extent of within-group communication, as well as outcomes of group dynamics, including such phenomena as the level of consensus within a group, innovation and turnover. According to Jackson et al (1991) group demographic composition involves identifying determinants of interpersonal attraction and sets the social context for relationships within an organization. The degree of an individual's similarity or dissimilarity to others in a workgroup may influence the processes that affect employee job satisfaction, organizational commitment, level of communication and are important predictors of turnover (Mobley et al, 1979).

Strategy, group and demography

Building on the pioneering theoretical work of Pfeffer (1983) and on earlier sociological theories of group interaction (Simmel, 1995; Blau, 1977) and demography (Ryder, 1964, 1965; McNeil and Thompson, 1971), organizational demography has been linked empirically to many important organizational outcomes: inter group cohesion, conflict and turnover (McCain, O'Reilly and Pfeffer, 1983; O'Reilly, Caldwell and Burnett, 1989; Pfeffer and Davis-Blake, 1992), culture (Carroll and Harrison, 1994), the distribution of power in organization (Shenhav and Haberfeld, 1992); innovation and adaptability (Reed, 1978; O'Reilly and Flatt, 1989) and organizational performance (Waldman and Avolio, 1986; Eisenhardt and Schoonhoven, 1990; Michel and Hambrick, 1992; Smith et al, 1994). Research regarding the consequences of organizational demography span widely from Kanter's (1977) study of how the proportions of men and women in corporations affect group process and individual outcomes, to Michel and Hambrick's (1992) study of how the diversity of top management teams affects organizational performance, and Ely's (1994) study of how the proportion of women at the top levels of law firms influences women's professional relationships.

Drucker (1974) posits that in large, complex organizations, material responsibilities are unlikely to be the exclusive domain of just one individual. Thus there is a need for studying the relationships amongst members of 'top teams' (Kakabadse, 1991) in relation to organization outcomes or strategic choice. As the strategic decision making process is by its very nature ambiguous, complex and unstructured, the perceptions and interpretation of a top management team's members critically affect strategic decisions (Dutton and Duncan, 1987). A top team's decision to initiate changes in strategy is based on members' perceptions of opportunities and constraints (Tushman and Romanelli, 1985). As top team members engage in the strategic decision making process, each top team member's perceptions and interpretations will reflect his or her own 'cognitive base' (Kahalas and Groves, 1979; Hambrick and Mason, 1984; Dearborn and Simon, 1985). The emerging empirical evidence shows that leaders and top management teams have considerable impact on organizational outcomes (Romanelli and Tushman, 1986; Finkelstein and Hambrick, 1990; Kakabadse, 1991, 1993; Kakabadse et al, 1996). While Finkelstein and Hambrick's (1990) study finds that in high discretion industries, such as the computer industry, managers seem to 'matter greatly', Kakabadse's (1991, 1993) extensive study of 'top teams' finds that leadership has the strongest impact on attaining and promoting organizational effectiveness.

According to Cyert and March's (1963) concept of the 'dominant coalition', Hambrick and Mason's (1984) 'upper echelons' theory and Kakabadse's (1991) discretionary leadership theory of 'top team' behaviour, upper level management has an important impact on organizational outcomes because of the discretionary decisions they are empowered to make on behalf of the organization. Since these managers make discretionary decisions consistent with their cognitive base, which is in part a function of their personal values and experiences, their past experiences and values can be linked to organizational outcomes (Kakabadse, 1991). Based on this discretionary leadership logic, scholars have linked top teams to organizational innovation (Bantel and Jackson, 1989; O'Reilly and Flatt, 1989), strategy (Finkelstein and Hambrick, 1990; Michel and Hambrick, 1992), strategic change (Grimm and Smith, 1991; Wiersema and Bantel, 1992) and performance (Waldman and Avolio, 1986; Murray, 1989; O'Reilly and Flatt, 1989; Eisenhardt and Schoonhoven, 1990; Michel and Hambrick, 1992; Hambrick and D'Aveni, 1992; Kakabadse, 1991, 1993; Smith et al, 1994; Kakabadse et al, 1996).

Three main conceptual perspectives emerge from 'top team' research, which focus on the top team's demography, process and organization performance. Top team demography refers to the aggregated external characteristics of the top team (heterogeneity, tenure, size). Process concerns the team's actions and behaviours, namely communication and psychological dimensions such as social integration. Broader, qualitative organizational goals, beyond traditional profit maximization are developed for performance, such as clear vision, unity of strategic direction and quality of dialogue.

Top teams: homogeneity and heterogeneity

Barnard (1938) was amongst the first theorists to argue that interpersonal and social consciences can affect the performance of a management team. He argues that there is a need for a tight knit 'informal executive organization' which fits, where 'questions of "fitness" involve such matters as education, experience, age, sex, personal distinction, prestige, race, nationality' (Barnard, 1938, p.224). Barnard's view that cohesion aids communication and collaboration is strongly reinforced by later research (Roberts and O'Reilly, 1979; Wagner, Pfeffer and O'Reilly, 1984). Although excessive cohesion may create a harmful insularity from external forces (Janis, 1972; Korac-Boisvert and Kouzmin, 1994), empirical data strongly indicate that cohesion facilitates the need for effective communication in situations of high interdependence. Solidarity, sponsorship and mutual choice are likely to occur among similar individuals (Pfeffer, 1983), leading to congruence of beliefs and perceptions of the organization and how it operates (Wagner, Pfeffer and O'Reilly, 1984; Tushman and Romanelli, 1985) in terms of high cohesion (Dutton and Duncan, 1987), continuity (Reed, 1978) and decision making. Such congruence can be particularly functional when high interdependence characterizes an organization's diversification posture, demanding integration amongst top team members. Michel and Hambrick (1992) find a positive association between team homogeneity and performance for vertically integrated organizations. Michel and Hambrick (1992) argue that in vertically integrated and related-constrained organizations, there is a need for ample internal communication through negotiation, compromise and collaboration. This communication process is greatly aided if top team members have a well developed rapport and a common outlook and language (Michel and Hambrick, 1992). Conversely, cohesion is not as important in situations of low interdependence, as in these organizations, top team members exist as discrete technical resources rather than as coordinative entities (Michel and Hambrick, 1992).

Homogeneous groups can also be expected to exhibit conformity and lack of openness to information. Social psychological research on decision making in groups shows that members' perceptions of similarity with others, particularly in values, beliefs and attitudes, increase group identification and cohesion (Lott and Lott, 1965; Zander, 1977). Cohesiveness in turn is associated with high conformity (Janis, 1972; Zander, 1977), high commitment to prior courses of actions (Janis, 1972), lack of openness to new information and interference with a group's ability to fully use information (Whitney and Smith, 1983). Janis (1972) argues that a crisis situation tends to produce demands for loyalty and conformity within the group that cause it to make faulty analyses and to miss obvious problems and other alternatives, which is worsened if the group is already homogenous in preference and outlook and has been chosen specifically to minimize the potential for conflict. In contrast, demographic heterogeneity represents diversity in a team's cognitive base. According to Hambrick and Masson's (1984) model, a heterogeneous team will gather information from a variety of sources and hold diverse interpretations and views. Dutton and Duncan (1987) posit that differentiation in an organization's belief structure, defined as high complexity with low consensus, enhances the search for information, the perception that change is feasible, and the momentum for change. Others suggest that high member diversity and variety enhance the ability of organizations to adapt (Weick, 1969; Katz, 1982). Group heterogeneity is shown to be associated with levels of creativity and innovation (Katz, 1982; Wanous and Youtz, 1986; Bantel and Jackson, 1989; Murray, 1989). The presumed benefits of a diverse group are that its members' different points of view lead to variety, novelty and comprehensiveness in the strategy for recommended solutions. The members of such a team will be able and willing to change others' viewpoints (Hoffman and Maier, 1961). Research findings suggest that a need to reconcile diverse solutions and viewpoints stimulates effective group discussion and internal high quality decisions (Hoffman, 1959). Demographic composition or demographic trait homogeneity suggests, in some cases, receptivity to change and a willingness to take risks, while demographic heterogeneity indicates diversity of information sources and perspectives, and creativity and inventiveness in decision making (Hambrick and Masson, 1984; Dutton and Duncan, 1987; Wiersema and Bantel, 1992).

Tushman and Romanelli (1985) find that the internal coordination requirement associated with an organization's strategy increases structural elaboration, which creates inertia that promotes the maintenance of the status quo, even if such clear dysfunctional consequences, as performance downturns, are evident. Such inertia will decrease the probability of the team perceiving the need for fundamental change (Normann, 1977). Thus, a top team must be proactive in its role of voicing views, if strategic change is to be initiated. The characteristics of a top team expected to be proactive in determining strategic change, include receptivity to change; willingness to take risk; diversity in information sources and perspectives; and creativity and inventiveness in decision making (Wiersema and Bantel, 1992). Receptivity to change suggests an openness to pursue different business approaches, essential to strategic change. Willingness to take risk is important because changing organizational strategy involves risk in abandoning established ways of conducting business in favour of making commitments to strategic directions for which the payoffs are not guaranteed. Novelty and strategic change on the other hand, result from a creative and innovative decision making style. Diversity in information sources and perspectives suggests differentiation in an organization's belief structure which in turn leads to a perception of the feasibility of change and momentum toward change (Dutton and Duncan, 1987).

APS demographics

Eleven demographic characteristics are reported in this survey.

Level in organization Of the 1,500 questionnaires distributed, 337 responses came from SES Bands 1, 2 and 3 and 375 from SO levels A, B and C and their equivalents (Table 4.1).[1] Thirty eight respondents did not specify the level occupied by them.

Table 4.1
Level in organization

Level	No. of respondents	%
SES 1	253	33.7
SES 2	66	8.8
SES 3	18	2.4
Senior officers	375	50.0
Not specified	38	5.1
Total	750	100.0

Years in job Just over 33 per cent of SESs and SOs indicate that they have spent 1-2 years in the job (Table 4.2). Just over 21 per cent indicate they have been 3-4 years in their present position. No significant difference exists between SESs and SOs in terms of time spent in the present job.

Table 4.2
Years in job

Years in job	SES	Senior Officers	No. of respondents	%
< 6 months	40	58	98	13.8
6-11 months	56	57	113	16.0
1-2 years	118	116	234	33.1
3-4 years	75	78	153	21.6
5-6 years	33	38	71	10.0
7-8 years	9	12	21	3.0
9-10 years	2	5	7	1.0
>10 years	2	9	11	1.5
Total	335	373	708	100.0
Not specified	-	-	42	-

Years in organization Sixteen per cent of SESs and SOs report they have spent 3-4 years in their present department/division, with the greater proportion of these being SOs (Table 4.3). A further 13.4 per cent have spent 5-6 years in their organization, again with the greater proportion of these being SOs. Just over 12 per cent report they have spent 1-2 years in their present department/division, with this grouping being more equally balanced between SESs and SOs. As far as SESs are concerned, a significant number have spent between 7-8 years in their department/division, with another significant cluster remaining in their department/division for 21-26 years or more. A substantial proportion of SOs have spent 5-6 years in their department/division.

Table 4.3
Years in the organization

Years in organization	SES	Senior Officers	No. of respondents	%
<6 months	11	10	21	3.0
6-11 months	11	12	23	3.2
1-2 years	43	47	90	12.7
3-4 years	40	74	114	16.0
5-6 years	34	61	95	13.4
7-8 years	41	28	69	9.7
9-10 years	14	19	33	4.6
11-15 years	39	41	80	11.3
16-20 years	29	34	63	8.9
21-25 years	35	23	58	8.2
>26 years	40	25	65	9.0
Total	337	374	711	100.0
Not specified	-	-	39	-

Years in the APS Just over 76 per cent of SESs and SOs have spent over 10 years in the APS (Table 4.4).

Table 4.4
Years in the APS

Years in the APS	SES	Senior Officers	No. of respondents	%
Under 2 years	13	9	22	3.1
2-5 years	21	33	54	7.7
5-10 years	26	61	87	12.5
Over 10 years	269	267	536	76.7
Total	329	370	699	100.0
Not specified	-	-	51	-

Number of senior management appointments Almost 24 per cent of SESs and SOs report that they hold their first senior management job, with another 23.5 per cent holding their second senior management appointment (Table 4.5). The greatest number of SOs hold their first or second senior management appointment, whereas the single largest number of SESs have held more than four senior management appointments.

Table 4.5
Number of senior management appointments

Is your current position your:	SES	Senior Officer	No. of respondents	%
First senior management appointment	70	86	156	23.9
Second senior management appointment	65	88	153	23.5
Third senior management appointment	65	51	116	17.8
Fourth senior management appointment	46	33	79	12.1
More than fourth senior management appointment	89	59	148	22.7
Total	335	317	652	100.0
Not specified	-	-	98	-

Appointments outside the APS Just over 67 per cent of SESs and SOs have held no previous appointments outside the APS (Table 4.6). Of those that have, the greatest number of entrants to the APS are from the private sector (8.5 per cent).

Table 4.6
Appointments outside the APS

Appointments outside the APS in the last 6 years	SES	Senior Officers	No. of respondents	%
State Government	24	17	41	5.8
Private sector	25	34	59	8.5
Non profit sector	11	10	21	3.0
Academic sector	16	16	32	4.6
International corporation	7	8	15	2.1
Other (varied)	21	41	62	8.8
No previous appointments held/specified	223	249	472	67.2
Total	327	375	702	100.0
Not identified	-	-	48	-

Structure of organization Thirty one per cent of the respondents consider that their department/division is functionally structured (Table 4.7). In the larger departments/divisions, divisional structures are reported as more commonplace.

Table 4.7
Structure of organization

Organization structure	%
Functional	31
Service/product	14
Divisional	26
Matrix	17
Combination	9
Other	3

Only nine per cent consider that the structure of their department/division is a combination of different structural forms.

Age of respondents Nearly 44 per cent of respondents fall into the 46-55 years old category and within that the greatest proportion are SESs (Table 4.8). Forty one per cent cover the 36-45 years old category, but within that the greatest number are SOs. Interestingly, 0.7 per cent of SOs are identified as under 25 years of age.

Table 4.8
Age of respondents

Age	SES	Senior Officers	No. of respondents	%
<25 years	0	5	5	0.7
26-35 years	13	63	76	10.7
36-45 years	120	171	291	41.0
46-55 years	180	129	309	43.7
56-65 years	21	6	27	3.8
>65 years	1	0	1	0.1
Total	335	374	709	100.0
Not specified	-	-	41	-

Background of respondents The greatest proportion of respondents (75.3 per cent) are identified as Australian born/English background (Table 4.9). The second greatest number are identified as foreign born but again with an English background (15.2 per cent).

Table 4.9
Background

Background	SES	Senior Officers	No. of respondents	%
Australian born/English background	261	273	534	75.3
Aboriginal	2	0	2	0.3
Australian born/non English background	8	21	29	4.1
Foreign born/English background	49	59	108	15.2
Foreign born/non English background	15	21	36	5.1
Total	335	374	709	100.0
Not specified	-	-	41	-

Gender Just over 79 per cent of the sample are males, equally split between SESs and SOs. Almost 21 per cent of the sample are women, the greater number of whom are SOs (Table 4.10).

Table 4.10
Gender of respondents

Gender	SES	Senior Officers	No. of respondents	%
Male	274	266	540	79.1
Female	50	93	143	20.9
Total	324	359	683	100.0
Not specified	-	-	67	-

Qualifications Just over 44 per cent of the sample have attained a first degree, university level standard of education (Table 4.11). A further 21.5 per cent report that they have achieved certificate/diploma recognition awarded by a professional body.

Table 4.11
Qualifications

Qualification	SES	Senior Officer	No. of responses[2]	%
Leaving certificate	35	33	68	7.5
High School certificate	31	44	75	8.2
TAFE/HND	16	20	36	3.9
BA/BSc	196	206	402	44.1
MBA/MPA	41	39	80	8.8
PhD	28	19	47	5.2
Professional certificate	82	114	196	21.5
No formal qualification	2	5	7	0.8
Total	431	480	911	100.0
Not specified	-	-	38	-

Notes

1. As far as this survey is concerned, the most senior public servants are SES Band 3.
2. Responses refer to the number of qualifications and not respondents, whereby any one respondent may identify that they hold multiple qualifications.

5 Culture of the Australian Public Service (APS)

Overview

The phrase 'culture of organization' refers to the sentiments, behaviours, deeply held values, routines and accepted ways of doing things held by staff and management that have become part of the fabric of the organization. It is assumed that the culture of any organization significantly influences and shapes staff and management's ways of doing and thinking about the challenges and issues facing the organization.

Two key elements of culture are identified, namely the predominant attitudes people hold towards work, ways of working and the organization, and the fundamental values that can substantially influence the shaping of opinions and behaviour of staff and management. Through factor analysis (a method for identifying patterns of response), five groups of attitudes and five separate groups of values emerge. The five attitudinal groupings are termed promoting a performance culture, work satisfaction, discipline, specialist orientation and independence. The five values factors are termed work practices, service orientation, professionalism and conduct, rights and duties and work place democracy.

In order to identify the possible impact of the attitudes and the shared values held by staff and management within the APS, particular measures of organizational and information technology (IT) performance are identified and cross correlated against the culture and values factors. The organizational factors are service delivery effectiveness, people performance effectiveness, clarity of strategic direction and effectiveness of organizational interfacing. The information technology factors are IT training meeting organizational needs, effectiveness of IT application, effectiveness of IT skills utilization and the impact of IT on the organization. The organizational culture factors, aspects of shared attitudes and shared values, measures of organizational and IT performance are described below. In effect, what are outlined are what the respondents consider organizational culture, organization performance and IT application to mean.

Attitudinal factors

- Performance culture: the respondents view a performance culture within the APS as one where the internal systems and controls are considered as helpful and supportive and curb wastage in the use of resources. Further, senior management acting in a reasonably cohesive manner, communicating effectively on key issues contributes considerably to growing a performance oriented environment. In addition, the respondents view a positive performance culture as one requiring that change be considered as meeting the demands of current and future challenges and that decisions are made on sound and accurate information. Also, daily work activities should be considered as sensibly organized in line with organizational goals which in turn are recognized as clear and reasonable.

- Work satisfaction: is considered to emerge from having a role which challenges and stimulates the role incumbent as well as providing the opportunity to utilize one's skills and abilities as appropriate. Being stretched and the effective use of skills combined with a feeling of recognition and respect that the job engenders, enhance work satisfaction and commitment to the organization.

- Discipline: it is recognized that being disciplined in the pursuit of tasks and initiatives is an important element of working as a senior person. Equally, attention to procedures and details is emphasized. Further, those who display high levels of discipline, respect people who stick to the rules and pay attention to details.

- Specialist orientation: the respondents also identify that work satisfaction comes from the pursuit of specialist rather than general management work. The respondents report that they value being members of a profession and being respected for their expertise. In fact, the respondents highlight that there should be more specialists in positions of authority.

- Independence and individuality: are highlighted as aspects of the senior manager experience. Interference and control applied by others is resented.

Values factors

- Work practices: the values driving particular work practices relate to those behaviours and orientations which are identified as supportive of high levels of individual contribution and performance. Attention to both internal and external interfaces is emphasized. Holding a service focus and responsiveness to client needs are equally placed with team working, flexibility and consultation. Further, respecting each person's unique approach is coupled with organizational considerations through terms as recognition, individuality, efficiency and particularist principles. Maximizing on opportunities in an environment of openness of communication motivates people to additionally attain high levels of performance.

- Service oriented values: highlight the need for respect of others, for supportive leadership and efficiency and effectiveness in the organization in order to provide for innovative and quality services to clients and value to the community. Characteristics of organizational and community values are social justice, morale of employees and organizational reputation. These two orientations emphasize the need for holding values which promote the provision of service, internally and externally.

- Professionalism and conduct values: refer to what the respondents consider promotes a high standard of personal conduct from individuals in the workplace. Being effective in one's job by providing quality results is related to holding a strong sense of loyalty and commitment to one's colleagues and the organization. Further, a personal sense of integrity in terms of how one goes about undertaking tasks, forming relationships and delivering on commitments made are seen as aspects of professionalism.

- Rights and duties values: highlight the importance of being held accountable for the discharge of responsibilities in public office. It is also considered that in order to be effectively held to account, it is important that the individuals concerned are able to take a broader view on issues, for example hold an opinion on natural justice. Participation of others in the process of accountability is equally coupled with a need for privacy and the protection of the individual.

- Workplace democracy values: emphasize respect and caring for people as well as the involvement of others in the dialogue and decision making process concerning work related issues.

Organizational performance factors

- Service delivery effectiveness: refers to the degree to which staff and management focus on key client groups and entertain a high level quality of discourse as to how to respond to clients' requirements. Equally, management's ability to deliver goods and services on time, be more responsive to meeting new initiatives and evolve a better thought through strategic policy for the future, are considered as equally important elements of effectiveness of service delivery.

- Performance of people: in the organization relates to issues of trust, morale, quality of internal relationships and a reduction in the number of inaccurate and unrealistic commitments being made to clients. Improvement in these areas is considered to stimulate overall better performance from the employees of the APS.

- Strategic direction: refers to the quality of thinking displayed by senior management as to how current changes generally, and changes in community requirements and demands specifically, are likely to affect the current running of the organization. Such clarity of understanding needs to equally be applied to the issues affecting long term strategy and how that will impact on the separate departments within the APS. Through such insights, the APS can be structured to address present and future challenges.

- Interfacing across the structure: relates to examining the quality of relationship between central office and regional offices, divisions and subsidiaries and the relationship between the regions, divisions and subsidiaries themselves. Equally, the style of management at the regional offices, divisions and subsidiaries, is viewed as an important element of interfacing.

Information technology (IT) factors

- Focus of IT training: refers to meeting both the IT development needs of individuals and their current job related requirements and the overall needs of the organization. It is also considered that IT training should be aligned with IT strategic planning driven at the corporate level and delivered in a just in time fashion.

- Effectiveness of IT applications: is considered as meeting the hardware and software needs of the organization, the operational needs of staff and management and assessing and responding to the degree of IT utilization amongst the staff and management in the organization.

- IT skills: are held as being the more specialist, advanced technical and the innovative skills required to meet new challenges.

- IT impact on organization: refers to aligning IT systems with the way the organization is structured and paying particular attention to those interfaces which need servicing. How effectively information is shared at those interfaces is equally considered important. Equally, attention is given to assessing the impact of IT on the performance of employees, on the decision process, and on the way in which the top team works. In order to effectively apply IT, it is viewed as necessary that attention be given to IT planning over the long term and the control measures to be applied to IT in the organization.

Impact of culture

In order to assess the impact of the culture of the APS on the way people behave and the organization functions, the five attitudinal factors of performance culture, work satisfaction, discipline, specialist orientation and independence are cross correlated against the five values factors, the organizational performance and IT factors (Figure 5.1).

The cross correlational tables (impact of shared attitudes and impact of shared values on organization) can be found in Appendix 4.

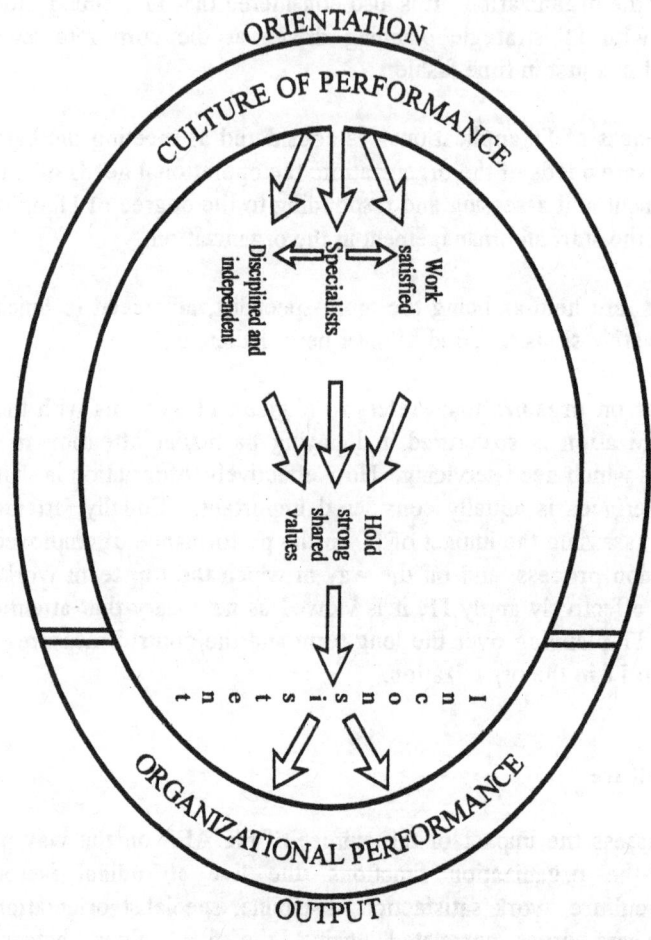

Figure 5.1 Impact of culture on performance of organization

Working within an organization in which people are performance oriented enhances the degree of work satisfaction experienced by staff and management. Further, within such an organizational environment, the respondents consider themselves as disciplined and focused. One strong reason why the respondents highlight their work environment as performance driven and display satisfaction with their work is that they consider themselves as specialists. Their specialist orientation and their interest in their work are stimuli in themselves, promoting positive and shared attitudes towards the organization. Working within a culture supportive of performance with a staff and management satisfied with their work, encourages the holding pursuing of values which promote best practice internally and externally in the community. Further, the more people in the organization who hold particular values concerning applying high standards of work practice, providing service and being professional in one's conduct within the workplace, the more others are encouraged to adopt these values. Only those individuals who value and encourage independence of action are recognized as undermining the generation of a performance environment and strongly held shared values. In effect, nurturing a culture of positive contribution and performance, enhances the sharing of values which promote service, the rights of individuals, appropriateness of conduct and involvement in the decision making processes in the workplace.

However, such a positive internal orientation does not promote equal consistency and effectiveness of performance at the organizational level and in the community. Working within a positively oriented performance culture is recognized as enhancing effectiveness of service delivery and promoting a better quality of interfacing. Being satisfied with one's work, motivates people to attempt to clarify the strategic direction of their organization, be more sensitive in terms of applying IT training to meet user needs and generally be flexible in how IT would be applied in the organization in order to effectively respond to user requirements. Further, being disciplined as a senior manager enhances clarity of debate over strategic direction and provides for the focus that effectively channels the contribution of people to meet particular goals.

Holding strong values concerning work practice, professionalism and conduct, provision of service, individual rights and workplace involvement in decision making, again only partly influences effectiveness of performance at an organizational and/or community level. Greatest impact is made by those people who hold strong values of service, whereby they are more likely to pay attention to enhancing the performance of people and be motivated to clarify the strategic direction being pursued by the organization. Those individuals who hold strong service values are equally likely to be more flexible in applying IT to meet needs within the organization.

Differences by level of organization

In order to determine whether differences of view exist between SESs and SOs, Table 5.1 highlights minimal differences across the four areas of attitudes to work and organization, values, organization performance measures and application of IT effectiveness. SOs are identified as more specialist oriented, and more adaptive and flexible in the way they apply their IT skills. However, SOs feel that IT training is not focused to meet their and the overall needs of the organization. The only remaining significant difference is that SES 1 level see themselves as holding more service oriented values than the other SESs and SOs.

Table 5.1
Differences of perception by level

Organizational factors	SO	SES 1	SES 2	SES 3
• *Attitudes to work and organization*				
Performance culture				
Work satisfaction				
Discipline				
Specialist orientation	XX			
Independence				
• *Values*				
Work practices				
Service oriented		X		
Professionalism and conduct				
Rights and duties				
Work place democracy				
• *Organizational performance*				
Effectiveness of service delivery				
Performance of people				
Strategic direction				
Interfacing effectiveness				

Organizational factors	Levels			
	SO	SES 1	SES 2	SES 3
Information technology				
Focus of IT training	-X			
Effectiveness of application				
IT skills adaptiveness	X			
Impact effectiveness on organization				

Key: Levels of significance:

SO   - Senior Officer   X - 05
SES 1 - Senior Executive Service 1   XX - 01
SES 2 - Senior Executive Service 2
SES 3 - Senior Executive Service 3

Summary

- Five key factors highlighting deeply held attitudes to work and organization are identified by the respondents, namely performance culture, work satisfaction, discipline, specialist orientation and independence.

- Five key values relating to aspects of personal and organizational performance are identified by the respondents, namely work practice values, service oriented values, professionalism and conduct values, rights and duties values and work place democracy values.

- The culture of the APS is identified as supportive of high quality performance, promoting higher levels of work satisfaction, especially amongst those who hold a strong sense of discipline in the discharge of their daily work activities and who display a confidence to think and act in a more independent manner. These individuals equally hold strong shared values concerning personal and organizational conduct.

- Holding strong personal, role related and organization related values is likely to promote a stronger sense of shared ethic of the rights and wrongs in the way people and organizations should conduct themselves.

- Working within a positively oriented work environment and holding strong values are identified as having a limited impact on effectiveness of performance externally in the community and internally within the APS.

- Very few differences in perceptions between SOs and SESs 1, 2 and 3 are identified in aspects of attitude to work and organization values, concerning individual and organization conduct, effectiveness of organizational performance and appropriateness of application of IT in the organization.

6 Impact of the Centre

Styles of management

In order to explore the impact of the Centre on regional and outlying offices, the effectiveness of application of four key styles of management are examined: styles that are sensitive to the needs of people, power oriented, rules and regulations oriented and ones that value and enhance performance and professionalism in others.

- People sensitive styles: refer to managers at the Centre being responsive to and respecting the needs, requests and areas of challenge facing the managers in regional or outlying offices.

- Power oriented styles: refer to those approaches adopted by managers in the Centre to influence others through personal dominance and/or power invested in office with a view to having their agenda adopted.

- Styles promoting rules and regulations: are ones that focus managers in the regional and outlying offices to comply with procedures and regulations emanating from Central Office.

- Styles valuing performance and professionalism: highlight the practice of open communication and feedback, establishing and working towards criteria for effective performance and promoting a shared sense of responsibility towards high quality performance.

As can be seen in Table 6.1, 11 per cent of respondents consider Central Office's management style to be sensitive to the needs of managers and their regional/outlying organizations. In addition, 21 per cent of responses consider Central Office managers to be power oriented. Further, 24 per cent of responses highlight Central Office management as holding a strong rules and regulations oriented perspective. However, the greater number of responses consider Central Office managers as respecting and promoting performance and professionalism in the management and staff of regional/outlying offices. In essence, 45 per cent of the responses emphasize the practice of more negative styles of management, with 55 per cent emphasising a more positively oriented approach. What is the impact of such variety of approaches and orientation at the Centre on the management of regional/outlying offices?

Table 6.1
Leadership demographics

How would you describe your corporate Central Office's management style?	SES	Senior Officers	No. of respondents	%
Sensitive to people	51	43	94	11
Power oriented	74	100	174	21
Rules and regulation oriented	93	108	201	24
Value performance and professionalism	191	172	363	44
Total	409	423	832	100
Not specified	-	-	38	-

Two key aspects of Central Office's management style are identified. The first explores the impact of Central Office's perceived style of management on particular aspects of organization including the effectiveness of IT application in the regional/outlying offices. The second examines the impact of these four styles on the shared attitudes held by management, their shared values, and on organizational performance. Throughout, particular attention will be paid to the consistency of behaviour and cohesion of perspective between the managers at the Centre and those in outlying offices.

Figure 6.1 highlights that the greatest impact on the regions through usage of the positive people sensitive and performance oriented styles is in terms of fostering and enhancing relationships with external agencies and client groups, the effective communication and meeting of objectives and in the appropriate usage and application of IT in the organization. The people sensitive styles are likely to have positive impact on the promotion and effective implementation of the organization's policies and services if managers at the Centre are recognized as being responsive to the needs of managers in the regional offices. Further, the development of effective client relations and relations with external agencies are likely to be enhanced if the managers at the Centre are supportive of the ideas and initiatives of managers from regional offices. It is equally recognized that in delegating responsibilities to regional offices, a people oriented style is supportive of building trust and positive relationships. In terms of IT application in the organization, managers in the Centre who practise a more people oriented approach are likely to motivate managers in the regions to more effectively apply IT technology to meet the needs of the regions. Specifically, through responding to the needs of managers in the regions, managers in the Centre are more motivated to focus IT training to meet organizational needs and apply IT technology to be supportive of the organization.

Further, when managers at the Centre adopt a style of valuing performance, the impact on managers in the regions is more profound. Managers in the regions are motivated to practise a similar philosophy which has a strong impact on infrastructure. Interagency relations are identified as enhanced. There is, equally, a visible improvement in the quality of services/products. Further, investment in R&D in terms of the time and effort invested into developing new services and approaches to client and community care, is reported to increase. The improvements in communication between the Centre and the regions lead to greater trust between the two sets of managers. As a result, greater delegation of authority over particular tasks and responsibilities to regional offices occurs.

Managers at the Centre practising styles valuing performance and professionalism have an equally profound impact on communications. Promotion of organizational policies and services, whether emanating from the regions or the Centre, improves, as does their effective implementation. Managers in the regions are more motivated to develop effective client relations and synergistic relations with other agencies. Also communication of objectives from the Centre or emanating from the regions/departments are identified as clearer and more focused.

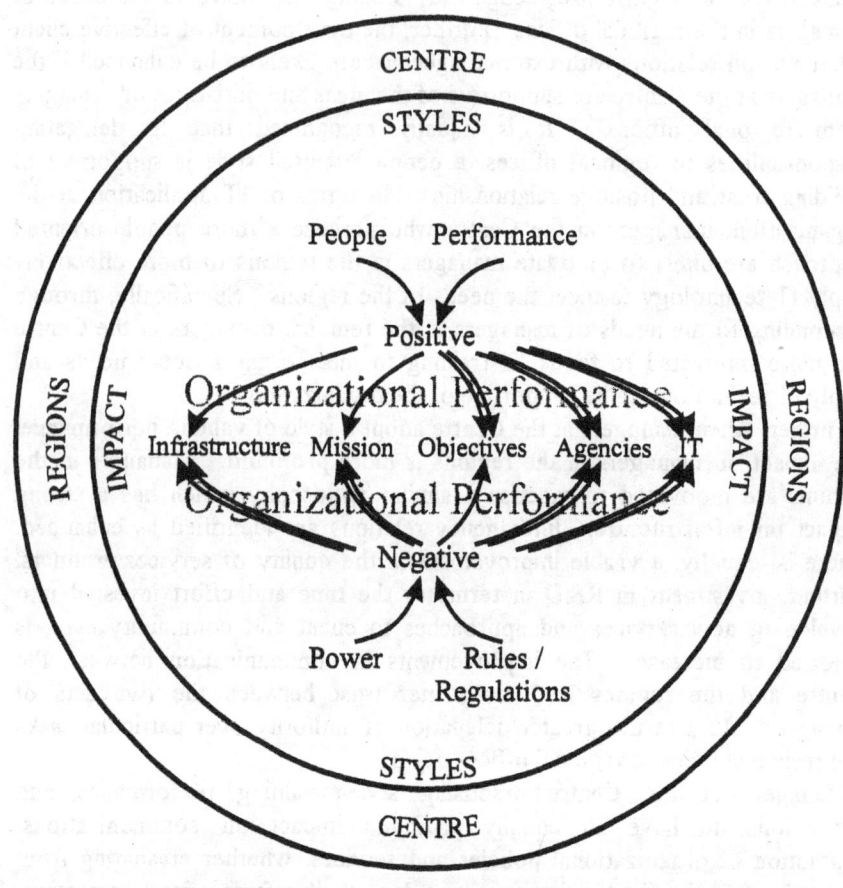

Figure 6.1 Leadership wheel: impact of Centre on regions - organizational performance

Valuing performance and professionalism at regional level positively impacts on senior management relationships. The consistency of promotion of the mission/vision of the department/regional office is improved by senior management in the regions when they witness positive example of leadership from the Centre. Similar findings are identified for effectiveness of IT application. It is recognized that if a performance oriented approach is adopted by the management at the Centre, regional managers are likely to be more concerned that IT training be focused to meet organizational needs and IT generally be applied to meet the requirements of staff and management.

Contrasting results emerge when managers at the Centre are viewed as applying power oriented styles. One immediate impact is on the infrastructure The automating of administrative processes, restructuring, downsizing and delayering are recognized as occurring through the application of power oriented styles. In effect, managers at the Centre more impose their views as to the shape, size and configuration of organization.

Similar negative impact is identified in terms of promoting cohesion of view over particular strategic initiatives. Power oriented styles do not encourage a consistency of approach in the promotion and implementation of policies/services in the regions. Equally, managers in the regions are unlikely to develop effective client relationships and meaningful relationships with other external agencies, if they feel themselves to be at the receiving end of a Centre management who adopt a power oriented approach. The mission/vision of the department/region is likely to be inconsistently promoted if power oriented styles are adopted by the managers at the Centre and by those in regional offices.

Comparably negative results emerge when Centre management promotes adherence to the organization's rules and regulations. The Centre's and regional offices' policies and services are both communicated and implemented in an inconsistent manner by a more demotivated regional management. Equally, their justification for their actions is unlikely to be coherently communicated. Similar inconsistencies are likely to emerge in the generation of desired relationships with key client groupings and external agencies. The will to promote positive synergies is likely to be diminished with regional management contributing on a just what is required basis. The more regional managers consider that they are required to function within a regime of rules and regulations, the less they are likely to identify with and actively promote the mission/vision of the organization.

The adoption of power oriented styles and the imposition of adherence to rules and regulations have a profoundly negative impact on the application of IT in the organization. Both of these approaches are unlikely to motivate staff and management in the regions to focus IT training to meet organizational needs. Equally, regional staff and management are less likely to be concerned with how effectively IT meets user needs. Within such perceived negative circumstances, management at regional level are unlikely to be driven to assess the impact of effectiveness of IT utilization on their organization.

The four styles identified as being practised by the management at the Centre equally influence the development of attitudes, shared values and effectiveness of delivery of services to clients and the community (Figure 6.2). People sensitive styles are recognized as supportive of service oriented values. Further, a management that is seen as sensitive and responsive to the needs of staff at regional offices are identified as enhancing the performance of people and providing positive example and stimulus for more effective interfacing across the structure (within regions, between regions and between the Centre and the regions).

The most positive impact is made by a management at the Centre that practises styles that value performance and professionalism. Discipline amongst staff and management in the regions is improved. Further, values that promote service, professionalism and conduct, rights and duties and workplace democracy are enhanced with a Centre management that displays its valuing of high quality performance from regional managers and staff. The biggest impact is on effectiveness of delivery. It is identified that effectiveness of service improves substantially under a management supportive of professionalism of performance. Equally, the performance of individuals improves as does the quality of interfacing behaviour. Staff and management in the regions become more motivated and consequently identify more with the strategic direction being pursued.

As valuing professionalism and high quality performance has such a beneficial impact on staff and management to enhance quality of delivery of services, so equally but negatively impactful are power oriented and rules and regulations oriented styles. Adopting a rules and regulations philosophy to regional management is identified as reducing regional staff and management levels of work satisfaction. Further, staff and management in the regions are likely to be less motivated to identify with and promote service oriented values when responding to a Centre management that is power oriented and requiring adherence to rules and regulations.

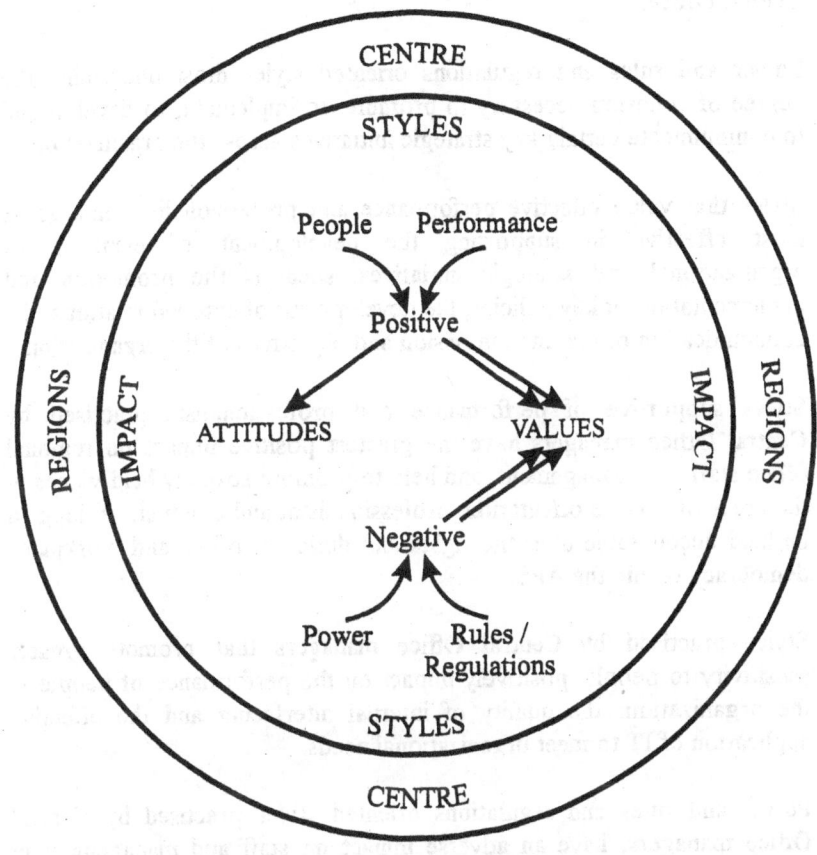

Figure 6.2 Leadership wheel: impact of Centre on regions - attitudes, values and effectiveness of delivery

Summary

- No significant differences emerge between SESs and SOs concerning the patterns of response across the four styles of management displayed by Central Office.

- Power and rules and regulations oriented styles most undermine the degree of cohesion necessary to promote, to implement, to develop and to communicate certain key strategic initiatives across the organization.

- Styles that value effective performance and professionalism emerge as most effective in supporting the development of elements of organizational and strategic initiatives, such as the promotion and implementation of key policies, the development of external relations, the communication of the mission, vision and objectives of the organization.

- Styles supportive of performance and professionalism practised by Central Office managers have the greatest positive impact on regional office staff and management, and help to promote strongly held values in the areas of service orientation, professionalism and conduct, wishing to be held accountable over the rights and duties of office and workplace democracy within the APS.

- Styles practised by Central Office managers that promote greater sensitivity to people, positively impact on the performance of people in the organization, the quality of internal interfacing and the effective application of IT to meet organizational needs.

- Power and rules and regulations oriented styles practised by Central Office managers, have an adverse impact on staff and management in regional offices in terms of the effectiveness of service delivery, the performance of people, the clarity of strategic direction, the effectiveness of internal interfacing and the application of IT to meet organizational needs.

7 Leadership

Introduction

A performance oriented culture of organization enhances work satisfaction, promotes far greater discipline of application and follow through and encourages the adoption of values supportive of service, professionalism, the rights of individuals and workplace democracy. Equally, a supportive and positively perceived culture goes some way to motivating individuals to enhance the performance of the organization externally within communities.

One interviewee stated:

> In many ways, this place is not bad and we have good people, but there is no vision, no leadership and our good people will just not stay here much longer. We desperately need decisive leadership.
>
> SES

The above comment of the SES respondent captures a particular perspective of leadership in the APS. Although the comment is more negative, the importance of leadership is emphasized.

One crucial lever towards gaining higher order performance as an organization is effective leadership. Clarity of direction, cohesion of intent and consistency of application, are considered the hallmarks of successful leadership and equally of successful enterprise promotion.

In this section, the impact of leadership on the APS is examined. The degree of cohesion over vision and consistency of behaviour, especially on issues of communication, are examined. Particular attention is paid to quality of dialogue at senior managerial levels, considered as the 'lubricant' of cohesion and consistency. Equally, exploration of different philosophies and practices of leadership is undertaken and attention given as to the impact of such differences of approach. Throughout, comparison is made with mid to large sized private sector business organizations representing 12 countries and National Health Service (NHS) Trust organizations in the UK.

Valuing leadership in the APS

In comparison to elements of organizational culture, the survey respondents provide their view as to how they rate the quality of leadership they experience in the APS. Table 7.1 presents the mean scores of elements of culture of organization, namely shared attitudes, shared values and a mean score for leadership in terms of perceived top team effectiveness, whereby scoring 1 represents not at all valued and 5, highly valued.

As can be seen from Table 7.1, aspects of shared attitudes are rated above average, with the lowest being independence (3.06). The values held by the respondents are rated considerably higher, with professionalism and conduct and rights and duties values being rated the highest. In contrast, top team effectiveness, on the above six dimensions, is rated lowest (2.23).

In essence, the respondents feel that the organization in which they work is oriented towards establishing a performance culture, with people being reasonably well satisfied, being sufficiently disciplined, coming from a specialist background and feeling marginally independent. Values are held in considerably higher esteem. Values concerned with high standards of work practice and holding a service orientation are rated as important and are actively promoted. Values concerned with high standards of professionalism and conduct and the rights and duties of office are most highly rated in the APS. Comparable emphasis is given to those values concerning workplace democracy.

Table 7.1
Benchmarking leadership in the APS (1 low - 5 high)

Culture of organization	Mean score
• *Attitudes*	
Performance culture	3.24
Work satisfaction	3.54
Discipline	3.23
Specialist orientation	3.2
Independence	3.06
• *Values*	
Work practices	3.9
Service orientation	3.8
Professionalism and conduct	4.52
Rights and duties	4.1
Workplace democracy	3.9
• *Leadership*	
Top team effectiveness[1]	2.23

The comparatively low scores on the leadership factor suggest that the respondents view their organization as reasonably satisfactory, well principled but lacking in cohesive leadership and clear direction. The implication is that introducing new or improved innovation and services, changing the structure of the organization or embarking on more fundamental change, are unlikely to work as intended, as the leadership contribution necessary for effective implementation is considered to be lacking.

Why leadership in the APS is less valued than aspects of culture of organization is examined in the following sections.

Strategic intent

One key question was asked in the private sector, NHS and APS surveys, namely 'Do the members of the Senior Executive (President, Chairmen, CEOs, MDs, EDs, Directors, GMs, SESs, SOs)[2] hold different views as to the future direction of the organization?' (Table 7.2) (see also Kakabadse, Okazaki-Ward and Myers, 1996).

Table 7.2
Fundamentally different views concerning the direction of the organization (%)

	Japan	UK	France	Ireland	Germany	Sweden
Yes	23	30	39	48	32	20

	Spain	Austria	Finland	USA	China	Hong Kong	NHS[3] Top Team	Board	APS
Yes	40	31	25	39	33	42	20	21	56

Fifty six per cent of the SESs (Bands 1, 2, 3) and SOs who completed this questionnaire consider that members of the senior management group hold fundamentally different views as to the shape and nature of the APS in general, and of their department and the future pathways that should be pursued, in particular. Of the NHS Trusts, distinction is drawn between the executive committee (top team) and the main board. Constitutionally, only two executive committee directors sit on the main board, accompanied by three non executives including the Trust chairmen. Twenty per cent of the top team members and 21 per cent of the board members highlight that fundamentally different views on vision, future direction and shape of organization are held by members of their respective groups. Of the private sector respondents, the Irish (48 per cent of respondents), Spanish (40 per cent) and French top managers (39 per cent) compare with such diversity of view. The Swedish (20 per cent) and Japanese (23 per cent) respondents highlight the least differences of view concerning strategic direction at senior management level.

Dialogue

Dialogue is explored as the capability to address and work towards resolving issues of sensitivity at senior management levels. One question was asked, namely 'Are there issues or sensitivities that merit attention but do not receive attention at senior management level?' (Table 7.3) (see also Kakabadse, Okazaki-Ward and Myers, 1996).

Table 7.3
Sensitivity of dialogue (%)

	Japan	UK	France	Ireland	Germany	Sweden
Yes	77	47	36	68	61	50

	Spain	Austria	Finland	USA	China	Hong Kong	NHS[3] Top Team	Board	APS
Yes	63	67	49	62	80	58	70	66	66

The Chinese (80 per cent) and Japanese (77 per cent) private sector respondents highlight the greatest number of concerns, indicating that important but unattended issues predominate senior management. The senior managers of the APS (66 per cent) follow the Irish (68 per cent) and Austrian (67 per cent) private sector senior managers. The British, Finnish and French senior managers identify the least number of sensitive issues impacting on the quality of dialogue at senior levels. The NHS top team respondents also report inhibited dialogue at senior levels (70 per cent). The executive committee of NHS Trust organizations is viewed as a more restrictive forum for dialogue than the main boards of Trusts.

Basically, other than for the French respondents, one-half to two-thirds of respondents report outstanding issues remaining unaddressed at senior levels but which need to be addressed in order to progress the organization. The Australian APS respondents are no different to the other sample of top managers, emphasising the strain senior managers are likely to experience in responding positively to difficult challenges.

Top team behaviour

Six aspects of senior manager behaviour in teams, that are identified in Table 7.1, namely approachability, addressing sensitivities, being understanding, trust, commitment to decision implementation and the long term/short term orientation of top managers, are contrasted for both the APS and private sector sample in terms of how senior managers behave (Table 7.4) (see also Kakabadse, Okazaki-Ward and Myers, 1996).

Distinction is made between the responses of SESs, Presidents, Chairmen, CEOs, MDs, EDs and those holding general manager (GM) and SO positions. The aim is to identify whether compatibility of view exists between top level managers and the general managers/SOs below them, concerning the behaviour and effectiveness of the top team.

Table 7.4
Managerial behaviours: comparative response by seniority (%)

	Japan		UK		France		Ireland		Germany		Sweden	
	TOP	GM	TOP	GM	TOP	GM	TOP	GM	TOP	GM	TOP	GM
Easy to talk to	82	62	73	65	80	76	87		78		84	83
Not easy to talk to		47		44		47		60		54		42
Discuss sensitive issues	69		66		71		52		68	63	66	
Address safe issues		61		70		48		67	41	68	63	48
Understanding	78		68		61		52		75		71	
Not understanding		61		68		48		67		69		66
Trust each other	73		65		66		61		83		79	
Not trust each other		76		72		74		91		64		73
Implement decisions made in top team	89					64		50				
Implement decisions that personally suit		62	54	58	58	48	61	66	68	42	56	50
Address long and short term issues	75											
Address short term issues												

156

	Spain		Austria		Hong Kong		US		APS	
	TOP	GM	TOP	GM	TOP	GM	TOP	GM	SES	SOs
Easy to talk to / Not easy to talk to	75	77	80	64	80	56	78	65	55	53
Discuss sensitive issues / Address safe issues	44	61	60	51	67	40	62	58	40	78
Understanding / Not understanding	53	61	58	51	53	66	60	48	33	76
Trust each other / Not trust each other	58	51	63	57	71	72	63	51	36	74
Implement decisions made in top team	70	69	65		78		78	60	52	
Implement decisions that personally suit				41		50				59
Address long and short term issues	61		62		64	67	73	60	50	
Address short term issues		60		49						63

Key: TOP Presidents/CEOs/Chairmen/MDs SES Senior Executive Service
      GM   General Managers   SOs Senior Officers
      APS Australian Public Sector

The Irish and Germans offer the greatest contrast of responses in terms of the members of the top team being 'easy, or not easy to talk to'. However, only 55 per cent of the SESs consider their own colleagues as easy to address. Fifty three per cent of the SOs highlight that the SESs are not easy to approach.

In contrast, substantial differences of response across all the country respondents emerge to the question 'Do the members of the top team openly discuss sensitive issues?' For example, 69 per cent of Japanese top managers consider they openly address sensitive issues, whereas 47 per cent of the Japanese GMs consider that the top team address more safe issues. In contrast, the Irish and Spanish responses indicate that 52 per cent and 44 per cent respectively of top managers consider they more openly address sensitive issues whereas 60 per cent and 61 per cent of their GMs respectively consider that safe issues are discussed. Equally, the APS respondents highlight similar results whereby 40 per cent of the SESs consider that sensitive issues are discussed and 78 per cent of the SOs feel that the SESs address only safe issues.

Regarding the issue of understanding, Japan is the only country where the views of both the top managers and GMs are positive and supportive. In contrast, the percentage of private sector GMs in the UK, Ireland, Germany and Spain who consider that their top management make little attempt to understand each other, is higher than that of the top managers who consider that they have a good understanding of each other. The APS results are in keeping with this finding, as 33 per cent of the SESs consider themselves understanding and supportive, whereas 76 per cent of SOs think otherwise. In France, Sweden and Austria, the percentage of private sector top managers who consider that they understand each other, is higher than that of their GMs who think that their top managers lack understanding of each other.

On the issue of trust, the Japanese responses highlight similar levels of compatibility to the Swedes. For both samples, the top managers indicate that the levels of trust amongst the members of the top team are high, an opinion that is shared by their GMs. The greatest degree of incompatibility of view of the private sector responses arises from the Irish, UK and German samples, wherein 67 per cent, 68 per cent and 69 per cent respectively of their GMs consider that the behaviour of their bosses is indicative of low levels of trust amongst the members of the Senior Executive. Of the APS sample, 36 per cent of SESs consider that they trust each other as top team colleagues, whereas 74 per cent of the SOs state that the members of their top team behave as if they do not trust each other.

Equally, compatibility of scores from the Japanese respondents emerge in response to the question 'Do the members of the top team implement decisions jointly made in the top team?'. Eighty nine per cent of the Japanese top management group indicate they do and 76 per cent of their GMs agree. A contrast of scores between the top management group and the GM sample is identified in the British, Irish and Austrian private sector respondences. The Irish respondents provide for the greatest contrast, with 91 per cent of top management indicating that decisions jointly made in meetings are implemented, whereas 50 per cent of their GMs consider that their senior managers implement only those decisions that personally suit the individual, irrespective of whatever was jointly agreed. For the APS, 52 per cent of the SESs consider that decisions jointly made in the top team are implemented, whereas 59 per cent of the SOs report that, in their opinion, the members of the top team implement only those decisions that personally suit the individual.

In response to the question 'Do the members of the top team address long and short term issues?', the Japanese respondents again provide the most comparable, positively oriented responses. Seventy five per cent of the respondents in the top management category consider that they address both long and short term issues and 62 per cent of the Japanese GM sample agree. In contrast, the Spanish respondents report that 61 per cent of top management and 60 per cent of the GMs consider that the top team addresses only short term issues. Equally, the APS responses highlight that 50 per cent of SESs consider that they address long and short term issues, whereas 63 per cent of SOs consider that the SESs address only short term issues. Similarly, the private sector respondents of the UK, France, Ireland, Germany and Sweden report comparable trends.

Top team dynamics

Four key themes have emerged from this part of the study. First, leadership in the APS is rated as least valued in comparison to aspects of culture of organization, namely shared attitudes towards work and those deeply held and actively pursued values concerning work related practices, the provision of service, conduct within the workplace and the rights and needs of individuals. Second, in comparison with the results of the private sector and NHS top managers, cohesion at senior levels within the APS over the shape, direction and purpose of the organization, is more problematic and an issue particularly worthy of attention. However, promoting a shared sense of cabinet responsibility is as much an issue of leadership in private as well as public sector organizations. Third, and again in keeping with the private sector and NHS experience, the sensitivity experienced over conducting meaningful dialogue highlights that particular concerns remain unresolved. Fourth, differences of perception do exist between top management and their immediate level below on six key dimensions of team leadership behaviour which, if allowed to continue, could substantially damagingly influence the implementation of innovations, policies and services. Again, these differences are a phenomenon of private sector organizations, NHS Trusts and the APS.

Impact of top teams (APS)

The question is, what is the impact of such leadership anomalies on the APS? Particular aspects of impact on organization and impact on individuals within the APS (Figure 7.1) are identified as a result of poor quality of dialogue and lack of substantial cohesion over visioning.[4]

As a result of perceived poor quality dialogue and splits in visioning, three areas of impact are identified, namely impact on people, impact on the direction being pursued by the senior management of the organization, and impact on the effectiveness of the infrastructure of the APS.

In a climate of more negatively oriented leadership, the styles of management adopted at senior and middle levels are affected. The approaches adopted by management are seen as sponsoring power and rules and regulations oriented approaches. Underplayed are performance and professionalism as is sensitivity towards staff and lower level management.

Within such a context, management in the regions are particularly critical. They highlight themselves as demotivated, lacking clear areas of responsibility and report that they and particularly their staff and junior management do just what is required of them. Innovation and invention are minimalized. Accompanying poor morale is a feeling of experiencing a considerable number of hindrances in the doing of one's job. It is also reported that within a more negative work environment, family life has become more strained as the tensions and lack of stimulus experienced at work are inevitably brought into the home environment.

Turning to the issue of future direction, the goals of various departments are considered unclear. Especially in those teams that experience serious divergence of views concerning the direction and shape of their organization, the more short term are the goals that, in reality, are being pursued, irrespective of the words used to communicate goals and objectives.

Impact on infrastructure is seen as variable and inconsistent. Two particular organizational operations are identified as affected, namely outsourcing and restructuring. It is identified that outsourcing and restructuring occur with greater frequency when top management are divided as to the future direction of the organization. In fact, in certain cases, outsourcing and restructuring are used by certain senior managers as a vehicle to promote the changes they desire.

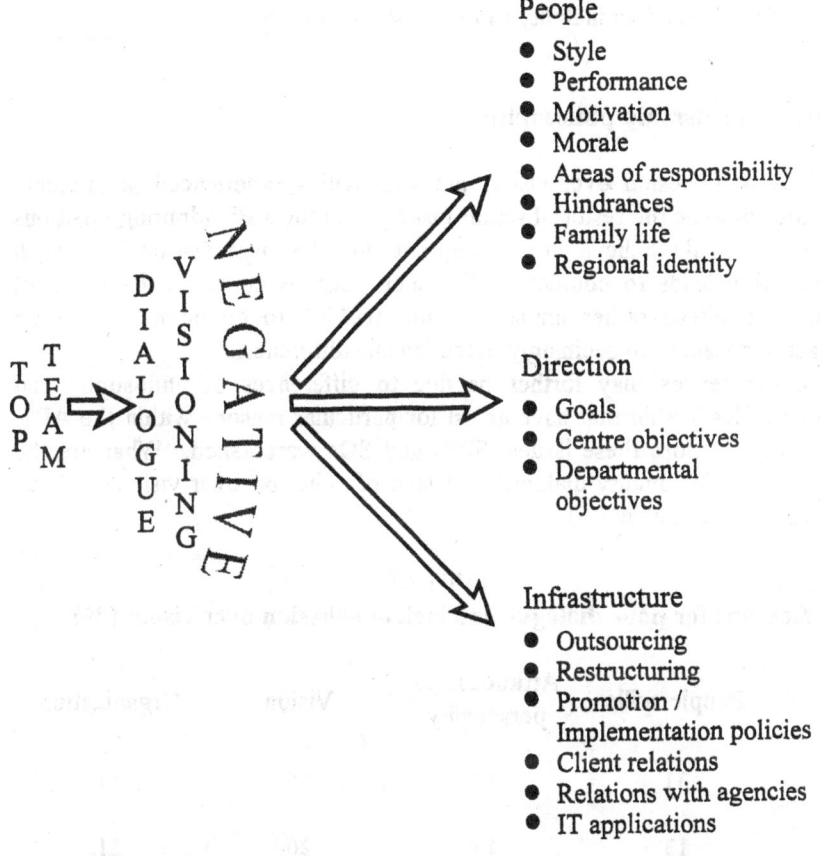

Figure 7.1 Top team impact: APS

Additional aspects of organization are reported as affected by senior management that do not address issues they know require attention. In particular, the promotion and development of external relations with various client and community groups and with other agencies is seen as undermined. Equally, the effective implementation of IT is seen as damaged by poor quality dialogue and an inability to form a shared vision.

Emerging leadership philosophies

The lack of cohesion over vision and sensitivities experienced in pursuing dialogue could be the result of senior managers in the APS adopting positions which they truly believe are appropriate for the organization, but such juxtaposition leads to conflict. Also, such tensions could be the result of certain individuals rather immaturely not wishing to cooperate, and their interactions leading to seemingly irreconcilable differences.

Such differences may further be due to differences of philosophy and practice of leadership that have arisen for particular reasons within the APS. In order to explore these issues, SESs and SOs were asked, 'What are the reasons for poor quality dialogue and lack of cohesion over vision?'. Four reasons emerge (Table 7.5).

Table 7.5
Reasons for poor dialogue and lack of cohesion over vision (%)

	People skills	Attitudes and personality	Vision	Organization
SESs	31	42	16	11
SOs	13	46	20	21

Both groups concur that a fundamental reason for tension and diversity at senior levels is due to differences of attitude and personality. Further, 16 per cent of SESs and 20 per cent of SOs feel that genuine differences of philosophy and perception as to the future purpose, shape, culture and configuration of the APS, inhibits greater cohesion and consistency at the top. Greatest divergence of opinion exists as to whether senior level tensions are the result of poor people skills or because of inherent tensions in the structure of the organization.

The view of SESs and SOs that differences due to styles, personalities and attitudes are a prime reason for poor top team behaviour, is borne out in an examination of approaches to leadership practice at senior levels in the APS. In fact, three fundamentally different philosophies, approaches and ways of thinking of leadership have emerged. These differences of leadership are significantly driven by four demographic factors, namely size of organization, years in the organization, years in the present job and the number of senior management appointments held in the APS by the individual. In effect, differences of demographics rather than the views held by individuals are likely to engender in people who occupy discretionary leader roles, substantially different perspectives on key issues, namely how differences, diversity and tensions in the APS should be managed, ways of working, manner in which the organization should be configured and reconfigured, and future strategies and mission to pursue. Level in organization is identified as not significant. That is, as many SESs and SOs are identified in any one leadership grouping as in any of the other two.

The three different leader groups are identified as the team players, the radicals and the bureaucrats.

Team players

Demographic characteristics:
Size	- 2,500-5,000 persons
Years in organisation	- 16-25 years
Years in job	- 5-10 years
Number of senior management appointments	- 2.8

Characteristics:[5]

Style:
Promoting performance
Discipline
Independent
Specialist

Philosophy:
Providing service
Promoting sense of responsibility
Leading through positive example
Responsing to challenge
Professionalism and conduct
Promoting personal development

Team players are typically employed in large sized government organizations, spanning between 2,500-5,000 employees. Of the emerging three leader profiles, team players have spent longest in any one organization, between 16-25 years. Equally, individuals who project this profile have spent more time in any one job than those who adopt the other two leader profiles, and have held, on average, 2.8 senior managerial appointments.

The long stay nature of team players is strongly influential in the forming of their views as to what it means to lead and promote a performance oriented culture in the organization. Part of generating a positive performance ethos in the organization is due to the fact that team players promote a positive attitude to most challenges. Team players indicate that they are satisfied with their job, are committed to the organization, find what they do challenging and, equally, display their appreciation of being challenged. Hence, team players consider that they stretch themselves and also provide for developmental on the job opportunities for others through exposure to challenging experiences. They consider themselves as hard working but within the context of a team working culture. Through endeavour and positive relationships with others, team players feel they establish clear goals. However, they are sensitive to the need for re-appraising their circumstances and hence are conscious of the need for inviting feedback, and making feedback an accepted way of working within the organization.

Team players lead through example. The positive orientation displayed towards subordinates, colleagues, superiors and towards work activities is extended to include the organization. They indicate that change initiatives undertaken in the past have attained positive results. They display equally positive views concerning present and likely future changes. One reason for their positive attitude towards change in the organization is that they actively encourage their subordinates and peers to undertake a broader corporate view over issues, a perspective they themselves adopt. In effect, working as a team and adopting an organization wide perspective, are for them, inter related. Team players highlight respect of tradition as well as of people. The team player's view of a positive performance oriented culture is one which allows for the recognition of the efforts and abilities of individuals, as well as respect for the organization.

Team players consider themselves as disciplined and attempt to enhance the levels of self discipline in those with whom they interact. They exhibit a clarity of decision making and encourage others to do likewise. They go about their daily activities in a structured manner by tending to work within procedural guidelines. Following through on commitments made, is another indicator of their disciplined approach in their achievement of objectives. Team players hold a strong desire for constantly improving performance, through effective follow through on initiatives embarked on, and by being guided by their longer term view over issues. In addition to the innovative application of skills, is their support for ministers. They consider that a prime area of duty for them is to promptly respond to the requirements of government ministers.

Despite their strong identity with the organization, team players also display a strong sense of independence. They equally indicate their preference for occupying a commanding role and further highlight their need for getting their own way. Resentment can be shown towards those who adopt a command style towards them. They, in turn, can be equally dismissive towards those whom they consider to have unnecessarily become involved in their affairs. The paradox with team players is their capability to link their strong organizational identity with their need for independence and their desire for the development of people. The reason these strong desires are accommodated, is that team players believe that providing opportunities for the development of people is essential for the enhancement of the organization. Their sense of independence heightens their distaste for a command structure but equally they recognize the need for stability. Hence, effectively working with others, bringing others forward with minimum disruption to the organization, creating an environment where views can be openly offered, and relying on collegiality and not command, are fundamental to their philosophy of leadership.

Integral to leading through people is providing service. Team players value being client driven and providing quality of service to communities. Engendering high levels of morale in their staff and management is their key lever towards attaining a positive orientation towards service within the organization. They recognize that in order to provide service externally they and, through example, others have to provide service to staff and lower level management, internally.

In both their style and philosophy, the theme of identification with the organization is strongly held by team players. Conscious of how the organization functions internally is matched by a sensitivity as to how the organization is perceived externally. Their strong identity with the organization is displayed by their desire to enhance the reputation of the organization. Efficiency of systems and procedures are held in equal esteem with effectiveness of service delivery.

As with their organization orientation, team players are identified as holding strong values concerning ways of working with others. Two key sets of values emerge: those highlighting professionalism and conduct in the workplace, and those concerned with quality of relationships and personal development. Work related values are identified in terms of professionalism in the discharge of one's duties, undertaken in a quality manner with the intent of striving for excellence. Appropriate personal conduct is viewed as loyalty and commitment to one's colleagues and the organization.

Quality of relationship values indicate a high regard for the generation of opportunity for people but in an environment where individuals can determine their own pathways and should especially feel fulfilled in whatever they do. Team players hold to universalistic principles of, for example, common pay standards and equal opportunity for appointments and promotion. Their openness is coupled with maintaining the rights of individuals in terms of protection of privacy over personal and non work related issues.

Teams players also highlight their specialist background. They display that the source of work satisfaction comes from the technical/specialist side of their job. They value being recognized and respected as an expert, as they do being a member of a profession.

Radicals

Demographic characteristics:
Size of organization	- 500-2,000 persons
Years in organization	- 1-4 years
Years in job	- 1-2 years
Number of senior management appointments	- 2.6

Characteristics:

Style:	*Philosophy:*
Critical	Outward focused
Job satisfied	Respect for people
Specialist	Service oriented
Independent	Accountable
	Freedom to act

    Radicals tend to have a background of having worked in smaller government departments/agencies, typically of 500-2,000 people. They have spent few years in any one organization (average between 1-4 years) and have the fewest number of senior management appointments than those in the other two leadership groupings.

    Radicals are identified as critical of their organization and its culture and values. The top team of which they see themselves as members, is viewed as lacking cohesion, with certain individuals pursuing their own course of action irrespective of whatever is agreed. Poor quality interaction at senior management levels is seen as leading to poor quality decision making, often because of not having or not wishing to have, appropriate information. On this basis, work is considered as not being sensibly organized.

    One reason why radicals are critical of senior management is that top management in the APS are seen as being functionally oriented, displaying little loyalty to a corporate philosophy. In addition, their senior management colleagues are seen as lacking in discipline in their work activities and lacking effective follow through, especially on new projects or initiatives. Senior management are equally viewed as lacking tolerance for the expression of alternative views and innovative ideas. Radicals consider that a management that behaves in such a manner promotes poor communication in the organization, leading to staff and management not being motivated to effectively interact with each other. An outcome of low motivation is poor attendance at meetings.

With poor example being provided by senior management, radicals feel that departments, agencies and the broader organization are lacking clear goals. Radicals consider that senior management are not sufficiently decisive and display inconsistency of behaviour on key issues which leads to confusion of messages in terms of communication. Overall, the feeling is that working in such an environment leads to a feeling of constantly being constrained and displaying little trust in management, especially under circumstances of change. As a reaction to such experiences, radicals see little need to display cabinet responsibility but project dissatisfaction with the internal functioning of their organization.

However, radicals highlight high levels of job satisfaction. They indicate that they are stimulated by the challenge of their role and are committed to their work and job. They feel they use their skills and knowledge as they consider appropriate to the demands of their work. Equally, in their dealings with their colleagues and subordinates, the quality of teamwork is considered as high and supportive of the individual. Radicals consider that recognition and respect comes from their job and from their level of positive contribution to their work.

Radicals are also identified as self disciplined in terms of their approach to their daily work activities. They are equally conscious of the need to promote discipline in others. They are insistent that regular briefings on developments in projects and other initiatives, are vital for effective communication. Hence, they report that they are regularly briefed and are disciplined about briefing others. They tend to follow established procedures and display a high respect for rules.

Effective teamwork is also viewed as resulting from being disciplined. Cohesive teamwork is recognized as necessary for effective policy implementation. They recognize that positive teamwork helps people to better identify with, and own, the challenges and activities they have undertaken. For radicals, teamwork and discipline are considered as the important levers for effective policy and strategy implementation.

However, being disciplined is accompanied by strong feelings of independence and a need for freedom to pursue their own courses of action. Radicals highlight that they dislike interference in their daily work activities. They are resentful of being directed on operational matters or broader policy matters. However, they highlight that they do find positions of command stimulating, as they can then pursue and apply their views and ideas in the organization. However, they dislike their ideas and initiatives being blocked.

Radicals equally emphasize their specialist background and specialist inclination. They report that their work satisfaction comes from being actively involved in their area of specialization. They value being part of a specialist professional group and gain greater stimulus from the application of their expertise than from involvement in general management work.

Apart from being specialist and independent, another reason why radicals find their internal working environment unsatisfactory is that they hold strong values as to the meaning of leadership, service and the overall management of people. Leadership is not just seen as command or taking charge, but the leadership necessary for the provision of service to communities and clients. Being innovative and efficient as a leader is placed in a context of providing value to the community and service to people. For radicals, loyalty to clients is considered as vital as their loyalty and support to ministers and more than their loyalty to the organization. Being held accountable for their use of powers of office and for the utilization of resources, are viewed as important in terms of keeping leaders on track concerning their service focus.

Radicals highly value competence and the effective application of skills, and despite their pro client orientation, support their employing organization but under particular conditions. Budget stability, organizational growth and high quality advice to ministers are aptly intertwined with respect for individuals, bonding, integrity, quality, competence, effectiveness of communication, caring and recognition. In essence, radicals are not anti organizational, but are demanding and require that their high standards be met. Their critical comments arise from the fact that they feel that they are either making little impact on their organization or that their organization is resisting reform.

Being demanding is highlighted by their values concerning performance, where being held accountable for personal performance and the management of people is linked with professionalism, commitment, consultation and excellence of endeavour. Hence, radicals are task and service oriented and are willing to have themselves held to account. They seem to find it difficult to understand why others cannot respond in a like fashion.

In the discharge of their professional duties, they combine self reliance with team work, networking and participation. The way they bridge the differences between being a member of a team and an individual, is by displaying their personal effectiveness in their work and over the longer term, in their track record. They equally attempt to inculcate the same high standards in others by working towards promoting trusting relationships. Their perspective is that if people trust each other, then they can accept feedback, then they can improve. The frustration of the radicals is that they expect high standards and when disappointed, they display their feelings about the organization and its management through critical comments.

Bureaucrats

Demographic characteristics:
Size of organization - 5,000-10,000 persons
Years in organization - 10-15 years
Years in job - 2-3 years
Number of senior management appointments - 3.4

Characteristics:
Styles: *Philosophy:*
Cynical   Impartial
Job satisfied   Positive conduct
Specialist   Service oriented
Disciplined   Accountable

Bureaucrats typically have worked in larger government departments, having spent 10-15 years in any one organization but having changed jobs considerably, with an average span of time of 2-3 years in any one job. Further, bureaucrats have held the greatest number of senior management positions (3.4) in comparison with the other two leader groups.

Bureaucrats are identified as displaying a cynical style of leadership in that they view their organization as being constraining and themselves as hard done by. Yet, these are the very same people who have more experience of senior management than others, but seem to be unwilling to do anything about their circumstances. They feel their organization has been misguided about the changes that have been undertaken in the past. The senior management (of which they are a part) are seen to be pulling in different directions which is viewed, by bureaucrats, as negatively impacting on their organization. Quality of decision making is seen as poor, as decisions are not seen to be based on reliable and/or relevant information. Poor coordination and poor internal controls are viewed as endemic of an organization that displays dysfunctional behaviour from its leaders. For bureaucrats, poor communication and poor follow through on agreed initiatives are additional symptoms of lack of cohesion. One reason for inadequate interaction at senior levels, is that bureaucrats, similar to radicals, view top managers as identifying with their functions and not with the department or organization as a whole.

The result of such poor discipline is that the goals of the organization are viewed as unclear and work is seen as poorly organized. The repercussions on people are viewed as dramatic. For bureaucrats, working within such an organization is seen by them as providing no encouragement to work hard. Bureaucrats feel that in an environment of inadequate controls and unsatisfactory communication, they lose track of new and existing initiatives. They feel they are not regularly informed of changes and developments that take place, leaving them with the feeling of being constantly out of touch. Bureaucrats express considerable levels of dissatisfaction with their working environment and consider themselves as unable to change their organization. Their dissatisfaction and feelings of powerlessness feed their cynical orientation which in turn negatively influences peers and colleagues. Bureaucrats feel themselves to be the victims of an unwelcoming working environment, despite the fact that they hold integral membership of the senior management strata.

In contrast, bureaucrats indicate that they are satisfied with their job. They feel they make good use of their skills and abilities in their present job. Equally, they feel they benefit considerably in terms of recognition and respect from the status accompanying their jobs. Bureaucrats feel they are approachable and responsive to others. They equally highlight that they can take, and work with, criticism. Despite their negative orientation towards the organization, bureaucrats indicate that they enjoy the challenge of their role.

Bureaucrats highlight that one element of job related satisfaction comes from the specialist aspect of their work. In fact, they consider that there should be more specialists in positions of authority. Part of the reason why bureaucrats gain considerable satisfaction from the specialist part of their job is that they consider this as the source of their recognition and status. They feel valued for their expertise. In contrast, they highlight that they dislike general management activities.

The bureaucrats' more cynical view of the organization does not undermine their drive for effective job related performance. Bureaucrats see themselves as disciplined in terms of attention to detail. Equally, the same degree of discipline is applied to following established procedures. They see themselves as setting realistic time targets for their direct reports. In particular, they consider that self discipline needs to be applied when under pressure, in order for them to be able to emotionally sustain themselves during such a demanding phase. Respect is shown for those who are disciplined and for those who respect the rules and procedures laid down in the organization. They feel that, generally, greater discipline needs to be applied by management. Bureaucrats strongly believe that greater discipline leads to greater success for the organization.

Bureaucrats equally hold strong values determining what they consider to be professionalism, standards of personal conduct, performance, service and the development of the organization through effective accountability. Professionalism for bureaucrats is a concern with high standards of application of skills and competencies, whilst maintaining impartiality, and a sense of fairness. Hence, displaying commitment, being timely, diligent and responsible, whilst at the same time being neutral, are important balances to achieve in order to provide for value to the community and equally protect and enhance the reputation of the organization.

In fact, the twin themes of effective service provision and the protection and development of the organization, are deeply held by bureaucrats. As far as work performance is concerned, personal attributes, as flexibility, openness, networking, innovation and caring are held in equal esteem with achieving and maintaining budget stability and efficiency of organization. Similarly, in terms of provision of client service, quality of work, skills, teamwork, consultation, effective internal communication and pursuing opportunities are coupled with probity, and loyalty to the organization. In terms of maintaining standards and controls within the organization, being held accountable for all aspects of performance is considered as crucial. Being held accountable for the use of resources and the powers and privileges of office are as important as being held accountable for the management of people and individual personal performance.

Leadership in action

What of the impact of these separate leadership approaches on the APS? The particular styles and philosophies of the three leader groupings are cross correlated against the same measures of organizational performance and IT effectiveness as utilized in Chapters 4 and 6 as well as the top team effectiveness measures identified earlier in this chapter. Further, an examination of the impact of splits in visioning and poor quality dialogue on the styles and philosophies of the three leaders is presented. For detailed information of the statistics underlying the impact of the three leadership approaches, see Appendix 7.

Team players in action

The styles and philosophy of team players are identified as having a favourable impact on the performance of the organization (Figure 7.2).

The team player's orientation to promoting a positive and supportive performance oriented culture has a beneficial impact on the six organizational performance measures. The performance of individuals and teams is seen as enhanced when working in a motivating environment. The senior management team is recognized as more able to respond positively to the challenges it faces. As the quality of dialogue and interactions improve, so does service delivery, partly due to the improvements of morale experienced by staff and management and partly due to the improvements in interfacing

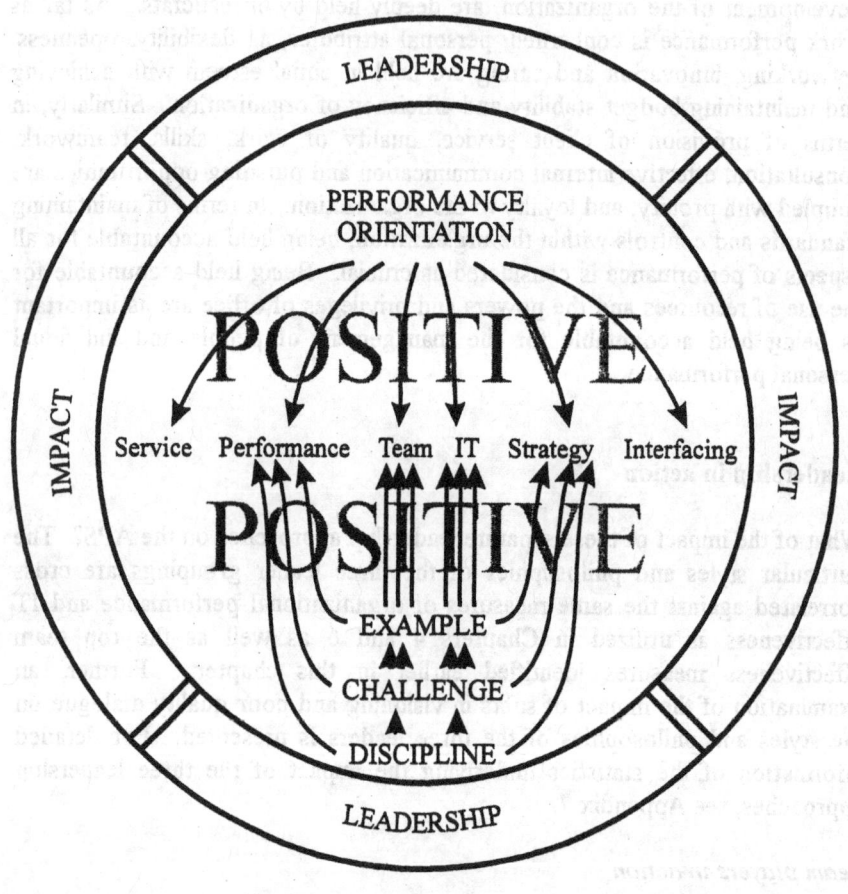

Figure 7.2 Leadership wheel: team players' impact on organization

across the structure. The better quality of communication and greater likely commitment to be supportive across the structure, provide for a more enriched service orientation within the organization.

Similar patterns are identified in terms of the effectiveness of application of IT in the organization. Operating in a culture where staff and management take pride in improving performance, enhances the likelihood that IT training will be more focused to meet the needs of users. Similarly, IT is likely to be more effectively applied in the job as people are likely to be more adaptive in their application of IT skills. Overall, IT is likely to be more effectively applied in the organization.

Equally effective in team players is their leading through example, which is viewed as having a positive impact across the six measures of organizational performance. Being responsive to challenge, being disciplined and holding high standards of professionalism and conduct are seen as further enhancing the performance of staff and management, and improving the quality of interactions amongst senior management.

Effective performance contributes to improvements in ownership and trust. Senior managers, staff and lower level management are more likely to gain greater confidence in themselves, their abilities and their capability to achieve, the more they maintain their focus on performance. Hence, the results highlight that there is likely to be greater belief in, and commitment to, the strategies being pursued, the more the leadership highlights performance and not orientation to organization.

However, working within a top team where the interactions amongst its members are more negative, has undesired consequences on the leadership style of team players (Figure 7.3). Poor quality dialogue in particular has the greatest undermining impact. The team players' motivation to apply their people skills is diminished, as is their drive to nurture a performance oriented culture. Equally, the team players' sense of discipline is undermined, leaving them less willing to lead by example. A reduced sense of discipline leaves team players considerably less motivated to promote service or to display the maturity needed for accepting responsibility for their own actions.

Working within an unsatisfactory environment leaves team players less willing to be openly held to account for their actions. Inevitably, their high standards for professionalism and conduct also drop.

Working in a team in which senior colleagues hold and pursue different views as to the shape and future of their organization equally dampens the performance and contribution of team players. Again, the team players' willingness to nurture a performance oriented culture is diminished, as is their drive to lead by good example. However, the results indicate that the team players' capability to effectively manage people and be supportive of others'

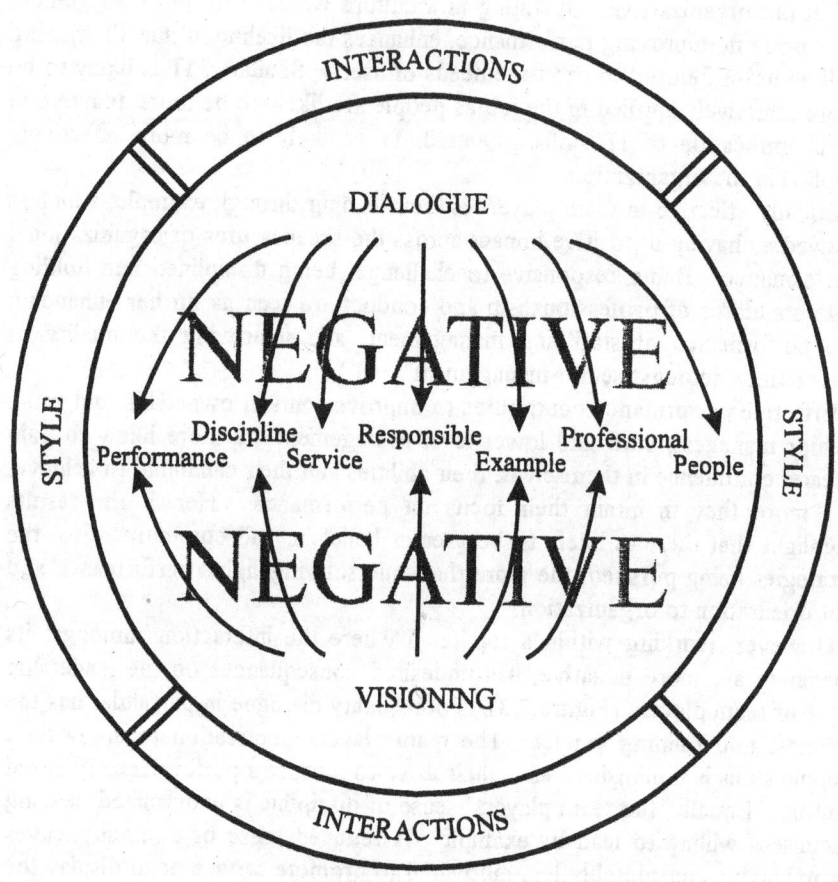

Figure 7.3 Leadership wheel: top team impact on team players

development whilst maintaining their own standards of services, are not diminished when working within a split top team.

Overall, team players attempt to create circumstances where they and others contribute their best. However, they are particularly prone to underperforming and experiencing poor morale in what they would interpret as a more negatively oriented organization. Their confidence in themselves to provide service and support in order to 'get the best out of others', is damaged.

Radicals in action

The ease with which radicals criticize and find fault with the organization is identified as particularly damaging (Figure 7.4). The fact that radicals openly express their dissatisfaction diminishes the motivation of staff and management to improve their performance and to enhance service delivery. Colleagues at senior management levels are likely to also feel threatened and become defensive when interacting with radicals. As defensiveness in the senior team increases, less effective becomes the quality of interfacing within the organization. Continuous expression of dissatisfaction with the organization and its leadership, is likely to undermine people's confidence in the capabilities of senior management and hence the necessary clarity, focus and ownership of strategy are unlikely to be forthcoming.

Equal damage is identified in terms of IT application in the organization. The more radicals state their grievances, the less effectively is IT training likely to be applied to meet the needs of the organization. Staff and management's confidence to experiment and try new approaches in order to adapt and grow their IT skills to meet new challenges, is likely to be equally diminished. Overall, the more critical the radicals, the less effectively is IT likely to be applied to meet the requirements of people's jobs, project teams or generally the organization's.

As stated, the reason for the critical nature of radicals is because their standards, sense of service and external orientation to meet community/client needs are so high. As radicals do not intend to damage but improve standards, they do, despite their critical stance, have a positive impact on the organization. The more radicals are satisfied with their job and are positively challenged to meet external agency, community and/or particular client needs, the more they are likely to engender positive attitudes and enhance morale in the organization. They are likely to work more closely with those individuals with whom they interact on a project or activity and provide a climate of openness and support which others could find stimulating. The performance of people improves as does team work. The quality of interfacing amongst those involved on projects or other activities is equally likely to improve. The

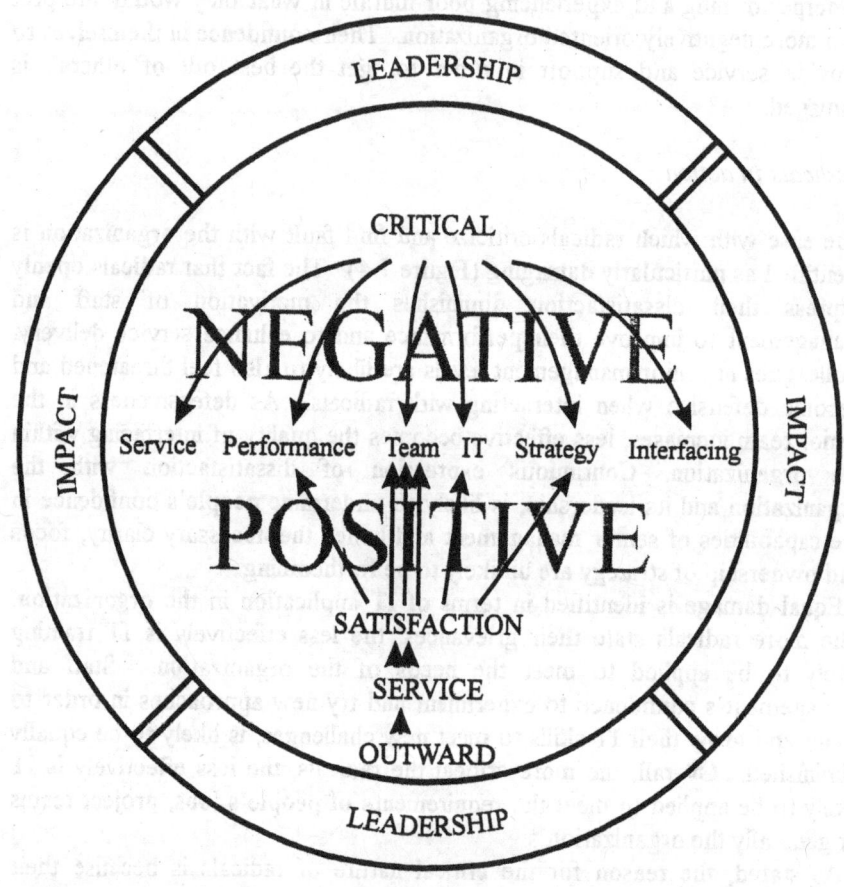

Figure 7.4 Leadership wheel: radicals' impact on organization

more radicals work to address problems externally, in the community or with other agencies, the more they will work towards clarifying strategic direction and help staff and management to gain greater ownership of the strategy and vision being pursued.

Under such circumstances, equal benefit is identified for the application of IT in the organization. The more satisfied are radicals with their job or project, the greater the emphasis on focusing IT to meet needs, either in terms of training or user needs. However, despite being positively challenged on projects or programmes, the outward focus of radicals may leave them with little time to assist peers and subordinates to learn and experiment to be more flexible in their use of IT

Radicals, unlike team players, are more adept at working within an environment of poor quality dialogue and with senior managers who may pursue different ends concerning the future of the organization (Figure 7.5). The radicals' ability to verbalize their dissatisfaction could leave colleagues fearful of them. In addition to feeling inhibited by radicals, the feelings of estrangement may extend to not trusting them or not identifying with their view as to the future shape and path of the organization. Hence, although critical of what is happening in the organization but with the intention of stimulating improvement, the behaviour of radicals could further deteriorate the quality of dialogue and splits of vision that already exist amongst senior managers. However, they as individuals are unlikely to be undeterred by working within a more negative environment.

Whether radicals are partly to blame or not for undermining dialogue and cohesion, their more positive features become less evident within a more negative senior management team. Their sense of job satisfaction diminishes. Their willingness to appropriately utilize discretion is equally likely to drop. In fact, their sense of independence may drive them to inappropriately utilize discretion in ways that promote greater disunity at senior levels. Radicals have learnt that in circumstances where senior management lack cohesion, they individually, or in particular cliques, attempt to promote their view as to how the organization should proceed.

The results highlight that the level of dissatisfaction and verbalization of their discontent with the organization and top management, leaves radicals having a particularly negative impact on the effectiveness of performance of the organization and on the effectiveness of IT application. It is unfortunate that the other positive aspects of radicals, namely their sense of purpose, drive, high standards and strong values make little impact on the development of their organization.

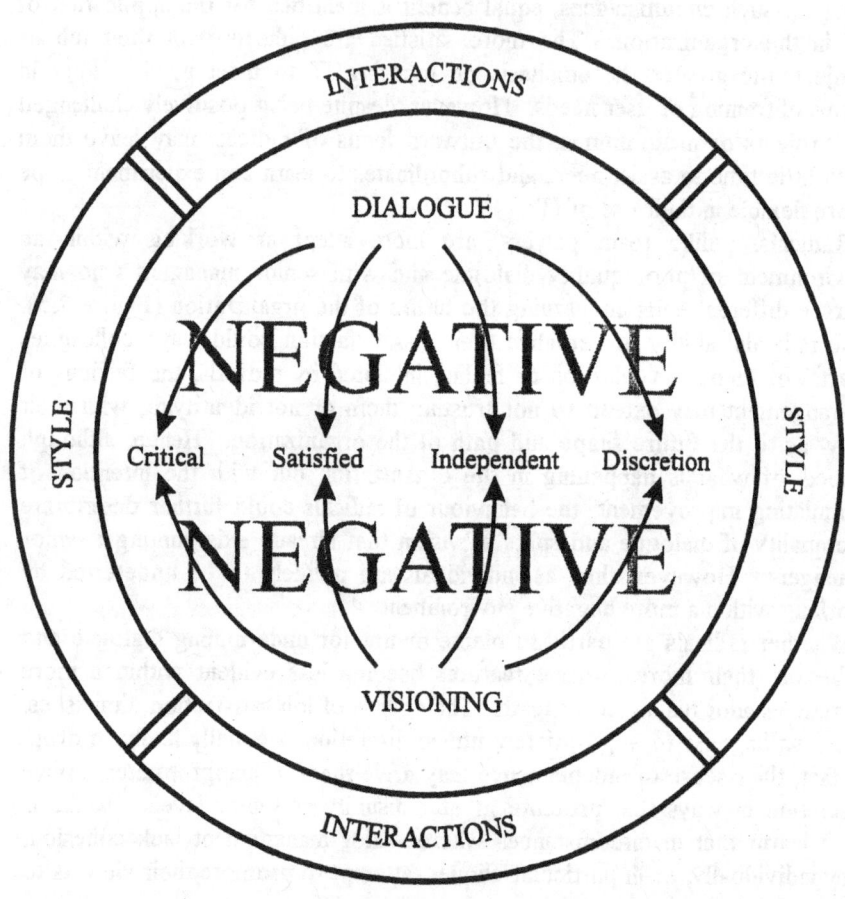

Figure 7.5 Leadership wheel: top team impact on radicals

Bureaucrats in action

The cynical perspective of the bureaucrats is identified as having a negative impact on the organization (Figure 7.6). Similar to radicals, bureaucrats are viewed as inhibiting people's drive to be innovative and undermining their confidence. Hence, the willingness by staff and management to adopt a more service oriented perspective to communities, clients and external agencies is considerably diminished. Bureaucrats are also identified as devoting less time and attention to improving the performance of people. They are recognized as undermining morale and damaging the quality of interfacing in the organization. In particular, bureaucrats are identified as promoting negative interactions at senior management levels. Added to that, their sense of impartiality and manner of conduct, strongly oriented towards accountability, are seen as impersonal and lacking in sensitivity. Their perceived coldness further inhibits others from effectively interacting with them, and hence further damaging relationships. Lack of positive interaction in dialogue inhibits the emergence of cohesion on issues of strategy and longer term direction for the organization.

Similar negativity of impact is applied to IT application in the organization. Their negative orientation inhibits individuals from focusing IT training to meet user needs. When led by bureaucrats, both users and IT specialists are less likely to be motivated to attempt to apply IT to address the job related needs of users or more generally to meet the overall requirements of the organization. Being managed by someone who is perceived as over critical and damning does little to invite flexibility and innovation. Similar to radicals, bureaucrats are identified as more capable of functioning in a negatively oriented environment (Figure 7.7). However, more than radicals, bureaucrats are likely to further promote poorer quality dialogue and splits of visioning where such concerns already exist. In effect, they are likely to feed such poor behaviour and become a negative role model for others to emulate. Their impartiality can be misinterpreted as lacking rapport and disinterest in their colleagues and subordinates. Hence, their seeming lack of involvement is likely to dampen the enthusiasm of others to explore issues of strategy and vision.

Leadership impact on the Centre

Chapter 6 identified four key styles of management being adopted by managers at the Centre and the impact of these on regional/outlying offices. Explored here is the impact of the three different leadership philosophies on the utilization of the four styles of management mentioned (Figure 7.8).

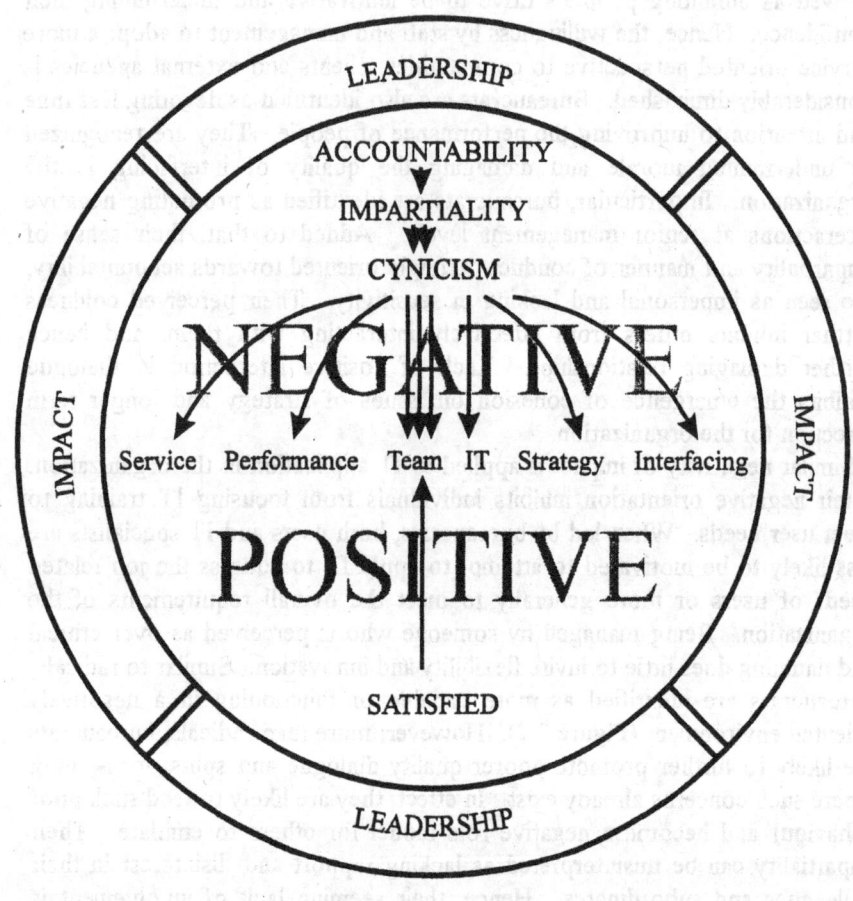

Figure 7.6 Leadership wheel: bureaucrats' impact on organization

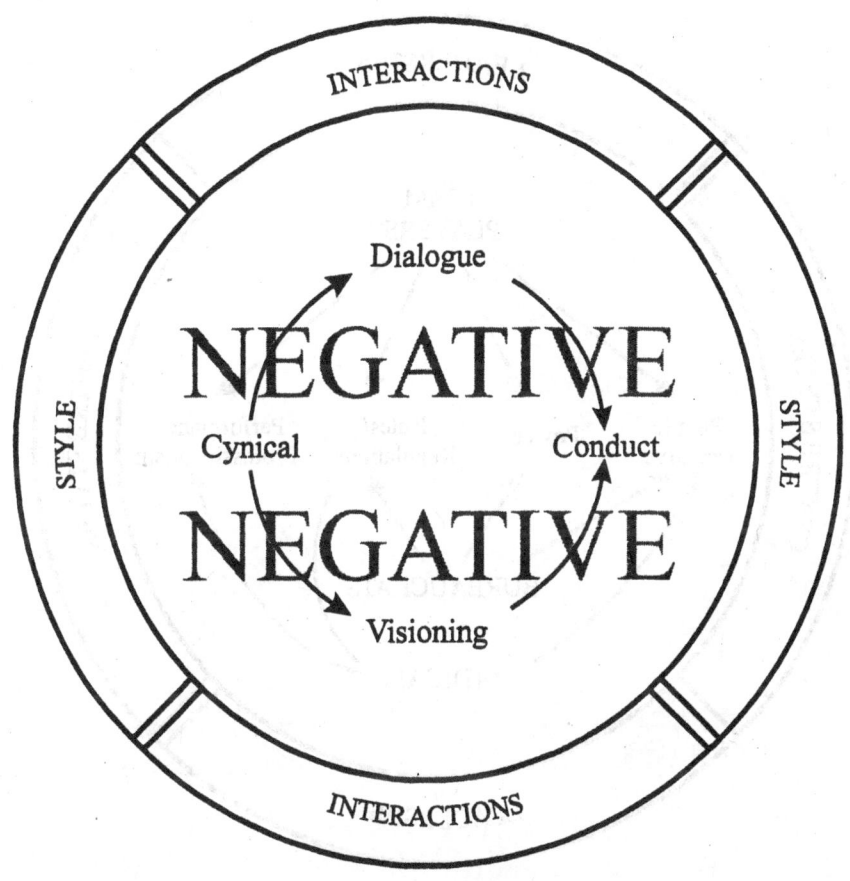

Figure 7.7 Leadership wheel: top team impact on bureaucrats

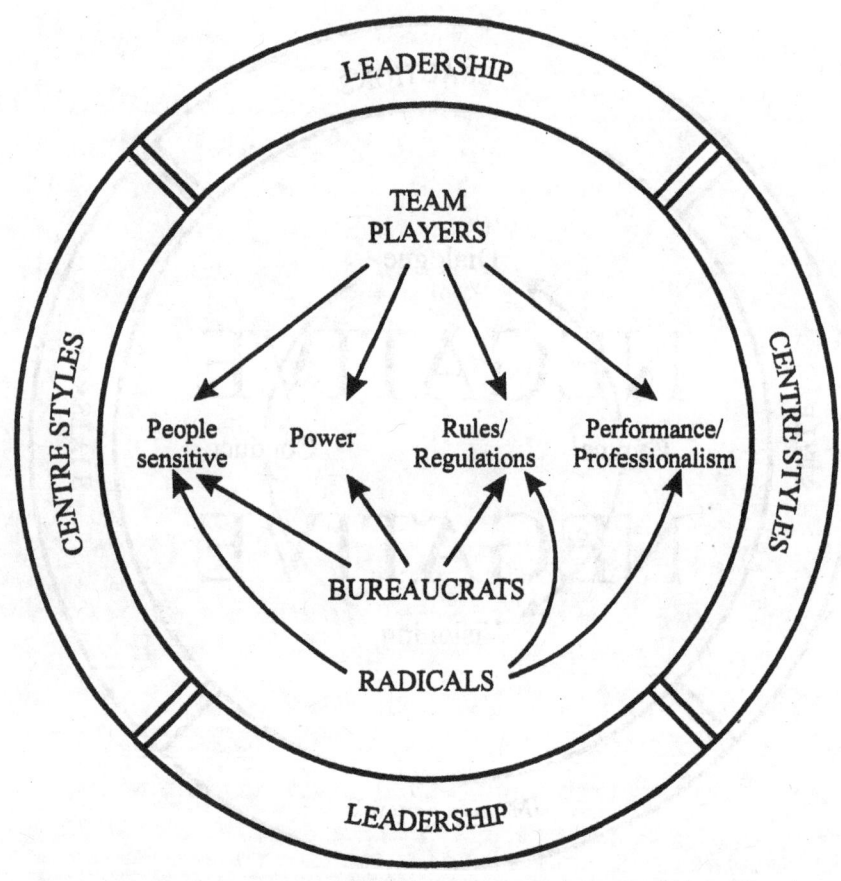

Figure 7.8 Leadership wheel: leadership impact on the Centre

Team players, radicals and bureaucrats are identified as practising people sensitive styles. Also, team players, radicals and bureaucrats are recognized as applying rules and regulations whenever required. However, only team players and bureaucrats are identified as significantly more applying power oriented styles. Further, only team players and radicals are identified as significantly more using styles that value performance and professionalism.

In essence, motivating people by being responsive to their needs and establishing clear parameters within the organization by application of rules and regulations, are practices commonly applied by the three different types of leader. However, when under pressure to influence, team players and bureaucrats would far more use manipulative/coercive styles (power oriented) in order to promote their perspectives. In contrast, team players and radicals are recognized as seriously attempting to promote higher standards of performance and induce a positive attitude towards being recognized as professional.

These findings are in keeping with the results emerging so far, whereby the team players would far more attempt to influence by working with people, irrespective of whether they use more people sensitive or power oriented styles. Radicals would be more abrupt, focusing on issues, but finding negotiating on key agendas through what they would consider as more manipulative means, distasteful. Bureaucrats would focus less on addressing key issues openly or through confrontation, but be more covert and distant in their approach.

Benchmarking leaderships: private sector comparison

Parallels exist between the APS findings and the results emerging from the Cranfield International private sector surveys. From the private sector surveys, spanning 12 countries, three distinctly different approaches to leadership emerge: those of senior managers who are drivers, politicians and strategists. Similar to the APS survey, profile differences are strongly influenced by demographic characteristics, five in this case, namely, size of organization, years spent in organization, years spent in job, number of senior management appointments held, and age of respondents. More detailed information concerning the characteristics of the three leadership orientations is provided in Appendix 3.

Table 7.6
Profile of leadership: private sector

Drivers	Politicians	Strategists
• Motivators	• Communicators	• Promote performance
• Dissatisfied	• Dissatisfied	• Manage diversity
• Cynical	• Disciplined	• Disciplined
• Independent	• Independent	• Specialist
• Specialist		

As can be see in Table 7.6, the need for independence, the specialist background and the reliance on discipline, parallel the leadership attributes of the leader profiles in the APS. The cynicism and dissatisfaction with job and organization, especially portrayed by those executives who are younger, with less experience and are more demanding and less compromising, namely the drivers and politicians, are comparable to the profile of the radicals and bureaucrats identified in the APS. Further, of the two most positively oriented leadership styles emerging from the private sector and from the APS, the strategists and team players, both are performance oriented and both attempt to positively manage strain, tension and diversity.

Further, a comparable distribution of valid cases emerges in each of the three categories for both the APS and the private sector (Table 7.7). Approximately two-thirds of the total sample fall into the more negatively oriented styles of leadership. The team players and strategists representing the more positive leadership contribution, emerge as occupying one-third of the APS and private sector samples, respectively.

Table 7.7
Leadership: sample distribution (valid cases)

APS:

Team players	Radicals	Bureaucrats
N = 216	292	242

Private sector:

Strategists	Politicians	Drivers
N = 1423	1207	1223

However, two major areas of differences exist. First, as can be seen in Appendices 2 and 3, identifying the particular attributes of leadership for both the APS and private sector samples, the three leadership styles of the private sector highlight a greater willingness and sensitivity to better manage and to better relate to peers and subordinates in order to attain greater effectiveness of performance. Making oneself more available to others, and trying to be more in tune with the needs of the organization in order to provide for greater attentiveness to external stakeholders, is strongly shared by the three leadership profiles emerging from the private sector. Although client service and promoting value to the community emerge as deeply held attributes from the APS sample, the close attention to and motivation of people in order to enhance the performance of the organization, is less apparent in the public sector approaches to leadership. Dissatisfaction and disdain for the organization emerge as the more powerful philosophies in the APS results.

Second, a fundamental difference exists between the team players and strategists. Team players are identified as having a background of working in more medium sized organizations. Strategists are identified as having spent most of their time in larger organizations. The cynicism that is expressed from having worked in a larger organization (bureaucrats) does not emerge from the private sector sample.

Private sector: impact on organization performance

Five key areas of organizational performance in private sector organizations are identified, namely promoting a performance culture, effectiveness of top team, morale of staff and management, gaining competitive advantage through high quality dialogue and effectively interfacing internally in the organization.

Promoting a performance culture involves top management practising an open management style, whereby staff and management feel comfortable to express what and where improvements need to take place. Such sensitivity helps make others feel comfortable to allow for a high level of communication to emerge, especially on being kept informed of progress on projects and key initiatives. The more open style enables staff and management to more quickly identify with where and how problems arise. Further, greater discipline on follow through on initiatives is encouraged in order for completion of projects or activities. Working in a positive environment promotes a shared sense of satisfaction with the work and with the organization, which in turn promotes positive interactions internally and with customers and suppliers externally.

An effective top team is considered by the survey respondents to be one where the quality of dialogue amongst its members is deemed to be high. The individuals feel sufficiently comfortable with each other to make whatever comments concerning performance they feel are appropriate. Equally, high levels of trust and respect for each other as people predominates. Further, there exists a strongly shared sense of cabinet responsibility concerning communication of key policies and strategies, and the implementation of decisions.

Morale refers to sentiments held by staff and management concerning satisfaction with work and organization, the quality of internal relationships and the quality of performance from the organization's employees. The greater the satisfaction in these areas, the higher the level of morale in the organization.

Gaining competitive advantage refers to management's ability to promote particular synergies that would gain advantage for the organization in its market place. Their understanding of the impact of competitors on the market is coupled with their views as to the degree of focus required to gain and keep customer accounts. Equally recognized as important, is for management to hold a shared view as to what is required in terms of sales and marketing so that a positive response is forthcoming from the organization to the management of external relationships and to new initiatives. Hence, a high quality dialogue amongst senior managers concerning competitive advantage is necessary in order to reach common agreement as to how the different elements of strategy combine and need to be effectively actioned.

Effective interfacing Crucial to effectively working the structure of the organization involves management appreciating how and why the organization is currently configured. Such an understanding then allows for a high quality of interfacing between the various functions and departments. Staff and management are likely to be more clear as to how improvements in communication will promote greater efficiency of organization.

Impact of drivers

Drivers are identified as having a mixed impact on the organization (Figure 7.9). Drivers are motivators of people and are disciplined in their approach. The people oriented aspects of their leadership style are identified as having a positive impact in terms of generating a performance oriented culture, in promoting effective teamwork at the top, in improving morale in the organization and in terms of displaying how to effectively interface in the organization. In effect, when adopting a more motivational approach, line management are more likely to appreciate how to gain competitive advantage. However, when drivers are being more disciplined and focused, line management are likely to feel reluctant to question and debate approaches to gaining competitive advantage. Subordinates are more likely to be fearful of making a mistake. Further, the fact that drivers are identified as dissatisfied, cynical, independent and specialist, is viewed as having a negative impact on the five key organizational performance measures.

Impact of politicians

Politicians are recognized as effective communicators, an attribute which is identified as having a positive impact on stimulating a performance oriented culture in the organization, as enhancing top team relationships and as improving the morale of staff and management (Figure 7.9). Being disciplined is equally viewed as having a positive impact on promoting a performance oriented culture.

However, their exhibited dissatisfaction and sense of independence are identified as having a negative impact on the growth of a performance culture, team relationships, morale and dialogue over competitive advantage. Politicians therefore are likely to promote mixed messages and, as a result, people are less likely to trust them.

Impact of strategists

For strategists, their capability to promote greater levels of performance from others and to manage diversity, are seen to have a positive impact on promoting a performance oriented culture in the workplace, enhancing relationships at senior management levels, improving morale internally, promoting a better quality dialogue concerning competitive advantage and providing good example concerning interfacing across the organization (Figure 7.9). The discipline applied by strategists is also recognized as enhancing a culture of performance and improving the quality of interfacing in the organization.

Similar to the APS results, strategists like team players portray a positive attitude and inclination to the effective management of people, which in turn improves performance within the organization in terms of enhancing morale and improving team interactions, and externally in terms of improving standards of service to the markets.

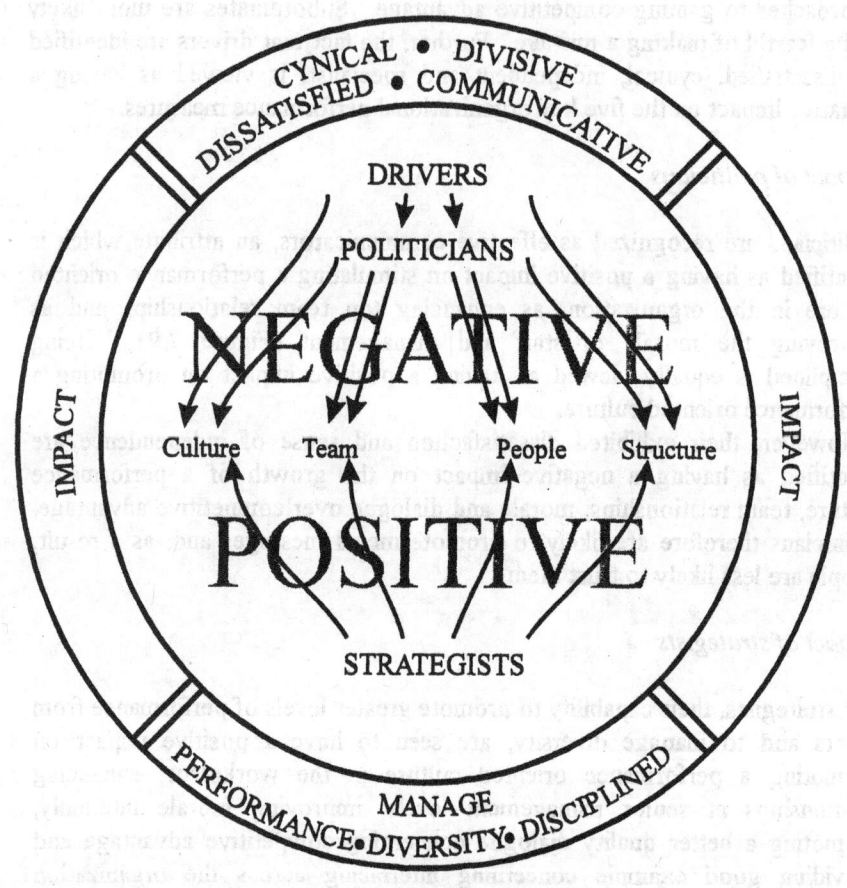

Figure 7.9 Leadership wheel: private sector

Summary

Leadership tensions

- Leadership within the APS is valued least in comparison with elements of culture of organization.

- Senior management in the APS are identified as more divided on issues of visioning and strategic intent when benchmarked against private sector business leaders and NHS Trusts (UK) management.

- Senior management in the APS are identified as comparable on issues of sensitivity of dialogue when benchmarked with private sector business leaders and NHS Trusts (UK) management.

- On examination of key managerial behaviours which lead to greater trust, improved communication, greater sense of cabinet responsibility and strategic capability, senior managers in the APS benchmark unfavourably against private sector business leaders.

Dialogue

- Poor quality dialogue at senior management levels leads to greater practice of power and rules and regulation oriented styles of management.

- Poor quality dialogue at senior management levels leads to poor communication, lack of clarity of organization goals and poor application of IT in the organization.

- Poor quality dialogue at senior management levels is seen as inhibiting the promotion and implementation of policies, as inhibiting the nurture of effective client relations and equally, as inhibiting the development of positive relations with other agencies.

- Poor quality dialogue at senior management levels leads to the management in regional offices feeling demotivated, lacking clear areas of responsibility and experiencing hindrances in their current position.

Visioning

- Splits of visioning at senior management levels encourage the practice of insensitive, power oriented styles of management.

- Splits of visioning at senior management levels lead to poor communication of organizational objectives.

- Splits of visioning at senior management levels lead to confusion as to which goals are being pursued and why.

- Splits of visioning at senior management levels lead to ineffective practice in terms of certain organizational operations, such as outsourcing, restructuring, the application of IT, the promotion and implementation of policies and the nurture of external relationships.

- Splits of visioning at senior management levels lead to management in the regions feeling demotivated.

Leadership philosophies

- In the opinion of SESs and SOs, the attitudes adopted and the personalities of senior managers are the principal reasons for tensions, blockages and inhibitions arising within the APS.

- Three contrasting philosophies of leadership are identified in the APS, termed the team players, radicals and bureaucrats. These orientations are more the result of people's experiences of having worked in different sizes of organization, having spent more or fewer years in the organization, more or fewer years on the job and having held varying numbers of senior management appointments.

- Team players are seen as making the most positive impact, in terms of enhancing organizational performance, supporting more effective application of IT in the organization, and nurturing the development of people.

- Team players are vulnerable to poor quality dialogue and division over the strategies and vision being pursued at senior management levels.

- Radicals are identified as outward focused and service oriented but over critical of the organization and its management.

- The critical style of radicals is seen to considerably demotivate people which in turn inhibits their contribution towards effective organizational performance and the effective application of IT in the organization.

- The critical style of radicals promotes poor quality dialogue and splits of visioning amongst senior managers in the organization.

- Bureaucrats are identified as cynical. They are also seen as impartial in terms of expressing opinions on issues, their impartiality being seen as cold and insensitive towards people.

- The cynical style of bureaucrats is seen to considerably demotivate people and undermine their contribution to enhancing organizational performance and to pursuing their interest in effectively implementing IT in the organization.

- The cynical style of bureaucrats promotes poor quality dialogue and splits of visioning amongst senior managers in the organization.

- Team players, radicals and bureaucrats are identified as influencing the styles of management at the Centre in different ways, with the team players more prepared to influence people through the use of both positive and negative styles, and the radicals being more open and confronting. Overall the bureaucrats are viewed as having the most negative impact which is undermining of the morale of staff and lower level management.

Benchmarking leadership

- Within the private sector, three philosophies of leadership emerge, namely, drivers, politicians and strategists, which in turn arise as the result of differences of experience of five key demographic characteristics, namely, size of organization, years spent in organization, years spent on the job, number of senior management appointments held, and age of respondents.

- Parallels between the leadership philosophies identified in the APS and in the private sector are identified except for the fact that, generally, private sector leaders highlight a greater willingness and sensitivity to relate to peers and subordinates in order to attain greater effectiveness of performance from the staff and management.

- Similar to the APS, the leadership philosophies identified in the private sector survey are recognized as significantly impactful on measures of organizational performance.

Notes

1. Respondents were asked whether the members of the top team were:
   - easy to talk to/not easy to talk to
   - people who openly discuss sensitive issues/people who address more safe issues
   - understanding of each other/not understanding of each other
   - people who trust each other/people who do not trust each other
   - people who will jointly implement decisions made in the top team/people who will implement decisions made in the top team which personally suit the individual
   - people who will address long and short term issues/people who will address more short term concerns.

2. CEO   Chief Executive Officer
   MD   Managing Director
   ED   Executive Director
   GM   General Manager
   SES   Senior Executive Service
   SOs   Senior Officers

3. NHS   National Health Service

4. For more indepth information, see Appendix 6 for a full analysis and account of impact of top team leadership within the APS. See also Chapter 6 and Appendix 5 providing a comprehensive analysis as to how leadership behaviour at the Centre impacts on the regions.

5. See Appendix 2 for a more indepth breakdown of the style and philosophy characteristics of team players.

8 Recommendations for management development

Positive culture is necessary but not sufficient, however, effective leadership is necessary and sufficient for promoting effective organizational performance.

Overview

The results of the study are clear. A positive culture of organization supportive of shared values such as providing service, professionalism and conduct, rights of individuals and workplace democracy, has limited impact on how people, teams and the overall organization performs. In this study it has been identified that leadership has a profound impact on the effectiveness of organizational performance, irrespective of whether the leadership orientation is more positive or negative. Further, the study also shows that contrasting philosophies of leadership promote poor quality dialogue and low cohesion over visioning, which in turn have a most powerful influence on people, teams and organizational performance measures (Figure 8.1). Individual leaders under such circumstances utilize those approaches they consider best for their situation, but the contrast between them promotes greater division and mistrust in the organization.

In particular, due to both poor quality dialogue, lack of unity over visioning, and the practice and pursuit of differing leadership philosophies, the style of management exhibited by the top management of the various government departments is considered as promoting an inconsistency of message and undermining the trust necessary in top management to sponsor innovative and high quality services to clients, the community and other agencies. Styles that value performance and professionalism are minimized. Further, due to the varying quality of dialogue at the top, the personal style of top managers is

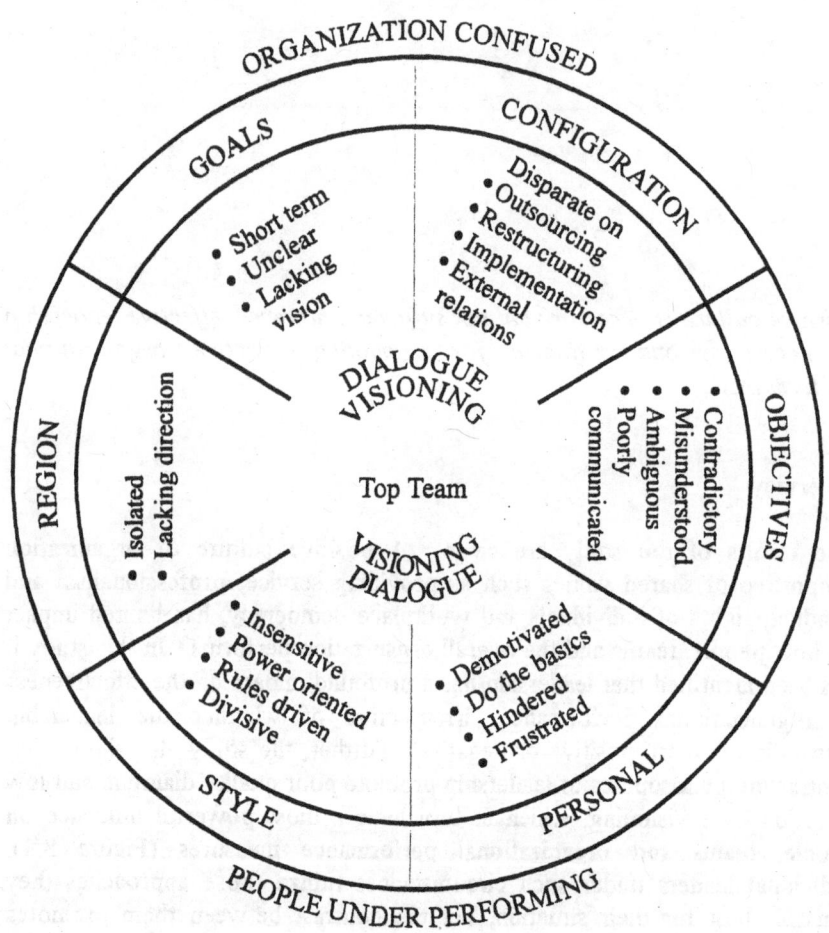

Figure 8.1 Leadership wheel: impact of top teams on the APS

considered as more insensitive and responding inappropriately to the needs of staff and lower level management within the APS.

In terms of clarity concerning future direction, the goals of the various departments are considered as more unclear. In fact, the greater the degree of splits of visioning, the more short term the orientation of senior managers in the way they pursue the goals of the organization. In addition, the poorer the quality of dialogue and the splits of visioning, the less effectively are Central Office and departmental objectives communicated.

As far as the introduction and management of particular organizational operations are concerned, the outsourcing of these operations, and the restructuring of departments and/or particular units, are considered to occur with greater frequency when top management are divided as to the future direction of the organization. The implication is that the respondents consider such innovations are more the endeavour of one senior individual, or small group of top managers, pushing through change, at times in opposition from colleagues and other sections of the organization.

Not surprisingly, when it comes to the promotion and development of external relationships, the process can be described as fraught. Due to perceived differences of view concerning the future, and poor quality dialogue, the promotion and implementation of policies and the development of effective relations with various client groupings and other agencies are seen as constrained. Such circumstances epitomize a stop/start practice to offering new developments to the community and other agencies. Further, the innovative application of IT is seen as equally hampered by poor quality dialogue and splits of visioning.

In terms of impact on individuals, due especially to perceived poor quality dialogue at senior levels, management in the regions view themselves and are seen as more demotivated, lacking clear areas of responsibility, experiencing substantial hindrances in their current position, are not driven to be performance oriented and fundamentally do just what is required of them. Not surprisingly, morale is considered as low in such circumstances.

In effect, growing a positive performance oriented culture within the organization is identified as necessary but not sufficient for effectiveness of performance at both the individual and organizational level. However, leadership is identified as both necessary and sufficient for impacting on individual, team and organizational performance, irrespective of whether the result is more positive or negative.

The results emphasize that the growth and development of high performing leaders is the vital ingredient to the promotion of an effective public service. The following sections examine the approaches to developing high performing leaders. The impact of poor, divisive and indecisive leadership on the APS, on private sector and health service organizations, is examined.

Equally explored is the impact of positive leadership on the APS if senior managers were to improve their leadership practice. Interestingly, most managers can see what needs to be done and how the organization will benefit if those known concerns within the APS are confronted. The challenge is 'doing it'! Part of 'doing it' is coming to terms with particular myths which inhibit the conduct of high quality dialogue. An examination of those myths is undertaken as a prelude to highlighting best practice leadership behaviours and the routes to the development of such behaviours. Further, in order to achieve greater cohesion in the organization, establishing a mission that binds the organization and the steps to take to its effective implementation, are examined. Finally, a blueprint for the development of leaders already in post, as well as emerging 'high flyers' is presented. In so doing, the concept of managing a paradox in leadership is introduced. In effect, managing differences and the concepts of the leadership gap are explored, highlighting the particularly demanding challenges facing leaders in today's organizations, when attention to issues of costs and infrastructure have to be managed in conjunction with the promotion of a quality philosophy and the nurture of trusting and responsive relationships in order to promote service to the community. In the discussion of how to develop leaders, particular attention is given to the nurture of key capabilities such as visioning, maturity, wisdom, quality of dialogue, resolution of tensions, communication and feedback. One theme is stressed, the capabilities required for effective leadership practice are developable. Leaders in today's corporate organizations are made, not born! Those that resist development are the ones unlikely to progress as effectively performing leaders.

Areas needing attention

Two areas that are worthy of attention are identified, the behaviour of leaders and current practices of dialogue.

Behaviour of leaders

Table 8.1
Need for change in leader behaviour: views of SESs and SOs
% of responses

Level	Leadership Behaviour	Communication	Team	Business focus	Performance management	New blood
SESs	18	29	9			
%		56		18	22	3

Level	Leadership Behaviour	Communication	Team	Business focus	Performance management	New blood
SOs	26 ↘	27 ↓	9 ↙			
%		62		16	19	2

% refers to percentage of responses identifying key issues requiring attention.

Interestingly, SESs and SOs seem to be aware of the impact they have on their organization. Four areas of change of practice of leadership are identified by SESs and SOs, namely changes in leadership behaviour, business focus (goals, vision, structure of organization, strategic planning), performance management, and new blood (recruits from outside the service) being brought into the APS. Fifty six per cent of the comments made by SESs concern changes of leadership thinking and practice, a finding similar to SOs of whom 62 per cent are concerned that leadership practice is needy of attention. Both SESs and SOs consider that the communication skills of leaders require the greatest attention. A certain disparity of view exists between SESs and SOs as to whether the behaviour of individual leaders requires attention in terms of development, with 26 per cent of comments of SOs highlighting that greater attention is necessary in this area. From thereon, both groups largely concur that the performance of management generally and the capability of management to focus, are worthy of development but are not a priority concern. Interestingly, both groups concur that introducing 'new blood' into the organization is not going to make much difference.

Below (Tables 8.2 and 8.3) outline comments made by participants highlighting areas for improvement in the above categories. For both groups, numerous comments refer to stronger, more decisive leadership, supported by comments outlining greater integration and sharing amongst key personalities. As far as communication is concerned, greater honesty, more openness, greater tolerance, more and better consultation, greater airing of differences, are examples of certain of the comments, all suggesting a need for a far improved quality of dialogue. Equal concurrence of comments is identified under the heading of 'Business focus', whereby clearer direction in terms of goals and strategic direction, better integration, more clearly thought through reorganization, less short term restructuring and overall better follow through practices, highlight some of the key themes to emerge. Under the performance management category, those issues requiring attention range from enhancing the change management skills of senior managers, to selection procedures, to greater cooperation and more hands on management.

Table 8.2
Comments highlighting improvements (SESs)

Leadership

Behaviour

- Stronger control from top
- More decisive leadership
- Stronger CEO
- Corporate leadership
- Control powerful personalities
- Greater shared vision
- Greater motivation for outlying offices
- More positive attitude from top team

Communication

- Better management meetings
- Greater openness and trust
- More open discussion
- Engage minister better
- Discuss differences
- Fewer interpersonal differences
- Better dialogue
- More understanding and tolerance of others
- Better consultation
- More strategic dialogue
- Improved quality of relationships
- Less divide and rule

Performance management

- Realistic briefings
- Nothing can help
- Develop diverse range of skills
- Reduce feeling of irreconcilable differences
- Better policy choices
- Better monitoring of change
- More senior management focus on performance
- Less focus on internal politics
- More hands on management
- Greater top management development
- Better selection at top
- More skills to overcome resistance

Business focus

- Restructuring needed
- Clearer goal direction
- More commercial debate
- Robust strategic planning process
- Better bonding
- Better planned change
- More conceptualization about the structure of the organization
- Less political interference
- Better strategic planning

Table 8.3
Comments highlighting improvements (SOs)

Leadership

Behaviour

- Stronger leadership*
- Strong CEO
- More training in strategic leadership
- More tolerant leadership
- More strategic leadership at top
- Greater caring attitude
- Less entrenched views at top
- Better leadership from CEO
- Clearer direction and leadership
- Better leadership
- More integrated leadership

Communication

- Communication of a clearer vision
- Better consensus
- Better dialogue over differences
- Greater open communication
- Better analysis and discussion
- Greater admission of problems
- Greater feedback required
- More listening to staff
- Better communication from top team
- Better consultation
- More senior management conferences for communication purposes
- More openness
- More willingness to confront
- More honest dialogue

Performance management

- Better selection of top managers
- Confront key issues
- Re-educate top in leadership
- Top management to better understand what is their problem
- Evaluate divisions in department
- Greater sense of responsibility
- More client sensitivity
- More career advancement
- More meaningful staff development
- Change management skills
- Value good staff
- Be more politically sensitive

Business focus

- Better planning
- Better reorganization
- Restructure on business lines
- Clearer future direction of organization
- Better shaping of vision
- Greater government decisiveness
- More integrated reorganization
- Better structured top team
- Greater clarity of strategic objectives
- Greater organizational integration
- Be more corporate focused
- Less restructuring of management

* Stronger leadership is one of the most quoted comments reported in the survey.

Dialogue

The theme of quality of dialogue and its impact on the organization is continued. Respondents were asked to identify the impact on people and the organization of dialogue at senior management levels that is perceived as restrictive and inhibits attending to particular challenges in the organization. Their views are highlighted in Table 8.4.

People issues are considered as the most crucial to address, with 37 per cent of comments highlighting the need to improve the morale of staff and management and 31 per cent emphasizing that the performance of the members of senior management needs improvement. Twenty eight per cent of comments relate to strategic issues and how these are not fully debated and examined. Further, a considerable percentage of comments refer to infrastructure issues, such as structure of organization, the manner in which regional offices are run, relationship between Central Office and the regions, quality of relationship between the regional offices, and differences of opinion concerning reorganization.

Table 8.4
Impact of restriction of dialogue (APS)

Issues identified as needing attention	%
• Morale of staff and management	37
• Performance of members of senior management	31
• Issues affecting the long term	28
• Structure of organization	24
• Relationship between SESs	22
• Relationship between Central Office/regions	22
• The way regional offices/divisions are run	20
• Future of the APS	18
• Differences of opinion concerning reorganization	17
• Relationship between regional offices	16
• Quality of services offered externally	13
• Changes in organization direction	13
• Cost management and control	12

% refers to percentage of comments identified as respondents had the opportunity to make multiple responses.

Interestingly, the quality of services offered externally is viewed as having been less restricted and less needy of attention than the people, strategic, structural and interfacing issues already highlighted.

In terms of supporting the infrastructure of the organization, concern is equally expressed over the application of IT in the APS. In response to the question, 'Are there IT issues that merit but do not receive attention at the senior management levels?', 44 per cent of respondents stated 'yes'. Table 8.5 highlights the concerns identified with issues of IT. Ineffective IT application is seen to negatively impact on the performance of the organization (21 per cent), negatively impact on the performance of employees (21 per cent) and is likely to hamper any long term planning concerning IT investment (20 per cent of comments).

Table 8.5
Sensitivities related to IT issues (APS)

Areas of concern	%
• Impact on organizational performance	21
• Impact on employees	21
• Issues affecting long term IT planning	20
• IT alignment with structure of organization	15
• Information control	13
• Impact on decision processes	12
• Choice of adopted IT	12

% refers to percentage of comments identified as respondents had the opportunity to make multiple responses.

Comparisons with the private sector and NHS Trusts in the area of impact are somewhat more difficult as, understandably, the impact measures vary considerably across the two sectors. However, a similar pattern of results emerge whereby issues such as productivity, cost management and control, profitability, clarity of strategic direction, morale and decision making in private sector organizations are viewed as directly related to the degree of cohesion (or lack of it) and the quality of dialogue (or lack of it) practised by the top team (Table 8.6).

Table 8.6
Impact of top team (private sector) on people and organization
Poor quality of dialogue and visioning

Areas needing attention	%
• Employee morale	42
• Profitability	39
• Clarity of strategic direction	35
• Productivity	35
• Employee performance	34
• Response to new initiatives	34
• Quality of decision making	30
• Trust	26
• Commitment to decisions	25
• Leadership style	24
• Cost management and control	22
• Relationship between departments	22
• Inaccuracies to clients/customers	21
• Poor focus on customer groups	20

% refers to percentage of responses identifying key issues requiring attention, with respondents having the opportunity to make multiple responses.

Equally, similar patterns emerge for NHS Trusts (UK), whereby morale, quality of relationships with external bodies and internal units, the interface between clinicians and management, are identified as more needy of attention than restructuring and cost management and control (Table 8.7).

Similar to the APS results, the British NHS Trust findings identify people, structure and strategic process issues as worthy of greater attention. Effectiveness of service delivery and ability to handle patient demands are placed low on the list of priorities which is not the case with the private sector, whereby response to new initiatives and productivity are placed high on the list of concerns requiring attention.

Table 8.7
Impact of top team (NHS Trusts) on people and organization
Poor quality of dialogue and visioning

Areas needing attention	%
• Trust	38
• Understanding between clinicians and management	34
• Quality of decision making	34
• Relationship with external bodies	28
• Clarity of decision making	26
• Clinician/nursing morale	26
• Interfacing internally	26
• Restructuring	24
• Commitment to decisions made	24
• Cost management and control	22
• Effectiveness of service delivery	22
• Ability to handle patient demands	22

% refers to percentage of responses identifying key issues requiring attention, with respondents having the opportunity to make multiple responses.

Enhancement of dialogue

Having identified key areas of concern due to poor leadership, the respondents were asked to list how much better would circumstances be if such tensions had been resolved earlier. Table 8.8 outlines those areas where improvement would be noticeable if quality of dialogue improved. Two key areas are discernible, namely people management/relationship improvements (i.e. morale of staff and management, relationships, trust issues) and effectiveness of service provision externally (improved response to new initiatives, improved ability to deliver goods/services on time and enhanced external relationships).

Table 8.8
Enhancement of quality of dialogue (APS)

Areas of improvement	%
• Morale of staff/management	53
• Internal relationships	45
• Trust of senior managers in each other	40
• Better performance from employees	38
• Improved strategic policy	34
• Improved response to new initiatives	32
• Better focus on key client groupings	30
• Improved ability to deliver goods/services on time	29
• Better relationship between the centre and the regions	26
• Enhanced external relations	25
• Fewer unrealistic commitments made to bosses/subordinates	22
• Fewer resignations/people leaving	20
• Better understanding of how to work the structure of the organization	19
• Better discussions concerning client impact	17
• Greater efficiency through cost cutting	16
• Improved ability of managers to handle clients	16
• Fewer unrealistic commitments made to clients	16
• More considered approach to financial management	16

% refers to percentage of comments identified as respondents had the opportunity to make multiple responses.

It is postulated that attention to the people issues provides the extra cutting edge in terms of effectiveness of service delivery, negotiating and maintaining positive relationships with other agencies and enhancing the level of satisfaction of the community in the delivery of government services.

The following questions were asked of private sector respondents:

Q: How would you rate your competitors?
A: Customer orientated (63 per cent of responses).

Q: What is involved in the marketing of your products/services?
A: Establishing longer term relationships with clients/customers (85 per cent of responses).

The evidence emerging from the Cranfield surveys suggests that the content of senior management dialogue should emphasize the 'softer' concerns of management, irrespective of whether the focus is private or public sector.

Consideration of the following questions may assist senior managers in the APS to explore avenues for improvement.

- What key concerns are known to exist in the APS department, project, region and are consistently not discussed at senior management levels?

- For how long have particular concerns been recognized as pertinent to address?

- What is the nature of the sensitivity that inhibits appropriate dialogue from taking place?

- What forums do senior management attend in order to examine and understand the workings of the organization?

- At these forums, who draws up the agenda, and how representative are the issues on the agenda in terms of drawing to the surface underlying but inadequately examined concerns?

- How responsive are senior management to giving and receiving feedback?

- To what extent do senior management seriously request feedback?

- How remote are senior management from the reality of organizational life?

- What are the opportunity costs for the organization of not entering into dialogue over these issues?

The response to these questions is likely to provide a view as to management's intent and capability to discuss the issues facing their organization. As management in the future are likely to experience even greater levels of ambiguity in responding to the conflicting demands of different stakeholders, the honest views emerging from the above questions are likely to highlight senior management's level of robustness to provide for effective leadership.

Dispelling myths

Of course, loyalty and support for ministers is crucial but at times this is used as an excuse to not address and face up to other problems.

SES

I think we lack courage .... so I get impatient. I don't think we collectively work to change what we don't like. In terms of managing upwards, I sometimes wonder how people have got to where they have ... well I suppose I can answer my own question, they never do anything controversial using the minister as the excuse.

SES

I should say that the relationships I have had with ministers over the last five years, with the exception of the current one, have been the most fantastic relationships. Ministers don't tell you go out and change this or do that and you sit there and say 'yes, yes, yes'. You use your own initiative and courage.

SES

Repeatedly in interview, the complexity of the senior manager's role was described in considerable detail. Particular attention was given to two issues, the specific and special relationship with ministers and the range of issues and of stakeholders that confront senior managers in the APS. The overall impression gained from interview is that few other senior managers in both private and public sector organizations face such a range of complexity of relationships and intellectual and pragmatic challenges. Although most concurred as to the range and nature of such challenges, considerable disagreement of view emerged as to how effectively such challenges were/are addressed.

Virtually all interviewees indicated that supporting ministers is of paramount importance. However, certain interviewees indicated that support for ministers is so demanding that it inhibited other considerations. The net effect is that particular problems are knowingly not addressed because attention is given to meeting ministerial requirements. Others however highlighted that support for ministers, although of exceptional importance, is also used as an excuse by senior managers to not confront issues that require their attention. As one stated:

If your boss does not want to do something, the minister is used as the excuse. The problem is, we all know what is happening. So as a technique, it just demotivates.

SO

SESs and SOs were asked to identify the five key values and attributes that they considered are of significant importance in effectively doing their job. The top 12 value items to have emerged for both groups are identified below (Table 8.9).

Out of 53 separately identified values and attributes, high quality advice to ministers was marked fourteenth by SESs, whilst support for ministers was forty-second. For SOs, high quality advice to ministers was ranked thirty-second, whilst support for ministers was ranked forty-third. Otherwise, there is a considerable degree of overlap on the key job related values and attributes between the two groups. The discernible differences are that SOs value opportunity and recognition, whilst SESs reflect more on career, position and ambition.

Table 8.9
Key job related values and attributes

Rank	SESs	Rank	SOs
1	Effectiveness	1	Communication
2	Communication	2	Teamwork
3	Integrity	3	Professionalism
4	Professionalism	4	Integrity
5	Competence	5	Probity
6	Accountability for powers/privileges	6	Respect
7	Teamwork	7	Quality
8	Quality	8	Opportunity
9	Probity	9	Excellence
10	Respect	10	Responsibility
11	Commitment	11	Recognition
12	Honesty	12	Competence

Key to developing robustness for effective leadership is dispelling myths which may inhibit effective performance. One of the myths is that providing high quality support and advice for ministers overrides all else. Provision of advice, support and concern for ministers is vital, but does not need to impede confronting particular problem areas.

A similar finding has emerged from the private sector survey whereby national cultural differences are viewed as impeding the management of internationally based companies. Closer examination reveals obvious differences of ethnic and national cultural background, but in well led organizations such differences do not undermine new initiatives, competitiveness, product investment and quality, programmes of change and leadership of the organization. Difference of ethnicity and cultural background is a charm not an impediment. However, companies facing interfacing tensions, internal division and confused leadership also display internal strife due to supposed ethnic differences. A division or subsidiary company located in a different country working to resist the initiatives or influence of Central Office, could produce 'the ethnic card', i.e. we in Germany, Japan, Britain, or wherever, do not operate in this way and hence cannot proceed with your request from Central Office. Ethnicity is an emotive subject. Because of the sensitivities involved, managers at the Centre may be unwilling to challenge the managers in the regions. Ethnicity is, in effect, used as a powerful lever for blocking change, hindering communication and resisting reform.

The second issue, repeatedly highlighted, of job related complexity, holds weight if comparison is to be made between the job of an SES (band) 3 and the managing director (MD) of a single product range company from the private sector. Under these circumstances, the SESs job is probably more complex and demanding in comparison to the job of the MD of a medium sized company. However, being an executive director of the Daimler Benz Corporation, for example, where the interests of the group range from household products, transportation (cars, railways, aeroplanes) and defence, i.e. from toaster to roadster, is likely be experienced as particularly challenging. Currently, a rationalization of Daimler Benz has been undertaken in order to attempt to steer the group back into profitability. As so many larger, private sector corporate organizations hold multiple interests, the challenge of effectively discharging the role of director, CEO, MD, general manager, is demanding, bearing in mind the need to manage the expectations of varying stakeholders who are unlikely to share compatible agendas.

The Cranfield surveys highlight job related complexity as an issue most senior managers of mid to large sized organizations have to face. Tables 7.3 and 7.4 highlight that inhibition and an unwillingness to address known concerns are phenomena of organizational life today, both for private and public sector senior managers. Where prioritization is difficult because of the sensitive nature of the issues involved, it is common place to 'shy away' from addressing known concerns. Alternatively, a diversion could be created, whereby ethnicity is the parallel tactic amongst private sector organizations, to support for ministers in the APS, in terms of being used as a blockage. There is little doubt that the senior manager's job in the APS is complex and, of course, support and advice for ministers are crucial. However, it is important to distinguish between the demands of genuine support for ministers and the issue being used as a smoke screen to resist initiatives and/or not face up to particularly sensitive or discomforting issues.

A crucial step to developing the capabilities of leadership is to recognize the nature of inhibitions which can prevent effective dialogue and airing of views from being pursued.

Developing leaders

The message is, similar challenges face international business leaders and leaders of health organizations as face top civil servant government leaders. The symptoms of problems may be different in different forums, but the underlying pressures are comparable.

An additional insight paralleling the private sector, the health sector and the APS government leaders is that all of those interviewed intuitively knew the situation they faced. The hurdle to overcome in interview was winning the confidence of the interviewees, so that the person felt comfortable to more openly discuss their experiences and often their anguish at their seeming powerlessness to overcome what are tense but challenging human problems. What has emerged from all three of the Cranfield studies is that the feeling of 'not getting one's act together' is, in fact, an experience of normality. The reason why this is the case, is that it is considered that being a leader in today's organizations places the person in a permanent paradox.

Paradox of philosophy

Principally, this study has shown that few differences of perceptions as to the strengths, weaknesses and areas for development exist between SESs and SOs in the APS. Similar conclusions are highlighted for private sector respondents. Equally, the recommendations for improvement combine hard/soft approaches, namely strong, decisive leadership is desired in combination with supportive, empowering styles. The question is how can educated, responsible, developed individuals make such juxtaposed comments? In response, the three areas of leadership, identified in this study, are explored in terms of their transformational and transactional identity; the impact of accommodating contrasting models of leadership philosophy is also examined; and recognizing what works in terms of desired leadership frameworks in different contexts, is given airing.

Transactional or transformational? From workshops conducted with private sector senior managers, with senior managers from health service organizations and from police organizations, and with senior civil servants (UK), the criteria for transformational and transactional leadership emerged and are identified in Tables 8.10 and 8.11. These criteria are used to benchmark the three leadership philosophies identified in the APS.

As can be seen, the radicals are identified as fitting far more into the transformational camp of leadership, whilst bureaucrats fall more into the transactional group of leadership, and team players somewhere in-between. For team players, they share similar characteristics to radicals in terms of adopting a broader view of current and future circumstances, promoting quality, being independent and being loyal to the mission. Bureaucrats equally display certain characteristics of radicals, such as valuing quality and the provision of service, externally in the community, but also by being uncomfortable to work with, being insensitive, being ends oriented and independent minded.

Table 8.10
Slotting team players, radicals and bureaucrats: transformational

Leadership	Team players	Radicals	Bureaucrats
Broad picture	✓	✓	
Externally oriented	✓	✓	
'Cuts through'		✓	
Can be insensitive		✓	✓
Ends oriented	✓	✓	✓
Loyalty to mission	✓	✓	
Independent	✓	✓	✓
Risk taker		✓	
Quality externally	✓	✓	✓
Quality internally		✓	
Low self concern		✓	
Sacrifice self and others		✓	
Low on tenure	✓	✓	
Impatient		✓	✓
Critical		✓	✓
Internally disruptive		✓	✓
Uncomfortable to be with		✓	✓
Destroys boundaries		✓	
Dramatic change		✓	

APS philosophies

Table 8.11
Slotting team players, radicals and bureaucrats: transactional

APS philosophies

Leadership	Team player	Radicals	Bureaucrats
Talks broad	✓	✓	✓
Acts micro	✓		✓
Self conscious	✓		✓
Sensitive to others	✓		
Status sensitive			
Loyalty to organization	✓		✓
Loyalty to team	✓		✓
Loyalty to individuals	✓		
Task/procedure oriented	✓		✓
Politically correct	✓		✓
Plays politics			✓
Needs/provides stability	✓		✓
Needs/provides structure	✓		✓
Patient	✓		
Supportive	✓	✓	
Cynical			✓
Uncomfortable to be with		✓	✓
Nice to your face			✓
Mountain boundaries	✓		✓
Efficient	✓	✓	✓
Incremental change	✓		✓

Equally, radicals display certain of the characteristics of team players and bureaucrats, such as being patient, being supportive to their own colleagues/subordinates and being able to present a broad overview of situations. The question is, does such polarity of leadership philosophies promote confusion, demotivation and even harm to staff and subordinates, and to the quality of service to the community in the APS? Do differences between people, especially of a fundamental nature, cause harm?

Analysis undertaken to determine the key influences impacting on quality of organizational performance and the effective adoption of IT in the organization, highlights the leadership approaches which enhance quality of performance at the organizational IT level.[1] Three organizational measures identified are clarity of strategic direction, effectiveness of service delivery to the community, and the quality of performance of people to promote quality of service (Figure 8.2). The IT measures are the four IT performance measures of, IT training, effectiveness of IT application, IT skills and the impact of IT in the organization (Figure 8.3).

In order to enhance organizational performance, high quality of interfacing across the structure is considered as necessary. In order to provide for clarity of strategic direction, positive, open and robust relationships are required of the senior managers in the top team. Such positive relationships promote high quality dialogue, which in turn nurtures the practice of ever improving quality of interfacing across the structure. In addition, adopting the behaviours of a disciplined team player adds to the cohesion and dialogue necessary for developing clarity of strategic direction. In order to enhance effectiveness of service delivery, adopting the approach of independent team players is identified as being of positive advantage. The enhancement of the performance of people is added by adopting the approach of disciplined team players and specialist oriented bureaucrats.

However, effectiveness of service delivery is undermined by managers who adopt the styles of independent and disciplined radicals and cynical and specialist bureaucrats. Similarly, the quality of performance of people in the organization is undermined by adopting the style of disciplined bureaucrats.

The theme of different leadership approaches being made more suitable and appropriate for differing challenges and circumstances, is continued in an examination of the effectiveness of IT adoption in the APS (Figure 8.3). Focused and needs related IT training is recognized as supportive of IT, including having a positive impact on the organization. The more IT is seen to be of value to the organization, the more managers and staff will wish to apply IT, which in turn will stimulate a greater desire to develop the appropriate IT skills in order to utilize the technology. Further, adopting the approach of independent radicals is viewed as enhancing the usage of innovative IT skills. In order to improve the chances of IT being utilized and being recognized as being of value to staff and management in the organization, the approaches of disciplined team players, impartial bureaucrats and independent radicals are seen as a positive influence.

Equally, detracting influences to the adoption of IT in the organization have been identified. Challenging and disciplined team players are more likely to promote the adoption of basic/adaptive approaches to training rather than innovative/high order approaches to training. Adopting the stance of independent team players promotes a similar effect in the area of IT skills, in that more basic/adaptive skills are likely to be adopted by IT users. In terms of IT adoption in the organization, two leadership influences are identified as having a detracting influence. Adopting the approach of independent team players and disciplined bureaucrats is seen to undermine the potential positive impact IT could make on the organization.

Figures 8.2 and 8.3 indicate that what it takes to make things happen in the APS is not dependent on uniformity of leadership philosophy, but more on the behaviours required to suit the circumstances. Inappropriate behaviours according to circumstances are equally identified. In order to improve the quality of performance of people (Figure 8.2), disciplined team player and specialist oriented bureaucrat behaviours are desired. The reason is that a disciplined team approach along with a clear emphasis on specialization are recognized as supportive influences.

However, the effectiveness of service delivery is hampered more, due to the greater anxiety provoking reaction that can be stimulated by independent and disciplined radicals and cynical and specialist oriented bureaucrats. To be effectively service oriented, requires sharing values, sharing mistakes and sharing best practice. In essence, people must feel comfortable to enter into dialogue about how to address the challenge of meeting the needs of different client groupings. Independent, disciplined radicals and cynical bureaucrats are unlikely to generate the warmth and comfort necessary for sharing. Specialist bureaucrats are equally unlikely to appreciate and hence stimulate broader ranging conversation, broad ranging in terms of topics and equally in terms of discussing issues, and also bringing to the surface the feelings of those public servants providing service. The radicals and bureaucrats are likely to be seen, and are seen, as not only inhibiting conversation on topics, but also as not stimulating catharsis, so that people can air their experiences of relating to service recipients.

Similar trends are identified for IT adoption in the organization. The reason that innovative radicals promote the adoption of innovative IT skills by staff and management, in contrast to independent team players who support the adoption of basic/adoptive skills, is that the team players are not sufficiently robust to stand apart from their context, and push for staff to further develop themselves. The fact that for IT to make a positive impact on the organization requires discipline, impartiality and independence from all three leader orientations indicates that, clarity of thought, focus, stand apart analysis of the organization and support for staff and management are necessary elements of the managerial input in leading change through using IT. Adopting the behaviour of disciplined bureaucrats and independent team players may introduce the necessary focus but not the support for staff and management nor the 'stand back-analytical' view of how progress is being made.

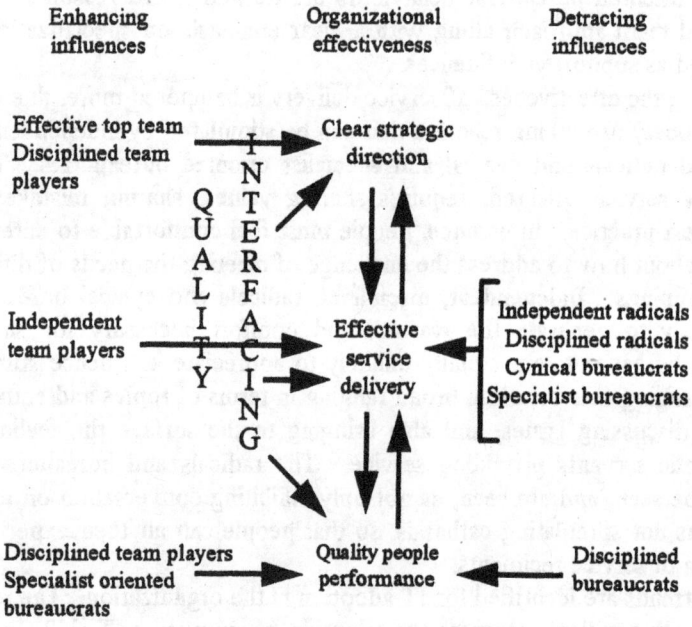

Figure 8.2 Leadership for effectiveness (APS)

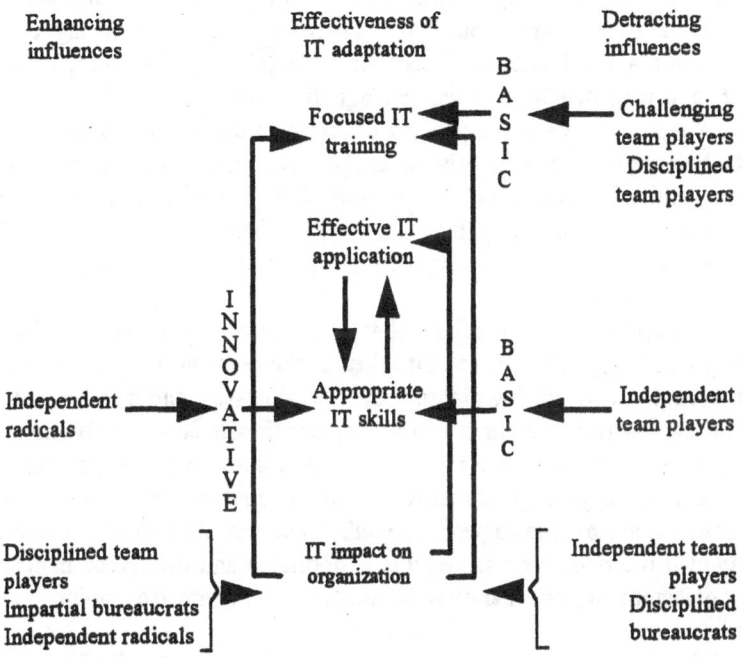

Figure 8.3 Leadership for IT adaptation (APS)

Similar results have been identified for the private sector (Figure 8.4). Whereas in order to attain effectiveness of performance at an organizational level, different approaches are viewed as acceptable, in order to attain clarity of strategic direction, to have an efficient running organization as a result of managing the structures of the enterprise well, and to have people who are high performers, a top team(s) which focuses on business issues and achieves openness of dialogue is important. Also desired are consistent managers who behave as drivers, disciplined politicians and disciplined performance oriented strategists and who display they can manage diversity.

What are seen to damage the process of strategic debate are managers who adopt the behaviour of cynical drivers, as their over critical and more negative comments inhibit others from freely conversing and exploring actions. Further, managers who are inconsistent in their behaviour are identified as poor role models in terms of quality of interfacing and for managing well the structure of the organization.

The private sector results highlight that if the process of strategic debate is managed positively, with due account taken of the relevant people by drawing on their strengths and not highlighting their weaknesses, and if the quality of interfacing across the structures of the organization is consistently high, far better levels of performance are extracted from staff and management. In fact, the clearer the strategic direction, the better managed the structure, the more motivated are people to perform well. However, that positive cycle can be damaged if the debate on strategy is undermined and the senior managers are not consistent in their handling of others at key interface points in the structure.

The results from both the private sector and the APS, highlight that appropriate transactional and transformational approaches are desired and workable in the management and leadership of an organization. As with the APS, a similar analysis of the distribution of transactional and transformational orientations indicate that the strategists fall more into the transformational camp, the politicians more into the transactional camp and the drivers straddling both, with the potential to damage daily interactions (transactions) and hence not building people's confidence to enter into transformational challenges. Equally, inappropriate transactional and transformational behaviours are identified as damaging to the organization.

Hence, the intervening variable is context! What is needed within particular contexts? What then happens to an organization if inappropriate behaviours become the norm? Analysis is undertaken exploring how damaging interactions are accommodated.

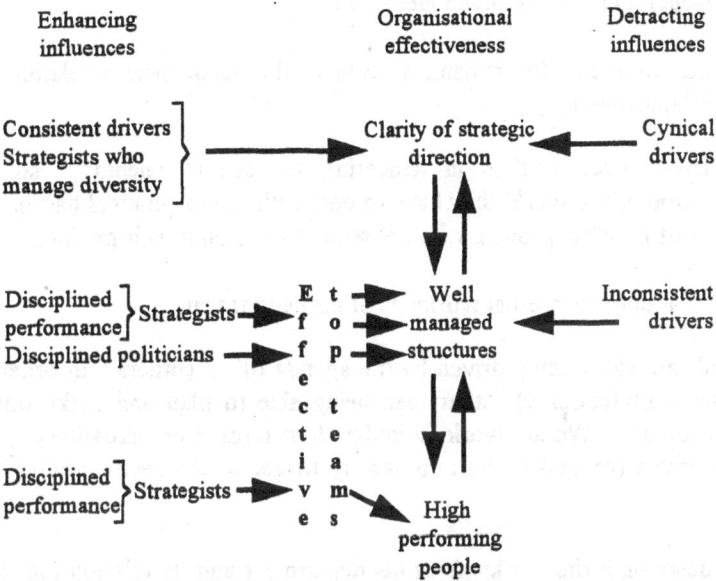

Figure 8.4 Private sector: leadership for effectiveness

Accommodating negative interactions

> I think there is tension, because of the Deputy Secretary. Mind you, he feels it's hopeless, so he can't cope. I think the Deputy Secretary has to strike that balance (i.e. between policy generation and management of a department), but with so much interference?

SES talking about his department, as well as the department's relationship with other departments.

> Most have never worked in delivering services to clients ... so the construction of the world they have to deal with ... is a political battlefield, with lots of fictional groups, who are seen as defending their position.

SES talking about the internal workings of his department.

> We find ourselves being driven by the agenda of .... (others - in order to maintain confidentiality) rather than being able to plan and make things happen for us ... We are working under short term stress situations ... we are not given (or make) the opportunity to get to the secondary/tertiary issues.

Manager describing the workings of his department and its relationship with other departments in the APS.

> Well I'll be honest with you. Any one of these guys (other SESs in other departments) could just screw you, often because they feel like it! Me, I play the game and when I get a chance, I just pay one of them back.

SES describing other SESs.

The above comments highlight a negative view of leadership. In keeping with the above comments, Table 8.1 indicates that the majority of comments referring to changes that are required in the APS, highlight changes of leadership. Yet, Tables 8.2 and 8.3 showed contrasting requirements for improvements in leadership and, furthermore, Figures 8.2, 8.3, and 8.4 highlighted that different leaders' behaviours can be equally effective. The concern is: does the behaviour adopted by senior management meet the contextual requirements of the organization?

Table 8.12
Subordinate managers' views of the top team

	As individuals	As team
Positive	66	33
Negative	34	67

Despite the negative comments made, Table 8.12 above highlights the comments made by SESs and SOs on their views of the top management of the APS. As individuals, top managers are seen in a mostly positive light (66 per cent of total comments made) with statements as 'my boss is intelligent, experienced, supportive, effective and focused,' being repeatedly made. However, the very same respondents offer substantially contrasting views of top management when bosses are assessed on working in a team. Sixty seven per cent of comments place top management in a negative light, with comments as, 'incapable, do not work as a team, destructive, self seeking' and particularly unkind comments as 'keystone cops', being made.

The evidence strongly points to quality of dialogue and team work being considered as substantially deficient in the APS. Whatever the capabilities of individual managers, the study results strongly suggest that the inappropriate behaviours outlined in Figures 8.2, 8.3 and 8.4 are the reality that is experienced in the APS. Hence, what do intelligent, experienced, reasonable managers do in circumstances of continuous damaging strain?

The findings of this study emphasize that inhibitive and unproductive interactions become a norm. In effect, managers in an attempt to appropriately function, revert to adopting the more negative behaviours commonly associated with power/politic interplays. Through continuous exposure to a deteriorating working environment, being political at work becomes a skill and an end in itself. After a while, managers may take pride in their capability to manage, be responsive and be proactive in the internal political game. It is relatively easy to come to believe that 'playing politics at work' is productive. In essence, managers will eventually believe that becoming proficient at power/political interplays predominantly moves agendas forward and contributes to the betterment of the organization. That mistaken assumption in turn, may become a belief that competence at power/political interplays is an attribute of transformational leadership.

As highlighted in Figure 2.1 (Chapter 2), power/politics falls into the transactional camp of leadership. However, it is possible to see why proficiency at internal power/politics can be misinterpreted as transformational leadership. First, Figure 2.1 highlighted power/politics as being recognized by theoreticians as a higher order form of transactional leadership. In essence, managers who adopt such behaviours have to consider context, how to influence people, for what reason, and how to work within the comfort zones of others, whilst manipulating agendas and pursuing alternative agendas. Second, it was equally shown in Figure 2.1 that linkage can be made between the concept of power and the concept of the 'Great Man', a perspective that is firmly placed in the transformational camp of the born to be great leader.

Hence, 'higher order' transactional leadership interactions can be mistakenly viewed as an element of transformational leadership and by so doing can become a way of life. Managers can come to believe that they are doing something transformationally worthwhile, when they are not. Hence, the behaviours adopted by management may be recognized as negative and damaging to the development of people and the organization, but if someone dares to express that, top managers do not accept it and may react punitively towards the person expressing such an observation.

Accommodation of alternative philosophies of leadership can be achieved, if it is recognized which appropriate behaviours are required in different contexts. However, to adopt inappropriate behaviours can lead managers to believe that differences of philosophy and style are undesired and the only way to counteract negative circumstances is through the adoption of power/political behaviours. Nothing could be further from the truth, even when the managers involved are seen as, and are, mature, responsive, responsible as individuals.

Part of breaking out of inappropriate philosophy and practice, is to recognize the damaging consequences of maintaining current modes of action. Part is also to recognize that a second paradox of leadership exists and that if both paradoxes are inappropriately handled, especially in organizations that have or are about to experience downsizing, then substantial damage to the fabric of the organization can occur. Appreciating the nature of both paradoxes is likely to then lead to more positive practice.

Paradox of intent

Why should an organization do anything different? One basic reason is to promote advantage for the communities and markets being served. In order to gain advantage, particular strategies have to be identified which take account of current challenges, the context of the organization at that moment in time, expected pressures, challenges and demands and where the organization should ideally position itself now and for the future, in order to enhance its value. Within such a scenario, considerable differences of view do exist concerning current circumstances, future developments and present and future purpose of the organization. To state the obvious, strategy and leadership are intimately linked, but these terms hold different meanings for different people. Such differences are captured and examined in an analysis of 'vertical' and 'horizontal' synergies. It is the particular combination, varying by circumstances, of vertical and horizontal synergies that gives strategy meaning and can equally highlight the differences between leaders.

Vertical synergies are concerned with economics, costs, structures of organizations, overheads; namely those aspects of organization that need constant attention and curtailment in order that the organization can operate efficiently. A vertically integrated organization is one that is economically well structured and administratively efficient in order to meet its key objectives. Clarity and cohesion of view emerge on issues of vertical integration through reliance on data. Is this organization too expensive? Do we have the cost/overhead base needed to respond to current and future demands? Do we have too many people? Such questions require information in order to support their resolution. If nothing else, top management can make unilateral decisions and then apply financial and organizational levers to ensure that the organization remains on course. On issues of vertical synergy, authoritarian oriented decision making works, despite people's dislike for such an approach, because once direction is set, too much debate and reconsideration can be disastrous in terms of not clearly focusing and hence not maximizing on the investment.

In contrast, horizontal synergies are concerned with issues of quality, being responsive to external needs, providing service and being sympathetic to the needs of clients and other agencies and to staff and management internally. In effect, horizontal synergies require a consultative management style, namely effective team work, open dialogue and an attitude of sharing and cooperation, all so as to be responsive to changing external demands.

Vertical synergies work better under centralized management control. Horizontal synergy promotion needs devolution of structures, the empowerment of people and reliance on informality rather than formality, and clarity of jobs and roles.

Therein lies the paradox (Figure 8.5). How can one control costs and prune expenses, and at the same time promote an internal environment of openness, trust and cooperation? How can one, as a senior manager, say to a subordinate or colleague, 'Give me feedback on what our clients need even if it is critical of me', and at the same time expect that person to freely respond when they fear that the very same senior manager who is asking the question, as that person may remove their job within the next financial year?

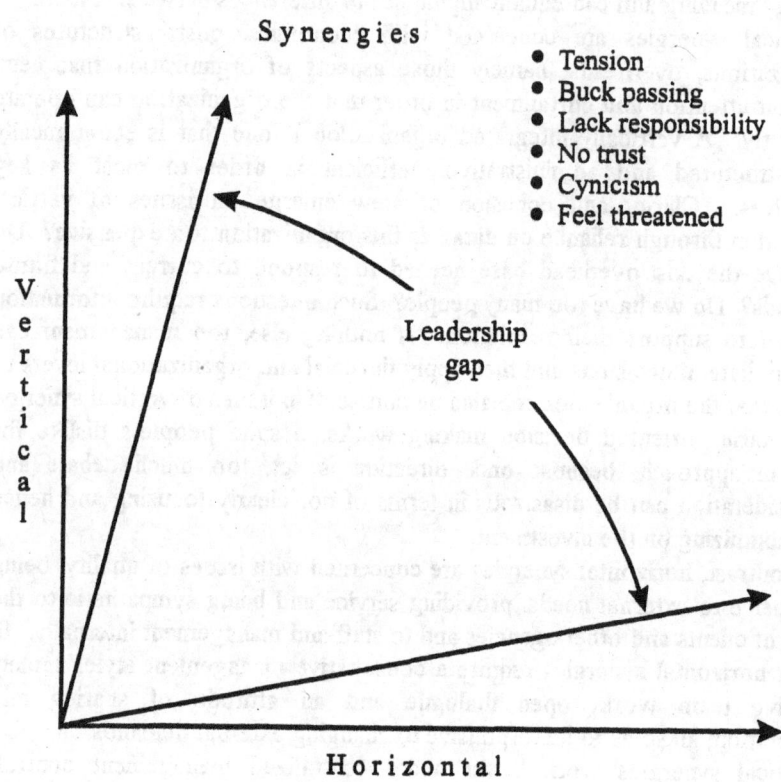

Figure 8.5 1990s leadership: a paradox

It is possible to effectively but separately lead for vertical and horizontal synergy strategies. However, to lead for both, coupled with an inability to effectively interact as a senior management team, promotes for a gap of leadership, a gap that may be filled by strife, division, tension, fundamental difference of view concerning the future, buck passing responsibility upwards, and feeling no sense of responsibility for one's leadership role. The tensions highlighted in Tables 8.2 and 8.3 of, namely, a need for openness as well as a need for stronger and decisive leadership; a need for more caring and yet a need for a stronger CEO; a need for greater focus and clarity and yet a need for more consultation and listening, are symptoms of the uncomfortable juxtaposition between vertical and horizontal synergies. Further, if management are unable to jointly and cohesively address such challenges, through effective teamwork, as shown to be the case in the previous section, then a gap of leadership may occur.

The phenomenon of the leadership gap is an experience common to top managers of both private and public sector organizations. Which organization today can afford to promote only vertical or only horizontal synergies? Which organization today can afford to continue with dysfunctionality at top team level? Very few - gaining advantage in markets or communities requires the pursuit of both vertical and horizontal synergies championed and nurtured by high performing teams, with a strong sense of cabinet responsibility and an openness of dialogue.

Aftermath of downsizing

Either for reasons of costs or for flexibility of response to client and/or market needs, downsizing has become a common experience for both private and public sector organizations. It is rarely reported that downsizing is a supportive, pleasant experience. Most senior managers tasked with downsizing report the unsatisfactory and disruptive nature of the exercise. Even a well conducted downsizing exercise is one where the demotivation of staff and management who leave and those who stay, and the disruption to the organization, are considerable. Disruption to varying degrees is an outcome of downsizing. The requirement then is for effective leadership to remotivate staff and management and refocus the organization towards meeting its newly shaped goals, objectives and mission.

Research work conducted at Cranfield School of Management (Doherty, 1994) identifies two phenomena to overcome in leading downsized, reconfigured organizations: the survivor syndrome, and the management support vacuum (Figure 8.6).

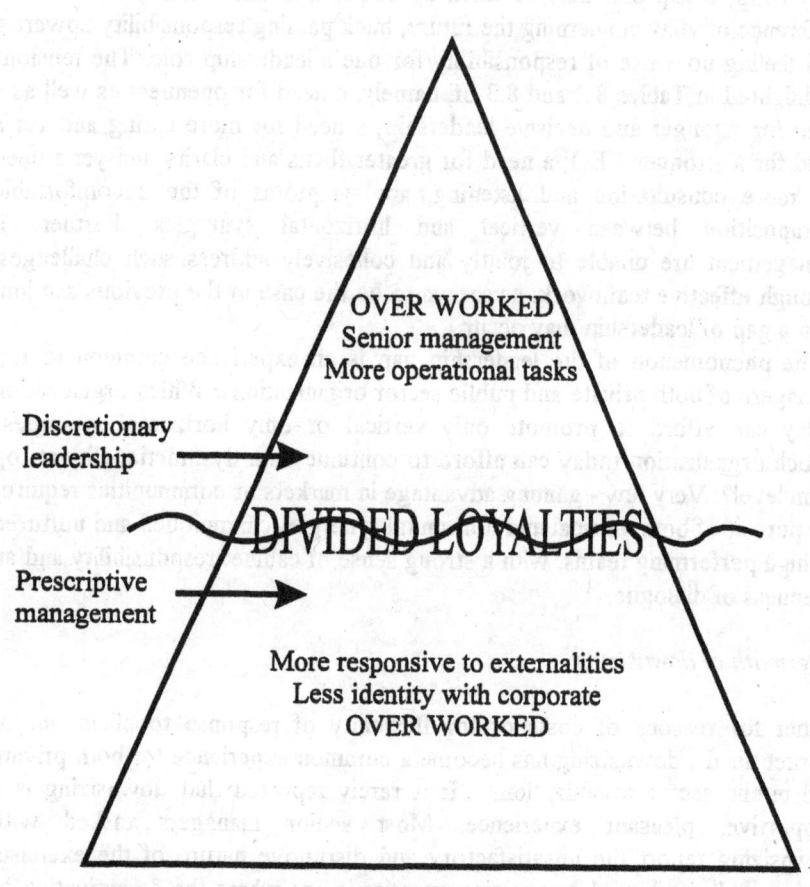

Figure 8.6 Aftermath of downsizing

- *Survivor syndrome:* The survivor syndrome refers to the shell shocked nature of those who survive the downsizing experience and their accompanying loss of confidence arising from what may seem (and may actually be) the arbitrary nature of job related termination without reference to ability, contribution, loyalty and years of experience. In many people's minds is the question, 'Am I next?' The feelings of insecurity and loss of confidence could inhibit any initiative being shown in case mistakes are made, resulting in the individual's job being terminated. Further, feelings of guilt may accompany the survivors as to why they are in full employment when, in their eyes, valued and trusted colleagues have been forced to leave. The net effect on staff and lower and middle level management is one of lack of trust in senior management and a substantial reduction of feelings of loyalty to the organization. If the organization has had to downsize for good reason, for example, to reduce its cost base or so that it can be that much more flexible to compete on horizontal synergy driven strategies, the leadership challenge is to recapture the goodwill of staff and management to provide an acceptable level of quality of service. Whether trust of management and feelings of loyalty to the organization can be recaptured, is dubious. The challenge is to promote effective performance without necessarily retaining the supportive feelings of the past.

- *Management support vacuum:* Downsizing initiatives tend to reduce the levels of management more in the middle of the organizational hierarchy. If equally accompanied by a move for decentralization in order to enhance flexibility and quality of response to meet client, community and customer needs, the result is that the number of discretionary leadership roles increases, but are filled by people who often lack the experience and maturity to perform effectively as leaders. Prior to downsizing, the very same newly appointed leaders in a more centralized organization would have been matured, on the job, by their progress through the traditional managerial ranks. Hence, the cohesiveness and sharing a sense of cabinet responsibility that would previously have taken place naturally, in the new organization are likely to be undermined, as entering into the leadership strata are individuals who are emotionally ill prepared to work as effective colleagues in senior executive teams. However, the individuals will rightly exercise their leader discretionary choice built into their role. Communicating the mission of the organization in a consistent manner and meaningfully displaying cabinet responsibility internally to staff and lower level management and externally to key stakeholders, so that all relevant parties can identify with and trust these initiatives, is likely to become an evermore fraught process.

An additional complication is that through downsizing, no shared agreement may exist as to who supports whom, even on matters concerning operational tasks. Senior management in the past may have delegated to middle management, tasks of an operational, managerial or administrative nature (Zemke, 1988). Such arrangements may no longer be possible due to the reconfiguration of the structure and the removal of jobs which provided substantial support. Hence, senior leaders may be left with a far greater task load, having less time to devote to strategic challenges, especially that of communication, at a time when the need for effective and visible communication is at its greatest.

Reducing the leadership gap

The challenge of leadership requires maximizing the synergies whilst attempting to constantly minimize potentially damaging strains. Those exposed to such stresses, know only too well what it means to live within an environment of contradiction and paradox, as has been seen only too clearly in this report when examining the respondents' views as to the impact of splits of visioning and poor quality dialogue on individuals, teams and the APS as a whole. The very people who have to manage their way through such challenges are the experts of their own problems. Hence, further insight is not required; actioning the insights that individuals hold about themselves, and their constituents, is required.

The following recommendations which emphasize both on and off the job development are in keeping with the spirit of the Karpin report except in one key area.[2] Karpin recognized that the challenge for greater economic prosperity requires effective leadership. Although leaders are identified as equally being enablers and coaches, a theme pursued in this report, Karpin does not refer to context. In this report, it is emphasized that universal guidelines towards effective leadership are only partly of value. Fundamental is to improve leadership capabilities by taking into account the dynamics of different organizational contexts. Only through this way can sense be made of the contradictory sets of statements identified in Tables 8.2 and 8.3. Only by responding to the demands of contexts can sense be made of the types of statements that appear in these tables, and Table 8.12.

Hence, the on and off the job recommendations made in this report take into account the mix of leadership philosophies that are identified in the APS and the context of the organization, both within a scenario of downsizing, decentralization and responsiveness to meeting client and community needs. In terms of on the job development, six key strategies are identified as mechanisms for reducing the gap of leadership and coping with the aftermath of downsizing.

- *Think issue, not territory*: Today's reality is that top managers are attending meetings, hearing agreement on key issues, walking out of meetings recognizing that commitment is not forthcoming, knowing that the agreements reached are worthless. Most have the insight as to what is happening around them but find it difficult to action such insight because of the personal discomfort experienced in addressing such problems. The first step to overcoming such difficulties of dialogue is to concentrate on organization wide issues and not be driven by territorial concerns.

    ... people who can learn ... have a broader perspective which they bring to bear on the analyses and contemplation of a problem. They can actually think about a range of options ... you can see the richness of their ideas.

    SES

    If the example provided by top management is that of being able to take an overview of a situation, such a perspective is more likely to emerge from staff and management lower down the organization. However, if the example from the top is 'preserve one's territory', that pattern of behaviour is equally likely to be replicated lower down.

- *Promote the qualities of leadership:* Apart from intellectually recognizing that need for a helicopter view, the challenge to emotionally accept and address sensitivities and concerns, is considerable. Two words capture the qualities for effective leadership, 'maturity' and 'wisdom'. Maturity can be defined as the capability to invite, receive and handle well, feedback. Wisdom can be defined as the capability to identify appropriate pathways forward when direction is obscure(d). In effect, the robustness and courage to stand back, recognize the nature of the current dynamics within the organization and then identify the best ways forward where guidance seldom exists, are the nature of the qualities of leadership. Part of that process is getting others to talk when relationships may be strained. On the job experience, discussions, mentoring and counselling can help develop such qualities. In effect, the individual is being taken from a state of professional skill to a higher order state of trusting their own judgement as to how to progress within demanding circumstances. The apt combination of intellectual, professional and 'street skills' forms the foundation for the personal qualities of leadership.

- *Get the dialogue right*: As stated, within any larger organization setting, differences, diversity and tension are normality. Differences should not be elevated to the status of a worrying problem, but should be kept at the level of irritant. Keeping irritants as irritants and not allowing for the emergence of undermining constraints, requires the establishment of a common language within the organization. That starts with a common language at the top. The question is, do senior management sufficiently respect themselves and the responsibilities of their roles to stand above daily frustrations and allow for the emergence of a process which helps them approach and meet current and future concerns? Process, how we talk to each other, is as important as content, what we talk about. The skill is to stimulate a debate in a manner that is workable to the key managers of the organization. Promoting a 'grit' in dialogue has to be matched with maintaining a level of comfort that allows for conversations to continue.[3] High quality dialogue needs to be crafted as much as any new service or product.

- *Get the interfaces right:* Making complex structures work is dependent on the quality of interfacing within the organization. Effective interfacing is a crucial lever to making strategies and policies work. If such practice is not held dear at the top, then distortion of policy during the phases of implementation is an expected and natural outcome. Hence, it is important to portray a consistency of message, so that in a disciplined way, important initiatives are effectively cascaded down the organization. The question is, do the managers as the key interface points in the structure recognize their degree of responsibility in terms of consistency, discipline and cabinet responsibility? The Cranfield results for both the civil servants, health services executives and the private sector indicate yes, if those managers feel themselves to be responsible members of the executive. Having clarified who is and is not in the broader executive, then such feelings of responsibility are inculcated by the setting of ground rules concerning dialogue and behaviour. Such ground rules are better promoted within a culture of learning.

- *Promote learning:* The policy and organizational agendas are set at the top. Promoting positive processes and context agendas requires nurturing a learning culture, sensitive to different environments and promoting the feeling of confidence to seek varying but cohesive ways through diversity and challenge. Such learning is seen to involve the following elements,

A   Be responsive to feedback. The freedom to engage in a conversation concerning continuous improvement emerges through having established a feedback culture.

B   Respect meetings. Executive work is conducted at meetings. Meetings are the forum where current issues and ways forward are aired and clarified, namely processes that are effective precursors to positive decision making and implementation. Making best use of meetings requires respecting the meetings forum. Learning to effectively conduct oneself at meetings demands a degree of flexibility. What issues should be raised and when? How should issues be raised? Do colleagues need to be informally forewarned and prepared so that they can better enter into the debate? The flexibility to think issue and process assists considerably in reaching resolution and ownership of that resolution, by all involved.

C   Behave the message. A member of staff or lower level management hearing one thing but then witnessing quite different behaviour from the manager speaking the words, does little for trust, drive and motivation. Winning the trust and commitment of staff and management relies heavily on top management behaving in a manner that is conducive to promoting the best practice they require others to display. Senior management, irrespective of the size and complexity of their executive, have to maintain a discipline to ensure for full participation of best practice behaviour.

D   Promote a networking culture. In addition to good example from the top, an additional finding of the Cranfield surveys towards promoting sound strategic and operational relationships, is effective networking. Building a network of relationships is an essential aspect of strategic management. The process takes time, requires patience and is achieved by displaying discipline, consistency and honesty at meetings and showing humanity and concern outside meetings. Effective dialoguing needs trusting relationships which are evolved over time. For any public servant, political intervention could disrupt job placement, but similar dynamics exist in private sector organizations whereby issues of profitability, meeting cost and revenue targets could place a question mark over any senior/middle manager's future. People in both sectors can just as easily lose their jobs. Experiencing vulnerability over job tenure is normal. The real question is how do senior managers see their jobs: as a series of tasks, as meeting particular managerial requirements, as hanging on to their job, or as leader of an organization, whereby the fabric of the organization and the morale of its employees are as important as meeting targets? The practice of promoting a networking culture is an active display of leadership.

- *Promote cabinet responsibility*: Do the members of the top team display that they desire cabinet responsibility in terms of how they behave rather than what they say? If certain senior colleagues disagree with a new initiative, do they fully challenge and debate the issue at meetings, or do they undermine and block the venture, displaying their resistance to the rest of the organization, and/or even the outside world, but outside the meeting? Is the greatest fear one has, one's own colleagues? If yes, cabinet responsibility does not exist. Where horizontal synergy strategies are being pursued, full acceptance of cabinet responsibility is vital. Staff, lower level management and external stakeholders need to witness the active support of all of the top team for key policies and initiatives. It is only through the communication of good example that demanding new ways of doing are accepted and cascaded down the organization. Attaining cabinet responsibility is a two step process. First, a conscious decision needs to be made; do we really want cabinet responsibility and intend to practice it or not? Second, its continuation is the result of having promoted a feedback culture. Could one, for example, face a colleague and say, 'You said you were going to do this and you have done the opposite!'? Only when a quality of dialogue which allows for such comments to be made and is seen as positive, does full cabinet responsibility exist. Otherwise, one is playing with words. Attaining and maintaining cabinet responsibility is a fraught process, but it does have its rewards. Full acceptance of cabinet responsibility provides for the 'grit' which stimulates positive debate as opposed to inhibition and back room conversation.

Direction and purpose: promoting the mission

It is more difficult to say that we the senior managers of the department have created the vision. But the mission and values of what we are about is up to us.

SES

I think as a department we are very professional. We are recognized outside as being very professional. I think the level of integrity is very high and I think ethical standards right down from the top are very good in terms of equal opportunity.

SES

I see my job as mainly articulating the vision, and then throwing it across government, the states and into the private sector. ... I am not here to prevent people from doing things. I am trying to add value across the government ... we empower to get departments together and I provide the broad mandate to do it.

SES

Well, everyone would say in this department that there is no vision, no leadership. So the people who are keen, who are bright, who want to contribute, they are the resources that are being wasted. People have got to a point where they feel as though there is not a lot of point in hanging around. People become dependent. They become cynical. I think we are creating the most awful legacy.

SES

Different views were expressed concerning the terms vision and mission. Certain SESs commented that the vision of their department or of the APS as a whole was not wholly their responsibility, as ministerial influence played a considerable part in determining the vision of the department/service in question. Others highlighted the term 'mission' as meaningful. Whatever is meant by the terms 'vision' and 'mission', the reality of promoting a set of values, improving standards and motivating and guiding staff to ever higher levels of performance, is recognized as a prime responsibility of the public servant leadership of the APS.

The survey respondents highlight that the direction and purpose of the department, irrespective of the words used, are fundamental to leadership in the APS. Overall, broader agreement concerning values, standards and conduct converges around the term 'mission', which will be the word used to highlight the need for attaining meaningful direction and purpose.

Promoting a mission is a primary contribution of leadership. To not do so is likely to allow for organizational chaos, short termism, in-fighting and a paradoxical empowerment of middle managers who may fill the gap of leadership but equally promote their own agendas, thereby adding to the confusion. Hence, the argument for creating a meaningful mission is powerful and in order to do so, the following two steps are highlighted.

- *Involve all of the top team*: Applying some or all of the leader best practice behaviours will help build a team displaying greater cohesion of purpose and consistency of behaviour. Equally, individual managers are likely to become more proficient and confident to work as a team. Against this background, quality of relationships is likely to improve as is the quality of dialogue. It is quality of dialogue that allows for relevant interchange of ideas and views. It is under these positive circumstances that people begin to express themselves as to the qualities they would wish to see in their department and the shortfalls that currently need addressing.

    In addition to evolving the confidence and skills for high quality interactions, consideration also needs to be given to membership, namely, who are in the top team. Those occupying discretionary leader roles need to be involved in the generation of the mission, irrespective of whether they sit on the relevant senior management committee(s). These are the people whose identity with the mission is crucial to its communication and acceptance throughout the organization and externally by key stakeholders. Hence, a crucial question to answer is, who is in the broader top team and who needs to be involved in 'working up the mission', in order for a meaningful mission to be operationalized?

- *Establish the platform*: Working towards improving the quality of dialogue is the first step towards establishing a basis for working towards a meaningful mission. However, senior managers do not have to wait to first establish a positive dialogue to embark on a process of identifying and communicating the mission of the organization. The mission generation process can be the 'kick off' for a more positive dialogue, an 'opening up' experience whereby the individuals involved would learn to better interact with each other and nurture a feedback culture in the organization.

    The second step to promoting a meaningful mission is to create amongst senior management a common experience of change and thereby build or rebuild new milestones concerning progress. Once a more common experience has been achieved, people will be more willing to, together, look to the future. In order to come near to generating a common experience, it would be important to first build a common experience of changing elements of the present before starting to influence the future. Focusing on potential in the here and now, can generate new energy, new beliefs and a new motivation to address the future and desire to change. It is obvious that this experience is contributory to influencing future agendas. It is a matter of finding ways to change elements of the here and now. One assumption in building up the skills for addressing the future is that time is not linear. Basically, the past is in the present as is the future. Many decision makers however act along the lines of a linear concept of time. The reality is that all have to carry the past into the future. By emphasizing the reasons for past and present success, new doors into the future can be opened.

From the comments made on questionnaire and in interview with APS respondents, it is unfortunate that so many experience the past, and even the present, as an unpleasant burden. This experience seems to be limiting the exploration of new possibilities. The missioning process gives senior management the chance to discover a new balance by finding new ways to behave through deciding what is needed now and how to move forward for tomorrow.

Improvement in dialogue, building a different logic for the team and even redesigning management's role, are experiences which are likely to stretch people. Part of the process of generating a common platform will involve a certain degree of reorientation by individuals. The messy stage of refocusing is an experience that needs to be undergone. This disruptive stage is likely to be resisted, as there exist elements of the present that are comfortable and which people do not wish to release. For the APS, the presence of a relatively performance oriented culture of organization, supportive of humanistic values but only marginally contributing to effective organizational performance, is counter balanced by a leadership that the respondents recognize as considerably damaging. Will improvements in leader behaviour necessarily take place? Experience and the research results suggest it is unlikely, unless senior management are willing to experience a change of 'logic' (mind set).

Helping senior managers through the emotionally challenging experience of changing mind set is vital. Workshops, counselling, mentoring and follow through, considerably assist the process. However, these approaches, in themselves, do little. The senior management have to commit to work towards establishing a mission for their organization and from there on, utilize qualitative techniques and the services of third parties to assist them through the more traumatic stage of entering into the new logic. The more senior management willingly go through the uncomfortable stages of change, the more likely these managers will open their minds, focus their energies and get themselves out of the logic where the context decides the ways forward for the person. The emerging shared platform of a new logic and experience, will stimulate the individuals to find alternative ways to influence their context. By so doing, the executive will learn how to lead change, as opposed to their situation leading them.

The emerging mission may be symbolized in a single word, a single sentence, a single image, but can only be really communicated through action. Written documents have no real importance. The emerging mission of the organization has to be behaved, so that lower level staff and management can clearly see that senior management share a common reference point which influences their action in providing purpose and direction to departments/the APS.

Developing the attributes of leadership

The steps towards generating a meaningful mission and utilizing the best practice behaviours outlined, share one common theme, 'context'. These recommendations are meaningful if the reality of the context of the organization is taken fully into account. In developing the attributes of leadership through off the job experiences, the same issue arises, help people to understand and effectively interact within different contexts. In this way can the themes of, be participative and yet provide strong decisive leadership, be respected as an individual but disliked as a member of the senior management team (Tables 8.2, 8.3, 8.12) be understood, accommodated and purposefully enacted.

Off the job leadership development provides opportunity for those already in a leader role, or for the high quality middle level managers, or individuals leading particular project groups or those displaying potential for responsibility and senior office, to explore and develop their leadership capabilities within a controlled and structured setting.

A programme of strategic leadership should expose its participants to the following inputs.

- *Resolving conflicting agendas*: Roles which are strategic and of leader status are ones where the role incumbents need to provide an identity as to the nature and purpose of the role; they need to provide a vision for that role. In essence, the individual needs to state what they are trying to do, why and towards what ends. The clarification and pursuit of agendas which take into account current and future circumstances, is a necessary process in the establishment of sense and meaning to leadership roles. What complicates the situation is that the number of agendas being pursued could potentially be as many as the number of discretionary roles and as varied as the personalities who occupy them. Hence, in any one strategic forum, it is likely that a number of strategic agendas may be promoted. Recognizing the reality of how key senior managers relate to each other and how they communicate mixed messages to the rest of the organization, whilst pursuing alternate visions and direction, is a reality that needs to be recognized and accommodated. Living in a world of conflicting realities whilst still having to manage the organization is a prospect that most are likely to face in the role of leadership. Once such a reality is accommodated, the confidence to begin to realign varying strategic options can emerge.

- *Conceptualizing restructuring*: Structuring work groups, departments, integrating and merging with other work groups or departments internally or with other agencies externally, are challenges of reconfiguring organization structures. The ability to visualize the form and shape of the desired organization, and to promote the appropriate quality of interfacing in newly designed structure, is a conceptual challenge. Being knowledgeable as to the different blueprints of organization structure, their strengths and weaknesses and how to configure an organization to achieve its purpose, are skills which can be developed. What is the purpose of the structure and do the key managers share compatible purposes? What are the design needs of a command structure? What are the attributes and people based requirements of a more interfacing structure? Under what circumstances should strong consideration be given to a top down as opposed to a bottom or middle up programme of change? Under what circumstances does structural change planning need to consider the morale of people, their trust in senior management, to the same degree as the details of structure and roles? These considerations need to be addressed as they are vital components of strategic leadership development.

- *Rituals, routine and culture*: Introducing change, especially of structures, impacts on the culture of the organization which in turn affects the rituals and routines that have become a part of most people's everyday work experience. The meaning and symbolism of everyday, recurring rituals and routines in people's lives and the power of such experiences to inhibit or enhance change, are additional considerations to structural reform. How to introduce new ways of doing, which will then consolidate as positive symbols of progress through enacted daily rituals and routines, are leadership considerations. Effective follow through on key initiatives, the nurture of individuals and work teams and the consolidation of change through new ways of working, enhance the prospects of a new forward looking, positively oriented culture being established in the organization. As so aptly highlighted in Chapter 7, positive leadership drives effective organizational performance, promotes a new culture and supports the emergence, internally, of more shared performance related attitudes. Although a positively oriented culture enhances the development of people, any programme of leadership needs to emphasize that positive leadership promotes performance related cultures and not vice versa, a point that is often intellectually appreciated, but emotionally disregarded.

- *Enhancing vision capability*: The Cranfield surveys highlight visioning as a key element of corporate leadership. What is visioning? The following are relevant questions posed for senior managers in the APS to address.

    A   What is the shape and configuration of key client, community and stakeholder groups?
    B   What is required now, and further required in the future, to service these user groups?
    C   What are the needs of important suppliers/distributors and how can such understanding be used to further nurture the relationship between them and the relevant departments in the APS?
    D   How prepared are various departments/functions/project groups to improve performance?
    E   How prepared are the various departments/functions/project groups to cooperate and more effectively interface, than is presently the case?
    F   What levels of expenditure are required to effectively provide for quality of services now and in the future?

The answers to these questions require an understanding of and access to details concerning the management of departments and units. It is through a detailed understanding of the expectations and requirements of stakeholder groups, the behaviour of suppliers, the needs and likely demands of external agencies, the likely life cycle of any service or provision, the level and speed of responsiveness required by different client/community groupings and the degree to which other agencies require supervision, that meaningful conclusions can be formed as to the level of expenditure required and the cost of service which needs to be taken into account. To form a view as to the size of the cost base to be accounted for, how departments and units need to be structured and how to position new and current services for them to be utilized by communities to the maximum, requires a detailed intimacy with the organization and equally an ability to extrapolate, from this detailed view, appropriate ways forward. Hence, the senior manager's ability to be concerned with detail and broader debate, with intimate day to day understanding of the functioning of the organization and yet see broader but realistic pictures as to how to proceed, are the distinguishing features of visioning. The Cranfield studies highlight that it is from relevant details that meaningful visions/missions are formed. In essence, effective visioning involves the capability for broad conceptualization, whilst having a discipline for, and an interest in, detail.

The Cranfield surveys equally emphasize that the capabilities required for discretionary leadership are developed and developable. These capabilities are not genetic/born with phenomena. Helping individuals recognize their current ability towards managing detail and broader extrapolation, can be achieved through feedback from questionnaire based exploration. This feedback can then be used as the basis for helping each person develop their capabilities in terms of greater discipline to effectively address day to day details and/or enter into debate over broader issues.

- *Ways towards reconciliation.* The APS respondents were asked:

   If the members of the top team hold different views as to the future direction of the organization, are such differences reconcilable?

   APS/Cranfield survey question.

   Of the 'yes' responses (i.e. differences are reconcilable), which accounted for 73 per cent of responses to the question, the greater majority indicate that improvements can be achieved by the way people are managed and also by changing their views as to the requirements of leadership. In effect, the respondents highlight that most leadership tensions within the organization are not the result of deeply held, fixed views but more the incumbents' inabilities to effectively address the processes of negotiating towards an acceptable shared perspective, further supporting the view that transactional and transformational leadership philosophies can sit side by side.

   Five steps to enhancing each manager's abilities to effectively work towards the resolution of differences and tensions are identified below.

- *Strengthening*: Strengthening individuals to fully partake in a process of reconciliation of differences is a crucial step. Coaching and mentoring individuals to greater 'robustness' enhance their ability to enter into and maintain dialogue. Part of the process is clarifying the issues dividing people. Part of the process equally involves venting feelings as to how others in the organization have behaved. Both elements of the process are a necessary catharsis, so that all involved can appreciate how deeply individuals have experienced the frustrations of interacting with their colleagues. However, the force of comments made could cause offence. At the receiving end, some may emotionally retreat, troubled by the comments made and as a result lose confidence or begin to display dependency on others. Others may retaliate aggressively, inflaming an already tense relationship. Strengthening individuals to embark on a journey of reconciliation requires them appreciating the dynamics of reconciliation and the impact that process is likely to have on them. Equally important is evolving a robustness to effectively work through aggressive feedback. The more focused and pertinent can be the feedback offered on a programme of development, the more prepared is the individual likely to be for a circumstance of negotiating reconciliation of conflicting visions or improving tense relationships.

- *Impact awareness*: In addition to helping individuals become more robust, feedback also helps a person to appreciate their impact on others. Whatever the intention of the person, their appreciation of how they are seen and why helps the individual to adjust to be more able to work issues through. Part of the process of helping individuals accurately assess their impact on others is to help the person become more sensitive towards others. However, part of the process equally involves challenging assumptions. For example, what one person means by robustness may be taken by others to mean aggression. The value in challenging assumptions is to assist people to be more responsive to the different meanings people attach to the same words but in different contexts. Being sensitive and responsive to contexts does not mean being driven by one's own circumstances. Understanding the dynamics of the context one is in, helps each person realistically recognize how far and at what pace they can introduce change. Most certainly, understanding context does not mean accepting the current context. Understanding how meanings vary by context simply provides each individual with more information which can equip them to better cope with the challenges they face.

- *Ego or vision?* What is the basis for the strategic identity being pursued once occupying a leader role, satisfying one's ego or a belief in the vision being pursued? What really motivates the individual, the belief in his vision or the fact that it is his vision, his ideal, himself as the key driving force? Basically what motivates for leadership, vision or ego?

Anyone in a role of command needs the confidence to clarify and pursue particular courses of action. However, to what extent do persons need to clarify and pursue their direction as opposed to accommodating alternate view points, winning the commitment of others and still maintaining their own particular course of action. Accommodating alternate viewpoints essentially requires a capability to work with contradiction. Understanding the agenda of others, the reasons as to why others hold their particular perspective and the degree to which others can be manoeuvred from their original position, requires a capability beyond an interpersonal skill of communicating effectively and being seen as accessible. What is required is a capacity to recognize the spread of strategic agendas, why people are committed to any one or more strategies or visions, and the possible pathways to a shared platform. Undoubtedly, the personal skills of winning confidence and working with others are important in the process of negotiation of reconciliation of differences, but so also are the conceptual skills of finding pathways through contrasting logics.

On a programme of leader development, exploration can be undertaken of an individual's current capability to work with contradiction and not easily aligned inputs. The person can begin to recognize the degree to which they need their view to predominate, as opposed to working with discomfort, so that elements of other viewpoints can be accommodated. Their current capabilities to address multiple meanings can then, through counselling and facilitation, be related to the perceived requirements of the person's context. Through relating the individual's present ways of discerning to current context, the person can emotionally experience the gap of learning that needs to be bridged. The more exercises of feedback, analysis and simulation can be related to the complexity of workplace circumstances, the more the individual is likely to be committed to pursue learning on the job.

If nothing else, the person could realistically recognize whether 'they just want their own way' or whether the direction being pursued realistically needs a clear, singular and disciplined approach in order to attain success.

Feedback, through exercises, case analysis, questionnaires and observation, is a vital lever for development, whether for enhancing robustness in the person, making them more aware of how they impact and influence people or for helping them to recognize whether they need to have their own way or equally live with the ways of others. However, feedback needs to be 'grounded' in context in order to be more effectively accommodated, that is, the relevance of feedback is to appreciate how to gain greater credibility in any one situation but which is unlikely to be replicated elsewhere. Equally, feedback can be grounded in 'purpose', that is, in questioning what purpose is served by providing feedback, for example, to help individuals be understanding of their impact on others, or to help them grow to greater robustness and maturity. The more grounded the feedback, the more the individual can discern how to use the data and pursue meaningful ways forward.

Discerning feedback data accurately is an especially important requirement when faced with substantially contradictory data. A commonly quoted experience for senior managers is to be 'wrongly' criticized or accused of satisfying their own aspirations at the expense of others - 'he/she only wants it their way!'. Exploration and analysis on a leader development programme may confirm a perception individuals have of themselves, that they are broad minded and genuinely trying to do the best for their organization. However, in their place of work they could be seen as singular minded, not listening and only caring that their objectives are achieved. Through exploration of impact of self, individuals may well recognize that they do have a capacity to broadly discern, perhaps also recognize that they can 'get on pretty well' with people, but their work related circumstances require a forcefulness of leadership, in order to establish a clear strategy for the future. What is to be learned, as far as the person on the leader programme is concerned: 'there is nothing wrong with you, you get on fine with others, just grit your teeth and push through with what you are doing'. Through grounding feedback in reality, the learning process is enhanced as individuals are more able to discern through the information they have been offered and identify what is of relevance to them.

It is especially important that leaders emotionally appreciate that different people hold different perceptions, leaving those persons receiving feedback with a query: which feedback is of value? Making sense of conflicting data involves an appreciation of the dynamics of the current situation, what the individual is trying to achieve within that context, which key opinion leader(s) the person is attempting to influence and, perhaps most important, which of the feedback given the person is willing to accept and utilize. It is a truism that in the world of discretionary leadership, perception is reality. If nothing else, the person is, at least, more prepared for the emotive nature of strategic processes.

- *Emotive nature of strategic change*: In the process of developing leaders, one point needs to be emphasized, namely outcomes and processes are totally intertwined. What any one individual or group of senior managers wishes to achieve is intimately linked with how they go about attaining their goals. The reason is that on broader based issues of a longer time perspective, a 'leap of faith' is required in identifying with those aspirations and becoming involved in actively promoting those targets. People need to believe that the goals, objectives, mission, targets that are being pursued are worthwhile for them, can be achieved and are the best goals, objectives, mission and targets to aim for. On more operational matters, it is far easier to prove, in a logical, linear manner, that what one wishes to achieve and how one goes about achieving it, are related. Why? As far as operational matters are concerned, time frames are shorter and far more distinct parameters surround tasks and activities (operations). On broader based issues, time frames are much longer, making it far more difficult to predict when an outcome will be attained or if that outcome will even be of similar shape to what was originally conceived. Second, the parameters providing shape to strategic issues are the result of dialogue at discretionary leadership levels. Over time, people's views alter as circumstances change, with the likelihood that agendas shift and hence the parameters of strategy equally alter. Therein lies the need for belief. People need to have faith that the journey upon which they have embarked is desired and of value to them. Once on the journey, it must be appreciated that it may not end up being the same as the one started by the individual.

No matter how appropriate and right are the goals and targets set by senior management, reinforcement of their value is as crucial as their appropriateness. As Table 7.4 highlighted, lack of shared perspective between top management and general management leads to dysfunctionality and unsatisfactory communication. Of the six behavioural issues examined in Table 7.4, the British, Irish and Australian samples benchmarked against the others, are identified as most problematic on issues of trust, cohesion, cabinet responsibility and openness of communication. Hence, how can lower level staff and management identify with and believe the mission and policies that are presented, if what they visualize is distortion?

Whatever strategic choices are made, who presents them, how they are presented and how communications are managed, are as important as the choices themselves. Deciding on strategic options involves an analysis of the options as well as identifying those people who are to be involved in the process of communicating decisions. Certain individuals may become identified with certain of the strategies being pursued. If strategic change is required, it may be important to signal such change by changing certain of the people involved in the strategic decision making process. The reality of rethinking options as well as the people makes the situation volatile, emotive and, more likely than not, tense. Recognizing that strategic choice is unlikely to be divorced from choices about the people involved in strategic process, then the emotive, not easy to handle nature of strategy needs to be appreciated on a programme of leadership development.

- *Learning displays of unity*: In developing leaders of potential, one fundamental precept is important to grasp, namely that the medium is as important as the message. Hence, unity over issues and clarity of communication are vital if leaders are going to be believed. Therefore, on any leader development programme, debate and analysis of the terms cohesion, consistency and cabinet responsibility, are vital.

Attendees of a leadership programme, again through questionnaire feedback and/or through case analysis or workshop discussion, have the opportunity to explore their loyalty to the mission of their organization and to the strategies being pursued. Further, in depth examination could also highlight the degree to which each senior manager's true feelings concerning the shape and future direction of the organization are visible and obvious to their colleagues and lower level staff and management. Conducting an analysis of cohesion and cabinet responsibility with an existing senior management team would truly emphasize the organizational implications concerning the likely success or failure of operationalizing particular strategies or the mission of the organization.

Attention to cohesion and sense of cabinet responsibility at senior levels in the organization not only surfaces the degree of agreement and identity with the shape of the organization, but equally highlights the behaviours senior managers display on issues of operationalization of strategy. The manner in which leaders communicate their commitment or lack of it to policies and strategies, is through behaviour. Subordinate staff and managers respond to behaviour, not words. In fact, the Cranfield surveys identified over 200 formal and informal channels of internal communication. However, it is postulated that if all the different channels of communication were serviced, at best 25 per cent of communication concerns would be adequately addressed. The remaining 75 per cent of communication challenges would only improve if the behaviour of senior management changed. Messages through spoken or written words highlight intentions. Effective leadership is communicated through good example, namely through the behaviours of the leaders of the organization.

Hence, examination of the behaviour of senior managers needs to be more focused, so that individuals can compare their perception of themselves with the perception others hold of them. The more workplace feedback can be introduced on to a leader development programme, the greater the likelihood individuals will concentrate on improving their effectiveness as leaders with behaviours that are contextually relevant. In so doing, an additional paradox of leadership is highlighted, namely that consistency of behaviour for leaders refers to the consistency required for attaining strategic intent and not necessarily consistency of daily behaviour. Hence, the paradox; for how can one be consistent in behaviour to achieve long term intents whilst needing to adjust to changing circumstances over the shorter term, hence appearing to be inconsistent?

Incremental change takes time. Leading incremental change is likely to require responding over time, to different agendas. Simply to acknowledge, let alone respond to, different agendas for internally politically valid reasons, could be seen by some in the organization as inconsistent. Accepting that perception is reality, then, even for perfectly valid reasons, the most effective leaders are likely to be accused of being inconsistent. Hence, the third paradox of leadership is that the consistency necessary for achieving strategic intent involves a certain degree of inconsistency of behaviour in the short term in adjusting to operational and immediate contextual circumstances and changes (Figure 8.7).

Identity with and acceptance of the vision and mission of the organization are crucial as a means of reducing the negative impact of the second paradox of leadership. Identity with the vision and mission provides for guideline parameters to decision making and behaviour. Cabinet responsibility then provides for the necessary discipline for the effective implementation of strategy. Through cabinet responsibility the way forward is clear, but at the same time each particular leader may have to make adjustments to suit his/her context. The complexity of relationship between cohesion, consistency and context needs to be highlighted on programmes of leader development.

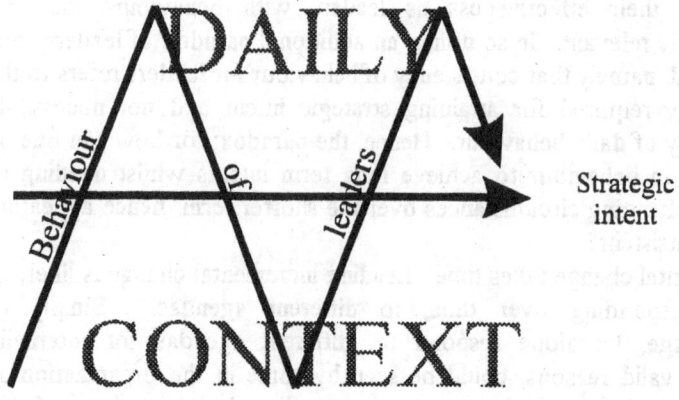

Figure 8.7 Discretionary leader behaviour

- *Broadening mental and educational sets: the confidential leadership consultation.* The experience of the inputs described above, no matter how well delivered, highlights two key learning points: utilizing already known insights and the power of context. Individuals who have held senior management positions are unlikely to be surprised by the learning they have gained. They are likely to have experienced the challenges, dilemmas, behaviours and circumstances outlined on the programme. The question is, to what extent are they prepared to action the insights that they already hold within their work context? Developing the will and robustness to address known challenges in workplace circumstances involves tying together the learning gained during the programme, with the opportunity for reflection. A programme of leadership in essence builds up the participants to allow themselves the intimacy of exploration, whereby through active reflection, contextually relevant ways forward and the courage to apply oneself to address known concerns, can be talked through with a third party. The leadership consultation is the bridge between knowing and application; between broadening mental and emotional sets and the wisdom and maturity to operationalize learning. In order to ensure for intimacy, confidentiality of conversation needs to be guaranteed. Whatever may be inserted or omitted from a programme of leadership development, the opportunity to discuss how to apply learning is the vital component.

Summary

Impact on organization

- Culture of organization is seen as necessary but not sufficient in terms of impacting on performance of organization.

- Leadership is seen as necessary and sufficient in terms of impacting on performance of organization.

- Within the APS, poor quality dialogue and lack of cohesion over visioning are identified as harmful to individuals, teams and the organization.

- SESs and SOs consider leadership as the one area needing most attention.

- The impact of restriction of dialogue and poor quality visioning on the APS is through comparison identified as similar to the results of the private sector and NHS Trusts (UK) samples.

Areas to address

- If improvements were to take place in quality of dialogue, visioning and leadership, the APS respondents identify where benefits to both individuals and the organization would occur.

- Providing support for ministers is a vital part of a senior manager's job in the APS but it is equally recognized that such commitments may be used as an excuse to not address other sensitive challenges in the organization.

- Perceived multiplicity of issues facing senior managers in the APS is used by some as a reason for not addressing known concerns in the organization.

- The phenomenon of the leadership gap is identified as a result of organizations attempting to pursue synergies emphasizing vertical integration (costs, infrastructure) and horizontal interactions (quality, teamwork and service), which can result in a management unable to face up to the emotionally demanding requirement of reconfiguring the infrastructure of the organization, whilst at the same time building trust and positive relationships with people.

- Equally identified as a challenge for management is attempting to introduce improvements in an organization that has experienced downsizing. The two phenomena of the survivor syndrome and the management support vacuum are additional strains on morale and the support senior management, especially, require in effectively pursuing their leadership task.

Steps for development

- Six on the job strategies for improving individual and team leadership behaviour are identified.

- Generating an effective mission of organization is considered vital to the development of public sector organizations. Two steps towards generating a meaningful mission for the organization are discussed.

- Six approaches to off the job leadership development are discussed. As part of the developmental process, understanding how to effectively work within the contradictory demands of different contexts and also influence events, is emphasized. Accommodating learning towards workplace application through confidential consultation, is strongly recommended.

Notes

1. For a more detailed analysis of the regression statistics supporting the conclusions presented in Figures 8.2 and 8.3, see Appendix 9.
2. Karpin (Chairman) 1995. 'Report of the Industry Task Force on Leadership and Management Skills, Enterprising Nation, Renewing Australia's Managers to Meet the Challenges of the Asia-Pacific Century', AGPS, Canberra.
3. Grit in dialogue refers to openness of conversation even when addressing issues that are sensitive and unwelcome to handle.

References

Adams, N. (1986), 'Efficiency Auditing in the Australian Audit Office', *Australian Journal of Public Administration*, Vol. 45, No. 3, September, pp. 180-200.

Adler, A. (1956), *The Individual Psychology of Alfred Adler*, edited by Ansbacher, H.L. and Ansbacher, R.R., Basic Books: New York.

Adler, N. (1986), *International Dimensions of Organisational Behaviour*, Kent Publishing: Boston.

Ahrne, G. (1990), *Agency and Organization: Towards an Organizational Theory of Society*, Sage: London.

Alban-Metcalf, B. and Nicholson, N. (1984), 'The Career Development of British Managers', Management Survey Report, British Institute of Management: Oxford.

Albrecht, K. and Zemke, R. (1985), *Service America*, Dow Jones-Irwin: Homewood.

Alderson, S. and Kakabadse, A.P. (1994), 'Business Ethics and Irish Management: A Cross-Cultural Study', *European Management Journal*, Vol. 12, No. 4, December, pp. 432-41.

Allan, R.W., Madison, D.L., Porter, L., Renwick, P. and Mayes, B.T. (1979), 'Organisational Politics: Tactics and Characteristics of Its Actors', *Californian Management Review*, Vol. 22, No. 1, pp. 475-83.

Allan, R.W. and Porter, L. (1983), *Organisational Influence Processes*, Scott Foresman: New York.

Allen, T. and Cohen, S. (1969), 'Information Flow in Research and Development Laboratories', *Administrative Science Quarterly*, Vol. 14, No 1, pp. 12-19.

Allison, G.T. (1971), *Essence of Decision*, Little Brown: Boston.

Anderson, C.R. and Paine, F.T. (1978), 'PIMS: A Re-examination', *Academy of Management Review*, Vol. 3, No. 3, pp. 602-12.

Anderson, C.W. (1988), 'Political Judgement and Public Policy', *Public Administration Quarterly*, Vol. 11, No. 4, Winter, pp. 439-62.

Anderson, P. and Tushman, M.L. (1990), 'Technological Discontinuities and Dominant Designs: A Cyclical Model of Technological Change', *Administrative Science Quarterly*, Vol. 35, No. 4, December, pp. 604-33.

Ansett, R. (1986), 'National Airlines: Efficiency and Reform', *Canberra Bulletin of Public Administration*, Vol. 13, No. 3, Spring, pp. 302-5.

Apter, D.E. (1965), *The Politics of Modernisation*, University of Chicago Press: Chicago.

Argyris, C. (1957), *Personality and Organisation*, Harper and Row: New York.

Argyris, C. (1962), *Interpersonal Competence and Organisational Effectiveness*, Dorsey Press: Homewood.

Argyris, C. (1976), *Increasing Leadership Effectiveness*, Wiley-Interscience: New York.

Argyris, C. (1982), *Reasoning, Learning and Action*, Jossey-Bass: San Francisco.

Argyris, C. (1991), 'Teaching Smart People How to Learn', *Harvard Business Review*, May-June, pp. 99-109.

Argyris, C. (1993), 'Education for Leading Learning', *Organisational Dynamics*, Winter, pp. 5-10.

Argyris, C. and Schon, D.A. (1974), *Theory and Practice: Increasing Professional Effectiveness*, Jossey-Bass: San Francisco.

Argyris, C. and Schon, D.A. (1978), *Organizational Learning: A Theory of Action Perspective*, Addison-Wesley: Reading.

Aristotle (1911), *The Nicomachean Ethics* (translated by Chase, edited by Dutton), Oxford University Press: London.

Aristotle (1946), *The Politics*, Clarendon: Oxford.

Arnold, W. and Plas, J. (1993), *The Human Touch*, Wiley: New York.

Asch, S.E. (1956), 'Studies of Independence and Conformity: A Minority of One Against Unanimous Majority', *Psychological Monograph*, No. 70, pp. 1-70.

Ashby, W.R. (1952), *Design for a Brain*, John Wiley: New York.

Ashby, W.R. (1960), *An Introduction to Cybernetics*, Chapman and Hall: London.

Attridge, E.J. (1991), 'Leadership Skills in the Australian SES', *Australian Journal of Public Administration*, Vol. 50, No. 4, December, pp. 328-46.

Aungles, S. and Parker, S. (1992), *Work, Organisations and Change: Themes and Perspectives in Australia* (Second Edition), Allen and Unwin: Sydney.

Australia Budget (1990), The Commonwealth Public Accounts (1990-91), 1990-91 Budget Paper Number 2, AGPS: Canberra.

Australia Budget (1991), The Commonwealth Public Accounts (1991-92), 1991-92 Budget Paper Number 2, AGPS: Canberra.

Australia Budget (1992), The Commonwealth Public Accounts (1992-93), 1992-93 Budget Paper Number 2, AGPS: Canberra.

Australia Budget (1993), The Commonwealth Public Accounts (1993-94), 1993-94 Budget Paper Number 2, AGPS: Canberra.

Australia Commonwealth Government (CG) (The Hilmer Report) (1993), 'National Competition Policy', Report by the Independent Committee of Inquiry, AGPS, Canberra: August.

Australia Commonwealth Government (CG) (1994), 'Working Nation: Policies and Programs', presented by The Prime Minister, The Honourable P.J. Keating, House of Representatives, 4 May 1994.

Australia Commonwealth Government (CG) (1995), 'Enterprising Nation: Renewing Australia's Managers to Meet the Challenges of the Asia-Pacific Century', (The Karpin Report), AGPS: Canberra.

Australia Department of Employment, Education and Training (DEET) (1995a), 'Client First: The Challenge for Government Information Technology', (Report of the Minister for Finance), Information Technology Review: Canberra, March.

Australia Department of Employment, Education and Training (DEET) (1995b), 'Corporate Technology Plan: 1995-1999', DEET Publishing Unit: Canberra, February.

Australia Industry Commission (IC) (1995), 'Computer Hardware, Software and Related Service Industries', Draft Report, Industry Commission: Canberra, 5 April.

Australia Industry Task Force on Leadership and Management Skills (Karpin, D., Chairman) (1995), 'Enterprising Nation: Renewing Australia's Managers to Meet the Challenges of the Asia-Pacific Century', AGPS: Canberra.

Australia MAB-MIAC Task Force on Management Improvement (1992), 'Evaluating Management Improvement in the Australian Public Service: First Report', MAB-MIAC Task Force on Management Improvement: Canberra.

Australia Management Advisory Board (MAB) (1992), 'The Australian Public Service Reformed: An Evaluation of a Decade of Management Reform', AGPS: Canberra, December.

Australia Management Advisory Board - Management Improvement Advisory Committee (MAB-MIAC) (1992), 'Building a Better Public Service', Number 12, AGPS: Canberra.

Australia National Audit Office (ANAO) (1992), 'Efficiency Audit: Commercialisation of the Commonwealth Reporting Service', The Auditor-General Report Number 6 (1992-93), AGPS: Canberra.

Australia National Board of Employment, Education and Training (NBEET) (1993), 'Crossing Innovation Boundaries: The Formation and Maintenance of Research Links Between Industry and Universities in Australia - Vols. 1 and 2', November, AGPS: Canberra.

Australia Parliament (1990), 'Not Dollars Alone: Review of the Financial Management Improvement Program' (Report of the House of Representatives Standing Committee on Finance and Public Administration), AGPS: Canberra.

Australia RCAGA (1976), 'Royal Commission on Australian Government Administration', (Chairman H.C. Coombs), Report, Australian Government Publishing Service: Canberra.

Avolio, B.J. and Gibbons, T.C. (1988), 'Developing Transformational Leaders: A Life Span Approach', in Conger, J.A. and Kanungo, R.N. (eds.), *Charismatic Leadership: The Elusive Factor in Organisational Effectiveness*, Jossey-Bass: San Francisco, pp. 276-308.

Avolio, B.J., Waldman, D.A. and Yammarino, F.J. (1991), 'Leading in the 1990s: The Four Is of Transformational Leadership', *Journal of European Industrial Training*, Vol. 15, No. 4, pp. 9-16.

Axel, H. (1993), *HR Executive Review: Downsizing*, Conference Board: New York.

Babson, S. (1993), 'Lean or Mean: The MIT Model and Lean Production at Mazda', *Labour Studies Journal*, Vol. 18, No. 2, Summer, pp. 3-24.

Bacherach, S.B. and Lawler, E.J. (1986), 'Power Dependence and Power Paradoxes in Bargaining', *Negotiation Journal*, Vol. 2, No. 2, pp. 167-74.

Bachrach, P. and Baratz, M. (1970), *Power and Poverty: Theory and Practice*, Oxford University Press: New York.

Baker, J.R. (1988), 'Contracting Out of Commonwealth Public Service Travel Arrangements', *Canberra Bulletin of Public Administration*, Vol. 15, No. 6, June, pp. 118-25.

Baker, W. (1992), 'The Network Organisation in Theory and Practice', in Nohria, N. and Eccles, R.G. (eds.), *Networks and Organisations: Structure, Form and Action*, Harvard Business School Press: Boston, pp. 397-429.

Bales, R.F. (1958), *Interaction Process Analysis*, Addison-Wesley: New York.

Bales, R. and Borgatta, E. (1955), 'Size of Group as a Factor in Interaction Profile', in Hare, A., Borgatta, E. and Bales, R. (eds.), *Small Groups: Studies in Social Interaction*, Knopf: New York, pp. 495-512.

Bandura, A. (1977), *Social Learning Theory*, Prentice-Hall: Englewood Cliffs.

Bandura, A. (1982), 'Self-efficacy Mechanism in Human Agency', *American Psychologist*, Vol. 37, pp. 122-47.

Bandura, A. (1986), *Social Foundations of Thought and Action*, Prentice-Hall: Englewood Cliffs.

Bandura, A. (1988), 'Self Realisation of Motivation and Action Through Goal Systems', in Hamilton, V., Bower, G. and Frijda, N. (eds.), *Cognitive Perspectives on Motivation and Emotion*, Kluwer Academic Publishers: Dordrecht, The Netherlands.

Banfield, E.C. (1960), 'The Training of the Executive', *Public Policy*, Vol. 8, No. 1, pp. 25-39.

Banner, D.K. and Blessingame, F. (1988), *Toward a Developmental Paradigm of Leadership*, School of Business and Public Administration, University of the Pacific: Stockton.

Bantel, K. and Jackson, S. (1989), 'Top Management and Innovations in Banking: Does the Composition of the Top Team Make a Difference?', *Strategic Management Journal*, Vol. 10, No. 1, pp. 107-24.

Barbour, G.P. and Sipel, G.A. (1986), 'Excellence in Leadership: Public Sector Model', *Public Management*, Vol. 68, August, pp. 24-9.

Bargo, Jr, M. (1980), *Choices and Decisions: A Guidebook for Constructing Values*, Californian University Associations: San Diego.

Barnard, C.I. (1938), *The Functions of the Executive*, Harvard University Press: Cambridge.

Barraclough, N. (1993), 'Of Power, Women and Influence, *The Sydney Morning Herald Good Weekend*, January, p. 7.

Barry, B. and Dowling, P. (1984), 'An Australian Management Style?', Australian Institute of Management Research Report, Canberra, pp. 1-49.

Bartlett, C.A. and Ghoshal, S. (1989), *Managing Across Borders*, Harvard Business School Press: Boston.

Bartlett, Sir F. (1932), *Remembering: A Study in Experiential and Social Psychology*, Cambridge University Press.

Bass, B.M. (1981), *Stogdill's Handbook of Leadership: Theory, Research and Managerial Implications*, Second Edition, Free Press: New York.

Bass, B.M. (1985a), 'Leadership: Good, Better, Best', *Organizational Dynamics*, Vol. 13, No. 4, Winter, pp. 26-40.

Bass, B.M. (1985b), *Leadership and Perfomance Beyond Expectations*, Free Press: New York.

Bass, B.M. (1988), 'Evolving Perspectives of Charismatic Leadership', in Conger, J.A. and Kanungo, R.N. (eds.), *Charismatic Leadership: The Exclusive Factor in Organisational Effectiveness*, Jossey-Bass: San Francisco, pp. 40-77.

Bass, B.M. (1990), *Bass and Stogdill's Handbook of Leadership: Theory Research and Management Applications*, Third Edition, Free Press: New York.

Bass, B.M., Avolio, B. and Goodheim, L. (1987), 'Biography and the Assessment of Transformational Leadership at the World Class Level', *Journal of Management*, Vol. 13, No. 1, pp. 7-20.

Bateson, G. (1973), *Step to an Ecology of Mind*, Granada: St Albans.

Bayne, P. (1984), 'Administrative Law', in Kouzmin, A., Nethercote, J.R. and Wettenhall, R.L. (eds.), *Australian Commonwealth Administration 1984: Essays in Review*, Canberra College of Advanced Administration in Association with ACT Division, Royal Australian Institute of Public Administration: Canberra, pp. 167-214.

Beer, M. (1980), *Organisations: Change and Development*, Goodyear: Santa Monica.

Beer, M. and Walter, A.E. (1987), 'Organisation Change and Development', *Annual Review of Psychology*, Vol. 38, No. 3, pp. 339-67.

Beiner, R. (1983), *Political Judgement, Chicago*, University Press: Chicago.

Belgard, W., Fisher, K.K. and Rauner, S. (1988), 'Vision, Opportunity, and Tenacity: Three Information Processes that Influence Formal Transformation', in Kilman, R. and Covin, T.J. (eds.), *Corporate Transformation*, Jossey-Bass: San Francisco.

Bell, C. (1971), *The Conventions of Crisis*, Oxford University Press: London.

Bell, D.V.J. (1975), *Power, Influence and Authority: An Essay in Political Linguistics*, Oxford University Press: New York.

Beniger, J. (1986), *The Control Revolution*, Harvard University Press: Cambridge.

Bennis, W. (1974), 'Conversation with Warren Bennis', *Organizational Dynamics*, Vol. 2, No. 2, pp. 51-66.

Bennis, W. (1982), 'The Art Form of Leadership', *International Management*, May, p. 21.

Bennis, W. (1984), 'Where Have All the Leaders Gone?', in Rosenbasck, W.E. and Taylor, R.L. (eds.), *Contemporary Issues in Leadership*, Westview Press: Boulder, pp. 42-60.

Bennis, W. (1988), 'Presidents as CEOs', *Los Angeles Times*, Part IV, 6 March, p. 3.

Bennis, W. (1989), *Why Leaders Can't Lead*, Jossey-Bass: San Francisco.

Bennis, W. (1993), *An Invented Life: Reflections on Leadership and Change*, Addison-Wesley: Reading.

Bennis, W. and Nanus, B. (1985), *Leaders: The Strategies for Taking Charge*, Harper and Row: New York.

Berger, P.L. and Luckmann, T. (1971), *The Social Construction of Reality: A Treatise in the Sociology of Knowledge*, Penguin: Harmondsworth.

Bernard, L.L. (1926), *An Introduction to Social Psychology*, Holt: New York.

Bierstadt, R. (1950), 'An Analysis of Social Power', *American Sociological Review*, Vol. 15, No. 4, pp. 730-33.

Bierstadt, R. (1974), *Power and Progress: Essays on Sociological Theory*, McGraw-Hill: New York.

Bingham, W.V. and Davis, W.T. (1927), 'Leadership', in Metcalf, H.C. (ed.), *The Psychological Foundations of Management*, Shaw: New York, pp. 56-74.

Bird, C. (1940), *Social Psychology*, Appleton-Century: New York.

Blainey, G. (1966), *The Tyranny of Distance*, Sun Books: Melbourne.

Blake, R. and Mouton, J.S. (1964), *The Managerial Grid*, Gulf Publishing: Houston.

Blandly, R. (1992), 'Multiple Schizophrenia, Economic Rationalism and Its Critics', *Australian Quarterly*, Vol. 64, No. 4, December, pp. 376-83.

Blau, P.M. (1970), 'A Formal Theory of Differentiation in Organisations', *American Sociological Review*, Vol. 35, pp. 201-18.

Blau, P.M. (1977), *Inequality and Heterogeneity*, Free Press: New York.

Blau, P.M. and Schoenherr, R.A. (1971), *The Structure of Organisations*, Basic Books Inc: New York.

Block, P. (1993), *Stewardship: Choosing Service Over Self-Interest*, Berrett-Koehler: New York.

Boettinger, H.M. (1989), 'And That Was the Future Telecommunications: From Future-Determined to Future-Determining', *Futures*, Vol. 21, No. 3, June, pp. 277-93.

Bohm, D. (1990), *On Dialogue*, David Bohm Seminars: California.

Bohret, C. (1993), 'The Tools of Public Management' in Eliassen, K.A. and Kooiman, J. (eds.), *Managing Public Organisations*, Sage: London, pp. 87-98.

Bolman, L.G. and Deal, T.E. (1991), *Reframing Organisations: Artistry, Choice and Leadership*, Jossey-Bass: San Francisco.

Bourdieu, P. and Passeron, J.C. (1990), *Reproduction in Education, Society and Culture* (Second Edition), Sage: London.

Bourgeois, III, L.J. (1980), 'Strategy and Environment: A Conceptual Integration', *Academy of Management Review*, Vol. 5, No. 1, pp. 25-39.

Bowditch, J.L. and Buone, A.F. (1982), 'Improving Software Productivity', *Computer*, Vol. 20, September, pp. 43-53.

Bower, J.L. (1983a), 'Managing for Efficiency, Managing for Equity', *Harvard Business Review*, August, pp. 83-90.

Bower, J.L. (1983b), *The Two Faces of Management: An American Approach to Leadership in Business and Politics*, Houghton Miffling: Boston.

Boyatzis, R.E. (1982), *The Competent Manager*, John Wiley.

Boyne, G.A. (1996), 'Competition and Local Government: A Public Choice Perspective', *Urban Studies*, Vol. 33, No. 6, pp. 703-21.

Bracey, H. (1993), *Managing from the Heart*, Dell: New York.

Bradford, D.L. and Cohen, A.R. (1984), *Managing for Excellence*, Wiley: New York.

Brassier, A. (1985), 'Strategic Vision: A Practical Tool', *The Bureaucrat*, Fall, pp. 23-6.

Broadbent, D.E. (1977), 'Hidden Pre-attentive Processes', *American Psychologist*, Vol. 32, pp. 98-109.

Brockner, J., Grover, S., O'Malley, M.N., Reed, T.F. and Glynn, M.A. (1993), 'Threat of Future Layoffs, Self-esteem and Survivors' Reactions: Evidence From the Laboratory and the Field', *Strategic Management Journal*, Vol. 14, Summer (Special Issue), pp. 153-66.

Brodie, M. and Bennett, R. (1979), *Perspectives on Managerial Effectiveness*, Thames Valley Regional Management Centre: London.

Brown, G.B. (1982), 'Leader Behaviour and Faculty Cohesiveness in Christian Schools', *Dissertation Abstract International*, Vol. 43, No. 7a, 2170.

Brown, H.R. (1978), 'Bureaucracy as Praxis: Towards a Political Phenomenology of Formal Organisations', *Administrative Science Quarterly*, Vol. 23, No. 3, pp. 365-82.

Brown, W. (1960), *Exploration in Management*, Heinemann: London.

Brown, W. and Jaques, E. (1964), *Product Pricing Analysis*, Heinemann Educational Books: London.

Bruner, J.S. (1972), *Process of Education*, Harvard University Press.

Bunyard, R.S. (1978), *Police: Organisation and Command: Police Studies Series*, Macdonald and Evans: Plymouth.

Burgelman, R.A. (1990), 'Strategy-Making and Organisational Ecology: A Conceptual Integration', in Singh, J.V. (ed.), *Organisational Evaluation: New Directions*, Sage: London, pp. 164-81.

Burk, J.P. (1989), 'Reconciling Public Administration and Democracy: The Role of the Responsible Administration', *Public Administration Review*, Vol. 49, No. 2, March-April, pp. 180-85.

Burke, W.W. (1964), 'Leadership Behaviour as a Function of the Leader, the Follower and the Situation', *Dissertation Abstracts*, Vol. 24, No. 3, pp. 2992.

Burke, W.W. (1976), 'Organisation Development in Transition', *Journal of Applied Behavioural Science*, Vol. 12, No. 1, pp. 22-43.

Burke, W.W. (1988), *Leadership Report*, (rev. ed.), W. Warner-Burke and Associates.

Burns, J.M. (1978), *Leadership*, Harper and Row: New York.

Burns, T. (1961), 'Micropolitics: Mechanisms of Organisational Change', *Administrative Science Quarterly*, Vol. 6, No. 2, pp. 267-81.

Burns, T. and Stalker, G.M. (1961), *The Management of Innovation*, Tavistock: London.

Burt, R.S. (1990), 'Kinds of Relations in American Discussion Networks', in Calhoun, C., Meyer, M.W. and Scott, W.R. (eds.), *Structures of Power and Constraint*, Cambridge University Press: New York, pp. 411-51.

Burt, R.S. (1992), 'The Social Structure of Competition', in Nohria, N. and Eccles, R.G. (eds.), *Networks and Organisations: Structure, Form and Action*, Harvard Business School Press: Boston, Chapter 2, pp. 57-91.

Burton, C. (1990), 'The Promise and the Price: Equal Employment Opportunity Programmes for Women in Australia', in Kouzmin, A. and Scott, N. (eds.), *Dynamics in Australian Public Management: Selected Essays*, Macmillan: Melbourne, pp. 72-84.

Cadbury, A. (1992), *Cadbury Report: The Financial Aspects of Corporate Governance*, Gee and Co Ltd: London.

Cadbury, A. (1995), *The Company Chairman: New Edition*, Fitzwillam Publishing: Hemel Hempstead.

Caiden, G.E. (1990), 'Australia's Changing Administrative Ethos; An Exploration', in Kouzmin, A. and Scott, N. (eds.), *Dynamics in Australian Public Management: Selected Essays*, Macmillan: Melbourne, pp. 29-49.

Caiden, G.E. (1991), 'Recent Administrative Changes in Australasia', *International Review of Administrative Services*, Vol. 57, No. 1, March, pp. 9-23.

Cameron, K.S., Freeman, S.J. and Mishra, A.K. (1993), 'Downsizing and Redesigning Organisations', in Huber, G. and Glick, W. (eds.), *Organizational Change and Redesign*, Oxford University Press: New York, pp. 83-97.

Canada External Affairs and International Trade Canada (EAITC) (1991), 'Information Technology Strategic Plan: 1991-1996', Information Systems Bureau (MSD): Ottawa, Canada, 18 December.

Canada Treasury Board of Canada (1994), 'Blueprint for Renewing Government Service Using Information Technology', Discussion Draft, Treasury Board of Canada: Ottawa.

Cantoni, V.J. (1993), 'Eliminating Bureaucracy - Roots and All', *Management Review*, Vol. 4, December, pp. 30-8.

Carlson, S. (1951), *Executive Behaviour: A Study of the Work Load and Working Methods of Managing Directors*, Stromberg: Stockholm.

Carnevale, A.P. and Stone, S.C. (1994), 'Diversity: Beyond the Golden Rule', *Training and Development*, Vol. 48, No. 10, October, pp. 22-39.

Carroll, G. (1984), 'Dynamics of Publisher Succession in Newspaper Organisations', *Administrative Science Quarterly*, Vol. 29, No. 2, pp. 303-29.

Carroll, G.R. and Harrison, R.J. (1994), 'Organisational Demography', Working Paper, Haas School of Business, University of California: Berkeley.

Carroll, M. (1995), 'IT Report 'Soft' but Thorough', *The Canberra Times*, 20 March, p. 13.

Cartwright, D. (1965), 'Influence, Leadership, Control', in March, J.G. (ed.), *Handbook of Organisations*, Rand-McNally: Chicago, pp. 93-112.

Cascio, W.F. (1992), *Managing Human Resources: Productivity, Quality of Work Life, Profits* (Third Edition), McGraw-Hill: New York.

Cascio, W.F. (1993), 'Downsizing: What Do We Know? What Have We Learned?', *Academy of Management Executive*, Vol. 7, No. 1, pp. 95-104.

Cascio, W.F. (1994), 'The Cost of Downsizing', *HRM Monthly*, February, pp. 8-13.

Castelles, M. (1989), 'High Technology and the New International Division of Labour', *Labour and Society*, Vol. 14, No. 1, pp. 7-42.

Cavalli-Sforza, L.L. and Feldman, M.W. (1981), *Cultural Transmission and Evolution*, Princeton University Press: Princeton.

Cerney, P. (1990), *The Changing Architecture of Politics: Structure, Agency and the Future of the State*, Sage: London.

Champy, J. and Arnoudse, D. (1992), 'The Leadership Challenge of Re-engineering', *Insights Quarterly*, Fall, pp. 70-93.

Cherry, C. (1978), *On Human Communication: A Review, a Survey and a Criticism*, (Third Edition), MIT Press: Cambridge.

Chevallier, J. (1996), 'Public Administration in Statist France', *Public Administration Review*, Vol. 56, No. 1, pp. 67-71.

Child, J. (1972), 'Organisation, Structure and Strategies of Control: A Replication of the Aston Study, *Administrative Science Quarterly*, Vol. 17, pp. 163-77.

Child, J. (1973), 'Parkinson's Progress: Accounting for the Number of Specialists in Organisation', *Administrative Science Quarterly*, Vol. 18, No. 3, September, pp. 324-48.

Choo, K.L. (1992), 'Strategic Management in Local Government: Guiding Principles for Effective Practice', *Local Government Policy Making*, Vol. 19, No. 3, December, pp. 42-9.

Coates, A.W. (1988), 'Economists in Government: An Historical and Comparative Perspective', *Canberra Bulletin of Public Administration*, Vol. 53, No. 4, December, pp. 45-55.

Cohen, A.R. and Bradford, D.L. (1990), *Influence Without Authority*, John Wiley: New York.

Coleman, S. (1993), 'Tightening The Belt', *Pacific Computer Weekly*, Vol. 905, 16 July, p. 8.

Collins, R. (1987), 'Interaction Ritual Chains, Power and Property: The Micro-Macro Connection as an Empirically Based Theoretical Problem', in Alexander, J.C., Giesen, B., Münch, R. and Smelzer, N.J. (eds.), *The Micro-Macro Link*, University of California Press: Berkeley, pp. 193-206.

Computerworld (1992), 'The MIS Budget', Vol. 14, No. 51, June, p. 58.

Conger, J.A. (1993), 'The Brave New World of Leadership Training', *Organisational Dynamics*, Vol. 21, No. 3, Winter, pp. 46-58.

Covey, S.R. (1989), *The Seven Habits of Highly Effective Leaders*, Simon and Schuster: New York.

Covey, S.R. (1990a), *The Seven Habits of Highly Effective People: Restoring the Character Ethic*, Simon and Schuster: New York.

Covey, S.R. (1990b), *Principle Centred Leadership*, Summit: New York.

Coward, L. (1990), 'Industrial Relations: Working Together', in Richards, C. (ed.), *Gathering Momentum: Commercialisation in the Public Sector*, Australian Government Publishing Service: Canberra, pp. 65-75.

Crozier, M. (1964), *The Bureaucratic Phenomenon*, Tavistock: London.

Culbert, S.A. and McDonough, J.J. (1980), *The Invisible War*, John Wiley and Sons: New York.

Currie, W. (1995), *Management Strategy for IT: An International Perspective*, Pitman Publishing: London.

Cyert, R.M. and March, J.G. (1963), *A Behavioural Theory of the Firm*, Prentice-Hall: Englewood Cliffs.

Daft, R.L. (1989), *Organisation Theory and Design* (Third Edition), West Publishing: New York.

Dahl, R.A. (1961), *Who Governs?*, Yale University Press: New Haven.

Dainty, P.H. and Anderson, M. (1996), *The Capable Executive: Effective Performance in Senior Management*, Macmillan Business: London.

Daniels, K. and de Chernatony, L. (1993), 'Differences in Cognitive Models of Buyers and Sellers', paper presented to the *International Workshop on Managerial and Organisation Cognition*, Brussels, Belgium.

Daniels, K., de Chernatony, L. and Johnson, J.G. (1993a), 'Validating a Method for Mapping Managers' Mental Models of Competitive Industry Structures', unpublished internal Cranfield School of Management Paper, ESRC Support Grant M036200E.

Daniels, K., de Chernatony, L. and Johnson, J.G. (1993b), 'Mental Models of Competitive Industry Structures: Issues in Mapping and Homogeneity', unpublished internal Cranfield School of Management paper, ESRC Support Grant M036200E.

Danish Ministry of Research (1994), 'Info-Society 2000', Ministry of Research: Denmark.

Darwin, C. (1964), *On the Origin of Species: By Means of Natural Selection*, Harvard University Press: Cambridge.

David, F. (1995), *Strategic Management*, (Fifth Edition), Prentice-Hall: New Jersey.

Davis, B. (1994), 'Our Managers Fall Down on the Job', *Australian Business Monthly*, Vol. 14, Issue 12, October, pp. 126-27.

Davis, E. and Lansbury, R. (1990), 'Industrial Democracy in the Australian Public Sector', in Kouzmin, A. and Scott, N. (eds.), *Dynamics in Australian Public Management: Selected Essays*, Macmillan: Melbourne, pp. 47-54.

Davis, J.A. and Warnath, C.F. (1957), 'Reliability, Validity and Stability of the Sociometric Voting Scales', *Journal of Social Psychology*, Vol. 45, pp. 111-22.

Davis, S.M. (1984), *Managing Corporate Culture*, Ballinger: Cambridge.

Davis, T.R. and Luthans, F. (1979), 'Leadership Examined: A Behavioural Approach', *Academy of Management Review*, Vol. 4, No. 2, pp. 237-48.

Dawkins, J. (1986), 'Privatisation and Deregulation: Myths and Practicalities', *Journal of Australian Political Economy*, 20 October, pp. 2-17.

Day, D.V. and Lord, R.G. (1988), 'Executive Leadership and Organisational Performance: Suggestions for a New Theory and Methodology', *Journal of Management*, Vol. 14, No. 3, pp. 453-64.

Deal, T.E. and Kennedy, A.A. (1982), *Corporate Culture: The Rites and Rituals of Corporate Life*, Addison-Wesley: Reading.

Dearborn, D.C. and Simon, H.A. (1985), 'Selective Perception: A Note on the Department Identification of Executives', *Sociometry*, Vol. 21, No. 2, pp. 144.

Denhardt, R.B. (1987), 'The Contemporary Critique of Management Education: Lessons for Business and Public Administration', *Public Administration Quarterly*, Vol. 10, No. 2, Summer, pp. 123-33.

Denison, D.R., Hooijberg, R. and Quinn, R.E. (1991), 'Paradox and Performance: A Theory of the Behavioural Complexity of Effective Leaders', Working Paper, The University of Michigan, School of Business: Michigan.

DePree, M. (1993), *Leadership Jazz*, Dell: New York.

Dicken, P. (1992), *Global Shift: The Internalization of Economic Activity*, PCP: London.

Dickenson, M. (1986), 'Industrial Relations and Personnel Management' in Kouzmin, A., Nethercote, J.R. and Wettenhall, R.L. (eds.), *Australian Commonwealth Administration 1984: Essays in Review*, Canberra College of Advanced Administration in Association with ACT Division, Royal Australian Institute of Public Administration: Canberra, pp. 26-39.

Dilton, T. (1993), 'Union Anger Over Government IT Outsourcing Plans', *Pacific Computer Weekly*, 16 July, pp. 77-88.

DiMaggio, P. (1986), 'Structural Analysis of Organisational Fields', in Staw, B. and Cummings, L.L. (eds.), *Research in Organisational Behaviour*, Vol. 8, JAI Press: Greenwich, pp. 335-70.

DiMaggio, P. (1988), 'Interest and Agency in Institutional Theory', in Zucker, L. (ed.), *Research on Institutional Patterns: Environment and Culture*, Ballinger Press: Cambridge, pp. 59-72.

Dixon, J., Kouzmin, A. and Korac-Kakabadse, N. (1996), 'The Commercialisation of the Australian Public Service and Accountability of Government: A Question of Boundaries', *The International Journal of Public Sector Management*, Vol. 9, No. 5/6, pp. 23-36.

Dizard, Jr, W.P. (1985), *The Coming Information Age*, Longman: New York.

Dodgson, M. (1989), 'National Policies - Research and Technology Policy in Australia: Legitimacy in Intervention', *Science and Public Policy*, Vol. 16, No. 3, pp. 159-66.

Dodgson, M. (1991), 'The Future for Technological Collaboration', Emerging New International Technology Order: Opportunities and Challenges For Korea, *STPI International Conference*, 5 September, Seoul, Korea.

Doherty, N. (1994), 'Survivor Syndrome Survey', Human Resource Research Centre, Cranfield School of Management.

Donaldson, L. (1976), 'Workload, Technology, Organisational Structure and Performance: A Critique of the Universal Generalisation', *Journal of Management Studies*, Vol. 13, pp. 255-73.

Dosi, G. (1984), *Technical Change and Industrial Transformation*, MacMillan: London.

Douglas, S.P. and Rhee, D.K. (1989), 'Examining Generic Competitive Strategy Types in US and European Markets', *Journal of International Business Studies*, Vol. 20, No. 3, pp. 437-63.

Dowling, P. and Nagel, T. (1986), 'National Work Practices: A Study of Australian and American Business Majors', *Journal of Management*, Vol. 12, No. 1, pp. 121-28.

Dowling, P.J. and Schuler, R.S. (1990), *International Dimensions in Human Resource Management*, PWS-Kent Publishing Company: New York.

Drath, W. and Plaus, C. (1994), *Making Common Sense: Leadership as Meaning Making in a Community of Practice*, Centre for Creative Leadership: Greensboro.

Drehmer, D.E. and Grossman, J.H. (1984), 'Scaling Managerial Respect: A Developmental Perspective', *Educational and Psychological Measurement*, Vol. 44, pp. 763-67.

Dror, Y. (1980), 'Think Tanks: A New Invention in Government', in Weiss, C.H. and Barton, A.H. (eds.), *Making Bureaucracy Work*, Sage: Beverley Hills, pp. 139-52.

Dror, Y. (1984), *Policymaking Under Adversity*, Transaction Books: New Brunswick.

Dror, Y. (1987) 'Retrofitting the Central Mind of Government', *Research in Public Policy Analysis and Management*, Vol. 69, No. 4, pp. 79-107.

Drucker, P.F. (1974), *Management: Tasks, Responsibilities, Practices*, Harper and Row: New York.

Drucker, P.F. (1978), *The Age of Discontinuity*, Harper Torchbooks: New York.

Drucker, P.F. (1988), 'The Coming of the New Organisations', *Harvard Business Review*, Vol. 66, January-February, pp. 35-53.

Drucker, P.F. (1990), *The New Realities*, Harper and Row: New York.

Drucker, P.F. (1992), 'The New Society of Organisations', *Harvard Business Review*, Vol. 70, No. 5, September-October, pp. 95-104.

Drucker, P.F. (1993), *Post-Capitalist Society*, Harper Business: New York.

Drucker, P.F. (1994), 'The Age of Social Transformation', *The Atlantic Monthly*, November.

Dubin, R. (1962), 'Business Behaviour Behaviourally Viewed' in Strother, G.B. (ed.), *Social Science Approaches to Business Behaviour*, Dorsey Press: Homewood, pp. 11-55.

Due, R. (1992), 'The Real Cost of Outsourcing', *Information Systems Management*, Winter, pp. 78-81.

DuGay, P. and Salaman, G. (1992), 'The Culture of the Customer', *Journal of Management Studies*, Vol. 29, No. 5, pp. 615-33.

Dumaine, B. (1994), 'Mr Learning Organisation', *Fortune*, 17 October, pp. 95-101.

Dunleavy, P. and Hood, C. (1994), 'From Old Public Administration to New Public Management', *Public Money and Management*, Vol. 14, Issue 3, July-September, pp. 9-16.

Dunphy, D. and Stace, D. (1988), 'Transformational and Coercive Strategies for Planned Organisational Change', *Organisational Studies*, Vol. 9, No. 3, pp. 317-34.

Dunphy, D. and Stace, D. (1990), *Under New Management*, McGraw-Hill: Sydney.

Durkheim, E. (1897), *Le Suicide*, F. Alcon: Paris.

Dutton, J. and Duncan, R. (1987), 'The Creation of Momentum for Change Through the Process of Strategic Issue Diagnosis', *Strategic Management Journal*, Vol. 8, No. 3, pp. 279-95.

Dyer, Jr, W.G. (1984), 'Organisational Culture: Analysis and Change' in Dyer, W.G. (ed.), *Strategies for Managing Change*, Addion-Wesley: Reading, pp. 1-24.

Eccles, T. (1992), 'Brief Case: Delayering Myths and Mezzanine Management', *Long Range Planning*, Vol. 25, No. 4, August, pp. 105-7.

Eden, D. (1990), *Pygmalion in Management: Productivity as a Self-fulfilling Prophecy*, Lexington Books: Lexington.

Eisenhardt, K. and Schoonhoven, C. (1990), 'Organisational Growth: Linking Founding Team, Strategy and Growth Among US Semi-Conductors Ventures 1978-1988', *Administrative Science Quarterly*, Vol. 35, No. 4, pp. 504-29.

Ely, R.J. (1994), 'The Effects of Organisational Demographics and Social Identity on Relationships among Professional Women', *Administrative Science Quarterly*, Vol. 39, No. 2, pp. 203-38.

Emery, F.E. and Trist, E.L. (1965), 'The Casual Texture of Organisational Environments', *Human Relations*, Vol. 18, pp. 21-32.

Erickson, B. (1988), 'The Relational Bias of Attitudes', in Wellman, B. and Berkowitz, S. (eds.), *Social Structures: A Network Approach*, Cambridge University Press: New York, pp. 99-121.

Erikson, E. (1964), *Insight and Responsibility*, Norton: New York.

Escobar, A. (1992), 'Reflection on 'Development': Grassroots Approaches and Alternative Politics in the Third World', *Futures*, Vol. 24, No. 6, pp. 411-36.

Etzioni, A. (1964), *Modern Organisations*, Prentice-Hall: New Jersey.

Evans, M.G. (1970), 'Leadership and Motivation', *Academy of Management Journal*, Vol. 13, No. 1, pp. 91-102.

Evans, P., Doz, Y. and Laurent, A. (eds.) (1990), *Human Resource Management in International Firms: Change, Globalizaton, Innovation*, St. Martin's Press: New York.

Evered, R. (1983), 'The Language of Organisation: The Case of the Navy', in Pondy, L., Frost, P., Morgan, G. and Dandridge, T. (eds.), *Organisational Symbolism*, JAI Press: Greenwich.

Faber, M. and Seers, D. (eds.) (1972), *The Crisis in Planning*, Chatto and Windus: London.

Fairbrother, P. (1991), 'In State of Change: Flexibility in the Civil Service', in Polert, A. (ed.), *Farewell to Flexibility*, Blackwell: Oxford, pp. 69-83.

Fairholm, G.W. (1991), *Values Leadership: Towards a New Philosophy of Leadership*, Praeger: London.

Fairholm, G.W. (1993), *Organisational Power Politics: Tactics in Organisational Leadership*, Praeger: London.

Fama, E.F. and Jensen, M.C. (1983), 'Separation of Ownership and Control', *Journal of Law and Economics*, Vol. 26, No. 3, pp. 301-25.

Farrell, D. and Petersen, T. (1982), 'Patterns of Political Behaviour in Organisations', *Academy of Management Review*, Vol. 7, No. 3, July, pp. 403-12.

Faulkner, R.R. (1973), 'Orchestra Interaction: Some Features of Communication and Authority in an Artistic Organisation', *Sociological Quarterly*, Vol. 14, No. 1, pp. 147-57.

Fenwick, M. and Edwards, R. (1994), 'Managing the British Subsidiary: Is Cultural Similarity Misleading?: A Study of Australian Manufacturers', paper presented at the Australian and New Zealand Academy of Management's (ANZAM) Annual Conference on *'Vanishing Borders: The Managerial Challenges'*, Wellington, December, pp. 1-20.

Fiedler, F.E. (1965), 'Engineer the Job to Fit the Manager', *Harvard Business Review*, Vol. 43, No. 5, pp. 115-21.

Fiedler, F.E. (1967), *A Theory of Leadership Effectiveness*, McGraw-Hill: New York.

Fiedler, F.E. (1987), 'When to Lead, When to Stand Back', *Psychology Today*, September, pp. 25-7.

Field, R.H.G. (1979), 'A Critique of the Vroom-Yetton Contingency Model of Leadership Behaviour', *Academy of Management Review*, Vol. 4, No. 2, pp. 249-57.

Filley, A., House, R. and Kerr, S. (1976), *Managerial Process and Organisational Behaviour* (Second Edition), Scott Foresman: Glenview.

Fillipowski, D. (1993), 'Downsizing Isn't Always Rightsizing', *Personnel Journal*, Vol. 72, No. 11, November, p. 71.

Finklelstein, S. and Hambrick, D. (1990), 'Top Management Team Tenure and Organisational Outcomes: The Moderating Role of Managerial Discretion' *Administrative Science Quarterly*, Vol. 35, No. 4, pp. 484-503.

Fischer, C.S. (1982), 'What Do We Mean By Friend? An Inductive Study', *Social Networks*, Vol. 3, No. 2, pp. 287-306.

Fleishman, E.A. and Harris, E.F. (1962), 'Patterns of Leadership Behaviour to Employee Grievances and Turnover', *Personal Psychology*, Vol. 15, No. 1, pp. 43-56.

Fligstein, N. (1992), 'The Social Construction of Efficiency', in Zey, M. (ed.), *Decision Making: Alternatives to Rational Choice Models*, Sage Publication: London, pp. 351-76.

Follett, M.P. (1942), *Dynamic Administration: The Collected Papers of Mary Parker Follett*, (edited by Metcalf, H.C. and Urwick, L.), Harper and Brothers: New York.

Forester, T. (ed.) (1985), *The Information Technology Revolution*, Blackwell: Oxford.

Forester, T. (1987), *High-Tech Society*, Basil Blackwell: Oxford.

Forester, T. (ed.) (1989), *Computers in the Human Context: Information Technology, Productivity and People*, Blackwell: Oxford.

Forrester Research Inc. (1993), 'Re-engineer Yourself', *Computerworld*, Vol. 15, No. 51, June, p. 70.

Foucault, M. (1965), *Madness and Reason: A History of Insanity in the Age of Reason*, Random House: New York.

Foucault, M. (1979), *Discipline and Punishment*, Vintage: New York.

Frank, L.K. (1939), 'Dilemma of Leadership', *Psychiatry*, Vol. 2, No. 3, pp. 343-61.

Franke, R. (1989), 'Technological Revolution and Productivity Decline: The Case of US Banks', in Forester, T. (ed.), *Computers in the Human Context: Information Technology, Productivity and People*, Blackwell: Oxford, pp. 281-90.

Frederickson, J. and Iaquinto, A. (1989), 'Inertia and Creeping Rationality in Strategic Decision Processes', *Academy of Management Journal*, Vol. 27, No. 4, pp. 445-66.

Freeman, C. and Perez, C. (1988), 'Structural Crisis of Adjustment, Business Cycles and Investment Behaviour', in Dosi, G., Freeman, C., Nelson, R., Silveberg, G. and Soete, L. (eds.), *Technical Change and Economic Theory*, Pinter: London, pp. 38-66.

Freeman, R.E. (1984), *Strategic Management: A Stakeholder Approach*, Pitman: London.

French, J.R. and Raven, B. (1959), 'The Bases of Social Power', in Cartwright Darwin (ed.), *Studies of Social Power*, Ann Arbor M.I. Institute of Social Research, The University of Michigan.

Freud, S. (1922), *Group Psychology and the Analysis of the Ego*, International Psychological Press: London.

Freud, S. (1953), *The Complete Psychological Works of Sigmund Freud*, Hogarth Press: London.

Frey, R. (1993), 'Empowerment or Else', *Harvard Business Review*, Vol. 71, No. 5, September-October, pp. 80-94.

Friedman, M. (1953), *Essays in Positive Economics*, University of Chicago Press: Chicago.

Fromm, E. (1941), *Escape from Freedom*, Farrer and Rinehart: New York.

Frost, P.J. and Hayes, D.C. (1979), 'An Exploration in Two Cultures of a Model of Political Behaviour in Organisations', in Frost, P.J. and Hayes, D.C. (eds.), *Organisational Functioning in a Cross Cultural Perspective*, Kent State University Press: Kent.

Fullan, M. (1991), *The New Meaning of Educational Changes*, Cassell: London.

Gaernter, K.M. and Gaernter, G.H. (1985), 'Proactive Roles of Federal Managers', *The Bureaucrat*, Vol. 14, No. 3, Fall, pp. 19-22.

Gandz, J. and Murray, V.V. (1980), 'The Experience of Workplace Politics', *Academy of Management Journal*, Vol. 23, No. 2, pp. 237-51 and 440-54.

Gardner, J.W. (1964), *Self-Renewal: The Individual and the Innovative Society*, Harper Colopon Books: New York.

Gardner, J.W. (1987), 'Constituents and Followers' (Vol. 8, Leadership Study Program), Independent Sector, Washington, November.

Garfinkel, H. (1967), *Studies in Ethnomethodology*, Prentice-Hall: Englewood Cliffs.

Garnett, J. and Kouzmin, A. (1995), 'Communication During Crises: From Bullhorn to Mass Media to High Technology to Organisational Networking', papers presented at the *Twenty-Third International Congress of Administrative Science*, Dubai, July, pp. 1-18.

Garson, J.P. and Puymoyen, A. (1995), 'New Patterns of Migration', *OECD Observer*, No. 192, February-March, pp. 8-12.

Gateway Information Service Inc. (1992), 'Re-engineering', *Computerworld*, Vol. 15, No. 24-25, December, p. 46.

Geisler, E. (1993), 'How Strategic is Your Information Technology?', *Information Technology*, January-February, pp. 31-2.

Ghiselli, E.E. (1971), *Explorations in Managerial Talent*, Goodyear: Glenview, Illinois.

Ghiselli, E.E. (1973), 'The Validity of Aptitude Tests in Personnel Selection', *Personnel Psychology*, Vol. 26, pp. 461-77.

Giddens, A. (1979), *Central Problems in Social Theory: Action Structure and Contradiction in Social Analysis*, Macmillan: London.

Giddens, A. (1984), *The Constitution of Society*, Polity Press: Oxford.

Gilbraith, J.R. (1974), 'Organisation Design: An Information Processing View', *Interfaces*, Vol. 4, No. 1, pp. 28-36.

Gilbraith, J.R. (1977), *Organisation Design*, Addison-Wesley: Reading.

Glasson, B.C. and Rusli, A. (1994), 'A Preliminary Examination of Some International Responses to Ten Populist BPR Questions: Unearthing BPR Concepts Throughout a Content Analysis', in *Proceedings of the 5th Australian Conference on Information Systems*, Melbourne, Vol. 1, September, pp. 99-112.

Gleeson, G. (1986), 'Managing Accountability', *Local Government Bulletin*, Vol. 49, No. 9, p. 22.

Goffman, E. (1974), *Frame Analysis: An Essay on the Organisation of Experience*, Penguin Books: Harmondsworth, Middlesex.

Goldhammer, H. and Shils, E.A. (1972), 'Types of Power and Status', *American Journal of Sociology*, Vol. 45, pp. 171-82.

Goleman, D. (1986), *Emotional Intelligence: Why it can Matter More than IQ*, Bloomsbury: London.

Goodstell, C. (1994), *The Case For Bureaucracy*, Chatham House Publishers: Chatham.

Gordon, G.G. (1986), 'The Relationship of Corporate Culture in Industry Sector and Corporate Performance', in Kilmann, R.H., Saxton, M.J., Serpa, R. and Associates (eds.), *Gaining Control of the Corporate Culture*, Jossey-Bass: San Francisco, pp. 103-25.

Gouldner, A.W. (1960), 'The Norm of Reciprocity: A Preliminary Statement', *American Sociological Review*, Vol. 25, pp. 161-78.

Gramsci, A. (1971), *Selection from Prison Notebooks*, International Publishers: New York.

Granovetter, M. (1973), 'The Strength of Weak Ties', *American Journal of Sociology*, Vol. 78, pp. 1360-80.

Granovetter, M. (1992), 'Problems of Explanation in Economic Sociology', in Nohria, N. and Eccles, R.G. (eds.), *Networks and Organisations: Structure, Form and Action*, Harvard Business School Press: Boston, Chapter 1, pp. 25-56.

Gransey, E. and Roberts, J. (1992), 'The Experience of Growth in Small High Technology Firms', paper presented to the *9th EGOS Colloquium*, May, Berlin.

Gray, A. and Jenkins, B. (1995), 'From Public Administration to Public Management: Reassessing a Revolution?', *Public Administration*, Vol. 73, No. 1, pp. 75-99.

Greengard, S. (1993), 'Don't Rush Downsizing: Plan, Plan, Plan', *Personnel Journal*, Vol. 71, No. 11, November, pp. 64-76.

Greenleaf, R.K. (1977), *Servant Leadership*, Paulist Press: New York.

Greenleaf, R.K. (1983), *Servant Leadership: A Journey into the Nature of Legitimate Power and Greatness*, Paulist Press: New York.

Grimm, C. and Smith, K. (1991), 'Management and Organisational Change: A Note on the Railroad Industry', *Strategic Management Journal*, Vol. 12, No. 4, 557-62.

Grob, L. (1984), 'Leadership: The Socratic Model', in Kellerman, B. (ed.), *Leadership: Multidisciplinary Perspectives*, Prentice-Hall: Englewood Cliffs.

Gross, T. (1996), *The Last Word on Power: Executive Re-Invention for Leaders Who Must Make the Impossible Happen*, Doubleday: New York.

Hackman, R.J. (1983), 'Group Influences on Individuals', in Dunette, M.D. (ed.), *Handbook of Industrial and Organisational Psychology*, Wiley: New York, pp. 1455-525.

Hage, J. and Aitken, M. (1966), 'Organisational Alienation: A Comparative Analysis', *American Sociological Review*, Vol. 31, pp. 497-507.

Hambrick, D.C. (1982), 'Environmental Scanning and Organisational Strategy', *Strategic Management Journal*, Vol. 3, No. 2, pp. 159-74.

Hambrick, D.C. (1989), 'Putting Top Managers Back in the Strategy Picture', *Strategic Management Journal*, Vol. 10, Special Issue, pp. 5-15.

Hambrick, D.C. (1995), 'Fragmentation or the Other Problems CEOs have with Their Top Management Teams', *California Management Review*, Vol. 37, No. 3, pp. 110-27.

Hambrick, D.C. and D'Aveni, R.A. (1992), 'Top Team Detonation as Part of the Downward Spiral of Large Corporate Bankruptcies, *Management Science*, Vol. 38, No. 6, pp. 1445-66.

Hambrick, D.C. and Finkelstein, S. (1987), 'Managerial Discretions: A Bridge Between Polar Views of Organisational Outcomes', in Cummings, L.L. and Staw, B. (eds.), *Research in Organisational Behaviour*, Vol. 9, JAI Press: Greenwich, pp. 369-406.

Hambrick, D.C. and Masson, P.A. (1984), 'Upper Echelons: The Organisation as a Reflection of its Top Managers', *Academy of Management Review*, Vol. 9, No. 2, pp. 193-206.

Hambrick, D.C. and Snow, C.C. (1977), 'A Contextual Model of Strategic Decision Making in Organizations', *Academy of Management Proceedings*, pp. 108-12.

Hamilton, S. (1990), 'The Restructuring of the Federal Public Service', in Kouzmin, A. and Scott, N. (eds.), *Dynamics in Australian Public Management: Selected Essays*, Macmillan: Melbourne, pp. 64-71.

Hammer, M. (1990), 'Re-engineering Work: Don't Automate, Obliterate', *Harvard Business Review*, Vol. 68, No. 4, July-August, pp. 104-12.

Hammer, M. and Champy, J. (1993), *Re-engineering the Corporation: A Manifesto for Business Revolution*, Harper Business: New York.

Hampden-Turner, C. and Trompenaars, F. (1993), *The Seven Cultures of Capitalism*, Piatkus: London.

Handy, C.B. (1976), *Understanding Organisations*, Penguin Books: Middlesex.

Harmon, M. (1989), 'Decisions' and 'Actions' as Contrasting Perspectives in Organisational Theory', *Public Administration Review*, Vol. 49, No. 2, March-April, pp. 144-50.

Harrison, R. (1972), 'Understanding Your Organisation's Character', *Harvard Business Review*, May-June, pp. 119-28.

Harvey-Jones, J. (1988), *Making it Happen: Reflections on Leadership*, Collins: London.

Haveman, H.A. (1993), 'Ghosts of Managers Past: Managerial Succession and Organisational Mortality', *Academy of Management Journal*, Vol. 36, No. 2, pp. 193-207.

Haydon, S. (1993), 'Intellectual Capital Pay Off in Result', *The Weekend Australia*, 14-15, August, p. 43.

Hayes-Roth, B. (1977), 'Evolution of Cognitive Structure and Processes', *Psychological Review*, Vol. 84, No. 2, pp. 260-78.

Heckscher, C. (1995), *White Collar Blues*, Basic Books: New York.

Hegel, G.W.F. (1971), *Philosophy of Mind*, (translators Wallace, W. and Miller, A.V.), Clarendon: Oxford.

Held, D. (1980), *Introduction to Critical Theory: Horkheimer to Habermas*, University of California Press: Berkeley and Los Angeles.

Henderson, J. (1991), *The Globalization of High Technology Production: Society, Space and Semiconductors in the Restructuring of the Modern World*, Routledge: London.

Henry, J. (1991), 'Making Sense of Creativity', in Henry, J. (ed.), *Creative Management*, Sage Publications: London, pp. 1-11.

Hersey, P. and Blanchard, K.M. (1969), *Management of Organisational Behaviour*, Prentice-Hall: Englewood Cliffs.

Hersey, P. and Blanchard, K.M. (1988), *Management of Organisational Behaviour: Utilising Human Resources*, (Fifth Edition), Prentice-Hall: Englewood Cliffs.

Hesse, H. (1995), *The Journey to the East*, Picador: London.

Hickman, C.C. and Silva, M. (1984), *Creating Excellence: Managing Corporate Culture, Strategy and Changing in the New Age*, American Library: New York.

Hickson, D.J., Hinings, C.R., Lee, C.A., Schneck, R.E. and Pennings, J.M. (1971), 'A Strategic Contingencies Theory of Intraorganizational Power', *Administrative Science Quarterly*, Vol. 16, No. 2, June, pp. 216-29.

Hickson, D.J., Hinings, C.R., McMillan, C. and Schwitter, J. (1971), 'The Culture Free Contexts of Work Organisations: A Tri-National Composition', Working Paper, School of Management, University of Bradford.

Hickson, D.J., Pugh, D.S. and Phesey, D. (1969), 'Operations Technology and Organisation Structure: An Empirical Appraisal', *Administrative Science Quarterly*, Vol. 17, pp. 44-54.

Higgins, W. (1988), 'Swedish Social Democracy and the New Democratic Socialism', in Sainsbury, D. (ed.), *Democracy, State and Justice: Critical Perspectives and New Interpretations*, Almquist and Wiksell: Stockholm, pp. 69-90.

Hill, S. (1989), *The Tragedy of Technology*, Pluto Press: London.

Hobbes (1929), *Leviathan*, Basil Blackwell: Oxford.

Hodgson, R. (1988), 'Purposing: The Fundamental Dynamics', *Business Quarterly*, Vol. 52, No. 4, Spring, pp. 8-11.

Hofer, C. and Schendel, D. (1978), *Strategy Formulation: Analytical Concepts*, West: St Paul.

Hoffman, R. (1959), 'Homogeneity of Member Personality and Its Effect on Group Problem-Solving', *Journal of Abnormal and Social Psychology*, Vol. 58, No. 1, pp. 27-32.

Hoffman, R. and Maier, N. (1961), 'Quality and Acceptance of Problem Solutions by Members of Homogeneous and Heterogeneous Groups', *Journal of Abnormal and Social Psychology*, Vol. 62, No. 2, pp. 401-17.

Hofstede, G. (1980), *Culture's Consequences: International Differences in Work-Related Values*, Sage: London.

Hofstede, G. (1993), 'Cultural Constraints in Management Theories', *Academy of Management Executives*, Vol. 7, No. 1, pp. 81-94.

Hogwood, B. (1995), 'Public Policy', *Public Administration*, Vol. 73, No. 1, pp. 59-73.

Homans, G.C. (1958), 'Social Behaviour as Exchange', *American Journal of Sociology*, Vol. 63, pp. 597-606.

Homans, G.C. (1961), *Social Behaviour: Its Elements and Forms*, Harcourt, Brace, Jovanovich: New York.

Homes, G.C. (1956), *The Human Group*, Harcourt, Brace: New York.

Hood, C. (1990), 'Public Administration: Lost an Empire, Not Yet Found a Role?', in Leftwich, A. (ed.), *New Development in Political Science*, Edward Elger: Aldershot, pp. 76-84.

Hooijberg, R. and Quinn, R.E. (1992), 'Behavioural Complexity and the Development of Effective Managers' in Phillips, R.L. and Hunt, J.G. (eds.), *Strategic Leadership*, Quorum Books: London, pp. 161-75.

Hopkins, D., Ainscow, M. and West, M. (1994), *School Improvement in an Era of Change*, Cassell: London.

Hoskings, D.M. and Schriesheim, C. (1978), 'Book Review of Fiedler, F.E., Chemers, M.M. and Mahar, L., Improving Leadership Effectiveness: The Leader Match Concept', *Administrative Science Quarterly*, Vol. 23, No. 3, pp. 496-505.

House, R.J. (1971), 'A Path-Goal Theory of Leader Effectiveness', *Administrative Science Quarterly*, Vol. 16, No. 3, September, pp. 321-39.

House, R.J. (1977), 'A 1976 Theory of Charismatic Leadership', in Hunt, J.G. and Larson, L.L. (eds.), *Leadership: The Cutting Edge*, Southern Illinois University Press: Carbondale, pp. 76-94.

House, R.J. (1988), 'Leadership Research: Some Forgotten, Ignored or Overlooked Findings', in Hunt, J.G., Baliga, B.R., Dachler, H.P. and Schriesheim, C.A. (eds.), *Emerging Leadership Vistas*, Lexington Books: Lexington, pp. 245-60.

House, R.J., Spangler, W.D. and Woycke, J. (1991), 'Personality and Charisma in the US Presidency: A Psychological Theory of Leader Effectiveness', *Administrative Science Quarterly*, Vol. 36, No. 3, September, pp. 364-96.

Howard, J. (1986), 'Federal Government: Administrative Chronicle', *Australian Journal of Public Administration*, Vol. 45, No. 3, September, pp. 271-75.

Howard, J. (1990), 'Attacking the Budget Problem', in Kouzmin, A. and Scott, N. (eds.), *Dynamics in Australian Public Management: Selected Essays*, MacMillan: Melbourne, pp. 72-93.

Howell, J.M. (1988), 'Two Faces of Charisma', in Conger, J.A. and Kanungo, R.N. (eds.), *Charismatic Leadership: The Elusive Factor in Organisational Effectiveness*, Jossey-Bass: San Francisco, pp. 213-36.

Hrebiniak, L.G. and Joyce, W.F. (1985), 'Organizational Adaptation: Strategic Choice and Environmental Determinism', *Administrative Science Quarterly*, Vol. 30, No. 2, pp. 336-49.

Huber, G.P. (1990), 'A Theory of the Effects of Advanced Information Technologies on Organizational Design, Intelligence and Decision Making', *Academy of Management Review*, Vol. 15, No. 1, January, pp. 47-71.

Huber, G. and McDaniel, R. (1986), 'Exploiting Technology to Design More Effective Organisations', in Jarke, M. (ed.), *Managers, Micros and Mainframes*, John Wiley: New York, pp. 221-36.

Huey, J. (1995), 'Eisner Explains Everything', *Fortune*, Vol. 131, No. 7, 17 April, pp. 44-68.

Hunt, J.G. (1984), 'Leadership and Managerial Behaviour', *SRA Modules in Management*, Science Research Association, Chicago.

Hunt, J.G. (1991), *Leadership: A New Synthesis*, Sage Publications: Newbury Park.

Hunter, F. (1959), *Top Leadership*, University of North Carolina Press: Chapel Hill.

Hunter, F. (1963), *Community Power Structure: A Study of Decision Makers*, Anchor Books: New York.

Huo, P.Y. and McKinley, W. (1992), 'Nation as a Context for Strategy: The Effects of National Characteristics on Business Level Strategies', *Management International Review*, Vol. 32, No. 2, pp. 103-13.

Iaccoca, L. and Novak, W. (1984), *Iaccoca: An Autobiography*, Bantam Books: New York.

Inkson, J.H.K., Hickson, D.J. and Pugh, D.S. (1970), 'Organisation Context and Structure: An Abbreviated Replication', *Administrative Science Quarterly*, Vol. 15, No. 3, pp. 318-29.

Jackson, S.E., Brett, J.F., Sessa, V.I., Cooper, D.M., Julin, J.A. and Peyronnin, K. (1991), 'Some Differences Make a Difference: Individual Dissimilarity and Group Heterogeneity as Correlates of Recruitment, Promotion and Turnover', *Journal of Applied Psychology*, Vol. 76, No. 4, pp. 675-89.

Jacobs, T.O. (1970), *Leadership and Exchange in Formal Organisations*, Human Resources Research Organisation: Alexandria.
Jacobs, T.O. and Jaques, E. (1987), 'Leadership in Complex Systems', in Zeidner, J. (ed.), *Human Productivity Enhancement: Organisations, Personnel and Decision Making*, Vol. 2, Praeger: New York.
Jacobs, T.O. and Jaques, E. (1990), 'Military Executive Leadership', in Clark, K.E. and Clark, M.B. (eds.), *Measures of Leadership*, Leadership Library of America: West Orange, pp. 281-95.
Jago, A.G. (1982), 'Leadership: Perspectives in Theory and Research', *Management Science*, Vol. 28, No. 3, pp. 315-36.
James, D. (1994), 'Theories on Knowledge Exports Go into Competition', *Business Review Weekly*, 17 October, pp. 78-80.
Janis, I.L. (1972), *Victims of Groupthink*, Houghton-Mifflin: Boston.
Janis, I.L. (1982), *Groupthink* (Second Revised Edition), Houghton-Mifflin: Boston.
Janis, I.L. and Mann, L. (1977), *Decision Making: A Psychological Analysis of Conflict, Choice and Commitment*, Free Press: New York.
Jaques, E. (1951), *Changing Culture of the Factory*, Tavistock Publications: London.
Jaques, E. (1956), *Measurement of Responsibility*, Townstore Publications: London.
Jaques, E. (1967), *Progression Handbook*, Heinemann Educational Books: London.
Jaques, E. (1979), 'Taking Time Seriously in Evaluating Jobs', *Harvard Business Review*, Vol. 57, No. 5, pp. 124-32.
Jaques, E. (1986), 'The Development of Intellectual Capacity', *Journal of Applied Behavioural Science*, Vol. 22, No. 3, pp. 361-81.
Jaques, E. (1989), *Requisite Organisation*, Arlington: Cason Hall.
Jarman, A.M.G. and Kouzmin, A. (1990), 'Decision Pathways From Crisis: A Contingency-Theory Simulation Heuristic for the Challenger Shuttle Disaster (1983-88)', *Contemporary Crises: Law, Crime and Social Policy*, Vol. 14, No. 4, December, pp. 399-433.
Jarman, A.M.G. and Kouzmin, A. (1994), 'Creeping Crises, Environmental Agendas and Expert Systems: A Research Note', *International Review of Administrative Sciences*, Vol. 60, No. 3, September, pp. 399-422.
Javidon, M. (1991), 'Leading a High-Commitment, High-Performance Organisation', *Long Range Planning*, Vol. 24, No. 2, pp. 28-36.
Jay, P. (1967), *Management and Machiavelli*, Hodder and Stoughton: London.
Jeannot, T.M. (1989), 'Moral Leadership and Practical Wisdom', *International Journal of Social Economies*, Vol. 16, No. 6, pp. 14-38.

Jenkins, R.L., Reizentein, R.C. and Rodgers, F.G. (1984), 'Report Cards on the MBA', *Harvard Business Review*, Vol. 65, No. 5, September-October, pp. 20-30.

Jenkins, S. (1995), *Accountable to None: The Tory Nationalisation of Britain*, Hamish Hamilton: London.

Jensen, M.C. (1986), 'Agency Costs of Free Cashflow, Corporate Finance and Take-overs', *American Economic Review*, Vol. 76, No. 3, pp. 323-29.

Johnson, G. and Scholes, K. (1993), *Exploring Corporate Strategy: Text and Cases*, Third Edition, Prentice-Hall: New York.

Johnson, R. and Lawrence, P.R. (1988), 'Beyond Vertical Integration: The Rise of the Value-Adding Partnership', *Harvard Business Review*, July-August, pp. 94-104.

Jung, C.G. (1953), *Collected Works*, Routledge and Kegan Paul: London.

Kahalas, H. and Groves, D. (1979), 'An Exploration of Graduate Business Students' Values', *Journal of Industrial Psychology*, Vol. 6, No. 1, pp. 18-24.

Kakabadse, A.P. (1977), 'Corporate Management in Local Government', *Journal of Management Studies*, Winter.

Kakabadse, A.P. (1982), *Culture of the Social Services*, Gower: Hampshire.

Kakabadse, A.P. (1983), *Politics of Management*, Gower: Hampshire.

Kakabadse, A.P. (1991), *The Wealth Creators: Top People, Top Teams and Executive Best Practice*, Kogan Page: London.

Kakabadse, A.P. (1993), 'Success Levers for Europe: The Cranfield Executive Competencies Survey', *Journal of Management Development*, Vol. 13, No. 1, pp. 75-96.

Kakabadse, A.P., Brovetto, P.R. and Holzer, R. (eds.) (1988), *Management Development and the Public Sector*, Gower: Aldershot.

Kakabadse, A.P., Korac-Kakabadse, N. and Myers, A. (1996), 'Leadership and the Public Sector: An Internationally Comparative Benchmarking Analysis', paper presented at *The Commonwealth Association for Public Administration and Management (CAPAM), Second Biennial Conference on The New Public Administration: Global Challenges - Local Solutions*, 21-24 April, Malta.

Kakabadse, A.P. and Myers, A. (1995), 'Qualities of Top Management: Comparisons of European Manufacturers', *Journal of Management Development*, Vol. 14, No. 1, pp. 5-15.

Kakabadse, A.P. and Myers, A. (1996), 'Boardroom Skills for Europe', *European Management Journal*, Vol. 4, No. 2, pp. 189-200.

Kakabadse, A.P., Okazaki-Ward, L. and Myers, A. (1996), *Japanese Business Leaders*, International Thomson.

Kakabadse, A.P. and Parker, C. (1984), 'Towards a Theory of Political Behaviour in Organisations' in Kakabadse, A. and Parker, C. (eds.), *Power, Politics and Organisations: A Behavioural Science View*, John Wiley and Sons: Chichester, pp. 87-108.

Kant, I. (1901), *Critique of Pure Reason* (revised edition), translated by Meiklejohn, J.M.D., Wiley Book Company: London.

Kant, I. (1909), 'Preface to the Metaphysical Elements of Ethics' in Abbott, T.K. (translator), *Kant's Critique of Practical Reason and Other Works on the Theory of Ethics* (Sixth Edition), Longmans, Green and Co: London, pp. 45-80.

Kanter, R.M. (1977), *Men and Women of the Corporation*, Basic Books: New York.

Kanter, R.M. (1979), 'Power Failure in Management Circuits', *Harvard Business Review*, July-August, pp. 83-92.

Kanter, R.M, (1984), *The Change Masters*, Unwin: London.

Kanter, R.M. (1991), 'Transcending Business Boundaries: 12,000 World Managers View Change', *Harvard Business Review*, Vol. 69, No. 3, May-June, pp. 151-67.

Kass, H. and Catron, B. (1990), *Images and Identities in Public Administration*, Sage: London.

Kast, E. and Rosenzweig, J.E. (1973), *Contingency Views of Organisation and Management*, Science Research Associates: Chicago.

Katz, D. and Kahn, R.L. (1978), *The Social Psychology of Organisations*, John Wiley: New York.

Katz, R. (1982), 'The Effects of Group Longevity on Project Communication and Performance', *Administrative Science Quarterly*, Vol. 27, No. 1, pp. 81-104.

Kauffman, R.J. and Weill, P. (1990), 'An Evaluative Framework for Research on the Performance Effects on Information Technology Investment', *Information Systems Research*, Vol. 1, No. 4, December, pp. 377-88.

Kauppinen, T.J. and Ogg, Jr, A.J. (1994), *Vision into Action: The Leader's Guide to Driving Change in Turbulent Times*, Leadership Studies International Inc: San Diego, California.

Keating, M. (1988), 'Managing for Results: The Challenge for Finance and Agencies', *Canberra Bulletin of Public Administration*, Vol. 15, No. 5, May, pp. 73-5 and 78-80.

Keck, S. (1991), 'Top Executive Team Structure: Does it Matter Anyway?', paper presented at *The Academy of Management Meeting*, August, Miami.

Keen, P.G.W. (1987), 'Telecommunications and Organizational Choice', *Communications Research*, Vol. 14, No. 5, pp. 588-606.

Keen, P.G.W. (1991), *Shaping the Future: Business Design Through Information Technology*, Harvard Business School Press: New York.

Kelley, L., Whatley, A. and Worthley, R. (1987), 'Assessing the Effects of Culture on Managerial Attitudes: A Three-culture Test', *Journal of International Business Studies*, Vol. 18, No. 2, Summer, pp. 17-31.

Kelly, G.A. (1955), *The Psychology of Personal Construct Theory*, Vols 1 and 2, Norton: New York.

Kerr, S. and Jermier, J. (1978), 'Substitutes for Leadership: Their Meaning and Measurement', *Organisational Behaviour and Human Performance*, Vol. 22, No. 3, pp. 374-407.

Kets de Vries, M.F. (1977), 'Crisis Leadership and the Paranoid Potential', *Bulletin*, Vol. 41, pp. 349-56.

Kevin, P.D. (1980), 'Why Subsidise State Transport Authorities?', *Australian Quarterly*, Vol. 59, No. 1, pp. 60-72.

Kilbourne, C.E. (1935), 'The Element of Leadership', *Journal of Coast Artillery*, Issue 37, pp. 45-8.

Kilmann, R.H. (1985), 'Introduction', in Kilmann, R., Saxton, M. and Serpa, R. (eds.), *Gaining Control of the Corporate Culture*, Jossey Bass: San Francisco, pp. i-ix.

Kilmann, R.H. (1986), 'Five Steps for Closing Culture-Gaps', in Kilmann, R.H., Saxton, M.J., Serpa, R. and Associates (eds.), *Gaining Control of the Corporate Culture*, Jossey-Bass: San Francisco, pp. 351-69.

Kilmann, R.H., Saxton, M.J. and Serpa, R. (1986a), 'Introduction: Five Key Issues in Understanding and Changing Culture', in Kilmann, R.H., Saxton, M.J., Serpa, R. and Associates (eds.), *Gaining Control of the Corporate Culture*, Jossey-Bass: San Francisco, pp. 1-16.

Kilmann, R.H, Saxton, M.J. and Serpa, R. (1986b), 'Conclusion: Why Culture is Not Just a Fad' in Kilmann, R.H., Saxton, M.J., Serpa, R. and Associates (1986) (eds.), *Gaining Control of the Corporate Culture*, Jossey-Bass: San Francisco, pp. 421-34.

Kingdom, J. (1990), 'Public Administration or Public Implementation: A Discipline in Crisis', *Public Policy and Administration*, Vol. 5, No. 1, pp. 5-29.

Kipnis, D. (1976), *The Powerholders*, University of Chicago Press: Chicago.

Kogan, M., Cang, S., Dixon, M. and Tolhday, H. (1971), *Working Relationships Within the British Hospital Service*, Bookstall Publications: London.

Kogan, M. and Terry, J. (1971), *The Organisation of a Social Services Department: A Blueprint*, Bookstall Publications: London.

Korac-Boisvert, N. (1993), 'Vulnerability Analysis of IT Strategic Planning in Commonwealth Countries: Patterns for IT Transfer', *Journal of Contingencies and Crisis Management*, Vol. 1, No. 1, March, pp. 58-63.

Korac-Boisvert, N. and Kouzmin, A. (1994), 'The Dark Side of Info-Age Social Networks in Public Organisation and Creeping Crisis', *Administrative Theory and Praxis*, Vol. 16, No. 1, April, pp. 57-82.

Korac-Boisvert, N. and Kouzmin, A. (1994a), 'Soft-Core Disasters: A Multiple Realities Crisis Perspective on IT Development Failures', in Klages, H. and Hill, H. (eds.), *Trends in Public Sector Renewal*, Peter Lang Publishing House: Berlin, pp. 71-114.

Korac-Boisvert, N. and Kouzmin, A. (1996), 'From the 'Captains of the Ship' to Architects of 'Organisational Arks': Communication Innovations, Globalisation and the 'Withering Away' of Leadership Steering', in Garnett, J.L. and Kouzmin, A. (eds.), *Handbook of Administrative Communication*, Marcel Dekker Inc: New York, Ch. 30.

Korac-Kakabadse, A.P. and Korac-Kakabadse, N. (1996), The Kakabadse Report 'Leadership in Government: Study of the Australian Public Service', Report submitted to the Commonwealth Government, Canberra, Australia, Cranfield School of Management.

Korac-Kakabadse, N. and Knyght, P.R. (1995), 'Inequality of Discourse and the Problem of Access to Justice', paper presented at *The Australian and New Zealand Academy of Management (ANZAM) Conference*, James Cook University, Townsville, 3-6 December.

Korac-Kakabadse, N. and Kouzmin, A. (1995), 'Managing Transnational Talent: Cultural Unity Within Globalized Diversity', paper presented at *The Australian and New Zealand Academy of Management (ANZAM) Conference*, James Cook University, Townsville, 3-6 December.

Korac-Kakabadse, N. and Kouzmin, A. (1996), 'Molecular Innovation and Molar Scanning Strategies for the Adoption of New Information Technology (IT) in Learning Organizations', *Public Productivity and Management Review*, Vol. 19, No. 4, June, pp. 434-54.

Korman, A. (1968), 'The Prediction of Managerial Performance: A Review', *Personnel Psychology*, Vol. 21, pp. 295-332.

Kosnik, R.D. (1987), 'Greenmail: A Study of Board Performance in Corporate Governance', *Administrative Science Quarterly*, Vol. 32, No. 2, pp. 163-85.

Kosnik, R.D. (1990), 'Effects of Board Demography and Directors: Incentives on Corporate Greenmail Decision', *Academy of Management Journal*, Vol. 33, No. 1, pp. 129-50.

Kotter, J.P. (1977), 'Power Dependencies and Effective Management', *Harvard Business Review*, July-August, pp. 125-36.

Kotter, J.P. (1982), *The General Managers*, Free Press: New York.

Kotter, J.P. (1988), *The Leadership Factor*, The Free Press: New York.

Kotter, J.P. and Heskett, J.L. (1992), *Corporate Culture and Performance*, Free Press: New York.

Kotter, J.P., Schelesinger, L.A. and Sathe, V. (1979), *Organisation: Text, Cases and Readings on the Management of Organisational Design and Change*, Richard, D. Irwin: Homewood.

Kouzes, J.M. and Posner, B.Z. (1987), *The Leadership Challenge: How to Get Extraordinary Things Done in Organisations*, Jossey-Bass: San Francisco.

Kouzmin, A. (1980), 'Control in Organizational Analysis: The Lost Politics', in Dunkerley, D. and Salaman, G. (eds.), *1979 International Yearbook of Organizational Studies*, Routledge and Kegan Paul: London, pp. 56-89.

Kouzmin, A. (1983), 'Centrifugal Organisations: Technology and 'Voice' in Organisational Analysis', in Kouzmin, A. (ed.), *Public Sector Administration: New Perspectives*, Longman Cheshire: Melbourne, pp. 232-306.

Kouzmin, A. and Jarman, A. (1989), 'Crisis Decision Making: Towards a Contingency Decision Path Perspective', in Rosenthal, U., Charles, M. and t'Hart, P. (eds.), *Coping with Crises: The Management of Disasters, Riots and Terrorism*, Charles C. Thomas: Springfield, pp. 397-435.

Kozlowski, S.W. and Doherty, M.L. (1989), 'Integration of Climate and Leadership: Examination of a Neglected Issue', *Journal of Applied Psychology*, Vol. 74, No. 4, August, pp. 546-53.

Kozmetsky, G. (1985), *Transformational Management*, Harper and Row: Cambridge.

Krebs, D.L. and Miller, D.T. (1985), 'Altruism and Aggression', in Lindzey, G. and Aronoson, E. (eds.), *Handbook of Social Psychology: Volume 2* (Third Edition), Random House: New York, pp. 143-57.

Krieger, L. and Stern, F. (eds.) (1968), *The Responsibilities of Power*, Macmillan: London.

Kriegler, R., Dawkins, P., Ryan, J. and Wooden, M. (1988), *Achieving Organisational Effectiveness: Case Studies in the Australian Services Sector*, Oxford University Press: Melbourne.

Krupp, S. (1961), *Pattern in Organisational Analysis*, Holt, Rinehart and Winston: New York.

Kuhn, T.S. (1970), *The Structure of Scientific Revolutions*, (Second Edition), Chicago University Press: Chicago.

Laeyendecker, L. (1989), 'Resistance to Change in a Religious Institution', *The Netherlands Journal of Social Sciences*, Vol. 25, No. 1, pp. 4-17.

Lamoreaux, N. (1985), *The Great Merger Movements in American Business*, Cambridge University Press: New York.

Lane, J.E. (1993), *The Public Sector*, Sage: London.

Larson, L.L., Hunt, J.G. and Osborn, R.N. (1976), 'The Great Hi-Hi Leader Behaviour Myth: A Lesson from Occam's Razor', *Academy of Management Journal*, Vol. 19, No. 4, pp. 628-47.

Lawrence, P. and Lorsch, J. (1967), 'Leadership and Organisational Performance: A Study of Large Corporations', *American Sociological Review*, Vol. 37, No. 1, 117-30.
Lazarsfeld, P.F., Berelson, B. and Gaudet, H. (1944), *The People's Choice*, Colombia University Press: New York.
Lazarus, R.S. (1963), *Personality and Adjustment*, Prentice-Hall: Englewood Cliffs.
Leavett, H.J. (1987), *Corporate Pathfinders: Building Visions and Values into Organisations*, Penguin: New York.
Levinson, H. (1968), *The Exceptional Executive; A Psychological Conception*, Harvard University Press: Cambridge.
Levinson, H. (1981), *Executive*, Harvard University Press: Boston.
Lewin, K. (1966), *Principles of Topological Psychology*, McGraw-Hill: New York.
Lewis, D. (1993), 'New Perspective on Transformation Leadership', paper presented at *The Australian and New Zealand Academy of Management's (ANZAM) Annual Conference*, December, Geelong.
Lieberson, S. and O'Conner, J. (1972), 'Leadership and Organisational Performance', *American Sociological Review*, Vol. 37, No. 2, pp. 117-30.
Likert, R. (1961), *New Patterns of Management*, McGraw-Hill: New York.
Limerick, D. and Cunnington, B. (1993), *Managing the New Organisation: A Blueprint for Networks and Strategic Alliances*, Business and Professional Publishing: Sydney.
Lindsay, W.M. and Rue, L.W. (1980), 'Impact of the Business Environment on the Long-range Planning Process: A Contingency View', *Proceedings of the Academy of Management*, Vol. 23, pp. 385-404.
Locke, J. (1971), *Social Contract*, Oxford University Press: London.
Lohman, D. (1992), 'The Impact of Leadership on Corporate Success: a Comparative Analysis of the American and Japanese Experience', in Clark, K.E., Clark, M.B. and Campbell, D.P. (eds.), *Impact of Leadership*, Centre for Creative Leadership: Greensboro, pp. 59-80.
Lorsch, J.W. and MacIver, E. (1989), *Power and Potentates: The Reality of America's Corporate Boards*, Harvard Business School Press: Boston.
Lott, A.J. and Lott, B.E. (1965), 'Group Cohesiveness and Interpersonal Attraction: A Review of Relationships with Antecedent and Consequent Variables', *Psychological Bulletin*, Vol. 4, No. 3, pp. 259-309.
Luis, M. (1992), 'Organisations as Culture-Bearing Milieu', in Schaftriz, J. and Ott, J. (eds.), *Classics of Organisation Theory* (Third Edition), Brooks and Cole Publishers: California, pp. 421-32.
Lukes, S.C. (1974), *Power: A Radical View*, Macmillan: London.

Luthans, F. and Lockwood, D.L. (1984), 'Towards an Observation System for Measuring Leader Behaviour in Natural Settings', in Hunt, J.G., Hosking, D., Schriesheim, C.A. and Stewart, R. (eds.), *Leaders and Managers: International Perspective on Managerial Behaviour and Leadership*, Pergamon Press: New York.

Macadam, R.D. and Bawden, R.J. (1986), 'Challenge and Response: Developing a System for Educating more Effective Agriculturists', *Prometheus*, Vol. 18, No. 3, pp. 125-37.

Machiavelli, N. (1950), 'The Discourse', translated by Detmold, C. in *The Prince and The Discourse*, Random House: New York.

Machiavelli, N. (1958), *The Prince* (translated by Marriott, W.K.), J.M. Dent and Sons Ltd: London.

Madison, D.L., Allen, R.W., Porter, L.W., Renwick, P.A. and Mayes, B.T. (1980), 'Organisational Politics: An Exploration of Managers' Perceptions, *Human Relations*, Vol. 33, No. 2, pp. 455-74.

Maier, N.R.F. (1967), 'Assets and Liabilities in Group Problem Solving: The Need for an Integrative Function', *Psychological Review*, Vol. 74, pp. 239-49.

Malone, T.W. and Rockhardt, J.F. (1991), 'Computers, Network and the Corporation', *Scientific American*, Vol. 265, No. 3, pp. 128-37.

Malone, T.W., Yates, J. and Benjamin, R.I. (1987), 'Electronic Markets and Electronic Hierarchies', *Communications of the ACM*, Vol. 30, pp. 484-97.

Mangham, I.L. (1978), *Interactions and Interventions in Organisations*, John Wiley: Chichester.

Manneramma, M. (1986), 'Futures Research and Social Decision Making: Alternative Futures as a Case Study', *Futures*, Vol. 18, No. 3, October, pp. 658-70.

Manz, C.C. and Sims, Jr, H.P. (1990), *Superleadership: Leading Others to Lead Themselves*, Prentice-Hall: Berkeley.

Manz, C.C. and Sims, Jr, H.P. (1991), 'Superleadership: Beyond the Myth of Heroic Leadership', *Organizational Dynamics*, Vol. 19, Summer, pp. 18-35.

Marceau, J. (ed.) (1992), *Reworking the World: Organisations, Technologies and Cultures in Comparative Perspective*, Walter de Gruyter: New York.

March, J.G. (1962), 'The Business Firm as a Political Coalition', *Journal of Politics*, Vol. 24, No. 4, pp. 662-78.

March, J.G. (1981), 'Footnotes to Organisational Changes', *Administrative Science Quarterly*, Vol. 26, No. 4, December, pp. 563-77.

March, J.G. and Simon, H.A. (1958), *Organisations*, John Wiley: New York.

Marr, A. (1995), *Ruling Britannia: The Failure and Future of British Democracy*, Michael Joseph: Middlesex.

Marsden, P.V. (1987), 'Core Discussion Networks of Americans', *American Sociological Review*, Vol. 52, No. 2, pp. 122-31.

Martin, K.J. and McConnell, J.J. (1991), 'Corporate Performance, Corporate Take-overs and Management Turnover', *Journal of Finance*, Vol. 46, No. 4, pp. 671-88.

Marting, D.D. and Shell, R.L. (1988), *Managment of Professionals: Insights for Maximizing Cooperation*, ASQC Press, Marcel Dekker: New York.

Marx, K. (1973), *Grundrisse: Foundations of the Critique of Political Economy*, (translated by Nicolaus, N.), Penguin: Harmondsworth.

Marx, K. (1976), *Capital: A Critique of Political Economy* (Vols. I-III) (translator Fowkes, B.), Penguin: Harmondsworth.

Maslow, A.H. (1962), *Toward a Psychology of Being*, Van Nostrand: Princeton.

Maslow, A.H. (1971), *The Further Reaches of Human Nature*, Penguin Books: Middlesex.

May, R. (1953), *Man's Search for Himself*, George Allen and Unwin: London.

May, R. (1972), *Power and Innocence*, W.W. Norton: New York.

Mayes, B.T. and Allen, R.W. (1977), 'Towards a Definition of Organisational Politics', *The Academy of Management Review*, Vol. 2, No. 4, October, pp. 672-78.

Mayo, E. (1933), *The Human Problems of an Individual Civilisation*, Macmillan: New York.

McAdam, N. (1993), 'In Search of the 'Sensitive New Age' Leader: Brain Dominance and Leadership Style', *Management*, November, pp. 5-8.

McAller, N. (1991), 'The Roots of Inspiration', in Henry, J. (ed.), *Creative Management*, Sage: London, pp. 12-15.

McAllister, I. and Vowles, J. (1994), 'The Rise of New Politics and Market Liberalism in Australia and New Zealand', *British Journal of Political Science*, Vol. 24, No. 3, pp. 381-402.

McCain, B., O'Reilly, III, C.A. and Pfeffer, J. (1983), 'The Effects of Departmental Demography on Turnover, *Administrative Science Quarterly*, Vol. 26, No. 4, pp. 626-41.

McCall, Jr, M.W. and Lombardo, M.M. (1983), 'What Makes a Top Executive?', *Psychology Today*, February, pp. 16-23.

McClelland, D.C. (1955), *Studies in Motivation*, Appleton-Century-Crofts: New York.

McClelland, D.C. (1958), 'Methods of Measuring Human Motivation', in Atkinson, J.W. (ed.), *Motives in Fantasy, Action and Society*, Van Nostrand: Princeton, pp. 7-45.

McClelland, D.C. (1961), *The Achieving Society*, D. Van Nostrand: New York.

McClelland, D.C. (1975), *Power: The Inner Experience*, Irvington: New York.
McClelland, D.C. and Boyatzis, R.E. (1982), 'Leadership Motive Pattern and Long-term Success in Management', *Journal of Applied Psychology*, Vol. 67, No. 4, pp. 737-43.
McClelland, D.C. and Burnham, D.H. (1976), 'Power is the Great Motivation', *Harvard Business Review*, Vol. 54, No. 2, pp. 100-10.
McClelland, D.C. and Winter, D.G. (1969), *Motivating Economic Achievement*, Free Press: New York.
McDermott, J. (1969), 'Technology: The Opiate of the Intellectual', *New York Review of Books*, 31 July, pp. 25-31.
McGregor, D. (1960), *The Human Side of Enterprise*, McGraw-Hill: New York.
McKevitt, D. (1993), 'Strategic Management in Public Services' in Willcocks, L. and Harrow, J. (eds.), *Rediscovering Public Service Management*, McGraw-Hill: London, pp. 40-58.
McNeil, K. and Thompson, J.D. (1971), 'The Regeneration of Social Organisations', *American Sociological Review*, Vol. 36, No. 4, pp. 624-37.
McPherson, M.J. (1990), 'Evolution in Communities of Voluntary Organisations', in Singh, J.V. (ed.), *Organisational Evaluation: New Directions*, Sage: London, pp. 224-45.
McPherson, P. (1984), 'Limits on Self-Seeking: The Role of Morality in Economic Life', in Colander, D. (ed.), *Neoclassical Political Economy: The Analysis of Rent-Seeking and DUP Activities*, Ballinger: Cambridge, pp. 71-85.
Meaney, C. (1995), 'Foreign Experts, Capitalism and Competing Agendas', *Comparative Political Studies*, Vol. 28, No. 2, pp. 275-305.
Meidle, J.R. and Ehrich, S.B. (1987), 'The Romance of Leadership and the Evaluation of Organisational Performance', *Academy of Management Journal*, Vol. 30, No. 1, pp. 90-109.
Meidner, R. (1978), *Collective Capital Formation through Wage-Earner Funds*, Allen and Unwin: London.
Merton, R.K. (1968), *Social Theory and Social Structure*, Free Press: New York.
Metzger, N. (1987), 'Beyond Survival to Excellency', *The Health Care Supervisor*, Vol. 5, No. 2, January, pp. 23-8.
Meyer, H.D. (1993), 'The Cultural Gap in Long-term International Work Groups: A German-American Case Study', *European Management Journal*, Vol. 11, No. 1, pp. 93-101.
Meyer, J. and Rowan, B. (1983), 'The Structure of Educational Organisations', in Meyer, J. and Scott, W. (eds.), *Organisational Environments: Ritual and Rationality*, Sage: Beverley Hills, pp. 71-97.

Michel, J. and Hambrick, D. (1992), 'Diversification Posture and Top Team Characteristics', *Academy of Management Journal*, Vol. 35, No. 1, pp. 9-37.

Miletti, D.S., Gillespie, D.F. and Morrissey, E. (1978), 'Technology and Organisations; Methodological Deficiencies Lacunae', *Technology and Culture*, Vol. 19, No. 1, pp. 83-92.

Milgram, S. (1974), *Obedience to Authority: An Experimental View*, Harper and Row: New York.

Miller, D. (1991), 'Stale in the Saddle: CEO Tenure and the Match between Organisation and Environment', *Management Science*, Vol. 37, No. 1, pp. 34-52.

Miller, W.C. (1995), 'Is Innovation Built Into Your Improvement Processes?', *Journal for Quality and Participation*, January/February, pp. 46-9.

Mills, W.C. (1940), 'Situated Actions and Vocabularies of Motive', *American Sociological Review*, No. 5, pp. 904-13.

Mills, W.C. (1957), *The Power Elite*, Oxford University Press: New York.

Mintzberg, H. (1973), *The Nature of Managerial Work*, Harper and Row: New York.

Mischel, W. (1977), 'Self-centred and The Self' in Mischel, T. (ed.), *The Self: Psychological and Philosophical Issues*, Bowman and Littlefield: N.J.

Misumi, J. and Peterson, M. (1985), 'The Performance Maintenance (PM) Theory of Leadership: Review of a Japanese Research Program', *Administrative Science Quarterly*, Vol. 30, No. 2, June, pp. 198-223.

Mitchell, T.R. and Scott, W.G. (1978), 'Leadership Failures, the Distrusting Public and Prospects of the Administrative State', *Public Administration Review*, Vol. 38, No. 6, November-December, pp. 445-52.

Mitroff, I.I. and Kilmann, R.H. (1984), *Corporate Tragedies: Product Tampering, Sabotage and Other Catastrophies*, Preager: New York.

Mittman, B.S. (1992), 'Theoretical and Methodological Issues in the Study of Organisation Demography and Demographic Change', in Tolbert, P.S. and Bacharach, S.B. (eds.), *Research in the Sociology of Organisation*, Vol. 10, JAI Press: Greenwich, pp. 3-53.

Mobley, W.H., Griffeth, R.W., Hand, H.H. and Meglino, B. (1979), 'Review and Conceptual Analysis for the Employee Turnover Process', *Psychological Bulletin*, Vol. 86, No. 5, pp. 493-522.

Montenare, J.R. (1978), 'Managerial Discretion: An Expended Model of Organisation Choice', *Academy of Management Review*, Vol. 3, No. 2, pp. 231-41.

Morgan, C. and Murgatroyd, S. (1994), *Total Quality Management in the Public Sector*, Open University Press: Buckingham.

Morgan, G. (ed.) (1983), *Beyond Method: Strategies for Social Research*, Sage: Beverley Hills.
Morgan, G. (1986), *Images of Organisation*, Sage: Beverley Hills.
Mouzelis, N.P. (1967), *Organisation and Bureaucracy: An Analysis of Modern Theories*, Routledge and Kegan Paul: London.
Muetzelfeldt, M. (1988), 'The Ideology of Consumption Within the Mode of Production', paper presented to the *Sociological Association of Australia and New Zealand Conference*, May, Canberra.
Muetzelfeldt, M. (1992), 'Organizational Restructuring and Devolutionist Doctrine: Organization as Strategic Control', in Marceau, J. (ed.), *Reworking the World: Organizations, Technologies, and Cultures in Comparative Perspective*, Walter de Gruyter: New York, pp. 295-316.
Münsterberg, H. (1913), *Psychology and Industrial Efficiency*, Management History Series, Vol. 19, Hive: Easton.
Murray, A. (1989), 'Top Management Group Heterogeneity and Firm Performance', *Strategic Management Journal*, Vol. 10, No 1, pp. 125-41.
Murray, V. and Gandz, J. (1980), 'Games Executives Play: Politics at Work', *Business Horizons*, pp. 11-23.
Myers, A., Kakabadse, A.P. and Gordon, C. (1995), 'Effectiveness of French Management: Analysing the Behaviour, Attitudes and Business Impact of Top Managers', *Journal of Management Development*, Vol. 14, No. 6, pp. 56-72.
Nader, J. (1995), 'Seers Look Forward to 2095', *ABM*, April, pp. 106-9.
Nadler, D.A. and Tushman, M.L. (1990), 'Beyond the Charismatic Leader: Leadership and Organisational Change', *California Management Review*, Vol. 32, No. 2, Winter, pp. 77-97.
Nagel, J.H. (1991), 'Psychological Obstacles to Administrative Responsibility: Lessons of the MOVE Disasters', *Journal of Policy and Analysis and Management*, Vol. 10, No. 1, Winter, pp. 1-23.
Naisbitt, J. (1994), *Global Paradox*, William Morrow and Company: New York.
Naulleau, G. and Harper, J. (1993), 'A Comparison of British and French Management Cultures: Some Implications for Management Development Practices in Each Country', *Management Education Review*, Vol. 24, Iss. 1, Spring, pp. 14-25.
Neisser, U. (1977), *Cognition and Reality*, John Wiley: New York.
Neustadt, R.E. (1960), *Presidential Power: The Politics of Leadership*, John Wiley: New York.
Newman, A.D. and Rowbottom, R.W. (1968), *Organisation Analysis, The Glacier Project*, Heinemann Educational Books: London.
Ng, S.H. (1980), *The Social Psychology of Power*, Academic Press: New York.

Nibly, H. (1984), 'Leadership Versus Management', *BYU Today*, February, pp. 16-47.
Nietzsche, F. (1976), *The Will to Power*, Vintage: New York.
Nohria, N. and Eccles, R.G. (1992), 'Face-to-Face: Making Network Organisations Work', in Nohria, N. and Eccles, R.G. (eds.), *Networks and Organisations: Structure, Form and Action*, Harvard Business School Press: Boston, pp. 288-308.
Nolan, R.L., Pollock, A.J. and Ware, J.P. (1988), 'Creating the 21st Century Organisation', *Stage by Stage*, Vol. 8, No. 4, pp. 1-17.
Nolan, R.L., Pollock, A.J. and Ware, J.P. (1989), 'Towards the Design of Network Organisations', *Stage by Stage*, Vol. 9, No. 1, pp. 1-11.
Nord, W.R. (1974), 'The Failure of Current Applied Behavioural Science: A Marxian Perspective', *Journal of Applied Behavioural Science*, Vol. 10, No. 4, pp. 557-78.
Norman, D.A. (1976), *Memory and Attention*, Wiley: New York.
Normann, R. (1977), *Managing for Growth*, Wiley: New York.
Nyberg, D. (1981), *Power Over Power*, Cornell University Press: New York.
O'Brian, C. and Banech, W.D. (1969), *Power and Consciousness*, New York University Press: New York.
O'Reilly, III, C.A., Caldwell, D.F. and Burnett, W.P. (1989), 'Workgroup Demography, Social Integration and Turnover', *Administrative Science Quarterly*, Vol. 34, No. 1, pp. 21-37.
O'Reilly, C.A. and Flatt, S. (1989), 'Executive Team Demography, Organisational Innovation and Firm Performance', Working Paper, Haas School of Business, University of California, Berkeley.
O'Tool, J.J. (1979), 'Corporate and Managerial Culture', in Cooper, C.L. (ed.), *Behavioural Problems in Organisations*, Prentice-Hall: Englewood Cliffs.
Ohmae, K. (1990), *The Borderless World*, Harper Business Press: New York.
Organization for Economic Cooperation and Development (OECD) (1987), 'Structural Adjustment and Economic Performance', OECD: Paris.
Organisation for Economic Cooperation and Development (OECD) (1995), 'The OECD Science and Technology Review', No. 15, OECD: Paris.
Osborne, D. and Gaebler, T. (1992), *Reinventing Government: How The Entrepreneurial Spirit is Transforming the Public Sector*, Addision-Wesley: Reading.
Ouchi, W. (1980), 'Markets, Bureaucracies and Clans', *Administrative Science Quarterly*, Vol. 25, No. 2, June, pp. 129-42.
Ouchi, W. (1981), *Theory Z*, Addison-Wesley: Reading.
Papp, D.S. (1984), *Contemporary International Relations: Frameworks for Understanding*, Macmillan: New York.

Parry, K.W. (1994), 'Transformational Leadership: An Australian Investigation of Leadership Behaviour', in Kouzmin, A., Still, L.V. and Clarke, P. (eds.), *New Directions in Management*, McGraw-Hill Book Company: Sydney, pp. 82-114.

Parsons, T. (1959), 'The Social Class as a Social System', *Harvard Educational Review*, Vol. 19, No. 4, pp. 297-318.

Pask, G. (1961), *An Approach to Cybernetics*, Harper and Row: New York.

Pauchant, T.C. (1991), 'Transferential Leadership: Towards a More Complex Understanding of Charisma in Organisations', *Organizational Studies*, Vol. 12, No. 4, pp. 507-27.

Peck, M.S. (1983), *The Different Drum*, Pan: London.

Pedler, M. (1988), 'Self-Development and Work Organisations', in Pedler, M., Burgoyne, J. and Boydell, T. (eds.), *Applying Self-Development in Organisations*, Prentice-Hall: London, pp. 76-92.

Pelz, D. and Andrews, F. (1966), *Scientists in Organisations*, Wiley: New York.

Pennings, J.H. (1973), 'Measures of Organisational Structure: A Methodological Note', *American Journal of Scociology*, Vol. 79, pp. 686-704.

Perez, C. and Soete, L. (1988), 'Catch up in Technology: Entry Barriers and Windows of Opportunity', in Dosi, G., Freeman, C., Nelson, R., Silverberg, G. and Soete, L. (eds.), *Technical Changes and Economic Theory*, Pinter: London, pp. 458-79.

Perrow, C. (1967), 'A Framework for the Comparative Analysis of Organisations', *American Sociological Review*, Vol. 32, No. 2, April, pp. 194-208.

Perrow, C. (1992), 'Small-Firm Networks', in Nohria, N. and Eccles, R.G. (eds.), *Networks and Organisations: Structure, Form and Action*, Harvard Business School Press: Boston, pp. 445-70.

Peters, T. and Austin, N. (1985), *A Passion for Excellence: The Leadership Difference*, Random House: New York.

Peters, T. and Waterman, R. (1982), *In Search of Excellence: Lessons from America's Best-Run Companies*, Harper and Row: New York.

Pettigrew, A.M. (1973), *The Politics of Organisational Decision-Making*, Tavistock: London.

Pettigrew, A.M. (1975), 'Strategy Formulation as a Political Process', *International Studies of Management and Organisation*, Vol. 7, pp. 78-87.

Pettigrew, A.M. (1979), 'On Studying Organisational Cultures', *Administrative Science Quarterly*, Vol. 24, No. 4, pp. 570-87.

Pettigrew, A.M. (1987), 'Context and Action in the Transformation of the Firm', *Journal of Management Studies*, Vol. 24, No. 6, pp. 18-26.

Pettigrew, A.M., Ferile, E. and McKee, L. (1992), *Shaping Strategic Change*, Sage: London.
Pfeffer, J. (1977), 'The Ambiguity of Leadership', *Academy of Management Review*, Vol. 2, No. 1, pp. 104-12.
Pfeffer, J. (1978), *Organisation Design*, AHM: Arlington Heights.
Pfeffer, J. (1981a), *Power in Organisations*, Pittman: Marshfield.
Pfeffer, J. (1981b), 'Management as a Symbolic Action: The Creation and Maintenance of Organisational Paradigms', in Cummings, L.L. and Staw, B.M. (eds.), *Research in Organisational Behaviour*, JAI Press: Greenwich, pp. 31-52.
Pfeffer, J. (1982), *Organisations and Organisation Theory*, Pitman: Boston.
Pfeffer, J. (1983), 'Organisational Demography', in Cummings, L.L. and Staw, B.M. (eds.), *Research in Organisational Behaviour*, Vol. 5, JAI Press: Greenwich, pp. 299-357.
Pfeffer, J. (1992), *Managing with Power: Politics and Influence in Organisations*, Harvard Business School Press: Boston.
Pfeffer, J. and Davis-Blake, A. (1992), 'Salary Dispersion, Location in the Salary Distribution and Turnover among College Administrators', *Industrial and Labour Relations Review*, Vol. 45, No. 4, pp. 753-63.
Pfeffer, J. and Salancik, G.R. (1978), *The External Control of Organisations: A Resource Dependence Perspective*, Harper and Row: New York.
Phillips, R.L. and Hunt, J.G. (eds.) (1992), *Strategic Leadership: A Multiorganisational-Level Perspective*, Quorum Books: Westport.
Piaget, J. (1978), *Essential Piaget*, Gruber, S. and Voreche, J. (eds.), Routledge and Kegan Paul: London.
Pijnenburg, B. and van Duin, M. (1991), 'The Zeebrugge Ferry Disaster: Elements of a Communication and Information Processes Scenario', in Rosenthal, U. and Pijnenburg, B. (eds.), *Crisis Management and Decision Making: Simulation Oriented Scenarios*, Kluwer Academic Publishers: Dordrecht, pp. 45-73.
Pirie, M. (1985), *Privatisation and the Public Sector: The British Experience and Its Application to Australia*, Adam Smith Institute: London.
Plato (1941), *The Republic*, Heinemann: Oxford.
Plato (1952), *The Statesman*, Routledge and Kegan Paul: London.
Plato (1956), *Apology*, translated by Church, F.J., Bobbs-Merrill: Indianapolis.
Plato (1957), 'Theaetetus', in *Plato's Theory of Knowledge: The Theaetetus and the Sophist of Plato*, translated by Conford, F.M., Bobbs Merrill: New York.
Plott, C.R. and Levine, M.E. (1961), 'A Model of Agenda Influence on Committee Decisions', *American Economic Review*, Vol. 68, No. 2, pp. 146-60.

Pollitt, C. (1993), *Managerialism and the Public Services*, Second Edition, Blackwell: Oxford.

Pollitt, C. (1996), 'Antistatist Reforms and New Administrative Directions: Public Administration in the United Kingdom', *Public Administration Review*, Vol. 56, No. 1, pp. 81-7.

Pollitt, C. and Harrison, S. (eds.) (1992), *Handbook of Public Services Management*, Blackwell: Oxford.

Ponder, Q.D. (1957), 'The Effective Manufacturing Foreman', in Young, E. (ed.), *Industrial Relations Resources Association Proceedings, 10th Annual Meeting*, Madison, pp. 41-54.

Pondy, L.R. (1978), 'Leadership is a Language Game', in McCall, M.W. and Lombardo, M.M. (eds.), *Leadership: Where Else Can We Go?*, Duke University Press: Durham.

Porat, M. (1977), 'The Information Economy', US Department of Commerce, Office of Telecommunications Special Publication, Number 77-12, Government Printing Office: Washington.

Porter, L.W., Allen, R.W. and Angle, H.L. (1981), 'The Politics of Upward Influence', in Staw, B.M. and Cummings, L.L., (eds.), *Research in Organisational Behaviour*, Vol. 3, JAI Press: Greenwich.

Porter, M.E. (1986), 'Government Regulation and Privatisation', *Canberra Bulletin of Public Administration*, Vol. 13, No. 3, Spring, pp. 204-10.

Porter, M.E. (1990), *The Competitive Advantage of Nations*, Free Press: New York.

Porter-O'Grady, T. (1984), *Shared Governance for Nursing: A Creative Approach to Professional Accountability*, Aspen System Corporation: Rockville.

Posner, B. and Low, P. (1990), 'Australian and American Managerial Values: Subtle Differences', *International Journal of Management*, Vol. 7, No. 1, pp. 89-97.

Powell, W.W. (1990), 'Neither Market Nor Hierarchy: Network Forms of Organisation', in Staw, B.M. and Cummings, L.L. (eds.), *Research in Organisational Behaviour: Volume 12*, JAI Press: Greenwich, pp. 295-336.

Power, M. (1994), *The Audit Explosion*, Demos: London.

Prahalad, C.K. and Bettis, R.A. (1986), 'The Dominant Logic: A New Linkage between Diversity and Performance', *Strategic Management Journal*, Vol. 7, No. 4, pp. 485-501.

Prior, D. (1993), 'In Search of the New Public Management', *Local Government Studies*, Vol. 19, No. 3, pp. 447-60.

Public Eye (1993), 'PS Stress Levels Underestimated', 3 June, pp. 1-2.

Pugh, C. (1991), 'Efficiency Auditing and the Australian Audit Office', *Australian Journal of Public Administration*, Vol. 46, No. 1, March, pp. 55-65.

Pugh, D.S. (1969), 'Organisational Behaviour: An Approach from Psychology', *Human Relations*, Vol. 22, pp. 345-54.
Pugh, D.S., Hickson, D.J., Hinings, C.R., McDonald, N.M., Turner, C. and Lipton, T. (1963), 'A Conceptual Scheme for Organisational Analysis', *Administrative Science Quarterly*, Vol. 8, pp. 289-315.
Pugh, D.S. and Payne, R.L. (1976) (eds.), *Organisational Behaviour in Its Context: The Aston Programme III*, Saxon House: Farnborough.
Pussey, M. (1991), *Economic Rationalism in Canberra: A Nation Building State Changes its Mind*, Cambridge University Press: Melbourne.
Quinn, R.E. (1981), 'Competing Values Approach to Organisational Effectiveness', *Public Productivity Review*, Vol. 5, No. 1, pp. 122-40.
Quinn, R.E. (1988), *Beyond Rational Management: Mastering the Paradoxes and Competing Demands of High Performance*, Jossey-Bass Publishers: San Francisco.
Quinn, R.E. and Cameron, K. (1983), 'Organisational Life Cycles and Shifting Criteria of Effectiveness: Some Preliminary Evidence', *Management Science*, Vol. 29, No. 1, pp. 33-50.
Quinn, R.E., Denison, D. and Hooijberg, R. (1989), 'An Empirical Assessment of the Competing Values Leadership Instrument', Working Paper, The University of Michigan, School of Business: Michigan.
Quinn, R.E., Spreitzer, G.M. and Hart, S. (1991), 'Challenging the Assumptions of Bipolarity: Interpretation and Managerial Effectiveness' in Srivastava, S. and Fry, R. (eds.), *Executive Continuity*, Jossey-Bass: San Francisco, pp. 79-98.
Radford, N. (1994), 'The School to Work Transition', *DEET Times*, Vol. 7, December, p. 2.
Ramos, A.G. (1981), *The New Science of Organisation: A Reconceptualization of the Wealth of Nations*, University of Toronto Press: Toronto.
Reed, R.L. (1978), 'Organisational Change in the American Foreign Service 1925-1965: The Utility of Cohort Analysis', *American Sociological Review*, Vol. 43, No. 3, pp. 404-21.
Reich, R.B. (1991), *The Work of Nations: Preparing Ourselves for 21st Century Capitalism*, Alferd A. Knopf: New York.
Reiman, B.C. (1973), 'On the Dimensions of Bureaucratic Structure: An Empirical Reappraisal', *Administrative Science Quarterly*, Vol. 188; pp. 462-76.
Reynolds, L. (1994), 'Can Government be Reinvented?', *Management Review*, January, pp. 14-21.
Rhinesmith, S.H. (1993), *A Manager's Guide to Globalization: Six Keys to Success in a Changing World*, The American Society for Training and Development, Irwin: New York.

Rhinesmith, S.H. (1995), 'Open the Door to a Global Mindset', *Training and Development*, May, pp. 35-43.
Rhodes, R. (1991), 'Theory and Methods in British Public Administration: The View From Political Science', *Political Studies*, Vol. 39, No. 5, pp. 533-54.
Rhodes, R. (1995), 'The State of Public Administration: A Professional History, 1970-95', *Public Administration*, Vol. 73, No. 1, pp. 1-15.
Rice, R.E. and Aydin, C. (1991), 'Attitudes Towards New Organisational Technology: Network Proximity as a Mechanism for Social Information Processing', *Administrative Science Quarterly*, Vol. 36, No. 2, June, pp. 219-44.
Rice, R.E., and Blair, J., (1984), 'New Organisational Media and Productivity', in Rice R.E. (ed.), *The New Media: Communication, Research and Technology*, Sage: Beverley Hills, pp. 185-216.
Rice, R.E., Grant, A., Schmitz, J. and Torobin, J. (1990), 'Individual and Network Influences on the Adoption and Perceived Outcomes of Electronic Messaging', *Social Networks*, Vol. 12, No. 1, pp. 27-55.
Richards, C. (ed.) (1991), *Gathering Momentum: Commercialisation in the Public Sector*, AGPS for the Department of Administrative Services: Canberra.
Riegel, K. (1973), 'Dialectic Operations: The Final Period of Cognitive Development', *Human Development*, Vol. 16, No. 3, pp. 346-70.
Roberts, K.H. and O'Reilly, III, C.A. (1979), 'Some Correlates of Communication Roles in Organisations', *Academy of Management Journal*, Vol. 22, No. 1, pp. 42-57.
Robinson, R.B. (1982), 'The Importance of 'Outsiders' in Small Firm Strategic Planning', *Academy of Management Journal*, Vol. 25, No. 1, pp. 80-93.
Robinson, R.B. and Pearce, J. (1984), 'Research Thrusts in Small Firm Strategic Planning', *Academy of Management Review*, Vol. 9, No. 1, pp. 128-37.
Rogers, C.R. (1951), *Client-Centred Therapy*, Houghton-Mifflin: Boston.
Rogers, E.M. and Kincaid, D.L. (1981), *Communication Networks: Towards a New Paradigm for Research*, Free Press: New York.
Rogers, E.M. and Shoemaker, F. (1971), *Communication of Innovations*, Free Press: New York.
Romanelli, E. and Tushman, M. (1986), 'Executive Leadership and Organisational Outcomes: An Evolutionary Perspective', in Hambrick D. (ed.), *The Executive Effect: Concept and Methods for Studying Top Managers*, JAI Press: Greenwich, pp. 129-40.

Romanelli, E. and Tushman, M. (1988), 'Executive Leadership and Organisational Outcomes: Towards a Competing Values Approach to Organisational Analysis', *Management Science*, Vol. 29, No. 3, pp. 367-77.

Ronen, S. (1986), *Comparative and Multinational Management*, Wiley: New York.

Roobeek, A.J.M. (1990), 'The Technological Debacle: European Technology Policy from a Future Perspective', *Futures*, Vol. 22, No. 6, November, pp. 904-14.

Rose, A.M. (1967), *The Power Structure*, Oxford University Press: New York.

Rosen, R.H. and Brown, P.B. (1996), *Leading People: Transforming Business from the Inside Out*, Penguin Books: Sydney.

Rosen, S., Levinger, G. and Lippitt, R. (1961), 'Perceived Sources of Social Power', *Journal of Abnormal Social Psychology*, Vol. 62, No. 3, pp. 439-41.

Rosenthal, U. and Kouzmin, A. (1993), 'Globalizing an Agenda for Contingencies and Crisis Management: An Editorial Statement', *Journal of Contingencies and Crisis Management*, Vol. 1, No. 1, March, pp. 1-12.

Rosenthal, U., t'Hart, P. and Kouzmin, A. (1991), 'The Bureau-Politics of Crisis Management', *Public Administration*, Vol. 69, No. 2, Summer, pp. 211-33.

Roszak, T. (1986), *The Cult of Information*, Lutterworth: Cambridge.

Rothstein, B. (1989), 'Argument før en Civil Socialism', *Omdaningen*, Sveriges Socialdemokratiska Undomsforbund: Kalmer, pp. 147-59.

Rotter, J.B. (1966), 'Generalised Expectancies for Internal Versus External Control of Reinforcement', *Psychological Monographs*, Vol. 80, No. 1, Whole No. 609.

Russell, B. (1938), *Power: A New Social Analysis*, W.W. Norton and Co: New York.

Ryder, N.B. (1964), 'Notes on the Concept of a Population', *American Journal of Sociology*, Vol. 30, No. 4, pp. 842-61.

Salancik, G.R. and Pfeffer, J. (1977), 'The Bases and Use of Power in Organisational Decision Making: The Case of a University', *Administrative Science Quarterly*, Vol. 22, No. 3, pp. 453-73.

Salancik, G.R. and Pfeffer, J. (1977a), 'Constraints on Administrator Decisions: The Limited Influence of Mayor on City Budget', *Urban Affairs Quarterly*, Vol. 12, No. 4, pp. 475-98.

Salancik, G.R. and Pfeffer, J. (1977b), 'Who Gets Power - And How They Hold on to It: A Strategic-Contingency Model of Power', *Organisational Dynamics*, Winter, p. 3-21.

Sappinen, J. (1992), 'Adjustment to a Foreign Culture and Measuring Expatriate Failure and Success: Two Case Studies of Finns in Estonia', Research Paper Series 2, Helsinki School of Economic and International Business Administration, Centre for International Business Research, Helsinki.

Sashkin, M. (1992), 'Strategic Leadership Competencies' in Phillips, R.L. and Hunt, J.G. (eds.), *Strategic Leadership: A Multiorganisational-Level Perspective*, Quorum Books: Westport.

Sashkin, M. and Burke, W. (1990), 'Understanding and Assessing Organisational Leadership', in Clark, K.E. and Clark, B. (eds.), *Measures of Leadership*, Leadership Library of America: West Orange, pp. 297-325.

Sashkin, M. and Morris, W.C. (1984), *Organisational Behaviour: Concepts and Experiences*, Prentice-Hall: Englewood Cliffs.

Sathe, V. (1983), 'Implications of Corporate Culture: A Manager's Guide to Action', *Organisational Dynamics*, Vol. 12, No. 2, Autumn, pp. 5-23.

Savoie, D. (1994), *Thatcher, Reagan, Mulroney in Search of a New Bureaucracy*, University of Toronto Press: Toronto.

Sayles, L.R. (1979), *Leadership: What Effective Managers Really Do and How They Do It*, McGraw-Hill Book Company: New York.

Schein, E.H. (1983), 'Role of the Founder in Creating Organisational Culture', *Organisational Dynamics*, Vol. 12, No.1, Summer, pp. 13-29.

Schein, E.H. (1985), *Organisational Culture and Leadership: A Dynamic View*, Jossey-Bass: San Francisco.

Schein, E.H. (1986), 'How Culture Forms, Develops and Changes' in Kilmann, R.H., Saxton, M.J., Serpa, R. and Associates (eds.), *Gaining Control of the Corporate Culture*, Jossey-Bass: San Francisco, pp. 17-43.

Schein, V.E. (1977), 'Individual Power and Political Behaviour in Organisations: An Inadequately Explored Reality', *Academy of Management Review*, January, pp. 64-72.

Schmitz, J. and Fulk, J. (1991), 'Organisational Colleagues' Information Richness and Electronic Mail: A Test of the Social Influence Model of Technology Use', *Communication Research*, Vol. 18, pp. 83-97.

Schneider, S.C. (1987), *Conflicting Ideologies: Structural and Motivational Consequences*, (Working Papers Insead 87/22), Fontainbleau: Insead.

Schneider, S.C. (1994), *Interpreting Strategic Issues: Making Sense of 1992*, (Working Papers Insead 94/01), Fontainbleau: Insead.

Schneider, S.C. and Meyer, A.D. (1991), 'Interpreting and Responding to Strategic Issues: The Impact of National Culture', *Strategic Management Journal*, Vol. 12, No. 2, pp. 307-20.

Schuler, R.S., Dowling, P.J. and Smart, J.P. (1988), *Personnel-Human Resources Managment in Australia*, Harper and Row: Sydney.

Schwartz, H.W. (1994), 'Public Choice Theory and Public Choices: Bureaucrats and State Reorganisation in Australia, Denmark, New Zealand and Sweden in the 1980s', *Administration and Society*, Vol. 26, No. 1, May, pp. 48-77.

Scott, W.E. (1977), 'Leadership: A Functional Analysis', in Hunt, J.G. and Larson, L.L. (eds.), *Leadership: The Cutting Edge*, Southern Illinois University Press: Carbondale.

Scott, W.E. (1992), *Organisations: A Rational, Natural and Open System*, Third Edition, Prentice-Hall: Englewood Cliffs.

Seibel, W. (1996), 'Administrative Science as Reform: German Public Administration', *Public Administration Review*, Vol. 56, No. 1, pp. 74-81.

Selznick, P. (1952), *The Organisational Weapon*, McGraw-Hill: New York.

Selznick, P. (1957), *Leadership in Administration: A Sociological Interpretation*, Harper and Row: New York.

Semler, R. (1993), *Maverick*, Arrow: London.

Senge, P.M. (1990a), *The Fifth Discipline: The Art and Practice of the Learning Organisation*, Century Books: London.

Senge, P.M. (1990b), 'The Leader's New Work: Building Learning Organisations', *Sloan Management Review*, Vol. 32, No. 1, Fall, pp. 7-23.

Senge, P.M. (1992), *The Fifth Discipline: The Art and Practice of the Learning Organization*, Random House: Sydney.

Senge, P.M., Ross, C., Smith, B. and Kleiner, A. (1994), *The Fifth Discipline Fieldbook: Strategies and Tools for Building a Learning Organisation*, Nicholas Brealey: London.

Shaw, M.E. (1976), *Group Dynamics: The Psychology of Small Group Behaviour*, McGraw-Hill: New York.

Shenhav, Y. and Haberfeld, Y. (1992), 'Organisational Demography and Inequality', *Social Forces*, Vol. 71, No. 1, pp. 123-43.

Sherwood, F.P. (1992), 'Comprehensive Government Reform in New Zealand', *Public Manager*, Vol. 21, No. 1, Spring, pp. 20-4.

Silverman, D. (1971), *The Theory of Organisations: A Sociological Framework*, Heinemann: London.

Simmel, G. (1955), *Conflict and the Web of Group Affiliations*, Free Press: New York.

Simon, H.A. (1947), *Administrative Behaviour*, Macmillan: New York.

Simon, H.A. (1957), *The Methods of Man*, John Wiley and Sons: New York.

Simon, H.A., Smithburg, W. and Thompson, V.A. (1950), *Public Administration*, Alfred A. Knopf: New York.

Sinclair, A. (1989), 'Public Sector Culture: Managerialism or Multiculturalism', *Australian Journal of Public Administration*, Vol. 48, No. 4, pp. 378-86.

Skelton, A. and Miller, W.C. (1993), 'Quality Innovation', *Executive Excellence*, September, pp. 15-16.
Skinner, B.F. (1953), *Science and Human Behaviour*, The Macmillan Company: New York.
Slater, P. (1976), *Exploration of Intrapersonal Space*, Vol 1, John Wiley: Chichester.
Slater, St. P., S. (1984), 'The Impact of Crisis on Managerial Behaviour', *Business Horizon*, May-June, pp. 65-8.
Slem, C.M., Llevi, D. and Young, A. (1986), 'The Effect of Technological Changes on the Psycho-Social Characteristic of Organisations', in Brown, Jr, O. and Hendrick, H.W. (eds.), *Human Factors in Organisational Design Management*, 2nd Edition, Elsevier Science Publishing: North-Holland, pp. 567-79.
Smelser, N. (1963), *Theory of Collective Behaviour*, Free Press: New York.
Smirchich, L. (1983), 'Concepts of Culture and Organisational Analysis', *Administrative Science Quarterly*, Vol. 28, No. 2, June, pp. 339-68.
Smith, K.G., Smith, K.A., Olian, J.D., Sims, Jr, H.P., O'Bannon, D.P. and Scully, J.A. (1994), 'Top Management Team Demography and Process: The Role of Social Integration and Communication', *Administrative Science Quarterly*, Vol. 39, No. 3, p 412-38.
Smith, S. (1984), 'Groupthink and the Hostage Rescue Mission', *British Journal of Political Science*, Vol. 14, No. 1, pp. 117-23.
Soesastro, H., Pangestu, M. and McKendrick, D. (1990), 'Summary of Chapters and Discussions', in Soesastro, H. and Pangestu, M. (eds.), *Technological Challenge in the Asia-Pacific Economy*, Allen and Unwin: Sydney, pp. 299-326.
Sofer, C. (1972), *Organisations in Theory and Practice*, Heinemann Educational Books: London.
Sonnenfeld, J. (1988), *The Hero's Farewell: What Happens When CEOs Retire*, Oxford University Press: New York.
Sproull, L. and Kiesler, S. (1991), 'Computers, Networks, and Work', *Scientific American*, Vol. 265, No. 3, pp. 1492-512.
Stanton, S. and Power, B. (1992), 'From Resistance to Results: Mastering the Organisational Issues of Re-engineering', *Insights Quarterly*, Fall, pp. 76-84.
Stark, A. (1993), 'What's the Matter with Business Ethics?', *Harvard Business Review*, Vol. 71, May-June, pp. 38-48.
Staw, B.M. and Ross, J. (1989), 'Understanding Behaviour in Escalation Situations', *Science*, Vol. 249, 13 October, pp. 216-20.
Sternberg, R.J. (1985), *Beyond I.Q.*, Cambridge University Press: New York.
Stevens, M. (1988), 'The Next Battle for Europe', *Business Review Weekly*, 6 May, pp. 58-61.

Stinchcombe, A.L., McDill, M.S. and Walker, D.R. (1986), 'Demography of Organisations', *American Journal of Sociology*, Vol. 74, No. 2, pp. 221-29.

Stogdill, R.M. (1948), 'Personal Factors Associated with Leadership: A Survey of the Literature', *Journal of Psychology*, Iss. 25, pp. 35-71.

Stogdill, R.M. (1974), *Handbook of Leadership*, Free Press: New York.

Stuart, P. (1993), 'HR Actions Offer Protection During Takeovers', *Personnel Journal*, Vol. 72, No. 6, June, pp. 84-95.

Swedish Prime Minister's Office (1994), 'Information Technology Wings to Human Ability', Government Commission on Information Technology, Prime Minister's Office: Stockholm.

Szilagyl, A.D and Wallace, Jr, M.J. (1983), *Organisational Behaviour and Performance*, Scott Foresman: Glenview.

t'Hart, P. (1990), *Groupthinking in Government: A Study of Small Groups and Policy Failure*, Swets and Zeitlinger: Amsterdam.

t'Hart, P., Rosenthal, U. and Kouzmin, A. (1993), 'Crisis Decision Making: The Centralisation Thesis Revisited', *Administration and Society*, Vol. 25, No. 1, May, pp. 12-45.

Tait, R. (1995), *Roads to the Top*, Macmillan Business.

Tannenbaum, A. and Schmidt, W.H. (1958), 'How to Choose a Leadership Pattern', *Harvard Business Review*, Vol. 36, March-April, pp. 95-101.

Tannenbaum, R.A. and Schmidt, W.H. (1973), 'How to Choose a Leadership Style', *Harvard Business Review*, Vol. 51, May-June, pp. 58-67.

Taylor, F.W. (1911), *Principles of Scientific Management*, Harper and Row: New York.

Tead, O. (1935), *The Art of Leadership*, McGraw-Hill: New York.

Terry, C. (1989), 'Leadership', in Tushman, M.L., O'Reilly, C. and Nadler, D.A. (eds.), *The Management of Organisations: Strategies, Tactics and Analysis*, Harper and Row: New York, pp. 252-67.

Thacker, J.B. (1990), 'Positioning Systems Management - the Major Problem for Management and Management Education', paper presented at the *Australian and New Zealand Academy of Management's (ANZAM) Annual Conference on Management Education*, Launceston, December, pp. 1-22.

The Canberra Times (1993), 'Compo Cases Surge Up by 61 Per Cent', 6 September, pp. 5.

The European Council (1994), 'Europe and the Global Information Society: Recommendations to the European Council', Bangemann Report, The European Chancel: Brussels, May.

Thibaut, J.W. and Kelly, H.H. (1959), *The Social Psychology of Groups*, John Wiley: New York.

Thomas, A.B. (1988), 'Does Leadership make a Difference to Organisational Performance?', *Administrative Science Quarterly*, Vol. 33, No. 3, pp. 338-400.

Thomasma, D.C. (1993), 'Moral Integrity and Healthcare Leadership', *Healthcare Executive*, Vol. 8, Iss. 1, January-February, p. 29.
Thompson, E.P. (1967), *The Making of the English Working Class*, Pelican: London.
Thompson, J.D. and Bates, F.L. (1957), 'Technology, Organisation and Administration', *Administrative Science Quarterly*, Vol. 2, No. 2, December, pp. 325-43.
Tichy, N. (1981), 'Networks in Organisations', in Nystrom, P.C. and Starbuck, W.G. (eds.), *Handbook of Organisational Design*, Vol. 2, Oxford University Press: New York, pp. 225-48.
Tichy, N.M. and Devanna, M.A. (1986), *The Transformational Leader*, John Wiley: New York.
Tichy, N.M. and Sherman, S. (1993), *Control Your Destiny or Someone Else Will: How Jack Welsch is Making General Electric the World's Most Competitive Corporation*, Doubleday: New York.
Toffler, A. (1980), *The Third Wave*, William Morrow: New York.
Tolman, E.C. (1924), *Behaviour and the Psychological Man*, University of California Press.
Trice, H. and Beyer, H.J. (1993), *The Culture of Work Organisations*, Prentice-Hall: Englewood Cliffs.
Tsui, A.S. (1994), 'Reputation Effectiveness: Towards a Mutual Responsiveness Framework', in Staw, B.M. and Cummings, L.L. (eds.), *Research in Organisational Behaviour*, JAI Press: Greenwich, pp. 257-307.
Tucker, R.C. (1981), *Politics as Leadership*, University of Missouri Press: Columbia.
Tushman, M.L. and Nelson, R.R. (1990), 'Introduction: Technology, Organisations and Innovation', *Administrative Science Quarterly*, Vol. 35, No. 1, March, pp. 1-8.
Tushman, M.L. and Romanelli, E. (1985), 'Organisation Evaluation: A Metamorphosis Model of Convergence and Reorientation', in Cummings, L.L. and Staw, B.M. (eds.), *Research in Organisational Behaviour*, Vol. 7, JAI Press: Greenwich, pp. 171-222.
Tutt, N., Neale, J. and Warburton, W. (1992), 'Strategic Management in Social Services' in Pollitt, C. and Harrison, S. (eds.) (1992), *Handbook of Public Services Management*, Blackwell: Oxford, pp. 268-80.
UK Department of Social Security (1989), 'Operational Strategy Pilot Evaluation Report: Management Summary and Main Report', HMSO: London.
Unger, R.M. (1987), *False Necessity*, Cambridge University Press: Cambridge.

USA National Performance Review Office of the Vice President (1993), 'Re-engineering Through Information Technology', Accompanying Report of the National Performance Review Office of the Vice President: Washington DC, September.

USA State of California (1994), 'Task Force on Government Technology Policy and Procurement', Report to Governor Pete Wilson, State of California, September.

Van Maanen, J. (1978), 'People Processing: Strategies of Organisational Socialising', in Dowling W. (ed.), *Organisational Dynamics*, Amacom: New York, pp. 19-30.

Van Maanen, J. (1994), 'An Interview with John Van Maanen', *OMT Newsletter, Academy of Management*, Winter, pp. 14-16.

Van Maanan, J. and Barley, S.R. (1985), 'Cultural Organisation Fragments of a Theory' in Van Maanan, J. and Barley, S.R (eds.), *Organisational Culture*, Sage Publications: Beverley Hills, pp. 31-53.

Vence, S.C. (1983), *Corporate Leadership: Boards, Directors and Strategy*, McGraw-Hill: New York.

Vroom, V. and Yetton, P. (1973), *Leadership and Decision Making*, University of Pittsburgh Press: Pittsburgh.

Wagner, W., Pfeffer, J. and O'Reilly, III, C.A. (1984), 'Organisational Demography and Turnover in Top Management Groups', *Administrative Science Quarterly*, Vol. 29, No. 1, pp. 74-92.

Waldman, D.A. and Avolio, B.J. (1986), 'A Meta-analysis of Age Difference in Job Performance', *Journal of Applied Psychology*, Vol. 71, No. 1, pp. 33-8.

Walton, R.E. (1989), *Up and Running: Integrating Information Technology and the Organisation*, Harvard Business School Press: Boston.

Wanous, J. and Youtz, M. (1986), 'Solution Diversity and the Quality of Group Decisions', *Academy of Management Journal*, Vol. 29, No. 2, pp. 149-58.

Warburton, F.E. (1993), 'Enhancing Competitiveness Through Leadership in Management', *Business Council Bulletin*, October, pp. 28-30.

Warner, T. (1989), 'Information Technology as a Competitive Burden', in Forester, T. (ed.), *Computers in the Human Context: Information Technology, Productivity and People*, Blackwell: Oxford, pp. 272-80.

Weber, M. (1920), 'Die Protestanticsche Ethik und der Geist des Kapitalismus, in *Gesammelte Aufsatze zur Religionssoziologie*, Vol. 1, Mohr und Siebeck: Tubingen, pp. 17-206.

Weber, M. (1947), *The Theory of Social and Economic Organisation*, The Free Press: Glencoe III.

Weber, M. (1949), "Objectivity' in Social Science and Social Policy', in Shils, E. and Finch, H.A. (eds.), *The Methodology of the Social Sciences*, Free Press: New York, pp. 49-112.

Weber, M. (1964), *Basic Concepts in Sociology* (translated by Secher, H.P.), Citadel Press: New York.

Weber, M. (1968), *On Charisma and Institution Building*, University of Chicago Press.

Weber, M. (1976), *Wirtschaft und Gesellschaft Volume 1-2* (ed. Winckelmann, J.) (Fifth Revised Edition), Mohr und Siebeck: Tubingen.

Weick, K.E. (1969), *The Social Psychology of Organising*, Addision-Wesley: Reading.

Weick, K.E. (1979), *The Social Psychology of Organising*, 2nd Edition, Adison Wesley: Reading, MA.

Weick, K.E. and Daft, R.L. (1983), 'The Effectiveness of Interpretation Systems', in Cameron, K.S. and Whetten, D.A. (eds.), *Organisational Effectiveness: A Comparison of Multiple Models*, Academic Press: New York, pp. 71-93.

Weill, P. (1992), 'The Relationship Between Investment in Information Technology and Firm Performance: A Study of the Value Manufacturing Sector', *Information Systems Research*, Vol. 3, No. 4, December, pp. 307-33.

Weiner, N. and Mahoney, T.A. (1981), 'A Model of Corporate Performance as a Function of Environmental, Organisational and Leadership Influence', *Academy of Management Journal*, Vol. 24, No. 3, pp. 453-70.

Weir, D. (1993), 'Not Doing the Business: Why There is No Decent Management Research', *The Times Higher Education Supplement*, 30 April, pp. 17.

Weisbach, M.S. (1988), 'Outside Directors and CEO Turnover', *Journal of Financial Economics*, Vol. 20, No. 4, pp. 431-60.

Wellman, B. (1983), 'Network Analysis: Some Basic Principles', in Collins, R. (ed.), *Sociological Theory*, Jossey-Bass: San Fransisco, pp. 155-200.

Wellman, B. (1988), 'Structural Analysis: From Method and Metaphor to Theory and Substance', in Wellman, B. and Berkowitz, S.D. (eds.), *Social Structures: A Network Approach*, Cambridge University Press: New York, pp. 19-61.

Western, J. (1983), *Social Inequalities in Australian Society*, MacMillan: Sydney.

Westley, F. and Mintzberg, H. (1989), 'Visionary Leadership and Strategic Management', *Strategic Management Journal*, Vol. 10, No. 1, pp. 17-32.

Wheatley, M. (1992), *The Future of Middle Management*, British Institute of Management: Oxford.

White, H. (1992), 'Agency as Control in Formal Networks', in Nohria, N. and Eccles, R.G. (eds.), *Networks and Organisations: Structure, Form and Action*, Harvard Business School Press: Boston, Ch. 3, pp. 92-117.
Whitney, J. and Smith, R. (1983), 'Effects of Group Cohesiveness on Attitude Polarisation and the Acquisition of Knowledge in a Strategic Planning Context', *Journal of Marketing Research*, Vol. 20, No. 2, pp. 167-76.
Wiersema, M. and Bantel, K. (1992), 'Top Management Team Demography and Corporate Strategic Change', *Academy of Management Journal*, Vol. 35, No. 1, pp. 91-121.
Wigforss, E. (1980), 'Om Provisoriska Utopier', in *Skrifter i Urval*, Vol. 1, pp. 274-313.
Williamson, O.E. (1981), 'The Modern Corporation: Origins, Evolution, Attributes', *Journal of Economic Literature*, Vol. 19, December, pp. 1537-68.
Williamson, O.E. (1985), *The Economic Institutions of Capitalism: Firms, Markets and Relations Contracting*, Prentice-Hall: Englewood Cliffs.
Winnicott, D.W. (1958), 'Transitional Objects and Transitional Phenomena', in *Collected Papers*, Tavistock: London.
Winter, D.G. (1987), 'Leader Appeal, Leaders' Performance and the Motive Profiles of Leaders and Followers: A Study of American Presidents and Elections', *Journal of Personality and Social Psychology*, Vol. 51, No. 1, pp. 196-202.
Winter, D.J. (1973), *The Power Motive*, Free Press: New York.
Wolfenstein, V.E. (1967), 'Some Psychological Aspects of Crisis Leadership', in Edinger, L.J. (ed.), *Political Leadership in Industrialised Societies*, Wiley: New York, pp. 155-81.
Womack, J. and Jones, D. (1994), 'From Lean Production to the Lean Enterprise', *Harvard Business Review*, Vol. 72, No. 2, March-April, pp. 93-103.
Woodward, J. (1965), *Industrial Organisation, Theory and Practice*, Oxford University Press: London.
World Commission on Environment and Development (WCED) (1987), 'The Brundland Commission Report', WCED: Paris.
Wright, V. (1994), 'Reshaping the State: The Implications for Public Administration', *West European Politics*, Vol. 17, No. 3, pp. 102-37.
Wrong, D.H. (1979), *Power: Its Forms, Bases and Uses*, Harper: New York.
Yavitz, B. (1993), quoted in Bennis, W., *An Invented Life: Reflections on Leadership and Change*, Addison-Wesley: Reading, pp. 99.
Yukl, G.A. (1981), *Leadership in Organisation*, Prentice-Hall: Englewood Cliffs.

Yukl, G.A. (1989), 'Managerial Leadership: A Review of Theory and Research', *Journal of Management*, Vol. 15, No. 2, pp. 251-89.

Yukl, G.A. and Van Fleet, D. (1982), 'Cross-Situational Multi-Method Research on Military Leader Effectiveness', *Organisational Behaviour and Human Performance*, Vol. 30, pp. 90-1.

Yukl, G.A., Wall, S. and Lepsinger, R. (1990), 'Preliminary Report on Validation of the Managerial Practices Survey', in Clark, K.E. and Clark, M.B. (eds.), *Measures of Leadership*, Leadership Library of America: West Orange, pp. 223-95.

Zaleznik, A. (1977), 'Managers and Leaders: Are They Different?', *Harvard Business Review*, Vol. 55, No. 3, May-June, p. 67.

Zander, A. (1977), *Groups at Work*, Jossey-Bass: San Francisco.

Zelany, M. (1982), 'High Technology Management', *Human System Management*, June, pp. 57-9.

Zemke, R. (1987), 'The Gulf of Mutual Incomprehension', *Training*, August, p. 8.

Zemke, R. (1988), 'Putting the Squeeze on Middle Managers', *Training*, November, pp. 67-74.

Zenger, T.R. and Lawrence, B.S. (1989), 'Organisational Demography: The Differential Effects of Age and Tenure Distributions on Technical Communication', *Academy of Management Journal*, Vol. 3, No. 32, pp. 353-76.

Zey, M. (1992), *Organisational Misconduct: Drexel and the Failure of Corporate Control*, Aldine de Gruyter: New York.

Zhou, X. (1995), 'Partial Reform and the Chinese Bureaucracy in the Post-Mao Era', *Comparative Political Studies*, Vol. 28, No. 3, pp. 440-68.

Zimbardo, P.G. (1970), 'The Human Choice: Individualisation, Reason and Order Versus Deindividualisation, Impulse and Chaos', in Arnold, W.J. and Levine, D. (eds.), *Nebraska Symposium on Motivation*, University of Nebraska Press: Lincoln, pp. 134-57.

Appendix 1
Culture of organization factor analysis: APS

- Attitude factors
- Values factors
- Organizational impact factors
- Information technology factors

Attitude factors

Factor 1: Performance culture (Alpha .87)

- Work is sensibly organized
- Decisions made on adequate/accurate information
- Members of top team do not pull in different directions
- Organization has goals that are clear cut and reasonable
- Organization has not been misguided in the changes it has carried out
- Senior management do not identify with the branch/department, but rather with the body corporate
- Money is not wasted because proper controls are in place
- Different units plan and coordinate their efforts
- Most people at my level are satisfied with their job
- Organization climate encourages me to work hard
- Most changes in the organization have been for the best
- Senior executives are tolerant of each other
- Senior management are disciplined at 'follow through'
- I am regularly informed about how new developments and initiatives are progressing
- Colleagues in the top team are supportive of me
- Systems and controls are not a hindrance to me

Factor 2: Work satisfaction (Alpha .78)

- I enjoy the challenge of my role in the organization
- Generally, I am satisfied with my job
- I do not feel like leaving this job
- The job brings me recognition and respect
- I am committed to the organization
- In my job I make use of my skills and abilities
- I feel stretched in this job

Factor 3: Discipline (Alpha .65)

- Need a structured and disciplined way to manage the business
- Important to follow established work procedures
- I like people to be tidy and well disciplined
- I respect people who stick to the rules
- I like people to pay attention to detail

- There is a right and wrong way of doing things
- I am more likely to observe protocol and then do what I think is best

Factor 4: Specialist orientation (Alpha .73)

- Work satisfaction comes from technical/specialist side of my job
- I enjoy the specialist aspects of my job more than the general management aspects
- I like to be considered an expert
- I enjoy getting others to understand the more technical aspects of my job
- I value being a member of a profession
- There should be more specialists in positions of authority
- I am valued for my expertise

Factor 5: Independence (Alpha .68)

- I do not like others to interfere in what I do
- I like being in a position where others do not have control over me
- I resent being told what to do
- I like to be left alone to do my work as I see fit
- Being my own boss is what turns me on
- I like to get my own way

Values factors

Factor 1: Work practices values (Alpha .90)

- Recognition
- Individuality
- Networking
- Opportunity
- Openness
- Teamwork
- Flexibility
- Innovation
- Trust
- Fun
- Consultation
- Service focus

- Communication
- Responsiveness
- Particularist principles
- Efficiency

Factor 2: Service oriented values (Alpha .87)

- Organizational leadership
- Client services
- Organizational efficiency
- Organizational effectiveness
- Quality
- Innovativeness
- Value to the community
- High morale
- Social justice
- Organizational reputation

Factor 3: Professionalism and conduct values (Alpha .86)

- Integrity
- Loyalty
- Professionalism
- Competence
- Fairness
- Commitment
- Quality
- Effectiveness
- Probity

Factor 4: Rights and duties values (Alpha .85)

- Accountability for use of powers/privileges
- Accountability for use of official resources
- Legality
- Accountability for personal performance of official duties
- Participation
- Accountability for management of people
- Natural justice
- Privacy

Factor 5: Workplace democracy (Alpha .83)

- Democratic principles
- Participation
- Equity principles
- Caring
- Respect for people

Organizational impact factors

Factor 1: Service delivery effectiveness (Alpha .82)

- Better discussions concerning client impact
- Improved ability of managers to handle clients
- Better focus on key client groups
- Better external relationships
- Improved ability to deliver goods/services on time
- Better thought through strategic policy for the future
- Improved response to new initiatives

Factor 2: Performance of people (Alpha .86)

- Improved employee morale
- Fewer resignations/people leaving
- Better internal relationships
- Greater trust
- Fewer inaccurate/unrealistic commitments made to clients
- Overall better performance from the corporation's employees

Factor 3: Top team effectiveness (Alpha .83)

- Understanding of each other
- People who openly discuss sensitive issues
- People who trust each other
- People who jointly implement decisions made in top team
- Easy to talk to
- People who address long/short term issues

Factor 4: Strategic direction (Alpha .74)

- Future of organization
- Structure of organization
- Issues affecting long term
- Changes in organization direction affecting how the organization functions
- How current changes will affect the future of the organization

Factor 5: Interfacing (Alpha .76)

- Relationship between central office and regional offices/divisions, subsidiaries
- Relationship between various offices/divisions/subsidiaries
- The way regional office offices/divisions/subsidiaries are run
- Improving the relationship between central office and functional areas/subsidiaries

Information technology factors

Factor 1: Focus of IT training (Alpha .87)

- Meeting employee requirements
- Meeting organizational needs
- Meeting employee development needs
- Aligning IT with strategic planning
- Delivered just in time
- Planned at the corporate level

Factor 2: IT application (Alpha .80)

- Hardware application
- Software application
- Satisfying operational needs
- Effectiveness of utilization

Factor 3: IT skills (Alpha .84)

- Specialist skills/generalist skills
- Technical skills/advanced skills
- Innovative/adaptive skills

Factor 4: IT impact on organization (Alpha .82)

- Long term IT planning
- Organizational performance
- Information control measures
- IT systems alignment with organization structure
- Impact on top team ways of working
- Impact on decision processes
- Impact on employees

Appendix 2
Leadership factors: APS

- Team players
- Radicals
- Bureaucrats

APS top team's demography measures

Measures of demographic attributes were collected for 750 Australian Public Service (APS) managers including senior executive service (SES) structure, Bands 1, 2 and 3; and Senior Officers (SO) structure level A, B and C; and their equivalents. The original demographic items introduced were level, age, gender, background, professional qualification, tenure in APS, organizational tenure, current job tenure, number of senior appointments, number of appointments outside APS and size of organization. However, only four demographic dimensions effectively differentiated three significant clusters: organizational tenure, current job tenure, number of senior appointments, size of organization.

Length of time in organization (organizational tenure)

Allen and Cohen (1969) find that a shared language reflects similarities in how individuals interpret, understand and respond to information, which results in part from a similar background and experience gained from tenure within an organization. In the APS, long tenured executives have been exposed to a variety of jobs. In addition, past organizational design making and experiences are shared and understood amongst those with similar tenures. Organizational tenure thus provides a frame of reference within which top team members operate. Katz (1982) points out that managers, with growing organizational experience, tend to rely increasingly on their past experiences and routine information sources rather than on new information. For example, Hayes-Roth (1977) argues that when an individual is provided with increased exposure to a given stimulus, a situation of 'over-learning' results, which leads to a clearly defined schema, and as a result only information consistent with the schema will be attended to.

Hambrick and Mason (1984) show that managers with long tenure tend to have a restricted knowledge base that will impede their response to environmental changes. Finkelstein and Hambrick (1990) find that longer tenured top team members tend to peruse strategic initiatives in line with industry trends. They suggest that such a pattern reflects a manager's risk aversion, commitment to prior actions, and restriction in information processes. Similarly, Miller's (1991) study of long tenured CEOs shows a link to strategies inappropriate to current environmental conditions. Executive succession has been supported by a variety of theories to play a role in overcoming organizational inertia by bringing about strategic change (Tushman and Romanelli, 1985). A top team with long organizational tenure is associated with high social cohesion (Michel and Hambrick, 1992) leading to a reluctance to change the status quo (Janis, 1972).

Research suggests that homogeneity of organizational tenure can lead to a common vocabulary (Rhodes, 1991), similar interpretation of events (Allen and Cohen, 1969; Lawrence and Lorsch, 1967), and can enhance communication among group members (March and Simon, 1968; Zenger and Lawrence, 1989). With frequent and accurate communication among top team members, the similarity of their beliefs and similarity of their perceptions of the organization increases (Rhinesmith, 1993, 1995). Such group communication patterns become stable and routinized over time (Roberts and O'Reilly, 1979; Katz, 1982), resulting in high levels of group cohesion and integration (O'Reilly et al, 1989). By contrast, heterogeneity of organizational tenure suggests that top team members will differ in their sets of experiences within an organization and will bring forward varied cognitive perspectives (Bantel and Jackson, 1989). However, communication difficulties will be high (McCain, O'Reilly and Pfeffer, 1983) and any ensuing conflict and power struggles will be based on dissimilar attitudes, values and beliefs (Pfeffer, 1983). Individuals with dissimilar attitudes, values and beliefs may experience feelings of isolation, lack of organizational attachment, and turnover (Roberts and O'Reilly, 1979).

Number of senior appointments (senior management tenure)

Hambrick and Mason (1984) contend that a manager's personal experiences and values can be inferred from observable demographic characteristics, such as years of experience, and that studying these observable characteristics overcomes the difficult problems of gaining access to executives to measure psychological or group dynamic variables, which may be the more direct underlying process characteristics linking the top team members' attributes to organizational outcomes. Building on the Hambrick and Mason (1984) study, scholars have empirically linked the top management team's demography to organizational performance (Waldman and Avolio, 1986; Murray, 1989; O'Reilly and Flatt, 1989; Eisenhardt and Schoonhoven, 1990; Michel, Hambrick and D'Aveni, 1992; Kakabadse, 1993; Smith et al, 1994; Kakabadse et al, 1996).

Length of time in current position (top team tenure)

The average tenure in organization of a top management team's members can be expected to indicate cohesion. Long tenures reflect a self selection process by which only those who embrace certain norms and perspectives are willing or allowed to stay in an organization (Pfeffer, 1983). Moreover, duration in a firm confers socialization, shared experiences and a common vocabulary (Katz, 1982). Managers with long tenure are more likely to have undergone common organizational experiences and thus are more likely to have developed similar schemata (Norman, 1976) or dominant logic (Prahalad and Bettis, 1986). Schemata are cognitive structures used to organize knowledge of past experiences and are particularly called upon when people make sense of new stimuli. Similarity of schemata among team members, developed via long tenure, can be expected to enhance cohesion, as managers adopt common platforms based on their beliefs and attributes arisen from past experiences. Long tenure is an indicator of experience in an organization and familiarity with a shrewd language which is likely to influence top team processes that may in turn affect the level of team turnover. A shared language reflects similarities in how individuals interpret, understand and respond to information; it results in part from similar backgrounds and experiences gained from tenure within an organization (Allen and Cohen, 1969).

Entry and length of stay in a group is an important determinant of a person's communication within the group (Allen and Cohen, 1969). Katz (1982) found that a group that had been together a long time tends to develop standardized ways of communication and homogeneity of perspective. Long age group tenure results in decreasing levels of verbal communication because group members feel they can anticipate other members' viewpoints and increased specialization occurs (Katz, 1982). In addition, longevity can lead to increasing isolation from outside sources of information (Pelz and Andrews, 1966) as members become less receptive toward communications that threaten their patterns of behaviour (Shenhav and Haberfeld, 1992). Heterogeneity of team tenure indicates that the various members of a top management team have been promoted at different times, suggesting that new and different perspectives on the strategic vision for the organization have been added. Team tenure homogeneity, by contrast, suggests shared socialization and group experience that reinforce the cohort phenomena.

Michel and Hambrick (1992) use the concept of social integration to explain links between average team tenure and diversification strategy and performance. They propose that the length of team tenure is a proxy for the level of team cohesion and that cohesion in turn affects performance. Similarly, Murray (1989) uses social integration and communication patterns to predict the form of the relationship between team heterogeneity and organization performance. He argues that team heterogeneity may lower performance in stable environments because the team would be less cohesive and require more formal communication. Eisenhardt and Schoonhoven (1990), Keck (1991) and Hambrick and D'Aveni (1992) all attribute the finding of links between team demography and organizational performance to unmeasured social psychological concepts. The assumptions in demographic studies are that team demography influences team processes, such as social integration and communication and these processes in turn affect organizational outcomes.

Organizational size

Increases in organization size add complexity with its attendant increases in structural variation and formalized systems for planning, control and resource allocation (Quinn and Cameron, 1983; Quinn, 1981). Some scholars (Hofer and Schendel, 1978; Lindsay and Rue, 1980; Frederickson and Iaquinto, 1989) posit that size of the organization is linked with the organization's strategic planning process, while others (Robinson, 1982; Robinson and Pearce, 1984) treat small size organizations as a separate category in their theoretical and empirical work. The dominant view in the literature is that as the size of the organization increases, there are a larger number of constituencies that organizations need to satisfy. Tushman and Romanelli (1985) posit that increases in organizational size can create progressively stronger resistance to fundamental change, as such large sized organizations show less likelihood of major changes in corporate strategy. Furthermore, large sized organizations are likely to have larger top teams, which are likely to influence demographic heterogeneity, since large groups have more potential for dissimilarity. In a small group, the addition of one person can increase team heterogeneity substantially (Bantel and Jackson, 1989). As the number of members in a top management team increases, structural elaboration is expected to change (Nadler and Tushman, 1990), including differentiation on perspective (Dearborn and Simon, 1985), specialization of skills and diversity of opinion (Bales and Borgatta, 1955). Such breadth of perspective should stimulate proactive strategic actions, as large sized organizations are more likely to exhibit the need for planning openness that ensures the needs of varied constituencies are being recognized. Eisenhardt and Schoonhoven (1990) find that large teams facilitate growth for new ventures. However as team size increases, group cohesion and communication intensity become strained (Shaw, 1976). Thus in low to moderate levels of largeness, a positive association with corporate strategic change is expected. However, the association will decrease if the team becomes very large (Wiersema and Bantel, 1992).

Team players

Demographic characteristics

Size - 2,500-5,000 (average)
Years in organization - 16-25 years (average)
Years in job - 5-10 years (average)
Number of senior management appointments - 2.8 (average)

Style

Promoting performance (Alpha .88)
- Job satisfied
- Committed
- Enjoy challenge
- Team players
- Hard working
- Encourage others
- Promote clear goals
- Stretch themselves
- Invite feedback
- Promote corporate view
- Promote team philosophy
- Positive about change
- Clear decision making
- Promote recognition/respect

Independent (Alpha .74)

- Dislike others' interference
- Like to get own way
- Self reliant
- Resent being told what to do

Philosophy

Providing service (Alpha .85)
- Network
- Respect for people
- Equity
- Service focus
- Participative in workplace
- Consultative
- Responsive
- Team oriented
- Bonding
- Budget stability
- Need for communication
- Neutrality

Promoting sense of responsibility (Alpha .85)
- Accountability for usage of resources
- Accountability for management of power
- Accountability for management of people
- Accountability for personal performance
- Timeliness
- Legality
- Seniority
- Impartiality
- Responsibility
- Honesty
- Integrity
- High productivity

Style

Specialist (Alpha .70)
- Satisfaction from technical/specialist side
- Expert
- Value being member of profession
- Prefer specialist work
- Promote specialists

Disciplined (Alpha .76)
- Structured in work
- Self disciplined
- Promote discipline in others
- Promote follow through
- Work within procedural guidelines
- Respect tradition

Philosophy

Leading through example (Alpha .83)
- Efficiency
- Leader driven
- Quality
- Client service
- Value to community
- Innovativeness
- Promoting high morale
- Track record
- Reputation (organizational)

Responding to challenge (Alpha .75)
- Diligence
- Effectiveness
- Support for ministers
- Competence
- Innovation
- Skills
- Efficiency
- Probity

Professionalism and conduct (Alpha .79)
- Quality
- Professionalism
- Excellence
- Trust
- Commitment
- Loyalty

Promoting personal development (Alpha .89)
- Flexibility
- Fun
- Opportunity
- Universalistic principles
- Privacy
- Natural justice
- Openness

Radicals

Demographic characteristics

Size of organization - 500-2,000 (average)
Years in organization - 1-4 years (average)
Years in job - 1-2 years (average)
Number of senior management appointments - 2.6 (average)

Style

Critical (Alpha .82)
- Top team seen as lacking cohesion
- See poor decision making in organization
- Work not sensibly organized
- Functional orientation of top management
- Misguided about changes
- Organization seen as lacking clear goals
- Lack of tolerance
- Critical of lack of discipline
- Critical of poor follow through
- Critical of poor controls
- Critical of poor communication
- Critical of poor meetings attendance
- Feel constrained

Job satisfied (Alpha .83)
- Job satisfied
- Stimulated by role challenge
- Committed to role
- Job oriented recognition
- Use skills as desired
- Supportive teamwork

Specialist (Alpha .65)
- Work satisfaction
- Expert driven
- Not general management oriented
- Value membership of profession
- Promotion of specialists

Philosophy

Outward focused (Alpha .86)
- Client service
- Innovative
- Social justice
- Provide value to community
- High morals
- Service focused
- Loyalty to clients
- Support for ministers
- Leadership for service
- Accountable over use of powers
- Accountability for use of resources
- Efficiency

Respect for people (Alpha .90)
- Caring
- Participative
- Recognition
- Democratic principles
- Respect for individuals
- Equity
- Organizational growth
- Natural justice
- Bonding/close ties
- Privacy
- Fun
- Communication

Style

Independence (Alpha .66)
- Dislike interference
- Resentful of being directed
- Enjoy command
- Do things own way
- Dislike being blocked
- Like to be left alone

Discipline (Alpha.66)
- Disciplined
- People to be tidy and disciplined
- Insist on being briefed
- Kept informed of progress
- Introduce appropriate controls
- Discipline fundamental to success
- Ability to handle top team
- Maintain group cohesion
- Follow established work procedures

Philosophy

Values for service (Alpha .84)
- Effectiveness
- Quality
- Competence
- Probity
- Skills
- Integrity
- Impartiality
- Diligence
- Timeliness
- High quality advice to ministers
- Responsibility
- Budget stability
- Effectiveness
- Neutrality
- Fairness
- Seniority

Values concerning effectiveness of individual performance (Alpha .88)
- Excellence
- Accountable for personal performance
- Accountable for management of people
- Professionalism
- Commitment
- Openness
- Consultation
- Honesty
- Efficiency

Valuing freedom to act (Alpha .72)
- Track record
- Opportunity
- Teamwork
- Responsiveness
- Networking
- Participative principles
- Individuality
- Trust
- High productivity
- Flexibility

Bureaucrats

Demographics

Size of organization — 5-10,000 persons (average)
Years in organization — 10-15 years (average)
Years in job — 2-3 years (average)
Number of senior management appointments — 3.4 (average)

Style

Cynical (Alpha .89)
- See misguided changes in past
- See unclear goals
- See work not sensibly organized
- No encouragement to work hard
- See top team pull in different directions
- Lose track of initiatives
- Dissatisfied with organization
- See poor controls
- See poor quality decision making
- See poor coordination
- Senior managers identify functionally
- Promote poor communication
- Not regularly informed
- Poor follow through
- Feel it difficult to keep up with changes
- Low tolerance for senior colleagues
- See managers moved too quickly
- Systems and controls are hindrance
- Receive poor feedback

Job satisfaction (Alpha .71)
- Make use of skills/abilities
- Recognition/respect from job
- Take criticism personally
- Generally satisfied with job
- Easy to talk to
- Enjoy challenge of any role

Philosophy

Impartiality (Alpha .88)
- Effectiveness
- Professionalism
- Skills
- Fairness
- Competence
- Value to community
- Diligence
- Organizational reputation
- Impartiality
- Responsibility
- High productivity
- Social justice
- Integrity
- Responsiveness
- Timeliness
- Commitment
- Excellence
- Neutrality

Personal conduct (Alpha .87)
- Recognition
- Flexibility
- Networking
- Openness
- Individuality
- Innovation
- Caring
- Track record
- Budget stability
- Service focus
- Fun
- Trust
- Efficiency
- Bonding/close ties
- Respect for people

Style

Specialist orientation (Alpha .70)
- Satisfaction from technical/specialist side of job
- Enjoy specialist activities
- Dislike general management
- Valued for expertise
- Like to be considered an expert
- Should have more specialists in authority
- Do not wish to leave job

Discipline (Alpha .70)
- Like people to be tidy/disciplined
- Discipline is fundamental to success
- Right and wrong way of doing things
- Attention to detail
- Set realistic time targets
- Show calm under pressure
- Follow established work procedures
- Respect people who stick to rules

Philosophy

Service orientation (Alpha .84)
- Communication
- Consultation
- Teamwork
- Quality
- Probity
- Client service
- Opportunity
- Loyalty to the organization
- Participation

Accountability (Alpha .76)
- Accountability for use of powers/privileges of public office
- Accountability for personal performance/official duties
- Accountability for use of official resources
- Accountability for the management of people
- Honesty
- Organizational growth

Appendix 3
Leadership factors: private sector

- Drivers

- Politicians

- Strategists

Drivers

Size of organization — 1,000-3,000 persons (average)
Years in organization — 6 months-1 year (average)
Years in job — 6 months-1 year (average)
Number of senior management appointments — 1.85 appointments (average)
Age — 26-35 years (average)

Motivators (Alpha .87)
- Open style
- Importance of people
- Enjoy challenge
- Have overview of business
- Application of controls
- Encourage checking out
- Committed
- Encourage discussion of work problems
- Focus on customer
- Sensitive to others
- Mature
- Enjoy specialist activities

Cynical (Alpha .71)
- Company misguided about change
- Systems and controls are hindrance
- Money wasted
- Poor controls in company
- Most people are dissatisfied
- Not regularly briefed
- Managers moved too quickly
- Company history of poor change management

Promote consistency (Alpha .78)
- Dislike interference
- Clear as to what is right/wrong
- Need for follow through
- Need for meetings discipline
- Insistent on regular briefings
- Specialist
- Respect traditions

Independent (Alpha .67)
- Dislike controls
- Get own way
- Need independence
- Need to be in charge

Politicians

Size of organization	- 4,000-10,000 persons (average)
Years of organization	- 4-7 years (average)
Years in job	- 2-3 years (average)
Number of senior management appointments	- 2.1 appointments (average)
Age	- 36-46 years (average)

Communicators (Alpha .87)
- Open style
- Importance of people
- Easy to talk to
- Overview of business
- Make oneself available to others
- Encourage checking out
- Committed
- Mature and tolerant
- Sensitive
- Enjoy general management
- Focus on customer
- Encourage being kept informed

Dissatisfied with organization (Alpha .74)
- Company misguided over change
- Feel like leaving job
- Most not satisfied with job
- Company history of poor change management
- Job dissatisfied
- Senior managers should be more tolerant of each other
- Systems and controls are hindrance
- Meetings changed too quickly
- Not regularly briefed
- Lose track of initiatives
- Colleagues lack understanding of their parts of business
- Managers moved on too quickly

Discipline (Alpha .83)
- Right/wrong way of doing things
- People to attend to detail
- Respect rules
- Respect people who stick to rules
- Follow established work procedures
- Need structured disciplined way to manage business
- People to be tidy/disciplined
- Insist on being regularly briefed
- People more disciplined in attending meetings
- Specialist oriented
- Communicate better with those from specialist background

Independent (Alpha .73)
- Dislike being controlled
- Need to be boss
- Do what I think best
- Like to get own way
- Like to be left alone
- Can see who will not fit
- Use protocol to own advantage

Strategists

Size of organization	- 4,000-10,000 persons (average)
Years in organization	- 4-7 years (average)
Years in job	- 4-5 years (average)
Number of senior management appointments	- 1.7 appointments (average)
Age	- 46-55 years

Promote performance (Alpha .89)
- Open style
- Importance of people
- Overview of business
- Committed
- Encourage checking out
- Enjoy challenge
- Sensitive
- Job placement needs managing
- Managers not moved on too quickly
- People should not feel isolated
- Mature/tolerant
- Customer is king
- Expect to be kept informed
- Systems and controls are helpful in job
- Need committed people in organization
- Encourage others to alter my views
- Regularly informed
- Encourage others to pay attention to detail
- Encourage others to make business profitable
- Encourage others to discuss their work problems

Manage diversity (Alpha .76)
- Company misguided about change
- Most changes have not been for best
- Others are dissatisfied with job
- Can lose track of initiatives
- Senior managers should be more tolerant
- Meetings changed too quickly
- Not regularly informed
- People should be more disciplined
- My colleagues understand my part of business
- Job satisfied
- Promote meetings discipline

Discipline (Alpha .79)
- Disciplined organization fundamental to success
- Important to show calm under pressure
- People to be tidy/disciplined
- Insist on being regularly briefed
- Need structured and disciplined way of managing business
- Attentive to group cohesion

Specialist (Alpha .74)
- Like to be considered an expert
- Valued for expertise
- Enjoy both specialist and general management aspects of job
- Work satisfaction from specialist activities
- Value being member of profession
- Promote identity with technical aspects of job

Appendix 4
Impact of culture of organization on organizational performance: APS

- Impact of culture on organization
- Impact of values on performance of organization

Table A4.1
Impact of culture of organization

Impact   *Culture factors*

Impact	PC	WS	D	Sp	Ind.
Attitudes to work and organization					
Performance culture	1.000	XX			X
Work satisfaction	XX	1.000		XX	
Discipline			1.00	XX	X
Specialist orientation		XX	XX	1.00	XX
Independence	X		X	XX	1.00
Values					
Work practices	XX	XX			
Service orientation	XX	XX	XX		-XX
Professionalism and conduct	XX	XX	XX	X	
Rights and duties	XX	XX	XX		-X
Workplace democracy	XX	XX			-XX
Organizational performance					
Effectiveness of service delivery	XX		X		-X
Performance of people			XX		-X
Strategic direction		XX	XX		
Interfacing effectiveness	XX	X			
Information technology					
Focus of IT training		XX	XX		
Effectiveness of application		XX	X		
IT skills adaptiveness	XX	XX		X	XX
Impact effectiveness on organization					-XX

Key   Levels of significance

PC - Performance culture   X - 05
WS - Work satisfaction   XX - 01
D   - Discipline
Sp   - Specialist
Ind. - Independent

- A positively oriented performance culture is positively correlated to the experience of satisfaction with the workplace.
- Respondents consider that operating in a positive work environment encourages the holding and pursuing of values which promote best practice internally and externally in the community.
- A supportive performance culture is seen to enhance the effectiveness of service delivery, of improving the quality of interfacing across the structure of the organization and of promoting a feeling of confidence in staff and management to adapt their IT skills to meet different challenges.
- Being satisfied with one's workplace is strongly determined by people recognizing that they are operating in a positive performance oriented environment.
- Those who display higher levels of work satisfaction are specialists or have a strong specialist orientation.
- Being satisfied with the workplace is likely to positively stimulate the adoption and application of the five key value areas held by staff and management.
- Satisfaction with the workplace is likely to enhance the debate on strategic direction and to stimulate people to be more conscientious to improve the effectiveness of their interfacing across the organization.
- The greater the staff and management in the workplace feel satisfied with their work environment, the more focused in terms of meeting needs is IT training likely to be, the greater the effectiveness of IT application and the more staff and management are likely to be flexible in their use of IT skills to meet the work related challenges they face.
- Being disciplined is strongly correlated with being specialist or having a specialist background.
- Being disciplined is correlated with being independence oriented.
- Being disciplined is considered as positively supporting the application of service oriented values, the values related to the promotion of people's performance and workplace conduct, and the application of values related to the discharge of rights and duties of office.
- Being disciplined is considered as having a positive impact on focusing IT training to meet needs, and on the effectiveness of IT application within the organization.
- The greater the degree of specialization, the greater the degree of work satisfaction experienced, the greater the discipline applied to the job and the greater the degree of independence that will be exhibited.
- Those who are more specialist and value greater specialization are likely to hold strong values concerning professionalism and conduct and are equally likely to be more adaptive in terms of IT skills application in different contexts.

- Being independently minded is more likely to undermine the promotion and acceptance of service oriented values, undermine practising the values concerning rights and duties in terms of accountability of office, and undermine participative work practices.
- A management holding a stronger independence orientation is likely to pay less attention to both the effectiveness of service delivery and the development and enhancement of the quality of performance of people.
- Managers who evolve a strong need for personal independence are likely to undermine the positive impact of IT on the organization.
- Independently minded staff and management are more likely to be flexible and adventurous in their application of IT systems in different circumstances.

Table A4.2
Impact of values on performance of organization

Impact   *Values factors*

	WP	SO	Prof and C	R&D	Wp. Dem.
• Values					
Work practices	1.00	XX	XX	XX	XX
Service oriented	XX	1.00	XX	XX	XX
Professionalism and conduct	XX	XX	1.00	XX	XX
Rights and duties	XX	XX	XX	1.00	XX
Workplace democracy	XX	XX	X	XX	1.00
• *Organizational performance*					
Effectiveness of service delivery	XX			X	X
Performance of people		XX			
Strategic direction		XX	X		
Interfacing effectiveness					
• *Information technology*					
Focus of IT training	X	XX	XX	XX	
Effectiveness of application	X	XX	XX		
IT skills adaptiveness		XX			X
Impact effectiveness on organization					

Key   Levels of significance

WP	- Organization performance	X - 05
SO	- Service oriented	XX - 01
Prof and C	- Professionalism and conduct	
R&D	- Rights and duties	
Wp. Dem.	- Workplace democracy	

- The five different sets of values strongly cross correlate with each other, suggesting that the more individuals hold any one of these values, the more likely are those people to accept, adopt and practice the other values.
- A more limited influence is identified in terms of a staff and management that strongly hold values and their impact on the measures of organizational performance and the effectiveness of application of IT in the APS.
- Values which promote effectiveness of work practice internally and externally, are more likely to inculcate in individuals a greater drive for effectiveness of service delivery, help people to focus IT training to meet individual and organizational needs and enhance an attitude of mind in staff and management of the need for effective IT application to assist the smoother running of the organization.
- Being more service oriented is likely to be supportive of wishing to improve the performance of people and promote their development in the workplace.
- Sharing strongly held service oriented values is likely to stimulate positive debate on the need for clearer strategic direction and promote a greater sense of ownership of the direction that is finally taken.
- Being more service oriented is likely to focus people's minds on how to apply IT training to meet the needs of the organization, make IT application more effective and help people understand why it is important to be flexible in the application of IT skills in different circumstances.
- Holding a strong sense of professionalism in terms of personal conduct in the discharge of one's daily work, is likely to help people become more aware of a clearer and stronger shared sense of strategic direction.
- Those who value professionalism in terms of daily conduct are more likely to appreciate the need for focusing IT training to meet organizational needs. Equally, they are more likely to attempt to ensure that IT is applied in a way that services the demands of different internal user groups.
- Those who hold strong rights and duties role values are likely to be more attentive to the effectiveness of service delivery internally and externally and recognize the need for focusing IT training to meet the needs of the APS.
- Those who hold rights and duties values are more likely to be flexible and adaptive in their application of IT skills to the needs of different situations.
- Valuing the practice and pursuit of democracy within the workplace, is perceived as likely enhancing the capability of the organization to effectively deliver its services to the community.

Appendix 5
Impact of the Centre

- Impact of corporate Centre's management style on demographics of organization

- Impact of Centre management's style on organizational culture and performance

Table A5.1
Impact of corporate Centre's management style on demographics of organization

		Style		
Organization demographics	SP	PO	R and R	P and P
• *Consistency on*				
Improving quality of services/products		-XX		XX
Improving relationship with clients	X			X
Improving inter agency relations		X		XX
Automating existing processes		X	X	
Restructuring		XX		-X
Downsizing/delayering	X			XX
Delegating to offices/departments				XX
R&D in new services/products				
• *Cohesion on*				
Promotion of organization's policies/services	XX	-XX	-XX	XX
Effective implementation of organization's policies/services	XX	-XX	-XX	XX
Develop effective client relationships	XX	-XX	-XX	XX
Develop effective relations with other agencies	XX	-XX	-XX	XX
Clear communication of Centre objectives			-XX	XX
Clear communication of departmental objectives				XX
Top team promotion mission/vision		-XX	-XX	XX

Key   Levels of significance

SP - Sensitive to people   X - 05
PO - Power oriented   XX - 01
R&R - Rules and regulations
P&P - Valuing performance and professionalism

- Managers at the Centre adopting people sensitive styles enhance the practice of delegation to other offices and departments in the regions.
- Greater effective promotion and implementation of the organization's policies and services is more likely to be achieved if managers at the Centre are seen to be responsive to the needs of managers in regional/outlying offices.
- The development of more effective client relationships and positive relationships with other agencies, is more likely with the pursuit of people sensitive styles by managers at the Centre.
- With the practice of power oriented styles, greater inconsistency of improvement in the quality of client services across regional offices is likely to emerge.
- The utilization of power oriented styles allows for the automating of existing processes, restructuring, downsizing and delayering. In effect, automation, restructuring and downsizing are more the result of certain central office managers' attempts to impose their own perspective as to the shape, size and configuration of the organization.
- Power oriented styles from central office are more likely to inhibit the development of a shared view concerning the promotion and implementation of the organization's policies and services.
- Power oriented styles from central office are likely to inhibit the development of effective client relationships and appropriate relationships with other agencies.
- Power oriented styles are not likely to induce a cohesive view to emerge from the senior management team at the Centre as to the effective promotion of the mission and the vision of the organization.
- A rules and regulation oriented style is likely to less stimulate the promotion and implementation of the organization's policies/services, less likely to develop effective relations with clients and other agencies, inhibit the clear communication of objectives of the Centre and less likely motivate the members of the senior management team to cohesively promote the mission and vision of the organization.
- Adopting a style of performance and professionalism by management at the Centre is likely to lead to improvements in the quality of services/products offered by the regions, and in positive relationships with clients and inter agency relationships.
- Management at the Centre adopting styles valuing performance and professionalism are more likely to delegate particular responsibilities to regional offices.
- Management at the Centre adopting styles of valuing performance and professionalism are more likely to be supportive of regional management

wishing to research and develop new services and products for the benefit of clients.
- Improvements are likely to occur in the promotion and effective implementation of the organization's policies/services and in the enhancement of positive client and external agency relationships, when management at the Centre adopt styles valuing performance and professionalism.
- Enhanced will be the clear communication of central office objectives as well as regional office objectives if the management at the Centre adopt styles valuing performance and professionalism.
- Working within an environment which values performance and professionalism is likely to stimulate the senior management in the regional offices to develop a greater sense of shared perspective on the mission and vision that should be pursued.

Table A5.2
Impact of Centre management's style on organizational culture and performance

Impact on organizational culture and performance	Style			
	SP	PO	R and R	P and P
• *Attitudes*				
Performance culture				
Work satisfaction			-X	
Discipline				XX
Specialist orientation				
Independence				-XX
• *Values*				
Work practices				
Service oriented	XX	-XX	-XX	XX
Professionalism and conduct				XX
Rights and duties	X	-X		XX
Workplace democracy				X

Impact on organizational culture and performance

	SP	PO	R and R	P and P
• *Organizational performance*				
Effectiveness of service delivery		-XX	-XX	XX
Performance of people	XX	-XX	-XX	XX
Strategic direction		-XX	-XX	XX
Interfacing effectiveness	XX	-XX	-XX	XX
• *Information technology*				
Focus of IT training	XX	-XX	-XX	XX
Effectiveness of application	XX	-XX	-XX	XX
IT skills adaptiveness	-XX		XX	
Impact effectiveness on organization	XX	-XX	-XX	

Key   Levels of significance

SP   - Sensitive to people   X - 05
PO   - Power oriented   XX - 01
R and R   - Rules and regulations oriented
P and P   - Value performance and professionalism

- A rules and regulations oriented style is likely to generate feelings of dissatisfaction with work amongst the staff and management in regional offices.
- Pursuing a style that promotes improvements in performance and sponsors a more professional attitude is likely to develop a greater sense of discipline and lessen the need for independence amongst staff and management in the regions.
- A people sensitive style is more likely to help staff and management in the regions to adopt more service oriented values.
- Power oriented and rules and regulations oriented styles are likely to undermine the adoption of service values.
- Respecting professionalism and high quality performance from the regional offices, is considered as most influential in the adoption of service oriented values, values that promote a stronger sense of professionalism and conduct, rights and duties values and values that allow for greater workplace democracy through involvement in the debate and decision making processes in the regional offices.
- Managers at the Centre who practice people sensitive styles are likely to induce improvements in the performance of people in the regional

offices. Also, the quality of interfacing between the Centre and regional offices, and between regional offices, is likely to improve.
- A positive impact in terms of focusing IT training to meeting organizational needs, and effectively applying IT technology to support the organization, are viewed as positive outcomes from the use of people sensitive styles by managers at the Centre.
- Being more sensitive to people's needs is likely to make staff and management in the regions less motivated to be flexible in the application of their skills to different contexts.
- Power oriented and rules and regulations oriented styles have a negative impact on the service oriented values adopted by staff and management in the regions.
- Effective service delivery to the community, the development of people, the clarity and cohesion required from management to promote clear strategic direction and the need for effective internal interfacing, are undermined at regional level by a Centre management who practice power and regulation oriented styles.
- IT training is likely to be less focused on meeting organizational needs as is the application of IT technology to support the organization if management at the Centre adopt power and rules and regulations oriented styles.
- A rules and regulations oriented style is likely to promote greater adaptiveness and flexibility in the application of IT skills in that staff and management are focused in the direction they need to pursue for the application of IT skills.
- Management at the Centre practising styles that enhance effective performance and promote an attitude of professionalism, aid the acceptance of values supportive of positive work practices, values that are service oriented, values of professionalism and conduct, values emphasizing accountability for the rights and duties of office and values supporting workplace democracy.
- Staff and management in regional offices are more likely to respect and wish to provide for greater levels of performance in the areas of delivery of service to the community, the development of people, clarity of strategic direction and cross functional relationships, if the management at the Centre are perceived as valuing performance and professionalism.
- With a positively oriented management at the Centre, IT training is more likely to be focused to meet organizational needs and IT generally is more likely to be applied according to the requirements of staff and management.

Appendix 6
Top team impact

- Top team impact (organizational) on the APS

- Top team impact (people) on the APS

Table A6.1
Top team impact (organizational) on the APS

Issues	Dialogue	Visioning
• *Management style*		
Sensitive to people	-XX	XX
Power oriented	XX	XX
Rules and regulations oriented	XX	-XX
Performance oriented	-XX	
• *Organizational goals*		
Medium term	-X	
Long term	-X	-XX
Unclear	XX	XX
• *Communication*		
Centre objectives	-XX	-XX
Departmental objectives	-XX	-XX
• *Organizational operations*		
Outsourcing		-XX
Restructuring		-XX
Promotion of policies	-XX	-XX
Implementation of policies	-XX	-XX
Effective client relations	-XX	-XX
Effective relations with other agencies	-XX	-XX
• Innovative application of IT	-XX	-XX

Levels of significance

X - 05
XX - 01

- Due to both perceived poor quality dialogue and lack of unity over visioning, the approach adopted by the senior management of various government departments is considered as more sponsoring power and rules and regulations oriented styles of management.
- Styles that value performance and professionalism are minimalized.

- Due to the varying quality of dialogue at the top, the personal style of top managers is considered as more insensitive to people.
- In terms of clarity concerning future direction, the goals of the various departments are considered as unclear.
- The greater the degree of split of visioning, the more short term are the goals being pursued.
- The poorer the quality of dialogue and the greater the divisions over visioning, the less effectively are departmental objectives communicated.
- The introduction and management of particular organizational operations, the outsourcing and the restructuring of departments and/or particular units, is considered to occur with greater frequency when top management are divided as to the future direction of the organization.
- Due to perceived differences of view concerning the future and poor quality dialogue, the promotion and implementation of policies and the development of effective relations with various client groupings and other agencies, are seen as hampered.
- The application of IT is seen as equally hampered by poor quality dialogue and splits of visioning.

Table A6.2
Top team impact (people) on the APS

Issues	Dialogue	Visioning
• Senior management (region/division)		
Demotivated	XX	XX
Performance oriented	-XX	
Do what is required	XX	X
Clear areas of responsibility	-XX	
• Morale	-XX	-XX
• Hindrances in current position	XX	XX
• Family life/career impact		-X

Levels of significance

X - 05
XX - 01

- In terms of impact on individuals, due to poor perceived quality dialogue at senior levels, management in the regions or divisions are identified as more demotivated, lacking clear areas of responsibility, experiencing substantial hindrances in their current position, are not driven to be performance oriented and fundamentally just do what is required of them. Morale is considered as low in such circumstances.
- In terms of impact on individuals, due to perceived splits of visioning at senior management levels, management in the regions/divisions are identified as more demotivated, doing just what is required of them and experiencing substantial hindrances in their current position. Morale is considered as low in such circumstances.
- Family life and career development are equally negatively impacted when the senior management is perceived as split on pursuing a consistent vision for the organization.

Appendix 7
Impact of leadership philosophies on the APS

- Team players
- Radicals
- Bureaucrats

Team players

Table A7.1
Team players' impact on organization performance

Elements of leadership	Organizational performance measures				
	SD	PP	TTE	S Dir.	IIE
• Promoting performance	XX	XX	XX	XX	XX
• Being disciplined		XX	X	X	
• Being independent			-X		
• Being specialist					
• Providing service			XX		
• Promoting responsibility		X	XX		
• Leading through example	X	XX	XX	XX	X
• Responsive to challenge		XX	XX	X	
• Professionalism and conduct			X	X	
• Promoting personal development					

Key Organizational performance   Levels of significance

    SD   - Service delivery   X - 05
    PP   - Effectiveness of people   XX - 01
    TTE - Top team effectiveness
    S Dir - Strategic direction
    IIE   - Internal interfacing effectiveness

- Promoting a positive performance oriented culture in the organization is seen as having a positive impact on the effectiveness of service delivery, on the performance of staff and management in the organization, on the manner in which the top team interacts, on the focus, cohesion and sense of ownership of staff and management of the strategies being pursued, on the direction the organization is taking and on the quality of interfacing internally.
- Being disciplined has less of an impact on organizational performance, except in the area of positively influencing the quality of performance of staff and management.
- Being too independently minded is seen as having a negative impact on the quality of top team relationships.

- Strongly held values supportive of provision of service to others and promoting a strong sense of responsibility amongst staff and management are viewed as enhancing the quality of interaction within the top team and improving levels of performance of people in the organization.
- Leading through example is viewed as having substantial positive impact across the five measures of organizational performance, in particular the development of people, the quality of interaction at top team level and the cohesion over strategic direction.
- Being responsive to challenge is seen to positively impact on the performance of people and on how effectively the top team interacts.
- Providing for high standards of professionalism and conduct is seen to marginally improve interactions amongst top team members and gain greater commitment from staff and management to support the strategies being pursued.

Table A7.2
Team players' impact on IT effectiveness

Elements of leadership	IT effectiveness measures			
	TMN	EA	SA	IEO
Promoting performance	XX	XX	XX	XX
Being disciplined	XX	X		X
Being independent				
Being specialist				
Providing service		XX		
Promoting responsibility	XX	XX		
Leading through example	XX	XX	XX	
Responding to challenge	XX	XX		
Professionalism and conduct	XX	XX		
Promoting personal development				

Key   Levels of significance

TMN - IT training meeting needs   X - -05
EA - IT effectiveness application (job) XX - -01
SA - IT skills adaptiveness
IEO - IT impact effectiveness on organization

- Promoting a performance oriented culture has a positive impact across the four relevant IT performance measures, namely the likelihood that IT training will be more focused to meet the needs of users, IT is likely to be more effectively applied on the job, people are likely to become more adaptive in application of IT skills, and IT is likely to be more effectively applied in the organization.
- Being disciplined provides for greater application of IT.
- Team players are seen to positively impact on IT training meeting the needs of users and the effectiveness of IT application on the job.
- Leading through positive example is seen as making a powerful impact on individuals in terms of their ability to become more adaptive and flexible in their usage of IT skills.

Table A7.3
Top team impact on team players

Elements of leadership	Top team impact	
	Dialogue	Visioning
Promoting performance	-XX	-XX
Being disciplined	-X	-X
Being independent		
Being specialist		-X
Providing service	-XX	
Promoting responsibility	-XX	-XX
Leading through example	-XX	-XX
Responsive to challenge		
Professionalism and conduct	-XX	-XX
Promoting personal development	-XX	

Key	Levels of significance
Dialogue - Poor quality dialogue	X - 05
Visioning - Lacking cohesion on vision	XX - 01

- Poor quality dialogue at top team level has the greatest negative impact, undermining the team players' willingness and capability to promote a performance oriented culture, undermining their sense of discipline, leaving them considerably less motivated to promote service or display the maturity needed for accepting the responsibility of their actions.

- The team player's drive to lead through positive example, to apply high standards for professionalism and conduct and promote greater personal development of others, is also undermined.
- Working with senior colleagues who hold and pursue different views as to the shape, configuration and future of their organization, equally inhibits the performance capabilities of team players, especially their willingness to promote a performance oriented culture and lead through positive example.

Radicals

Table A7.4
Radicals' impact on organizational performance

Elements of leadership   *Organizational performance measures*

Elements of leadership	SD	PP	TTE	S Dir.	IIE
• Critical	-XX	-XX	-XX	-XX	-XX
• Job satisfied		XX	XX	XX	
• Disciplined					
• Specialist					
• Independent					
• Outward focused leadership			XX	X	
• Respect for people					
• Service orientation			XX		
• Accountability			X		
• Freedom to act					

Key   Organizational effectiveness   Levels of significance

     SD   - Service delivery   X - 05
     PP   - Performance of people   XX - 01
     TTE   - Top team effectivensss
     S Dir. - Strategic direction
     IIE   - Internal interfacing effectiveness

- The dissatisfaction of radicals with their organization and the fact that they express their views openly, negatively impact on the five measures of organizational performance.
- Their influence on others in the organization to enhance effective service delivery externally is also negative.

- The effectiveness of interaction within teams and the focus, clarity and ownership of strategy are unlikely to be forthcoming in those groups whose membership includes radicals.
- The quality of interfacing within the organization is seen to deteriorate the more radicals express their dissatisfaction with the organization and its leadership.
- The more radicals are satisfied with their job, the more likely they are to motivate those others with whom they are more closely involved to improve their performance, promote a climate of openness within the senior management team and work towards attaining greater clarity and focus of strategy.
- The outward focus orientation of radicals in terms of being principally concerned with value to the community and service to clients, positively impacts on the interaction within the senior team and on clarifying strategic direction.
- Their high drive towards effective service provision and emphasis on effectiveness of performance, have a positive impact on their peers and subordinates in terms of promoting effective teamwork.

Table A7.5
Radicals' impact on IT effectiveness

Elements of leadership *Measures of IT effectiveness*

	TMN	EA	SA	IEO
• Critical	-XX	-XX	-X	-XX
• Job satisfied	X	XX	XX	
• Disciplined				
• Specialist				
• Independent				
• Outward focused			-XX	
• Respect for people	X			X
• Service orientation				
• Accountability				
• Freedom to act				

Key   Levels of significance

TMN - IT training meeting needs   X - 05
EA - IT effectiveness of application (job) XX - 01
SA - IT skills adaptiveness
IEO - Impact effectiveness on organization

- The impact of radicals on the application of IT in the organization indicates that the more they verbalize their complaints, the less effectively IT training is seen to meet needs in the organization, the less effectively IT is applied in terms of people's jobs and generally across the organization, and the less likely are staff and management to adapt and grow their skills to meet different challenges.
- The more satisfied radicals are with their job, the more they are likely to help focus IT training to meet user needs, help peers and colleagues effectively apply IT services to assist them to improve their performance in the job and generally support people to become more adaptive in the use of IT.

Table A7.6
Top team impact on radicals

Elements of leadership	Top team impact	
	Dialogue	Visioning
• Critical	XX	XX
• Job satisfied	-XX	-X
• Disciplined		
• Specialist		
• Independent		-X
• Outward focused		
• Respect for people		
• Service orientation		
• Accountability		
• Discretion		-X

Key	Levels of significance
Dialogue - Poor quality dialogue	X - 05
Visioning - Lacking cohesion on vision	XX - 01

- Poor quality dialogue and a senior team that has individual members who pursue different views concerning the future of the organization, add to the radicals' dissatisfaction with the organization and its leadership.
- The expressed dissatisfaction of radicals further undermines the interactions amongst senior managers, possibly leaving colleagues fearful of relating to those who display a strongly critical perspective, thereby adding to the unsatisfactory nature of top team dynamics.

- Radicals pursuing their need for independence further promote disunity with the senior management over visioning.

Bureaucrats

Table A7.7
Bureaucrats' impact on organizational performance

Elements of leadership	Measures of organizational effectiveness				
	SD	PP	TTE	S Dir.	IIE
- Cynical	-XX	-XX	-XX	-XX	-XX
- Job satisfied			X		
- Specialist					
- Disciplined					
- Impartial				-X	
- Conduct					
- Service orientation					
- Accountability				-X	

Key   Levels of significance

SD   - Service delivery   X - 05
PP   - Performance of people   XX - 01
TTE - Top team effectivensss
S Dir. - Strategic direction
IIE - Internal interfacing effectiveness

- Bureaucrats emerge as inhibiting initiatives concerned with service delivery, paying less attention to the performance of people, promoting more negative interactions within the top team, inhibiting the emergence of cohesion on issues of strategic direction and inhibiting or even damaging the quality of internal interfacing in the organization.
- Their sense of impartiality and strong instinct towards accountability are seen as damaging of relationships within the senior management team.
- Only when more satisfied with their work do bureaucrats have a more positive effect on top team relationships.

Table A7.8
Bureaucrats' impact on IT effectiveness

Elements of leadership *Measures of IT effectiveness*

	TMN	EA	SA	IEO
• Cynical	-XX	-XX	-XX	-XX
• Job satisfied				
• Specialist				
• Disciplined				
• Impartial	-X			
• Conduct			-X	
• Service orientation				
• Accountability				

Key   Levels of significance

TMN — IT training meeting needs   X - 05
EA   — IT effectiveness of application (job)   XX - 01
SA   — IT skills adaptiveness
IEO   — Impact effectiveness on organization

- The bureaucrat's cynical style is likely to inhibit others from focusing IT training to meet user needs or promote a willingness amongst staff and management to adapt their IT skills to meet different challenges.
- Users and IT specialists are likely to be less motivated to apply IT to address user job needs or to meet the overall requirements of the organization when faced with the cynical approach of bureaucrats.
- The impartial stance of bureaucrats does not motivate others in the organization to attempt to focus IT training to meet user needs.
- The attitude of bureaucrats towards appropriate workplace conduct inhibits others from adapting their IT skills to meet new challenges.

Table A7.9
Top team impact on bureaucrats

Elements of leadership   *Top team impact*

	Dialogue	Visioning
• Cynical	XX	XX
• Job satisfied		
• Specialist		
• Disciplined		
• Impartial		-X
• Conduct		
• Service oriented		
• Accountable		

Key   Levels of significance

Dialogue - Poor quality dialogue   X - 05
Visioning - Lacking cohesion on vision XX - 01

- The cynical approach of bureaucrats is heightened when the quality of dialogue within the top team is poor and when there is lack of cohesion on issues of vision and strategic direction.
- The distance and seeming lack of involvement of bureaucrats is likely to dampen enthusiasm to examine issues of strategy and vision.

Table A7.10
Leadership utilization of the four key styles of management

Centre styles   *Leadership*

	Team players	Radicals	Bureaucrats
• Sensitive to people	X	X	X
• Power oriented	X		X
• Rules and regulations oriented	X	X	X
• Valuing performance and professionalism	XX	XX	

Levels of significance

X - 05
XX - 01

- Team players, radicals and bureaucrats are equally likely to adopt people sensitive styles.
- Team players, radicals and bureaucrats are equally likely to adopt styles that promote rules and regulations.
- Team players and bureaucrats are more likely to adopt power oriented styles.
- Team players and radicals are more likely to adopt styles that display that they value performance and professionalism.

Appendix 8
Impact of private sector leadership philosophies

- Impact of drivers
- Impact of politicians
- Impact of strategists

Table A8.1
Impact of drivers

Organizational performance   *Elements of leadership*

	Motivators	Disciplined	Dissatisfied
Performance culture	XX	XX	-XX
Top team	XX	X	-XX
Morale		XX	-XX
Dialogue	XX	-XX	
Interfacing	XX		-XX

	Cynical	Independent	Specialist
Performance culture	-XX	XX	-XX
Top team	-XX	-XX	-X
Morale	-XX	-XX	-XX
Dialogue	-XX	-XX	-X
Interfacing	-XX	-X	-XX

Levels of significance

X - 05
XX - 01
- Negative Impact

- The more drivers attempt to motivate others, the more they enhance an internal culture supportive of performance, encourage positive relationships and positive dialogue amongst members of the top team and encourage more open and honest interfacing across the structure of the organization.
- The more disciplined are drivers in the discharge of their duties and activities, the more a performance oriented culture is enhanced internally, the more top team relationships improve, the morale in the organization improves, but the more sensitive becomes dialogue, especially at senior levels.
- The more drivers are dissatisfied and cynical, the more they undermine people's willingness to grow an internal culture supportive of performance, the more top team relationships and quality of dialogue at senior levels and throughout the organization are diminished, the poorer

the morale in the organization becomes and the poorer the quality of interfacing across the structure.
- The more drivers display their need for independence, the more top team relationships and quality of dialogue across the organization are damaged, the poorer the morale of staff and management in the organization becomes, and the poorer the quality of interfacing across the organization, but the more enhanced is a performance oriented culture in the organization.
- The more drivers portray themselves as specialists and promote operating in a more focused, expert oriented manner, the more an internal culture supportive of performance is undermined, the more top team relationships are undermined as is the quality of dialogue across the organization, the more morale in the organization suffers and the more the quality of interfacing across the structure diminishes.

Table A8.2
Impact of politicians

Organizational performance	*Elements of leadership*			
	Communicators	Dissatisfied	Disciplined	Independent
Performance culture	XX	-XX	XX	XX
Top team	XX	-XX	-X	XX
Morale	XX	-XX	-X	-XX
Dialogue		-XX		-XX
Interfacing		-XX		X

Levels of significance

X - 05
XX - 01
- Negative Impact

- The more politicians attempt to be effective at clearly communicating, the more an internal culture of performance is enhanced, the more positive are relationships amongst members of the top team, and the more morale in the organization improves.
- The more politicians display their dissatisfaction, the more the culture in the organization becomes less focused on effectiveness of performance, the more relationships within the top team and quality of dialogue across

the organization are undermined, the more morale in the organization suffers and the more the quality of interfacing across the organization is damaged.
- The more disciplined are politicians in the discharge of their duties, the more they provide positive example supportive of effective performance to the rest of the organization, but the more relationships in the top team are damaged and the more morale in the organization is undermined.
- The more politicians display their need for independence, the more they enhance the nature of an internal culture supportive of performance, the more relationships within the top team improve, the more the quality of interfacing across the organization improves, but the more morale in the organization diminishes and the poorer the quality of dialogue becomes.

Table A8.3
Impact of strategists

Organizational performance	Elements of leadership				
	Promote performance	Manage diversity	Disciplined	Independent	Specialist
Performance culture	XX	XX	XX	XX	XX
Top team	XX	XX			
Morale	XX	XX			
Dialogue	XX	XX	X		
Interfacing					

Levels of significance

X - 05
XX - 01

- The more strategists promote a positive, performance oriented way of working, the more an internal culture of effective performance is enhanced, the more top team relationships improve, the more positive does the morale of staff and management become and the more the quality of interfacing across the structure is enhanced.
- The more disciplined, independent and specialist the strategist portrays him/herself, the more an internal culture of performance is enhanced.
- The more disciplined the strategist, the more the quality of interfacing across the structure improves.

Appendix 9
Leadership impact on organization: regression analysis

- Service delivery
- Performance of people
- Strategic direction
- IT training
- IT application
- IT skills
- IT impact
- Private sector: strategic direction
- Private sector: management of structures
- Private sector: people management
- Private sector

Service delivery

Table A9.1
Regression analysis: leadership factor influence on organizational impact measures

Service delivery
R Square .46224

Significance T.	Factor
.0025	High quality of interfacing
.0002	Positive impact of independence orientation of team players
.0060	Negative impact of discipline orientation of radicals
.0000	Clear strategic direction
.0000	Effective performance of people
.0008	Negative impact of critical orientation of radicals
.0406	Negative impact of cynical orientation of bureaucrats
.0001	Negative impact of independence orientation of radicals
.0080	Negative impact of specialist orientation of bureaucrats

- Elements of organizational functioning, namely quality of interfacing and clarity of strategic direction are identified as having a positive impact on the quality of service delivery.
- The effective performance of people in the organization is identified as having a positive impact on the quality of service delivery.
- The independence orientation of radicals is identified as having a positive input on the quality of service delivery.
- The discipline, independence and criticism orientation of radicals is identified as having a negative impact on the quality of service delivery.
- The cynical and specialist orientation of bureaucrats is identified as having a negative impact on quality of service delivery.

Performance of people

Table A9.2
Regression analysis: leadership factor influence on organizational impact measures

Performance of people
R Square .54951

Significance T.	Factor
.0000	High quality of interfacing
.0000	Effectiveness of service delivery
.0000	Clarity of strategic direction
.0100	Negative impact of discipline orientation of bureaucrats
.0044	Positive impact of discipline orientation of team players
.0310	Positive impact of specialist orientation of bureaucrats

- Elements of organizational functioning, namely quality of interfacing, effectiveness of service delivery and clarity of strategic direction are identified as having a positive impact on enhancing the performance of people in the organization.
- The discipline orientation of team players is identified as having a positive impact on enhancing the performance of people in the organization.
- The specialist orientation of bureaucrats is identified as having a positive impact on enhancing the performance of people in the organization.
- The discipline orientation of bureaucrats is identified as having a negative impact on the performance of people in the organization.

Strategic direction

Table A9.3
Regression analysis: leadership factor influence on organizational performance measures

Strategic direction
R Square .43142

Significance T.	Factor
.0037	High quality interfacing
.0012	Effectiveness of top team
.0000	Effectiveness of service delivery
.0000	Effectiveness of performance of people
.0037	Positive input of discipline orientation of team players

- Elements of organizational functioning, namely the quality of interfacing and the effectiveness of service delivery are identified as having a positive impact on the process of clarifying the strategic direction of the organization.
- The high quality of performance of the top team and of the performance of people in the organization are identified as having a positive impact on the process of clarifying the strategic direction of the organization.
- The discipline orientation of team players is identified as having a positive impact on the process of clarifying the strategic direction of the organization.

IT training

Table A9.4
Regression analysis: leadership factor influence on IT training

R Square .81

Significance T.	Factor
.0047	Positive effect of IT impact on organization
.0222	Responding to challenge (team players) induces basic training
.0140	Discipline (team players) induces basic training

- The needs driven impact of IT in the organization is identified as having a positive impact on the application of IT training in the organization.
- The responding to challenge orientation of team players is identified as inducing only basic/adaptive IT training in the staff and management of the APS.
- The discipline orientation of team players is identified as inducing only basic/adaptive IT training in the staff and management in the organization.

IT application

Table A9.5
Regression analysis: leadership factor influence on IT application

R Square .73

Significance T.	Variable
.0059	Positive IT - impact on organization
.0285	Positive impact of IT skills

- Other IT factors, namely the quality of IT impact on the organization and the development of innovative/advanced IT skills, are identified as positively influencing the quality of IT application in the organization.

IT skills

Table A9.6
Regression analysis: leadership factor influence on IT skills

R Square .70

Significance T.	Variable
.0031	Independence (radicals) induces advanced/innovative IT skills
.0369	Effective IT application induces advanced/innovative IT skills
.0386	Independence (team players) induces basic/adoptive IT skills

- Quality IT application is identified as inducing advanced/innovative skills development amongst staff and management in the organization.
- The independence orientation of radicals is identified as inducing advanced/innovative IT skills development amongst staff and management in the organization.

- The independence orientation of team players is identified as inducing only basic/adoptive IT skills development amongst staff and management in the organization.

IT impact

Table A9.7
Regression analysis: leadership factor influence on IT impact

R Square .80

Significance T.	Variable
.0047	Positive application
.0086	IT training induces positive impact
.0094	Independence (team players) induces negative impact
.0066	Discipline (team players) induces positive impact
.0184	Professional impartiality (bureaucrats) induces positive impact
.0293	Independence (radicals) induces positive impact
.0368	Discipline (bureaucrats) induces negative impact

- Such IT factors as the quality of IT application in the organization and the quality of IT training, are identified as having a positive influence on the impact of IT on the organization.
- The independence orientation of team players is identified as having a negative influence on the impact of IT on the organization.
- The discipline orientation of team players is identified as having a positive influence on the impact of IT on the organization.
- The orientation of professional impartiality of bureaucrats is identified as having a positive influence on the impact of IT on the organization.
- The discipline orientation of bureaucrats is identified as having a negative influence on the impact of IT on the organization.
- The independence orientation of radicals is identified as having a positive influence on the impact of IT on the organization.

Private sector: strategic direction

Table A9.8
Regression analysis: leadership factor influence on clarity of strategic direction

R Square .38

Significance T.	Factor
.0000	Well managed organization structure
.0000	High performing people
.0452	Undermining cynical drivers
.0091	Consistent drivers
.0457	Strategists who effectively manage diversity

- A well managed structure of organization is identified as having a positive impact on the process of clarifying strategic direction in the enterprise.
- Effectively performing people in the organization are identified as having a positive impact on the process of clarifying strategic direction in the enterprise.
- The consistency orientation of drivers is identified as having a positive impact on the process of clarifying strategic direction in the enterprise.
- The diversity capability of strategists is identified as having a positive impact on the process of clarifying strategic direction in the enterprise.
- The cynical orientation of drivers is identified as having an undermining influence on the process of clarifying strategic direction in the enterprise.

Private sector: management of structures

Table A9.9
Regression analysis: leadership factor influence on effective management of structures

R Square .36

Significance T.	Factor
.0000	Clarity of strategic direction
.0000	Effectiveness of people performance
.0000	Effective performing top teams
.0093	Disciplined strategists
.0204	Inconsistent drivers have negative impact
.0026	Disciplined politicians
.0053	Performance oriented strategists

- A high performing top team which enters into a process of clarifying strategic direction in the enterprise, is identified as having a positive impact on the effective management of the structure of the organization.
- High performing people in the organization are identified as having a positive impact on the effective management of the structure of the organization.
- The discipline and performance orientation of strategists is identified as having a positive impact on the effective management of the structure of the organization.
- The discipline orientation of politicians is identified as having a positive impact on the effective management of the structure of the organization.
- The inconsistency orientation of drivers is identified as having a negative impact on the effective management of the structure of the organization.

Private sector: people management

Table A9.10
Regression analysis: leadership factor influence on effectiveness of people management

R Square .44123

Significance T.	Factor
.0000	Effectively managed structure of organization
.0000	Clear strategic direction
.0000	Effectively performing top team
.0096	Effective discipline (strategists)
.0002	Effectively promoting performance (strategists)

- A well managed structure of organization is identified as having a positive impact on the effective management of people in the organization.
- A high performing top team which enters into a process of clarifying strategic direction in the enterprise, is identified as having a positive impact on the effective management of people in the organization.
- The discipline and performance orientation of strategists is identified as having a positive impact on the management of people in the organization.

Private sector

Table A9.11
People management (Alpha .81)

Factor analysis

Improved employee morale
Better internal relationships
Greater trust
Fewer resignations/people leaving
Fewer inaccurate commitments made to bosses/subordinates
Overall better performance from the company's employees

Index

Adams, N. 109
Adler, A. 68
Administrative Appeal Tribunal Act (1975) 108
Administrative Decisions (Judicial Review) Act (1977) 108
agency theory 35
Ahrne, G. 49, 54, 72-3
Albrecht, K. and Zemke, R. 82
Alderson, S. and Kakabadse, A.P. 58, 64
Allan, R.W. et al 67, 72; and Porter, L. 67
Allen, T. and Cohen, S. 121, 307, 308, 309
Allison, G.T. 87
Anderson, C.W. 114
Anderson, P. and Tushman, M.L. 100
Apter, D.E. 75, 80
Argyris, C. 31-2, 48, 51; and Schon, D.A. 48, 51, 76
Aristotle 42, 53, 72
Arnold, W. and Plas, J. 43
Ashby, W.R. 48
Aston School 47
attribution theory 23
Attridge, E.J. 112

Aungles, S. and Parker, S. 104
Australia National Audit Office (ANAO) 110
Australia, Parliament 110
Australian Commonwealth Government 101
Australian Department of Employment, Education and Training (DEET) 103, 113
Australian Management Advisory Board 97
Australian Public Service (APS) 2, 5, 105; and averting 'red tape' syndrome 113-14; and customer service 113, 114, 354; and deregulation of public agencies 109, 113; and developing managers 112-16; enquiry into 107-8; and flexibility 113; growing commercialization of 109-10, 113; leadership in 5, 114-16; managerialist reforms of 106-16; and responsible action 111, 113; and shift from social to economic good 107; survey 5, 119-20, 193, 195-6; *see also* culture; demographics (survey); leadership (survey); recommendations; and

values 116
Avolio, B.J. et al 17, 79, 81
Axel, H. 103

Babson, S. 99
Bacherach, S.B. and Lawler, E.J. 67
Bachrach, P. and Baratz, M. 65, 80
Baker, J.R. 75, 109
Bales, R.F. 30, 31; and Borgatta, E. 310
Bandura, A. 39, 45
Banfield, E.C. 114
Banner, D.K. and Blessingame, F. 17, 20, 54
Bantel, K. and Jackson, S. 122, 308, 310
Barbour, G.P. and Sipel, G.A. 82
Bargo, M. Jr 115
Barnard, C.I. 19, 21, 65, 68, 80, 123
Barraclough, N. 113
Barry, B. and Dowling, P. 61
Bartlett, C.A. 45
Bass, B.M. 22, 25, 29, 79, 81, 82; et al 53, 70, 82, 83
Bayne, P. 107
Beer, M. 23; and Walter, A.E. 67
behaviour 45; improvement of 196-9; theories of 21-2
Beiner, R. 114
Belgard, W. et al 48
Bell, C. 50
Bell, D.V.J. 65
benchmarking 153, 183-8, 191
Beniger, J. 74
Bennis, W. 15, 16, 52, 53, 54, 66, 82; and Nanus, B. 17, 38, 39, 53, 54, 82
Berger, P.L. and Luckmann, T. 48
Bernard, L.L. 17, 19, 20
Bierstadt, R. 67
Bingham, W.V. and Davis, W.T. 19, 20

Blainey, G. 61
Blake, R. and Mouton, J.S. 21, 31
Bland Committee 107
Blandly, R. 108
Blau, P.M. 47, 120, 121
Block, P. 83
Boettinger, H.M. 11, 54, 73, 74, 75, 81
Bohm, D. 114
Bohret, C. 114
Bolman, L.G. and Deal, T.E. 100, 104
Bourdieu, P. and Passeron, J.C. 100
Bowditch, J.L. and Buone, A.F. 101
Bower, J.L. 26, 71
Boyatzis, R.E. 76
Boyne, G.A. 92
Bradford, D.L. and Cohen, A.R. 52, 53, 82
Brassier, A. 116
Brockner, J. et al 101, 103
Brodie, M. and Bennett, R. 82
Brown, G.B. 25
Brown, H.R. 46, 48
Brown, W. and Jaques, E. 86
Brunel University Institute of Organizational and Social Studies (BIOSS) 86
Bruner, J.S. 45
Bunyard, R.S. 86
bureaucrats 183, 190, 191, 210-11, 213; in action 179; cynical view of 169, 170, 185, 191; and decision making 169; demographics 315-16; and discipline 169, 170; impact on IT effectiveness 346; impact on performance 345; and job satisfaction 170; leadership wheel 180-2; loyalty and accountability of 171; top team impact on 347; and values 170-1; as victims 170; and work performance 171

Burgelman, R.A. 52
Burk, J.P. 111
Burke, W.W. 21, 72
Burns, J.M. 14-15, 16, 51, 53, 54, 81
Burns, T. 71; and Stalker, G.M. 71
Burt, R.S. 49
business cycles 100

Cadbury, A. 33, 34, 36, 37-8
Caiden, G.E. 90, 108
California, Task Force on Government Technology Policy and Procurement 98
Cameron, K.S. et al 99
Canada Treasury Board 98
Canberra Times 103
Cantoni, V.J. 81
Carlson, J. 83
Carlson, S. 33
Carnevale, A.P. and Stone, S.C. 45, 65
Carroll, G.R. 25; and Harrison, R.J. 121
Cartwright, D. 67
Cascio, W.F. 99, 100, 101, 103
Castelles, M. 87
Cavalli-Sforza, L.L. and Feldman, M.W. 115
central office: impact on culture and performance 331-3; impact on demographics 329-31; and style of management 143-5, 146, 147-8, 149, 150
Cerney, P. 87, 107
Champy, J. and Arnoudse, D. 99
charisma 14-15, 51, 81-3, 85
Cherry, C. 50
Chevallier, J. 93
Child, J. 24, 47
Choo, K.L. 96
Coates, A.W. 108
Coleman, S. 103

Collins, R. 50
Commonwealth Government 97, 103
Computerworld 97
Confucius 53
Conger, J.A. 79, 83
contextual perspective 4; theories of 24-38
contingency theory 29-30
core periphery employment model 104
Covey, S.R. 43
Cranfield surveys 183, 208, 209, 223, 228, 229, 236-7
Crozier, M. 67, 71
Culbert, S.A. and McDonough, J.J. 67
culture: changing 58; effective 57-8; global differences in 59-65; impact of 5; negative 57; positive 57; sensitivities of 208; strength of 56-7; and values 58-9
culture (survey): attitude factors 134-5, 141, 300-1; differences by level of organization 140-1; impact of culture 137-8, 139, 323-5; information technology factors 137, 304-5; organizational factors 136, 141, 303-4; overview 133-4; summary of 141-2; value factors 135-6, 141, 301-3
Currie, W. 88
Cyert, R.M. and March, J.G. 22, 122

Daft, R.L. 68, 70
Dahl, R.A. 65, 68
Daniels, K. and de Chernatony, L. 76; et al 76
Danish Ministry of Research 98
Darwin, C. 66
David, F. 94
Davis, B. 94, 113
Davis, E. and Lansbury, R. 109

Davis, J.A. and Warnath, C.F. 19, 20
Davis, S.M. 57
Davis, T.R. and Luthans, F. 22
Dawkins, J. 109
Day, D.V. and Lord, R.G. 26
Deal, T.E. and Kennedy, A.A. 56, 81
Dearborn, D.C. and Simon, H.A. 122, 310
decision making 23-4, 169
delayering 99
demographics (survey): age of respondents 130; appointments outside the APS 128-9; background of respondents 130-1; gender 131; homogeneity/heterogeneity in top teams 123-5; impact of Centre on 329-31; number of senior management appointments 128; organizational 120-1, 125, 129; qualifications 132; strategy, group 121-3; of team players 311-12; years in the APS 127; years in job 126; years in organization 126-7
Denhardt, R.B. 112
Denison, D.R. et al 116
developmental perspective 4, 38-40; capabilities v. competencies 51-6; enlightenment 40-2; and group dynamics 49-51; meanings 45-7; philosopher leader 42-4; and reality 47-9; and structure of organizations 47; unconscious/organizational anxiety 44-5
dialogue: enhancement of 203-6; grit in 228, 246; impact of restriction of 200-1, 245; improvement in 233; as poor 162-3, 179, 189, 193, 335-6, 341, 344; public/private comparisons 201-3; sensitivity of 154-5
Dicken, P. 87
Dilton, T. 103

DiMaggio, P. 68
directors, boards of 36-8
discretionary leadership 16, 75-9, 244
Dixon, J. et al 110-11
Dizard, W.P. Jr 11, 113
Dodgson, M. 97, 104
Doherty, N. 223
Donaldson, L. 47
Dosi, G. 100, 106
Douglas, S.P. and Rhee, D.K. 61
Dowling, P.J. and Nagel, T. 61; and Schuler, R.S. 64
downsizing 99, 103; aftermath of 223, 224, 225-6; and management support vacuum 225-6; and survivor syndrome 225
Drath, W. and Plaus, C. 89
Drehmeer, D.E. and Grossman, J.H. 82
drivers 186-7, 191, 318; impact of 350-1
Dror, Y. 48
Drucker, P.F. 25, 34-5, 36, 37-8, 48, 74, 122
Dubin, R. 32
Due, R. 101
DuGay, P. and Salaman, G. 100
Dunleavy, P. and Hood, C. 88, 94
Dunphy, D. and Stace, D. 67
Durkheim, E. 31
Dutton, J. and Duncan, R. 122, 123, 125
Dyer, W.G. Jr 58

Eccles, T. 100
Eden, D. 39
effective leadership 3, 16, 26-7, 45, 212-13, 214-15, 217
Efficiency Scrutiny Unit 108
Eisenhardt, K. and Schoonhoven, C. 121, 122, 308, 310
Ely, R.J. 122

Emery, F.E. and Trist, E.L. 54
Epictus 79
Erickson, B. 49
Erikson, E. 20
European Council 98
Evans, M.G. 22
Evered, R. 48
exchange theory 23
External Affairs and International Trade Canada 113

Faber, M. and Seers, D. 49
Fairholm, G.W. 12, 17, 51, 52, 53, 54, 58, 65, 67, 69-70, 71, 74, 79, 82, 116
Fama, E.F. and Jensen, M.C. 35, 36
Farrell, D. and Petersen, T. 67
Fenwick, M. and Edwards, R. 61
Fiedler, F.E. 21, 24, 29-30, 67
Filley, A. et al 24, 28-9
Fillipowski, D. 101, 103
Financial Management Improvement Programme (FMIP) 108
Finkelstein, S. and Hambrick, D. 122, 307
Fischer, C.S. 49
Fleishman, E.A. and Harris, E.F. 31
Fligstein, N. 68, 70
Follett, M.P. 66
Forester Research Inc 99
Forester, T. 11, 45, 73, 75, 87, 113
Foucault, M. 63
Frank, L.K. 20
Frederickson, J. and Iaquinto, A. 310
Freedom of Information Act (1982) 108
Freeman, C. and Perez, C. 88
Freeman, R.E. 95
French, J.R. and Raven, B. 65, 66, 68
Freud, S. 19, 20, 44, 51, 79, 80, 82
Frey, R. 53, 67, 70, 80, 82, 84
Friedman, M. 33

Fromm, E. 20
Frost, P.J. and Hayes, D.C. 71
Fullan, M. 111
functionalist approach 16

Gaernter, K.M. and Gaernter, G.H. 82
Gandz, J. and Murray, V.V. 71
Gardner, J.W. 68, 82
Garfinkel, H. 50
Garnett, J. and Kouzmin, A. 97
Garson, J.P. and Puymoyen, A. 63
Gateway Information Service Inc 99
Geisler, E. 97
Ghiselli, E.E. 76
Giddens, A. 46, 50, 100
Gilbraith, J.R. 23
Glasson, B.C. and Rusli, A. 99
Gleeson, G. 108
globalization 70, 84; and cultural differences 59-65; effect on public administration 87-9
Goffman, E. 45
Goldhammer, H. and Shils, E.A. 65
Goodstell, C. 90
Gordon, G.G. 57, 58
Gouldner, A.W. 67
governance: and economic performance 33-4; and stakeholders 34-8
Gramsci, A. 48
Granovetter, M. 49
Gransey, E. and Roberts, J. 104
Gray, A. and Jenkins, B. 91-2
great man theory 19, 20, 78, 220
Greengard, S. 101
Greenleaf, R.K. 69
Grimm, C. and Smith, K. 122
Grob, L. 48
Gross, T. 71

Hackman, R.J. 50, 56
Hage, J. and Aitken, M. 47
Hambrick, D.C. 26, 27; and D'Aveni, R.A. 122, 310; and Finkelstein, S. 81; and Mason, P.A. 26, 122, 124, 307, 308
Hamilton, S. 109
Hammer, M. 99; and Champy, J. 99, 100
Hampden-Turner, C. and Trompenaars, F. 111
Handy, C.B. 69
Harmon, M. 109, 112
harmonious team 13
Harvard University 30
Harvey-Jones, J. 83
Haveman, H.A. 25
Haydon, S. 101
Hayes-Roth, B. 307
Heckscher, C. 111
Held, D. 48
Henderson, J. 87
Henry, J. 52, 53, 84
Hersey, P. and Blanchard, K.M. 27-8, 31
Hickman, C.C. and Silva, M. 84
Hickson, D.J. et al 24, 47, 67
Higgins, W. 84, 105
high-high leadership myth 31
Hill, S. 99
Hobbes, T. 68, 70
Hodgson, R. 53
Hofer, C. and Schendel, D. 310
Hoffman, R. 124; and Maier, N. 124
Hofstede, G. 61, 63-4, 84
Hogwood, B. 87
Homans, G.C. 21, 23, 67
Hood, C. 87, 90-1
Hoojiberg, R. and Quinn, R.E. 116
Hopkins, D. et al 111
House, R.J. 24, 25, 82; et al 82
Howard, J. 112

Howell, J.M. 85
Hrebiniak, L.G. and Joyce, W.F. 38
Huber, G.P. 73, 74; and McDaniel, R. 74
Huey, J. 44
human resource strategies 104
humanistic models 30-2
Hunt, J.G. 25, 38
Huo, P.Y. and McKinley, W. 61

Iaccoca, L. 83; and Novak, W. 26
ideology 105-6
ignorance paradox 40
individual/s: attributes 2; character of 19-20; concept of 4; impact of top team on 336-7; role demands 2; theories of 20-4
Industry Task Force on Leadership and Management Skills 113
information technology (IT) 86, 304-5; adoption of 74-5, 211-12, 213; application of 137, 145, 150, 195, 201, 358; as benefit to community 98; and competitive advantage 97-9; development of 72-4; as enabling tool 97; impact of bureaucrats on 346; impact of 137, 359; impact of radicals on 343-4; impact of team players on 340-1; investment in 97; and reengineering 99-106; skills in 137, 324, 358-9; and training 137, 324, 357
Inkson, J.H.K. et al 47
institutional investors paradox 35-6
institutional leader 13
interaction expectancy theory 22

Jackson, S.E. et al 121
Jacobs, T.O. 21; and Jaques, E. 39
Jago, A.G. 25
Janis, I.L. 49, 50, 51, 56, 124, 308; and Mann, L. 49, 50, 56

Jaques, E. 39, 44, 75, 86
Jarman, A.M.G. and Kouzmin, A. 79, 83
Javidon, M. 26
Jay, P. 71
Jeannot, T.M. 85
Jenkins, R.L. et al 115
Jenkins, S. 89
Jensen, M.C. 35
Johnson, G. and Scholes, K. 76
Johnson, R. and Lawrance, P.R. 73
Jung, C.G. 19, 51

Kahalas, H. and Groves, D. 122
Kakabadse, A.P. 16-17, 27, 38, 39, 48-9, 52, 54, 61-2, 65, 68, 71, 86, 99, 106, 111, 115, 121, 122, 308; et al 52, 116, 122, 153, 154, 155, 308; and Myers, A. 61, 64, 77-8; and Parker, C. 71, 72
Kant, I. 42, 53
Kanter, R.M. 6, 49, 52, 53, 64, 66, 70, 80, 111, 121
Karpin report (1995) 226
Kass, H. and Catron, B. 90
Kast, E. and Rosenzweig, J.E. 23
Katz, D. and Kahn, R.L. 21, 23
Katz, R. 124, 307, 308, 309
Kauffman, R.J. and Weill, P. 97
Keating, M. 108
Keck, S. 310
Keen, P.G.W. 11, 63, 83, 84, 113
Kelley, L. et al 61
Kelly, G.A. 45
Kerr, S. and Jermier, J. 25
Kets de Vries, M.F. 19, 21, 79-80
Kevin, P.D. 59, 109
Kilmann, R.H. 57-8, 106; et al 56, 57, 59
Kingdom, J. 91
Kipnis, D. 67
knowledge 48

Kogan, M., et al 86; and Terry, J. 86
Korac-Boisvert, N. 54, 97; and Kouzmin, A. 11, 54, 56, 73, 75, 76, 77, 88, 97, 101, 105, 123
Korac-Kakabadse, A.P. and Korac-Kakabadse, N. 79
Korac-Kakabadse, N. and Knyght, P.R. 78
Korman, A. 21, 51
Kosnick, R.D. 35
Kotter, J.P. 19, 20, 27, 67, 76, 82, 83; et al 67
Kouzes, J.M. and Posner, B.Z. 39, 42
Kouzmin, A. 12, 68; and Jarman, A. 79, 80
Kozlowski, S.W. and Doherty, M.L. 83
Kozmetsky, G. 79, 81
Krebs, D.L. and Miller, D.T. 51
Krieger, L. and Stern, F. 79
Kriegler, R. et al 104
Krupp, S. 65
Kuhn, T.S. 87, 92

Laeyendecker, L. 66
Lamoreaux, N. 70
Lane, J.E. 92
Larson, L.L. et al 31
Lawrence, P. and Lorsch, J. 308
Lazarsfield, P.F. et al 49
Lazarus, R.S. 19
leader match concept 30
leader-follower relationship 22, 23, 41-2, 53; and transference 44-5
leader-manager differentiation 51-6
leadership 11-13; behaviour 27, 196-7; changing role of 72-5; character of individuals 19-24; and confidential consultation 244, 246; and context 1-2, 24-38; and culture 56-65; as definition of reality 47-9; development of 38-54, 56, 104-6;

enhancement of 5-6; history of 1;
negative interactions 218-20; and
organizational politics 70-2; and
outcomes 25-7; overview and
definitions of 13-17, 19; paradox of
51; philosophies of 190-1; and
power 14, 65-70; skills of 114-16;
style of 29; tensions in 189
leadership gap 222, 223, 245-6; get
dialogue right 228; get interfaces
right 228; promote cabinet
responsibility 230; promote learning
228-30; promote qualities of
leadership 227-8; reducing 226-30;
think issue, not territory 227
leadership (survey) 151-2; in action
171, 173, 175, 177, 179, 183;
benchmarking 153, 183-7; and
dialogue 154-5; emerging
philosophies in 162-71; and
strategic intent 153-4; valuing of
152-62; see also team players; top
teams
lean production 99
learning organization 43-4
Leavett, H.J. 51
Levinson, H. 20, 51
Lewin, K. 82
Lewis, D. 67, 80
Lieberson, S. and O'Conner, J. 25, 26
Likert, R. 21, 32
Limerick, D. and Cunnington, B. 73
Lindsay, W.M. and Rue, L.W. 310
Locke, J. 47
Lohman, D. 26
Lorsch, J.W. and McIver, E. 35
Lott, A.J. and Lott, B.E. 124
Luis, M. 81
Lukes, S.C. 70
Luthans, F. and Lockwood, D.L. 27

MAB-MIAC 105, 108
McAdam, N. 52, 53
Macadam, R.D. and Bawden, R.J. 114
McAller, N. 20, 53, 84
McAllister, I. and Vowles, J. 93
McCain, B. et al 121; and O'Reilly, C.A. 308
McClelland, D.C. 31, 66, 68; and Boyatzis, R.E. 76; and Burnham, D.H. 68; and Winter, D.G. 31
McDermott, J. 52
McGregor, D. 30
Machiavelli, N. 68, 69, 70
McKevitt, D. 94
McNeil, K. and Thompson, J.D. 121
McPherson, P. 115
Madison, D.L. et al 71, 72
Maier, N.R.F. 56
Malone, T.W. et al 73; and Rockhardt, J.F. 74
management: behaviour 156-7; complexity of role 206, 208-9; discretionary role 2; as independent 325; prescriptive role 2; process of 94-6; styles of 5, 143-5, 146, 147-8, 149, 150, 347-8; see also leader-manager differentiation
Mangham, I.L. 45
Manz, C.C. and Sims, H.P. Jr 11, 51, 52, 54, 64, 80, 83, 84
Marceau, J. 11, 113
March, J.G. 71; and Simon, H.A. 22, 121, 308
Marr, A. 89
Marsden, P.V. 49
Martin, K.J. and McConnell, J.J. 34
Marting, D.D. and Shell, R.L. 101
Marx, K. 68
Maslow, A.H. 53, 61, 64, 68, 82
May, R. 80

Mayes, B.T. and Allen, R.W. 66, 69, 70, 71
Meaney, C. 93
Meidle, J.R. and Ehrich, S.B. 25
Merton, R.K. 39
metanoia 42-3
Metzger, N. 53, 82
Meyer, H.D. 60, 61
Meyer, J. and Rowan, B. 50
Michel, J. et al 308; and Hambrick, D. 121, 123, 308, 309
Miletti, D.S. et al 90
Milgram, S. 51
Miller, W.C. 85, 307
Mills, W.C. 50, 56, 68
Mintzberg, H. 28, 32-3
Mischel, W. 45, 65
mission, promoting 230-2, 246; communication of 225-6; establish platform 232-4; involve all of top team 232
Misumi, J. and Peterson, M. 21
Mitchell, T.R. and Scott, W.G. 114
Mitroff, I.I. and Kilmann, R.H. 67
Mobley, W.H. et al 121
Montenare, J.R. 75
Morgan, C. and Murgatroyd, S. 104-5
Morgan, G. 44, 50, 52, 56, 64, 72-3, 73, 81, 89, 106, 115
Mouzelis, N.P. 47
Muetzfeldt, M. 89, 90
Münsterberg, H. 80
Murray, A. 122, 308, 309
Murray, V. and Gandz, J. 71
Myers, A. et al 77

Nadler, D.A. and Tushman, M.L. 310
Nagel, J.H. 111
Naisbitt, J. 78

National Health Service Trusts (UK) 2, 202
Naulleau, G. and Harper, J. 61
Neisser, U. 45
network structures 49-51, 56, 59, 74, 84
Neustadt, R.E. 65
new age concept 44, 54, 83-5
Newman, A.D. and Rowbottom, R.W. 86
Ng, S.H. 53, 82
Nibly, H. 52, 53
Nietzsche, F. 68
Nohria, N. and Eccles, R.G. 11, 56, 75, 113
Nolan, R.L. et al 56
Nord, W.R. 72
Norman, D.A. 309
Normann, R. 124
Nyberg, D. 65, 66, 69

Ombudsman Act (1976) 108
O'Reilly, C.A. et al 121, 308; and Flatt, S. 121, 122, 308
Organisation for Economic Cooperation and Development (OECD) 89
organizations: Anglo-American v. Continental European concepts of 37-8; demographics of 120-1, 125, 129; as networks 49-51, 56, 59; power and authority in 37; power and politics in 65-6, 70-2; and satisfaction with workplace 324; size of 310; structure in 46-7
Osborne, D. and Gaebler, T. 88, 89, 99
O'Tool, J.J. 58
Ouchi, W. 56, 58, 60
outsourcing 99

Papp, D.S. 65, 69, 85
paradox: of ignorance 40; of institutional investors 35-6; of intent 220-1, 223; of leadership 51, 222; of philosophy 209; of progress 83-5
Parry, K.W. 80
Parsons, T. 24
Pask, G. 48
path-goal theory 24-5
pathway through leadership model 17, 18, 19
Pauchant, T.C. 82
Peck, M.S. 43
Pedler, M. 84
Pelz, D. and Andrews, F. 121, 309
Pennings, J.H. 47
perceptual/cognitive theories 22-3
Perez, C. and Soete, L. 88
performance 25-7, 355; and bureaucrats 345; and the Centre 331-3; of people 355; and radicals 342-3; and team players 339-40; and values 326-7; valuing of 143, 144-5, 147
Perrow, C. 37
Peters, T. and Austin, N. 32, 81; and Waterman, R.H. 21, 37, 44, 53, 56, 58, 81, 88
Pettigrew, A.M. 23, 58, 66, 71, 106, 111
Pfeffer, J. 21, 23, 25, 28, 66, 70, 120-1, 123, 308, 309; and Davis-Blake, A. 121; and Salancik, G.R. 66
Phillips, R.L. and Hunt, J.G. 39
philosophy 42-4
Piaget, J. 45
Pijnenburg, B. and van Duin, M. 81
Pirie, M. 108
Plato 40-2, 53, 66, 68
Plott, C.R. and Levine, M.E. 71

politicians 15, 70-2, 187, 191, 319; impact of 351-2
Pollitt, C. 92; and Harrison, S. 94, 95
Ponder, Q.D. 32
Pondy, L.R. 12, 48
Porat, M. 11, 113
Porter, L.W. et al 71
Porter, M.E. 61, 108, 109
Porter-O'Grady, T. 83
Posner, B. and Low, P. 61
Powell, W.W. 54, 74-5
power: and alignment/contingency theory 67; centralization of 37, 89, 93, 99-100; and exchange theory 67; and group dynamic theories 66-7; and leadership 14, 68-70; and politics 65-6, 70-2, 219-20; and social action 68; as style of management 143, 144, 147-8, 330; transformational perspective 67-8
Power, M. 89
Prahalad, C.K. and Bettis, R.A. 309
prescribed leader 16
Prior, D. 92
programming 99
psychological approaches 20-1
public administration 4-5; and application of management theory to 92-6; and change through political initiative 89-91; global diffusion of 87-9, 94; and information technology 97-106; managerialist reforms of APS 106-16; and public choice theory 91-2
public choice theory 91-2
Public Eye 103
public/private sectors 94-6; and commercialization process 96; comparisons 183-7, 188, 192, 201-3, 208, 216, 217; and competitive advantage 186; and

effective interfacing 186; and
effective top teams 186; and impact
of drivers 186-7, 191; and impact
on organization performance 185;
and impact of politicians 187, 191;
and impact of strategists 187, 191;
and management of structures 361;
and morale 186; and people
management 362; and promoting
performance culture 185; and
strategic direction 360
Pugh, C. 109
Pugh, D.S. 47; et al 47; and Payne,
R.L. 24
Pussey, M. 108
Quinn, R.E. 27, 310; and Cameron,
K. 310; et al 27, 116

Radford, N. 106
radicals 175, 177, 183, 190, 191,
210-11, 213; in action 175, 177;
background 166; as critical of
management 166-7, 191;
demographics of 313-14; and
discharging of professional duties
168; and impact on IT effectiveness
343-4; and impact on performance
342-3; and impact of top team on
344-5; as independent 168; and job
satisfaction 167; leadership wheel
176, 178, 182; as self disciplined
167; as specialists 167-8; and
teamwork 167; and values 168
Ramos, A.G. 79, 90
rational/deductive perspective 23-4
recommendations: accommodating
negative interactions 218-20;
adoption of IT 212-13; and
aftermath of downsizing 223, 224,
226, 246; application of IT 201;
areas to address 145-6; behaviour
of leaders 196-9; cultural

background 208; developing
leaders 209, 234-44; dialogue
200-5, 245; direction and purpose
230-4; dispelling myths 206-9;
impact on organization 245; job
complexity 208; overview of survey
193, 195-6; and paradox of intent
220-1, 222, 223; and paradox of
philosophy 209; reducing leadership
gap 226-30, 245-6; relationship
with ministers 206-9, 245; steps for
development 246; top teams 202-3;
transactional or transformational
leaders 210-13, 216
Reed, R.L. 121, 123
reengineering: dark side of 104-6;
and human costs 100-1, 102,
103-4; and public management
99-100
regional/outlying offices, and impact
of the centre on 143-5, 146, 147-8,
149, 150, 332-3
Reiman, B.C. 47
relationship management 95
restructuring 99-100
Reynolds, L. 80, 98, 114
Rhinesmith, S.H. 308
Rhodes, 308
Rhodes, R. 87, 90, 91
Rice, R.E. and Aydin, C. 49, 50; and
Blair, J. 50; et al 49
Richards, C. 111
Riegel, K. 115
Roberts, K.H. and O'Reilly, C.A.
123, 308
Robinson, R.B. 310; and Pearce, J.
310
Rogers, C.R. 82
Rogers, E.M. and Kincaid, D.L. 50,
56; and Shoemaker, F. 121
Romanelli, E. and Tushman, M. 26,
122

Ronen, S. 61
Roobeek, A.J.M. 63
Rose, A.M. 68
Rosen, R.H. and Brown, P.B. 39
Rosen, S. et al 71
Rosenthal, U. et al 50, 51, 89; and Kouzmin, A. 39, 51, 80
Roszak, T. 91
Rothstein, B. 92
Rotter, J.B. 39
Royal Commission on Australian Government Administration (RCAGA) 107-8
Russell, B. 66, 68

Salancik, G.R. and Pfeffer, J. 45, 80
Sappinen, J. 60
Sashkin, M. and Burke, W. 31, 39; and Morris, W.C. 24
Sathe, V. 58
Savoie, D. 105
Sayles, L.R. 16
Schein, E.H. 56, 58-9, 67, 71
Schmitz, J. and Fulk, J. 49
Schneider, S.C. 61; and Meyer, A.D. 61
Schuler, R.S. et al 101
Schwartz, H.W. 108
Scott, W.E. 22, 25
Seibel, W. 93
Selznick, P. 13, 16, 45, 54, 93, 106
Semler, R. 43
Senge, P.M. 17, 20, 42-4, 54, 83, 84; et al 44
service delivery 113, 114, 202, 212, 354
Shaw, M.E. 310
Shenhav, Y. and Haberfeld, Y. 121, 309
Sherwood, F.P. 108
Silverman, D. 47
Simmel, G. 120, 121

Simon, H.A. 67; et al 65
Sinclair, A. 107
situational theory 27-9
Skelton, A. and Miller, W.C. 85
Skinner, B.F. 21
Slater, P. 45, 101
Slem, C.M. et al 101
Smelser, N. 105
Smith, K.G. et al 121, 122, 308
Smith, S. 78
Society for Worldwide International Funds Transfer (SWIFT) 59
Socrates 40-2
Socratic leadership 40-2
Soesastro, H. et al 97
Sofer, C. 47
Sonnenfeld, J. 26
Sproull, L. and Kiesler, S. 74
stakeholders 33, 34, 95
Stanton, S. and Power, B. 99
Stark, A. 84
Staw, B.M. and Ross, J. 51
Sternberg, R.J. 47
Stevens, M. 61
Stinchcombe, A.L. et al 120
Stogdill, R.M. 12, 20
strategists 184-5, 187, 191, 320-1, 356; broadening mental/ educational sets 244, 246; conceptualize restructuring 235; and emotive nature of strategic change 240-2; enhance vision capability 236-7; and feedback 239-40; impact of 352; and learning displays of unity 242-3; resolve conflicting agendas 234-5; rituals, routine and culture 235-6; and strengthening of individuals 237-8; vision or ego as motivator 238-40; and ways towards reconciliation 237
Stuart, P. 101

Swedish Prime Minister's office 98
synergies, vertical/horizontal 221, 222, 223, 225
Szilagyi, A.D. and Wallace, M.J. Jr 67

Tait, R. 44
Tannebaum, A. and Schmidt, W.H. 21
Tavistock Institute (London) 75
Taylor, F.W. 52, 64, 80
Tead, O. 19, 20
team players 183, 184-5, 190, 212, 213; in action 171, 173, 175; demographics of 311-12; as disciplined 164; and identification with the organization 164, 165; impact on IT effectiveness 340-1; impact on performance 339-40; impact of top team on 341-2; as independent 164-5; lead through example 164; leadership wheel 172; long stay nature of 163-4; specialist backgrounds of 166; values of 165; *see also* leadership (survey); top teams
Terry, C. 26
Thacker, J.B. 56
t'Hart, P. 49, 50, 51, 56, 80; et al 83
Theory X and Theory Y 21, 30-1
Thibaut, J.W. and Kelly, H.H. 67
Thomas, A.B. 26
Thomasma, D.C. 17
Thompson, E.P. 23
Thompson, J.D. and Bates, F.L. 89
Tichy, N.M. 56; and Devanna, M.A. 17, 81
time, as managerial lever for leaders 32-3
Toffler, A. 81
Tolman, E.C. 45
top teams 122; behaviour 155, 156-7, 158-9; characteristics of 124-5; and decision making 158-9; and demography 123, 307; discretionary leadership in 122; dynamics of 159-60; heterogeneity in 124; homogeneity in 123-4; impact on bureaucrats 347; impact of 160, 161, 162, 194; impact on radicals 344-5; impact on team players 341-2; involvement of 232; leadership wheel 174; length of time in current position 308-10; length of time in organization 307-8; and long/short term issues 159; number of senior appointments 308; organizational impact 335-6; people impact 336-7; performance of 123; process and organization in 123; and sensitive issues 158; and trust 158; and understanding 158; *see also* leadership (survey); team players
total quality management (TQM) 104
trait theory 19, 20-1
transactional leadership 14, 17-19, 86, 96, 210-13, 216, 219-20
transformational leadership 1, 4, 14, 17-19, 79, 79-85, 210-13, 216, 219; and charisma 81-3; and paradox of progress 83-5; and response to crisis 79-81
Trice, H. and Beyer, H.J. 79, 79-80
Tsui, A.S. 26
Tucker, R.C. 15, 16
Tushman, M.L. and Romanelli, E. 122, 124, 307, 310
Tutt, N. et al 95

UK Department of Social Security 113
upper echelon perspective 26
US National Performance Review

Office (NPROVP) 98, 113
values 116, 301-3; impact on performance 326-7
Van Maanen, J. 49, 106; and Barley, S.R. 81
Vence, S.C. 35, 36
vision 15, 190, 231; cohesion of 162-3, 193, 221; enhancing 236-7
Vroom, V. and Yetton, P. 21, 23

Wagner, W. et al 123
Waldman, D.A. and Avolio, B.J. 121, 122, 308
Walton, R.E. 74
Wanous, J. and Youtz, M. 124
Warburton, F.E. 51-2, 53, 67, 81, 82, 85
Weber, M. 12, 21, 47, 65, 68, 82
Weick, K.E. 46, 124; and Daft, R.L. 26
Weill, P. 73
Weiner, N. and Mahoney, T.A. 26
Weir, D. 106
Weisbach, M.S. 35
Welch, J. 54
Wellman, B. 50, 56
Western, J. 61
Westley, F. and Mintzberg, H. 77
Wheatley, M. 97, 99
White, H. 49
Whitney, J. and Smith, R. 124
Wiersema, M. and Bantel, K. 122, 124-5, 310
Williamson, O.E. 34
Winnicott, D.W. 45
Winter, D.G. 66, 68
Wolfenstein, V.E. 51, 80
Womack, J. and Jones, D. 99
Woodward, J. 90
World Commission on Environment and Development (WCED) 106

Wright, V. 93
Wrong, D.H. 65, 67

Yukl, G.A. 20, 21, 22, 27, 65, 68; et al 27; and Van Fleet, D. 21

Zaleznick, A. 53, 54
Zander, A. 124
Zelany, M. 74
Zemke, R. 54, 226
Zenger, T.R. and Lawrence, B.S. 308
Zey, M. 67, 68
Zhou, X. 93
Zimbardo, P.G. 51